Agatha Christie

MARPLE

EXPERT ON WICKEDNESS

MARK ALDRIDGE

HarperCollins*Publishers*

HarperCollins*Publishers*
1 London Bridge Street
London SE1 9GF
www.harpercollins.co.uk

HarperCollins*Publishers*
Macken House, 39/40 Mayor Street Upper,
Dublin 1, D01 C9W8, Ireland

Published by HarperCollins*Publishers* 2024
24 25 26 27 28 LBC 6 5 4 3 2

A catalogue record for this book is available from the British Library.

ISBN 978-0-00-852269-8

Printed and bound in the United States of America

CV 08.05.2024 1239

DEDICATION

For the much-missed Catherine Brobeck, co-host of the *All About Agatha* podcast, originator of the Dark Marple theory, and a shining light in the world of Agatha Christie.

A NOTE FROM THE AUTHOR

Although arranged chronologically, this book is designed so that you may read it however you choose - whether from cover to cover, or by dipping into sections that you particularly want to find out more about (or, indeed, skip sections that you are less interested in). There are no major spoilers in the main text, although a handful are in the endnotes (and clearly sign-posted as such).

ACKNOWLEDGEMENTS

This is my third book about Agatha Christie, and as ever I am extremely grateful for the kindness of other Christie fans and scholars. There is so much of her life and legacy that is only just starting to be discovered, and I would like to thank everybody who has spoken to me about their ideas, discoveries, and suggestions when it comes to exploring the world of Miss Marple. I would also like to apologise to anyone who I have overlooked.

I would particularly like to thank John Curran and Tony Medawar, whose ongoing research continues to uncover fascinating material about the Queen of Crime. John and Tony both happily responded to queries and theories of all types, and were kind enough to offer hugely helpful corrections and suggestions. Thanks also to the brilliant Claire Hines, Michelle Kazmer and Jana Ohnesorg, who all read a draft of this book, and whose feedback made me double check, clarify and correct several points before they made it into print.

One of the best things about researching Agatha Christie is that you get to share your findings with such a warm-hearted and enthusiastic community of fans and scholars. I would like to thank the organisers at the Agatha Christie and Golden Age of Crime conferences: J.C. Bernthal, Mia Dormer, Sarah Martin and Stefano Serafini. I'd also like to thank Heather Norman-Soderlind, Matt Newbury and Tony Medawar for the ever-brilliant International Agatha Christie Festival, which

takes place in Torquay every September, as well as Ana Castillo
of Tenerife's Agatha Christie Festival Internacional, which is
held in Puerto de la Cruz every other November. Both festivals give the opportunity to discuss Agatha Christie with an
amazing group of fans and experts. I can't begin to list all of
those with whom I have had fruitful conversations over the
years, but thanks to everyone who has chatted with me at one
of these events. I have particularly enjoyed picking up conversations with Kemper Donovan (of the indispensable *All
About Agatha* podcast) and Sophie Hannah at various points,
whether on panels or just in the bar after a talk.

Several people gave up their time to answer queries about
their work or gave a full interview. In particular, thanks to
Geraldine Alexander, Annette Badland, Trevor Bowen, Phil
Clymer, George Gallaccio, David Horovitch, Gemma Jenkins,
Julia McKenzie, Mary McMurray, Richard Osman, Guy Slater
and Enyd Williams.

Much of the work for this book has been based on archival
research, and I would like to thank the University of Exeter's
Special Collections team for their prompt and helpful service
and advice when going through the material held there. I
would also like to thank Louise North and her colleagues
at the BBC's Written Archives Centre who located so much
material for me, and then approved its reproduction in this
book.

Agatha Christie's Marple would not have been written were
it not for the invaluable support of Mathew Prichard, who
has always taken an interest in my research into his grandmother's work and legacy. I am eternally grateful that he has
continued to allow me access to material held by the Christie
Archive Trust. A special thanks also to Joe Keogh who suggested and searched for a great deal of fascinating and helpful
material held by the Trust, as well as Lucy Prichard, for her
insight and kindness.

I would also like to thank James Prichard and all at Agatha Christie Ltd for their help and kind co-operation. Many years ago, at the beginning of my research, I wondered if I should worry how the company may react to a new researcher. It has been great to discover that they are so supportive and enthusiastic about new Agatha Christie projects that help to keep her legacy alive, and remind us all why she remains the Queen of Crime.

At Solent University, Southampton, I would like to thank my colleagues, both current and former, including Stuart Joy, Darren Kerr, Paul Marchbank and Donna Peberdy. All have supported my ambitions and even enabled me to have the time and opportunity to occasionally dash off for an essential (to me!) archive visit or talk.

Thanks are due to people who helped me with specific queries, some of whom are steeped in the world of Agatha Christie, while others dug deep into their own specialisms to help me out. Just some of those who confirmed or supplied facts and material for me are Steve Arnold, Scott Wallace Baker, Shauno Butcher, Gary Cooper, Andrew Ferguson, Ian Greaves, Julius Green, Danil Guryanov, Haruhiko Imatake, David Morris (of the essential Collecting Christie website) and John Williams. I would also like to acknowledge the important work of Christie biographers Janet Morgan, Laura Thompson and Lucy Worsley.

At HarperCollins I would particularly like to thank David Brawn, whose support for both this and my Poirot book has made the process such a pleasure. These are not just difficult books to write, but also difficult to publish – and I am very pleased that it is David who puts in the hard work getting the illustrations in order, and thanks to designer Terence Caven for then making the final book look so attractive. The marvellous cover image is the work of the supremely talented Bill Bragg, who took the brief and managed to make it even better than I had envisaged. Thanks are also due to Anna Hervé, for her wonderfully helpful feedback on the submitted draft, and also Dawn Sinclair, formerly of the HarperCollins archives, who located so much material and was a genuine pleasure to work with. I am also hugely grateful to Lucy Foley for writing such a wonderful foreword, and to Jane Slavin for her marvellous work reading the audiobook.

I would like to give a special thanks to Gray Robert Brown, co-host and co-producer of *The Swinging Christies*, our podcast about Agatha Christie in the 1960s. Gray's feedback on an early version of this book was hugely helpful, just when my energy was beginning to flag. You can find out more about our Agatha Christie projects at ChristieTime.com.

A final, and extra special, thanks must go to my friends and family and, especially, my partner James, who has never complained about the endless Agatha Christie chat, and still takes pleasure in finding interesting editions of her books.

CONTENTS

FOREWORD

One of the very great pleasures for me, as an Agatha Christie fan and a writer of mysteries myself, is re-reading her books, watching adaptations of her stories and being able to talk about the Christie world with others – all the 'geekery' of true fandom. Imagine my delight, then, at not only having the chance to devour Mark Aldridge's wonderful new compendium of all things Marple in advance of publication, but also the honour of being asked to write the introduction. Especially (my apologies, *cher Monsieur*) because Miss Marple has always been my favourite.

Who is Miss Marple? A lace-capped little old lady surrounded by skeins of fleecy white wool? A prudish Victorian spinster? A petty village gossip, a traditionalist who mourns a lost way of life? A frail, rheumatic creature? Or an unshockable expert in all areas of human weakness and folly, a feminist figure, a Nemesis of wrongdoers: one who goes forward to do battle with evil, even risking life and limb in her valiant efforts to ensnare the guilty? As it turns out, she is all of these things, and more besides, as Mark Aldridge so expertly, entertainingly and comprehensively demonstrates in this book.

Of the entire Christie oeuvre, I believe the Marple books are the ones that most reward the reader on a second or third reading. This is because they rely less upon killer hooks (though there are some brilliant ones – see *A Murder is Announced* or *Sleeping Murder*) and more on a deep understanding of character. They have at their heart a detective who solves crimes, not through physical evidence, but via an unparalleled insight into the souls of other human beings, a formidable ability to scent out evil wherever she goes. Miss Marple is a character who changes through the books as a real person would: who ages, who grows more philosophical and tolerant in some respects and more formidable and severe in others.

This book is the greatest of treats for any Marple fan: a thorough examination of the plots of the books, of the many portrayals of the great lady herself in film and TV (with varying degrees of success!), and of the way in which the central character evolves across the canon as the world around her changes. Far from being the cliché of the Golden Age detective novel set in a perma-pastoral, quasi-feudal 1930s setting, Mark Aldridge shows us how the Marple books provide a fascinating portrait of mid-twentieth-century England and a changing social order. We may begin with the shadow of death visiting sleepy English villages and country houses, unchanged for decades with their full complement of servants, but we move swiftly on to the uncomfortable post-war accommodations of the haunted Fifties and then beyond to the technicolour social mobility of the Swinging Sixties. The book explores how St Mary Mead itself grows and modernises as the old order dies away, country estates are encircled by modern housing and industry, traditional hotels develop disturbing new identities. I think I only truly appreciated the extent to which Christie engages with the modern and keeps up with the changing times after reading it.

Rather like Miss Marple herself, this book wears its great cleverness and knowledge lightly. It will delight scholars and lay readers alike. Also like her, it displays wonderful wit and gossip and is full of amusing asides and anecdotes. You can dip into it at any point or read it from cover to cover and I know that, like the novels themselves, it will still entertain on a second - or third - reading.

I only wish I'd had the book to refer to while writing my story for the recent *Marple* collection, as it is an invaluable resource for any writer or reader trying to understand Christie's brilliance. Perhaps we will never fully understand it, because I think what lay behind it was a unique kind of genius - nowhere more in evidence than in the creation of her wise, loveable, frightening, amusing, enigmatic, terrifyingly intelligent elderly detective. But this book proves an indispensable companion to anyone making the attempt. Thank you to Mark Aldridge for writing it.

LUCY FOLEY
Summer 2024

MEET MISS MARPLE

It should be no surprise to anyone that Agatha Christie's Miss Marple has always been a reassuring presence. After all, her first appearance followed an exciting but also tumultuous time for Christie. The beginning of the 1920s saw the publication of her debut novel, *The Mysterious Affair at Styles* – the first of many adventures for the Belgian detective Hercule Poirot. Christie then went on to write short stories and thrillers alongside her mystery novels, while her day-to-day life was enhanced by a 'Grand Tour' in 1922, which saw her travelling the world alongside her husband, Archie. However, by the time that Miss Marple made her debut in December 1927, Christie's life had been turned upside down. In 1926, she had a breakdown following the death of her mother and Archie's decision to leave her for another woman. Both this breakdown and the subsequent well-publicised disappearance took some time to recover from, and yet these difficult events also coincided with the publication of *The Murder of Roger Ackroyd*, a novel that has since taken pride of place as one of Christie's masterpieces.

Agatha Christie's career was flourishing just as her life seemed to be falling apart. So it is notable that it was shortly

OPPOSITE: 'What can I do for you, madam?' Miss Marple carries out her gentle art of investigation in *Sleeping Murder*, illustrated by David Cuzik for one of six limited editions celebrating Agatha Christie's centenary in 1990.

after these events that she created a new character, whose entire raison d'être was to be a calm point in a stormy sea. Miss Jane Marple is an unmarried older lady who has spent most of her life in the small village of St Mary Mead, and her quiet observations of people and relationships give her great insight into character. For Miss Marple, these observations serve to prove that, whatever else is happening, human nature remains fundamentally the same. Miss Marple herself rarely seeks the spotlight, and, in the earlier short stories, almost functions as a punchline to a joke being played on other characters as the thoughtful old lady in the corner outwits her more forthright acquaintances. In doing this, Miss Marple shows that things will be all right in the end. Whatever the drama, the truth prevails, which was and is a reassuring fact for both readers and, we can presume, for Agatha Christie herself. Nevertheless, Miss Marple is not simply some kind grandmotherly figure. She has a steely streak, and an unerring ability to frustrate almost as many people as she charms, while her quest for the truth knows few barriers. In *Nemesis*, the final Marple story to be written, she finally concedes that 'you know, I *could* be ruthless ...' By this point, Miss Marple has gained a reputation as a person who can detect and remedy the 'wickedness' that she sees in everyday life. She is happy to do this, suggesting that 'I hope you dear young people will never realise how very wicked the world is.'[1]

This book charts the progress of Miss Marple from her short-story origins to later ventures on stage, screen and beyond, which now includes new mysteries written by some of the best crime writers working today – a true testament to the staying power of Agatha Christie's creation. Miss Marple's appearances in other media have resulted in some more radical versions of the character, from Margaret Rutherford's comical sleuthing in the films of the 1960s to the quirky Geraldine McEwan portrayal of the twenty-first century, in which she mourned a lost love. Each interpretation has its own fans and, as we shall see, even Christie's original Miss Marple stories show subtle changes to the character as society develops. Contradictory evidence doesn't allow us to pinpoint precisely when Miss Marple was born; she is both an elderly lady of the Victorian era in 1927 as well as an elderly lady of the World Wars generation in the 1970s. For Christie, 'Miss Marple was born at the age of sixty-five to seventy', but nevertheless she lives on to witness the rise of modern society, which she views with fascination.[2] Miss Marple may be nostalgic for a lost past, but she isn't a reactionary.

For fellow mystery writer Christianna Brand, Miss Marple was surely created to be the antithesis to Hercule Poirot, who Brand considered to be 'all shine and show-off'. Brand described Miss Marple as 'the very pink of modest self-deprecation', with her 'quiet confidence in her own powers', which is 'robustly bolstered up, should it ever fail her, by the adulation of her somewhat unremarkable friends.'[3] These 'unremarkable' associates include her novelist nephew Raymond West, while other important figures in Miss Marple's life drift in and out as stories demand it. Many of them are residents of St Mary Mead, from the local servants to the well-heeled Arthur and Dolly Bantry of nearby Gossington Hall.

It may be easy to think of Miss Marple as a character who had much in common with Agatha Christie, but it's wrong to do so. For one thing, Christie was only in her thirties when she created the character, and she later complained that 'I never can see why anybody thinks that I resemble Miss Marple in any way', before acknowledging that she may be more like Ariadne Oliver, the fictional mystery writer who appears in several of Christie's novels.[4] As Christie told a fan, Miss Marple tended her garden and 'lived all her life in the country, which is why her nephew considered (quite falsely) that she knew nothing about life. I have spent a great part of my life

Dame
Agatha Christie DBE
1890-1976

MISS MARPLE

Character name inspired by Marple

Unveiled by Mathew Prichard,
grandson of
Agatha Christie

A blue plaque at Marple Station near Stockport, unveiled by Mathew Prichard in 2015, in recognition of the town's role in apparently inspiring the name of his grandmother's character.

travelling in all sorts of interesting and exciting places, and, nomadic by temperament, my hobby has been travelling and music, and a love of gardens, but not much practical gardening.'[5]

Although Christie rejected the idea that she was a feminist, strong female protagonists were an important feature of many of her novels, and the intelligence and determination shown by Miss Marple is just one example of this. Some of the other examples are obvious, including the likes of Prudence Cowley (better known as Tuppence Beresford), whom we first meet in 1922's *The Secret Adversary*, and is shown to be more than a match for her eventual husband Tommy when it comes to solving mysteries through adventurous escapades. But in Christie's work a 'strong woman' can mean many things, from professional nurse Amy Leatheran (who narrates *Murder in Mesopotamia*) to the icy manipulation of Romaine Vole in *Witness for the Prosecution*, a woman who will do anything to prove her husband is innocent of murder.[6] The strength of Miss Marple may not always be obvious, because she plays her cards close to her chest, but her determination always shines through by the end of each mystery. This determination is important both in terms of proving that her conclusions are correct, and her unerring belief that justice must be done.

In terms of Miss Marple's origins, Christie often cited relatives and family friends as influences, which is unsurprising given her strongly matriarchal family background.[7] 'There is no particular model for Miss Marple,' she confessed; 'some of her remarks and points of view are reminiscent of my own two grandmothers, and of their friends and acquaintances, whom I knew in my youth.'[8] There exists a letter that appears to show that Christie thought that the name must have been inspired by the 'beautiful old manor' Marple Hall, near to Abney Hall (now in Greater Manchester), which was where her sister lived.[9] Readers are given relatively little background to the character herself, and instead learn much more from the way that she reacts to other people and events. In 1970 Christie wrote to a scholar who had penned his own biography of Miss Marple and confessed that 'If you know "the career of Miss Marple" from childhood upwards, you know more than I do! Indeed, I have never thought very much about her childhood.'[10] In terms of Miss Marple's character, a recent creation was an important influence: 'I think it is possible that Miss Marple arose from the pleasure I had taken in portraying Dr Sheppard's sister [Caroline] in *The Murder of Roger Ackroyd*,' Christie wrote in her autobiography. 'She had been my favourite character in the book – an acidulated spinster, full of curiosity, knowing everything, hearing everything: the complete detective service in the home.'[11] It was when the story was adapted for the stage by another writer that Christie realised the potential for a reworked version of the character, as the play changed Caroline into a younger love interest, renamed Caryl. 'I resented the removal of Caroline a good deal,' she later complained. 'I liked the part she played in village life: and I liked the idea of village life reflected through the life of the doctor and his masterful sister.' This turn of events was to have greater significance for Christie: 'I think at that moment, in St Mary Mead, though I did not yet know it, Miss Marple was born and with her Miss Hartnell, Miss Wetherby, and Colonel and Mrs Bantry – they were all there lined up below the border-line of consciousness, ready to come to life and step out on to the stage.'[12]

Miss Marple – the underestimated but ruthless sleuth of St Mary Mead – had arrived.

CHAPTER ONE:

Miss Marple's Early Mysteries
(1927-38)

I t is a common misconception that Miss Marple made her first appearance in the 1930 novel *The Murder at the Vicarage*, when in fact she made her debut three years earlier, in the 1927 short story 'The Tuesday Night Club'.[1] This is an understandable mistake, as the early Miss Marple stories weren't collected into a book until 1932, when they were published within *The Thirteen Problems*. However, this distinction is important for two reasons. Firstly, because reading these short mysteries first gives a good sense of her early characterisation, as well as providing a loose story arc for Miss Marple's development as a sleuth. Secondly, the particular importance of this period of Agatha Christie's

OPPOSITE: The very first portrait of Miss Marple, drawn by Gilbert Wilkinson to accompany 'The Tuesday Night Club', which in December 1927 began a series of six stories in *The Royal Magazine*.

life means that the wider context of Christie's world cannot be completely divorced from the contents of her writing. Agatha Christie's disappearance in December 1926 has been the source of endless fascination, and has inspired writers of both fiction and non-fiction to speculate about what happened. These numerous theories, which have covered everything from revenge conspiracies to science fiction, should not blind us to the severity of the real-life events. Less than a year before she penned the first Miss Marple story, Agatha Christie had hit rock bottom.

Decades later, Christie would write in a personal letter that the cause was simply 'Too many troubles all at once'.[2] This, she pointed out, 'breaks anybody down', and 'then some things happen – earache, toothache, gastritis, lapses of memory, sleep walking and even buckets of tears – just because one can't start the car!'[3] As early as 1928, she was honest about what had gone on:[4]

> On the day of my disappearance I drove over in the afternoon to Dorking with my daughter to see a relative. I was at this time in a very despondent state of mind. I just wanted my life to end. As I passed by Newlands Corner that afternoon I saw a quarry, and there came into my mind the thought of driving into it. However, as my daughter was with me in the car, I dismissed the idea at once.[5]

In her later letter, Christie explained why she so rarely referred to the painful subject: 'The least said, the less notice taken,' she wrote. 'The press has always made out it was a "publicity stunt". I considered at the time, and now long after still consider that that is preferable to airing my private life in public as everyone is so fond of doing nowadays! Anyone who knows me at all will know that publicity has always embarrassed me horribly.'[6]

Agatha Christie in the 1920s with her wire hair fox terrier Peter.

Despite these personal agonies, Christie remained a determined woman. In 1927 she spent some time recuperating, including in the beautiful town of Puerto de la Cruz in Tenerife.[7] She now had to support not only herself but her young daughter, Rosalind, and the best way to do this was to write more stories to generate an income. In this scenario Christie could have churned out unremarkable thriller stories that, by her own admission, were much easier to write than her mystery novels. And yet, as she had stated years earlier, 'crime is like drugs. Once a writer of detective stories and, though you may stray into the by-paths of poetry or psychology, you inevitably return – the public expect it of you!'[8] As a result, one of the most immediate outcomes of this time of crisis was one of the greatest creations in the history of mystery fiction. Just like Miss Marple, Agatha Christie was not to be underestimated.

The Mysteries of 'The Tuesday Night Club'
(Short stories, 1927–8)

Agatha Christie once insisted that 'Miss Marple insinuated herself so quietly into my life that I hardly noticed her arrival', and indeed she made a typically understated debut.[9] The first six Miss Marple stories were originally published in *The Royal Magazine*, a British monthly publication, commencing in December 1927. In the first mystery, readers are introduced to 'The Tuesday Night Club' (also the story's title), accompanied by the magazine's typically hyperbolic claim that this would be 'The first of a thrilling series of Mystery Stories – the best this famous author has ever written.'[10] In these loosely-linked stories, each of the six members of the club presents a mystery that they have encountered, with the others challenged to

ABOVE: The members of the 'Tuesday Night Club', as depicted by Gilbert Wilkinson in *The Royal Magazine* (1927).

solve the case; a particularly neat premise that allows Miss Marple to shine.

Christie 'chose six people whom I thought might meet once a week in a small village and describe some unsolved crime', starting with Miss Marple:

the sort of old lady who would have been rather like some of my grandmother's Ealing cronies – old ladies whom I have met in so many villages where I have gone to stay as a girl. Miss Marple was not in any way a picture of my grandmother; she was far more fussy and spinsterish than my grandmother ever was. But one thing she did have in common with her – though a cheerful person, she always expected the worst of everyone and everything, and was, with almost frightening accuracy, usually proved right.[11]

The five characters who join Miss Marple in the informal club would all appear to have their own strengths when it comes to solving mysteries, from solicitor Mr Petherick ('dry, shrewd, elderly') to clergyman Dr Pender, who reminds those present that those in his position 'hear things, we know a side of human character which is a sealed book to the outside world'.[12] Most significant of these further characters is Miss Marple's nephew, Raymond West, whose inclusion allows for some amusement about the generational divide and the pitfalls of dismissing people on the grounds of age or gender. Christie described him as 'a modern novelist who dealt in strong meat in his books, incest, sex, and sordid descriptions of bedrooms and lavatory equipment – the stark side of life was what Raymond West saw.'[13] It's worth remembering that Christie was somewhat closer to Raymond's age than Miss Marple's at this point, and yet it's clear where her sympathies lay. She created a convincingly patronising character, whose 'dear, pretty, old, fluffy Aunt Jane he treated with an indulgent kindness as one who knew nothing of the world'.[14] Any reader of this book will know how wrong he was.

In this first story, Miss Marple is described in a way that may surprise those who have come to view her as the smart, tweed-wearing woman of many adaptations. Here, she wears 'a black brocade dress, very much pinched in round the waist. Mechlin lace was arranged in a cascade down the front of the bodice. She had on black lace mittens, and a black lace cap surmounted the piled-up masses of her snowy hair'. As the accompanying magazine illustration shows, she is very much a Victorian, knitting her orange wool. Despite Christie's attempts to distance Miss Marple from any real-life individual, the description of this elderly woman sitting in a 'big grandfather chair' has similarities to Christie's description of her own grandmother, who 'passed her life in Victorian contentment', and whom she remembered sitting 'in a huge leather-backed carver's chair'.[15] At this stage the character must have been born in around 1860, although this would change as time moved on in the real world, and Miss Marple's own ageing slowed.[16] Here, she is described as taking pleasure from surveying the room with her kindly blue eyes. At this gathering, Raymond's girlfriend, Joyce, suggests that there might be some interesting stories to tell, although initially Miss Marple is forgotten when only five members of this new 'club' are included in the count. Once awkwardly acknowledged, the older lady humbly suggests that it will be an interesting evening, 'especially with so many clever gentlemen present'. By the time the six stories have been shared, however, Miss Marple will have outwitted all of these 'clever gentlemen' at some point.

Sir Henry Clithering, ex-Commissioner of Scotland Yard, is the first of the men to present a mystery for the club to discuss. Even readers who have never encountered these characters before are given an early clue that Miss Marple may be the one to solve this puzzle, given how keenly she notes the minutiae of village life. This includes the question of precisely what happened to Mrs Carruthers' picked shrimps, half of which disappeared between the shop and her home. Even this tiny mystery is enough to excite Miss Marple, whose cheeks grow pinker while mulling it over. Tantalisingly, the solution is never revealed, even when this and similar mysteries are alluded to in later stories, but we are sure that Miss Marple will have worked everything out. For Raymond, this is an example of his aunt only being capable of thinking on a smaller scale, but it is precisely this attention to small details that will help to reveal Miss Marple as a remarkable analyst of human nature.

The mystery itself concerns a poisoning in the Midlands, which is initially believed to have been accidental. The victim, Mrs Jones, ate tinned lobster, which is a food to be treated with great caution in the world of Agatha Christie. As the author remembered, 'tinned food was regarded with disapproval by all in the days of my girlhood. All girls were warned when they went to dances: "Be very careful you don't eat lobster for supper. You never know, *it may be tinned!*" - the word "tinned" being spoken with horror. Tinned crab was such a terrible commodity as not even to need warning against.'[17] Accordingly, ptomaine poisoning is initially attributed as the cause of death, but village gossip casts suspicion on the dead woman's husband and companion, with the result that an exhumation and new tests confirm arsenic as the lethal poison.[18] The question for the Tuesday Night Club (and the reader) is not only *who* poisoned the dead woman, but *how* she was poisoned. On the latter point, the ease with which the reader may deduce the true method

The 1958 Avon paperback cover by Daniel Stone depicted a Tuesday Night Club comprising Miss Marple and five men - and a skull.

is divided along national lines. When the Los Angeles-based podcast *All About Agatha* covered this story, the hosts casually mentioned that the relevant clue seemed obscure. They were then inundated with messages from those in Britain and other countries for whom the clue was obvious thanks to differences in the national cuisines; the podcast still receives occasional corrections on this point, which if nothing else is a helpful reminder that different readers can experience the same story in their own way.

One key accomplice in the crime elicits some indirect sympathy from Miss Marple, who, early on in proceedings, argues that 'so many people seem to me to be either not bad or good, but simply, you know, very silly', which is an observation that may apply to one member of the guilty party. 'There was no unkindness in Miss Marple,' said Christie, 'she just did not trust people. Though she expected the worst, she often

The Dell 'mapback' edition, with its cover by George A. Frederiksen, featured the fictional Grove of Astarte on the edge of Dartmoor (1943).

accepted people kindly in spite of what they were.'[19] This first story is an early indication of the sadness that Miss Marple can sometimes feel about those who are guilty but may have been misled or manipulated into the criminal act. 'I suppose they will hang [them] too,' she says, concerning the accomplice: 'poor thing'.

As well as featuring helpful illustrations of key characters and events, the initial magazine publication of this story in *The Royal* was structured slightly differently to the version now published within *The Thirteen Problems*, and most significantly removed the coda.[20] This concluding paragraph is where Miss Marple's methodology is reinforced, and her approach to working out the truth behind events and people is set up for the future. Earlier in the story she mentions her knowledge of an adulterous man called Mr Hargraves, which is initially dismissed as irrelevant by the impatient and short-tempered Raymond, but proves to be an essential part of Miss Marple's process. As she then reminds her nephew in this final section, 'you don't know as much of life as I do'.

The next story, 'The Idol House of Astarte', is told by Dr Pender.[21] This mystery takes place at a house called Silent Grove on the edge of Dartmoor in Christie's beloved Devon, and it concerns attendees at a fancy-dress party at the house. Several partygoers decide to roleplay a mystic act outside a newly built 'idol house' in the grounds, which has been placed where the owner feels a temple should have been. The result is murder 'by apparently no mortal agency', in which one member of the party collapses, and is then found to have been stabbed despite there being nobody close enough to have carried out the murder. The placement of this as the second story immediately indicates the extent to which this collection of stories was to be diverse in the choice of mystery

Dr Pender.

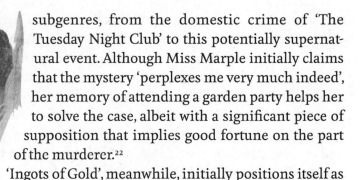
Raymond West.

subgenres, from the domestic crime of 'The Tuesday Night Club' to this potentially supernatural event. Although Miss Marple initially claims that the mystery 'perplexes me very much indeed', her memory of attending a garden party helps her to solve the case, albeit with a significant piece of supposition that implies good fortune on the part of the murderer.[22]

'Ingots of Gold', meanwhile, initially positions itself as a story about the locating of lost treasure.[23] Raymond West's tale moves along the English coast to Cornwall, specifically the 'wild and rocky' spot of Polperran, although despite the setting and story, he is annoyed by his aunt's suggestion that this marks him out as a romantic.[24] Nevertheless, in these early stories Raymond (who sports a natty bowtie alongside his angular features in the magazine illustration) is trying to impress his 'modern painter' girlfriend, Joyce Lemprière, who is happy to tease him. 'Raymond just likes the sound of the words and of himself saying them,' she informs everyone during the first story. None of his friends leap to his defence. This tale of gold carried by a sunken ship from the Spanish Armada is more than a simple treasure hunt in the end, of course. Miss Marple cuts through the atmospheric window-dressing of 'an awful foreboding of evil' and instead concentrates on tyre marks and deception, even though her attention is split between Raymond's storytelling and her own knitting. 'You wouldn't like my opinion dear,' she suggests to her nephew, 'young people never do.' She is probably right, as the solution includes her gently chastising him. This solution also highlights how much Miss Marple knows about the ways of the world, from the habits of gardeners to the significance of Christian holidays. 'You are so credulous, dear,' she tells Raymond. 'I suppose it is being a writer and having so much imagination.'

Joyce is the next guest to tell her story. Soon to become engaged to Raymond, she would appear to later change her name to Joan; such are the whims of creative types.[25] In 'The Tuesday Night Club', Joyce perceives her femininity to be a strength when it comes to the 'game' of deduction. 'I bet I could beat you all,' she says. 'I am not only a woman — and say what you like, women have an intuition that is denied to men — I am an artist as well. I see things that you don't. And then, too, as an artist I have knocked about among all sorts and conditions of people.' Such claims seem reasonable in isolation, until she drops her final, ill-judged, bombshell. 'I know life as darling Miss Marple here cannot possibly know it.' Christie herself was contradictory when it came to the strength of women's thinking versus men's. Miss Marple is one of many examples of Christie's women outwitting the opposite sex, but in a 1966 interview the author claimed that 'Very few people really stimulate you with the things they say. And those are usually men. Men have much better brains than women, don't you think? So much more originality.'[26] By the time Joyce comes to share the mystery of 'The Blood-Stained Pavement', she is more aware of Miss Marple's true strengths.[27]

'The Blood-Stained Pavement' returns to Cornwall, this time to the village of Rathole, seemingly based on the real location of Mousehole.[28] The accompanying illustration of Joyce in *The Royal* shows her to be a fashionable woman of the era, with short and slicked hair and precisely defined make-up creating an almost androgynous look. Her story concerns what seems to be blood appearing on a pavement, which is taken to be a warning of forthcoming death, and this apparently comes true when there is then a fatal incident at sea. Joyce is inevitably patronised

Joyce Lemprière.

by Raymond, who despairs of her referring to the Spanish 'shelling' some of the village ('Do try to be historically accurate, Joyce'), and the story requires quite some deduction to put all the pieces together, as the chain of clues leads to confusion more than anything. In the real world, Joyce's vision may have had its origins in Christie once seeing her sister Madge's face covered in blood ... only to learn that it was actually dyed nougat.[29]

While the men insist that 'there is very little data to go on', Miss Marple merely smiles, before making a point that may appear to be superficially modest but demonstrates how little the men of the 'club' know about life. 'Of course it is different for me,' Miss Marple insists, before solving the mystery that Joyce had failed to work out for herself. As well as claiming that women take more notice of clothes than men (an important element of the story's resolution), Miss Marple states that 'it is much easier for me sitting here quietly than it was for you - and being an artist you are so susceptible to atmosphere, aren't you?' In typical fashion, this comment from Miss Marple may be read as either a compliment or a criticism. By this point even Raymond is forced to accept his aunt's skills, which she explains neatly: 'There is a great deal of wickedness in village life.'

In the fifth story, local solicitor Mr Petherick presents the curious case of 'Motive v Opportunity'.[30] Petherick reassures his fellow guests that the case will be without jargon, perhaps feeling threatened by Miss Marple shaking a knitting needle at him while insisting 'No legal quibbles, now'. After all, these mysteries are for an evening's entertainment, rather than readers of legalese. Nevertheless, the mystery does concern a legal document - specifically, a will - which appears to have been replaced with a blank piece of

Mr Petherick.

paper. Miss Marple solves the case with such ease that she produces 'a long and prolonged chuckle'. This time, it is the memory of 'little Tommy Symonds' that brings the solution to mind. This 'naughty little boy' liked to tell riddles that could catch out his teacher, and although Raymond insists that surely Tommy Symonds has nothing to do with Mr Petherick's story, Miss Marple demonstrates that it does. 'Is there anything you do not know?' asks Mr Petherick. Very probably, but so far Miss Marple has solved each case even while preoccupied with her knitting.

Miss Marple.

Finally, it is the turn of Miss Marple herself to tell a story in 'The Thumb Mark of St. Peter', a title that Christie admitted was 'somewhat ridiculous'.[31] The story opens with Miss Marple reinforcing the fact that she is a keen observer of life. As Christie later said in a letter to a fan, Miss Marple 'had many hobbies – watching birds, gardening, a little gossip about the neighbours, perhaps more than you know about'.[32] It is the latter point that allows her to be so consistently underestimated, as few were paying any attention to what Miss Marple was really doing. Some light gardening, yes, but at the same time she is keeping a close eye on the village goings-on. To coincide with the publication of this story, Christie penned a short article called 'Does a Woman's Instinct Make Her a Good Detective?'[33] It's an interesting piece, not least because it seems so contradictory. Christie appears to be keen to play down women's skills, just as she was discreetly emphasising them in the stories themselves. 'Women are not methodical,' she stated, and generously we may consider this to demonstrate a differentiation between the precision of Hercule Poirot, and the more instinctive understanding of Miss Marple. More puzzlingly, the article claims that:

William Teason's 'Tuesday Club' cover for Dell (1963).

women are not really interested in crime. The criminal, when all is said and done, is just this – an enemy of society, and women do not really care about anything so impersonal as that. If a man has acquired a plethora of wives, or murdered his spouse for the sake of another, they are interested. It is the personal side that attracts them.

Superficially this is a bizarre claim, given that we know Christie herself was certainly interested in crime, as were many of the female characters she created. Perhaps we may substitute 'crime' for 'the criminal justice system', which would make more sense in an era when women had little to do with the mechanics of catching, trying and punishing criminals, although criminality is rarely 'impersonal'. Christie did not underemphasise the innate skills that she perceived many women to have. She claimed that:

> in a private and personal capacity women are wonderful detectives. They know all about Mr Jones and Miss Brown, and that the Robinsons aren't getting on as well so they did, and that Mr White married Mrs White for her money. There is no deceiving them. They just know! Because, you see, they are interested. The Whites live next door, and the Robinsons just over the way. And that is what matters in this life.

Christie appears to be underplaying not only her own strengths but those of her entire gender here, but she is also making a fair point about women's expertise, which can differ from men's, especially in an age when women were generally at home while men went to work. This meant that they honed different skills, and understood subtleties of societal and character change that may go unnoticed by men.

'Now you are laughing at me, my dears,' says Miss Marple at the beginning of this story, when Joyce teases her with a sarcastic expectation of something 'really spicy'. It is not yet clear how many times Miss Marple must outwit her companions in order to be granted proper respect, but clearly it takes more than five 'wins' for her to be certified champion of the club. Once more, village life is important to Miss Marple's deductions, but here it is also the setting. Other mysteries that she has encountered are teased without further elaboration: *why did* Mrs Sims only wear her new fur coat once? And *who did* cut the strings on Mrs Jones' bag? We are never told, although the later revelation that Mrs Jones

Another US 'Tuesday Club' cover by William Teason (1971).

'went off her head' (to use Miss Marple's words) may provide a clue.[34] We also meet a new relative of Miss Marple's, her niece Mabel, who doesn't appear to be Raymond's sister, and so is presumably the child of a second sibling (we are never given any definitive answer regarding the details of the Marple family tree). Mabel is described as 'silly', and she is clearly not the type who Miss Marple believes could be a murderer. Nevertheless, when Mabel's husband dies after two years of marriage, she is the subject of village gossip that suggests precisely that. Miss Marple then sets out to clear her niece's name.[35]

Miss Marple is not one for beating around the bush, even when it comes to her own family. 'There is no smoke without fire,' she insists when speaking to Mabel. Now that she is the protagonist of a story rather than an observer, Miss Marple takes on a new lease of life, using much blunter language with her niece than she has used in the polite get-togethers where we have seen her previously. 'If you have done anything silly, don't for Heaven's sake keep it back now,' she chastises Mabel,

Miss Marple and Raymond West, drawn by Alan J. Bowyer for William Collins' *Hush Magazine*, which reprinted 'The Thumb Mark of St Peter' in February 1931.

as she is already fed up with her niece's inability to help herself; 'no doubt that conduct of yours has done nothing to help', she adds later. Miss Marple also reveals what she trusts, and what she doesn't; she has faith in God, as she says a prayer to help her situation, but she is suspicious of doctors, which may explain why she is so keen to send at least one of them to the gallows in a later story. 'I have no truck with doctors and their medicines myself,' she insists, later claiming that an old tea recipe 'is worth any amount of your drugs'. Miss Marple's 'ever true faith' does indeed help her to solve the mystery, in a surprisingly direct way.

By the story's end not only has the mystery been resolved, but so has the question of the burgeoning romance simmering in the middle of each meeting of the club, as Miss Marple works out the answer to the question of exactly why Joyce always thinks of her as 'Aunt'. This frustrates Raymond, who is not permitted to break the news himself, and snobbishly recoils at the suggestion that his Aunt Jane recognised similarities between his proposal and that made by the milkman. 'Everybody is very much alike, really,' Miss Marple insists. 'But fortunately, perhaps, they don't realise it.'

These first half-dozen Miss Marple stories were so well received that Christie soon set to work on creating more mysteries for the character to solve. However, the author also set herself up for the same difficulty that she encountered with Poirot. Creating older detectives like Miss Marple 'proved most unfortunate', Christie later wrote, 'because she was going to have to last a long time in my life. If I had had any second sight, I would have provided myself with a precocious schoolboy as my first detective; then he could have grown old with me.'[36] However, Christie was not a cynical creator of detective stories, and she wrote about things and people that interested her, and the fact that these stories have also brought so much joy to others is almost a pleasant side effect. No matter how successful a schoolboy detective may have been, there are surely few readers who would swap Miss Marple for any alternative.

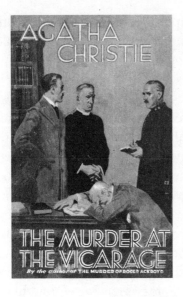 

The Murder at the Vicarage
(Novel, 1930)

When Agatha Christie first introduced Miss Marple as a 'spinster', it seems plausible that she was thinking of her own circumstances as much as her memories of elderly relatives. Although she did not fit the definition of 'spinster', having been married and had a child, for a while Christie saw her future as a single woman, and perhaps Miss Marple was an indication of her optimism for this new course of her life.[37] 'Spinster' is a word that has fallen out of fashion because of its problematic connotations that a woman without a husband is somehow to be marked out as different, or even lesser. Certainly, that is much of the point of the early Miss

ABOVE LEFT: The UK first edition of *The Murder at the Vicarage* was the first Agatha Christie book published in the company's new Crime Club imprint (1930). **ABOVE RIGHT:** The US first edition published by Dodd Mead (1930).

Marple appearances; who would listen to an older woman who had not even known true and lasting love, and failed to become a part of established society through supporting a husband and family?

Agatha and Archie Christie divorced in 1928, but she did not remain single for long. In 1930 she met the archaeologist Max Mallowan, fourteen years her junior, and the joy he brought her is immediately obvious in her correspondence. 'It's a wonderful year', Christie wrote to her friend Allen Lane, the publisher, in July.[38] In September she wrote again, two days after marrying Max, asking Lane to forgive 'an incoherent letter', as 'I am off to Venice and a wander through Greece – and with a husband too – I don't quite know how it happened as I was absolutely determined never to do it again – A great surprise to me!'[39] She went on to describe Max:

Griselda Clement and Miss Marple, as depicted in the *Chicago Daily Tribune* on 5 September 1930.

> He's a good deal younger than me and it's all very unsuitable – like everything else that's enjoyable! He's an archaeologist and of course I'm mad on that – we shall have a marvellous life wandering about the strange places – You met him – but you wouldn't remember him because he never speaks!! I can't think how I can be such a fool! – But safety at all costs is really a repulsive creed![40]

1930 also saw a significant professional development for Christie, as *The Murder at the Vicarage* was published in the latter half of the year. It first appeared as a serialisation in the *Chicago Tribune* (with illustrations showing an angular and large-nosed Miss Marple) alongside other newspapers from August, and then as a novel on 13 October, as the first Christie book to join the new imprint of the Collins Crime Club.[41]

It was likely written in 1929, which means that this is the only Miss Marple novel that Christie wrote as an unmarried woman.[42] This may explain why single women are given such prominence in the book (including not only Miss Marple, but other older ladies in St Mary Mead, such as Miss Hartnell and Miss Wetherby), as is the casual dismissiveness towards them that is ultimately proven to be ill-advised. Our narrator for this story is the village's vicar, Leonard Clement, whose wife Griselda describes Miss Marple as 'terrible' and 'the worst cat in the village'. The vicar disagrees a little, appreciating Miss

Le Masque published in 1932 as *L'Affaire Prothero*, with art by Jean Bernard.

Marple's sense of humour, which is no surprise since Christie imbues him with a tremendous sense of wit and honesty. The latter is particularly evident on the first page, when the vicar casually remarks that 'anyone who murdered Colonel Protheroe would be doing the world at large a service'. The bullying, overbearing Colonel is certainly an unpopular figure, even among his family, and few tears are shed when he is shot dead in the vicarage's study.

Despite the viciousness levelled at her by some characters, Miss Marple is initially described as a 'white-haired old lady with a gentle, appealing manner', although this outward appearance is acknowledged as deceptive. While her friend Miss Wetherby is 'a mixture of vinegar and gush', it is Miss Marple who is 'much the more dangerous'. She is not above patronising others on the basis of their youth in the same way that she is patronised for her old age, such as when Griselda suggests an innocent explanation for a relationship between two characters who appear to be having an affair. Miss Marple pats her on the arm: 'My dear,' she says, 'you are very young. The young have such innocent minds.' As ever, Miss Marple's own mind is preoccupied with the truth of her observational skills, both past and present. She remembers village incidents that have parallels with the unfolding events, while she is also no stranger to good old-fashioned nosiness and spying.[43] 'Miss Marple always sees everything,' remarks the vicar. 'Gardening is as good as a smoke screen, and the habit of observing birds through powerful glasses can always be turned to account.' Although his wife may think that Miss Marple is a 'nasty old cat', the vicar correctly concludes that 'That kind of cat is always right'. As Miss Marple claims, in St Mary Mead at least, 'idle tittle-tattle is very wrong and unkind, but it is so often true, isn't it?' When a character notes that Miss Marple knows a great deal, the vicar explains that she is 'rather unpopular on that account'. This knowledge extends beyond the village, and her reading of American detective stories help to influence her investigation, which is complicated by the contradictory confessions of Colonel Protheroe's wife, Anne, and her lover, the painter Lawrence Redding.

 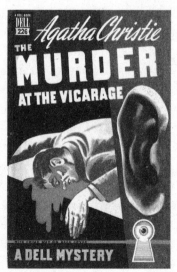

The 1948 'mapback' edition from Dell, illustrated by George A. Frederiksen, with a helpful plan of St Mary Mead.

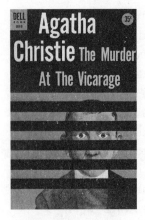

Dell's 1956 cover by Milton Glaser.

'Clever young men know so little of life,' states Miss Marple, when thinking about the impending arrival of her novelist nephew, Raymond. The vicar is no fan of Raymond's 'books about unpleasant people leading lives of surpassing dullness', but does note Miss Marple's amused twinkle during her nephew's arrogant speeches. Raymond dismisses St Mary Mead as 'a stagnant pool', a metaphor his aunt agrees to, but for her this is because nothing 'is so full of life under the microscope as a drop of water from a stagnant pool'. Although Raymond may consider St Mary Mead to be dull, there is a great deal going on in the village. Nevertheless, it is still a place where servants are seen as a necessity, as the traditional British class system gasps its last before the Second World War disrupts the status quo for good at the end of the decade. Of course, the residents have no foreknowledge of this while they bemoan the low quality of the 'help'. The vicar is particularly despairing of his own maid, who 'seemed to have taken a perverse pleasure in seeing how best she could alternate undercooking and overcooking', although he also understands that if she were to get too good then they would no longer be able to afford her services. The outside world has its own influences, and shell shock from the First World War is even cited as a possible defence for one suspect. At this point St Mary Mead is stated to be in the fictional country of Downshire, although it seems that there is some redrawing of county boundaries in the coming decade, as, by 1942, it is located in Radfordshire (also fictional).[44] Christie was happy to be vague, stating that 'There is no exact location for St Mary Mead, but it can be reached from London by train, or by car, in roughly about 1½ hours, and is about the same distance possibly from the south coast.'[45] Decades later, she would object to a claim that the village was in the real county of Berkshire, simply stating that it was '30 to 40 miles from London – South rather than North'.[46]

The formal investigation into the murder is undertaken by Inspector Slack and Colonel Melchett, who are both assisted and frustrated by the villagers. Slack is described as 'rude and over-bearing in the extreme', something that creates problems for him when he won't even allow the vicar to pass on important information because it doesn't fit with his current methodology for detection. Slack's superior, Colonel Melchett, is little better but neatly handled by Miss Marple; he is nearly apoplectic when she tells him that 'I'm afraid there's a lot of wickedness in the world. A nice honourable upright soldier like you

Collins White Circle paperbacks added the author to the front cover in 1958.

doesn't know about these things.' Melchett would certainly not appreciate being lectured by a member of the opposite sex, as he refuses to give them much credit. Following Anne Protheroe's confession, he states that 'She's a woman, and women act in that silly way. I'm not saying she did it for a moment ... You wouldn't believe the fool things I've known women do.'

Those who encounter Miss Marple are forced to accept her powers, which appear to be almost supernatural, such as when she spookily casts a shadow at the vicarage's breakfast table at a key point of the investigation. While the vicar despairs that she 'systematically thinks the worst of everyone', he also acknowledges that there 'is no detective in England equal to a spinster lady of an uncertain age with plenty of time on her hands'. However, even Miss Marple needs some help to draw her investigation to a close, as her instinct can only bring the case so far, and she is forced to set a trap to bring the guilty to justice. Once arrested and caught, the realities of the

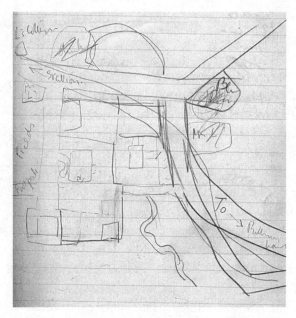

Agatha Christie's own sketch of St Mary Mead from her notebooks, showing most of the locations that appear in the novel.

criminal justice system in 1930 are passed over quickly, but any murderer will surely hang. One resident considers this point briefly, suggesting that 'We think with horror now of the days when we burnt witches. I believe the day will come when we will shudder to think that we ever hanged criminals.'

St Mary Mead's residents have immersed themselves in each other's lives and, in the vicarage at least, in the world of detective fiction. Villagers have been reading the adventures of Arsène Lupin, Sherlock Holmes, the writings of G. K. Chesterton and the mystery novel *The Stain on the Stairs*. This last title is a fictional book, but more than half a century later it was cited as one of the novels written by Jessica Fletcher, of the television series *Murder, She Wrote*; as her character was inspired by Miss Marple, this is unlikely to be a coincidence.[47]

One influence on *The Murder at the Vicarage* was Christie's own short story 'The Love Detectives', which was first published in 1926. This mystery also features a pair of lovers who each claim responsibility for a murder, and it reaches a similar conclusion to this novel.[48] The crime is investigated by the mysterious Mr Quin and his friend Mr Satterthwaite, but it was not included in the collection of Quin short stories that was also published in 1930, probably because of the similarities to *The Murder at the Vicarage*.

Reflecting on the novel years later, Christie confessed that 'I cannot remember where, when or how I wrote it, why I came to write it, or even what suggested to me that I should select a new character – Miss Marple – to act as the sleuth in the story. Certainly at the time I had no intention of continuing her for the rest of my life. I did not know that she was to become a rival to Hercule Poirot.'[49] Although it would become acknowledged as a classic Christie text, the author was less sure of it when revisiting it during the writing of her autobiography.[50] 'I am not so pleased with it as I was at the time,' she wrote. 'It has, I think, far too many characters and too many sub-plots.'[51] Christie is quite right here; it makes sense that archaeologist Dr Stone and his secretary Gladys Cram are generally removed from adaptations, for example. 'But,' Christie went on to say, 'at any rate the *main* plot is sound. The village is as real to me as it could be – and indeed there are several villages remarkably like it, even in these days. Little maids from orphanages, and well-trained servants on their way to higher things have faded away, but the daily women who have come to succeed them, are just as real and human – though not, I must say, nearly as skilled as their predecessors.'[52]

Readers tend to enjoy the novel more than Christie seemed to, as the central mystery works well alongside the amusing and insightful

Fontana Books' artwork cover from 1961.

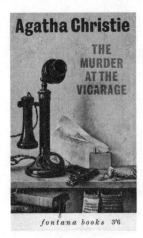

Tom Adams' first cover for the book in 1963.

Tom Adams' iconic second painting from 1977.

comments from the narrator. This can be difficult to achieve, as Christie later told an interviewer: 'I suppose it's just like making sauce. Sometimes you get all the ingredients just right and you have success.'[53] Reviews were generally good, with the *Daily Mirror* finding that 'Bafflement is well sustained', while the *Times Literary Supplement* felt that 'As a detective story, the only fault of this one is that it is hard to believe the culprit could kill Prothero [sic] so quickly and quietly ... It is Miss Marple who does detect the murderer in the end, but one suspects she would have done so sooner in reality.'[54] The *Yorkshire Post* argued that 'in less skilful hands these village-dwellers might easily have proved boring in the extreme. But even the most prosaic characters borrow something of Miss Christie's astuteness.'[55] *The Observer*'s reviewer H. C. O'Neill found 'distinct originality in her new experiment for keeping the secret. She discloses it at the outset, turns it inside out, apparently proves that the solution cannot be true, and so produces an atmosphere of bewilderment.'[56]

Reviewers in the United States were a little more cautious in their praise. The *News Chronicle* thought that Christie 'ought to be a village scandal-monger – she does it so well', but that 'I do want to know all about the other casually mentioned cases of this village life ... Could not Mrs Christie write a new *Cranford* – a *Cranford* of crime?'[57] The *New York Times* found village life tiresome, stating that 'The talented Miss Christie is far from being at her best in her latest mystery story. It will add little to her eminence in the field of detective fiction ... the average reader is apt to grow weary of it all, particularly of the amiable Miss Marple.' Even the ending was judged to be 'a distinct anti-climax'.[58] The *Brooklyn Citizen* praised the inhabitants of village life, with the residents and suspects 'less mechanical puppets dangling on strings than real honest to goodness, flesh and blood, living figures ... we have here a book which Agatha Christie fans may well term her best book.'[59] Contrarily, a year after publication the apparently slow-reading reviewer of the *Beatrice Daily Sun* concluded that 'Agatha Christie has written much better stories than this one, which drags interminably.'[60]

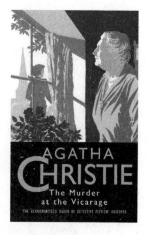

HarperCollins' 1996 design with art by Andrew Davidson.

Possibly the most welcome feedback was not from a reviewer, but an author who, alongside Christie, Margery Allingham and Ngaio Marsh, has been widely dubbed one of the 'Queens of Crime', Dorothy L. Sayers. Sayers was corresponding with Christie about another matter, but made time to express her adoration of this book. They were not close friends, and Sayers addressed her letters to 'Mrs Christie', with a note that – mindful of Christie's divorce and remarriage – she was unsure what name she should use for the author 'rendered illustrious by the exploits of M. Poirot'.[61] In December 1930, Sayers wrote to offer:

congratulations and applause for *Murder at the Vicarage*. Not only did you take me in very completely – which is nice – I like to be taken in – but, oh, gosh! Don't you know all about village life!!! Are you a pastor's daughter? (*Who's Who* not to hand). I am, so I can recognise every dreadful truth in the story. The parson and the old pussies are simply splendid. I did enjoy it all so much. Dear old tabbies are the only possible right kind of female detective, and Miss M is lovely – and really not half a bad old soul in the end – which is what is so clever of you. I think this is the best you have done – almost – though I am very fond of *Roger Ackroyd*. But I like this better because it hasn't got a Dictaphone in it; I have an anti-dicta-gramophone complex.[62]

Perhaps it was the congratulations of a fellow esteemed author that convinced Christie that Miss Marple could continue beyond one novel and a collection of short stories, although more than a decade would pass before the appearance of a second full-length mystery starring St Mary Mead's most famous resident. Even Miss Marple's neighbours have started to consider her more kindly by the end of *The Murder at the Vicarage*. 'I wonder, Miss Marple,' says the vicar, 'if you were to commit a murder whether you would ever be found out.' Miss Marple is shocked: 'What a terrible idea,' she retorts, 'I hope I could never do such a wicked thing.' She then laughs, and hints that she knows the vicar's own 'little secret', which is that his wife is pregnant. This time, our narrator seems pleased with the 'old cat', concluding that 'Really Miss Marple is rather a dear …'

The Thirteen Problems
(Short Story Collection, 1932)

The Thirteen Problems brings together all the Miss Marple short stories that Agatha Christie had written by the time of its publication, 6 June 1932.[63] This includes not only the six original 'Tuesday Night Club' mysteries, but also a further six stories published in *The Story-Teller Magazine* from December 1929, plus one more. 'I enjoyed writing the Miss Marple stories very much, conceived a great affection for my fluffy old lady, and hoped that she might be a success', Christie remembered two decades later. 'She was. After the first six stories had appeared,

ABOVE LEFT: William Collins' first edition of *The Thirteen Problems* sported the Crime Club's generic dark green jacket featuring the imprint's Hooded Gunman (1933). **ABOVE RIGHT:** The US first edition published by Dodd Mead featured Miss Marple herself and a completely different title, *The Tuesday Club Murders*, illustrated by Leon Louis des Rosiers (1933).

An illustration by J. A. May for 'Death by Drowning' in *Nash's Pall Mall Magazine* in 1931.

six more were requested.'[64] The magazine publication of these six new stories prefaced the arrival of *The Murder at the Vicarage*, while the thirteenth mystery, 'Death by Drowning', was first seen in *Nash's Pall Mall Magazine*'s November 1931 edition. This indicated that Miss Marple's adventures were to be an ongoing series even after she starred in her own novel, although her appearances would be highly irregular for quite some time. Nevertheless, as Christie said: 'Miss Marple had definitely come to stay'.[65]

For the second set of six stories, Christie adopted a similar format to the 'Tuesday Night Club'. Sir Henry Clithering has returned to St Mary Mead, and this time is lodging with Colonel Arthur Bantry and his wife, Dolly, at Gossington Hall. This is our first chance to meet the Bantrys, but at this stage they are not exactly enamoured of the village's ruthless sleuth. Dolly considers her to be 'Quite a dear, but hopelessly behind the times'. Nevertheless, the Bantrys indulge a request from Sir Henry and invite Miss Marple, hoping that she will perform her 'trick' of solving mysteries; they particularly want to get to the bottom of their own 'ghost story'. Miss

Marple duly arrives, this time wearing black lace mittens and shawl, as well as lace atop her hair; she is still very much an old lady in the Victorian mould. The two other attendees at dinner are the elderly Dr Lloyd and the beautiful actress Jane Helier.[66]

Colonel Bantry's 'ghost story' is the first of the crimes to be discussed by the group, and bears the title 'The Blue Geranium'. As originally printed in the magazine, the tale opened with Mrs Bantry's thoughts during her dinner party, including her recalling that Sir Henry had suggested Miss Marple attend the dinner; these events were rearranged and condensed for the later book publication. The story concerns one George Pritchard, who is recently widowed, although nobody seems upset about his wife's death. Colonel Bantry insists that most men 'would have hit her over the head with a hatchet long ago', and his wife agrees that Mrs Pritchard was 'a dreadful woman', adding that 'If George Pritchard had brained her with a hatchet, and there had been any woman on the jury, he would have been triumphantly acquitted.' The Bantrys may be at the top of the local social and economic ladder, but they are not exactly genteel in their conversation. Colonel Bantry then goes on to say more about the death of Mrs Pritchard, as he explains that she had started to seek guidance from fortune tellers, one of whom told the bed-ridden woman to avoid blue flowers, and that a blue geranium would mean death. When a flower on her bedroom's wallpaper appears to change to blue on the night of a full moon, Mrs Pritchard is concerned, and even more so when it happens again, despite the room being locked. When it happens for the third time it is indeed a geranium that turns blue, and this time Mrs Pritchard is found dead. This patterned wallpaper appears to have been inspired by Christie's

A variant edition, *Mystery of the Blue Geranium and Other Tuesday Club Murders*, issued by Bantam Books in Los Angeles circa 1941.

AGATHA CHRISTIE
THE THIRTEEN
PROBLEMS
6ᵈ

A DETECTIVE THRILLER

A 1938 sixpenny
paperback from Collins.

own nursery from her childhood, which had 'mauve irises climbing up the walls in an endless pattern'.[67]

George Pritchard is an obvious suspect, as is a nurse who tended his wife, but it is the mysteriously changing flower that is perhaps most intriguing. Just like Agatha Christie herself, Miss Marple has nursing experience that will help here, ably assisted by the information that the dead woman made use of smelling salts, and that there was a faint odour of gas when she was found. The practicalities of the crime may be more complicated than they need to be, but both Christie and Miss Marple are too clever to fall into the trap of believing the victim was scared to death. Miss Marple muses that 'if I were going to kill anyone – which, of course, I wouldn't dream of doing for a minute . . . I don't like killing – not even wasps . . .', before stating that she would need to choose something more definite than simply the idea of fear and a weak heart. 'Miss Marple,' replies Sir Henry, 'you frighten me.' Some readers have since teasingly speculated on the possibility of 'Dark Marple', a woman with a killer's instinct wrapped in a cuddly exterior, and the possibility is never clearer than here.[68]

When *The Thirteen Problems* was reviewed by the *Daily Mirror*, the reviewer stated that 'The plots are so good that one marvels at the prodigality which has been displayed, as most of them would have made a full-length thriller.'[69] The next story, 'The Companion', is a particularly good example of this, as it relies on a clever twist that would later be reused and reworked by Christie for a full-length Miss Marple novel, albeit placed within an entirely different surrounding story.[70] It is Dr Lloyd's turn to share this tale, which takes place in the Canary Islands, where Christie had recuperated in 1927 following her disappearance. The mystery concerns two English women, Mary Barton and her paid companion, Amy Durrant. Both go into the sea, but Miss Durrant gets into trouble and is drowned. One witness claims to have seen Mary Barton holding her companion's head under the water, although this is dismissed as a misreading of panicked events, not least because there would seem to be no particular motive for such a murder. Dr Lloyd later learns that Miss Barton is reported drowned in Cornwall, having apparently confessed to some crime. It isn't clear precisely what crime has occurred, if any, but Miss Marple is soon on the case, especially regarding one of the women's apparent weight gain, which stirs a memory of small-time fraudster Mrs Trout of St Mary Mead. Thanks to an extraordinary coincidence, her theory can be proven right, and although Miss Marple is now used to being gently teased, Jane Helier fails to understand the relevance of village life. 'But nothing ever happens in a village, does it?' she sighs.

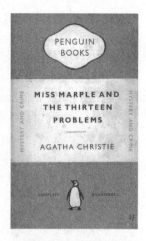

Penguin added 'Miss Marple' to the title in 1953.

'The Four Suspects' opens with a rumination on how many crimes lie undiscovered; Miss Marple believes that there must be a great many. Miss Marple's character has now been softened a little more, as she is described as 'charming', and most of her fellow dinner guests seem to enjoy hearing about the small village mysteries

The 1961 Pan edition.

that inform her detection skills. This case most definitely reaches beyond the confines of St Mary Mead, with a German secret society providing the background to Dr Lloyd's story, in which a man dies after falling down the stairs, having previously indicated that he expected someone to 'get him'. Dr

Lloyd has not been able to solve the crime himself, but Miss Marple draws on written clues of the type that Christie often supplies, in which a statement can be interpreted in multiple ways. She is also helped by a window into the wider world that was supplied by her German governess, who apparently taught two Miss Marples, the other being young Jane Marple's (unnamed) sister.

In 'A Christmas Tragedy', Miss Marple tells a story so extraordinary that it seems remarkable that she has not mentioned it before.[71] The mystery concerns the murder of a woman in a hotel where Miss Marple stayed. This hotel is a hydro, which treats and relaxes its guests using water-based 'hydropathic' methods, such as swimming and spas; this was exactly the sort of recuperative environment to which Christie had retreated in 1926. Initially, Dolly Bantry is horrified by the idea of the women in the group having to tell a story, arguing that by simply listening to the men they 'have displayed the true womanly attitude – not wishing to thrust ourselves in the limelight!' In Agatha Christie's introduction to this collection, she remembered that although her grandmother had 'led the most sheltered and Victorian of lives', she 'nevertheless always appeared to be intimately acquainted with all the depths of human depravity', which is what we see in this vicious story. As Christie went on to say, 'One could be made to feel incredibly naïve and credulous by her reproachful remark: "But did you *believe* what they said to you? You shouldn't do that. *I* never do!"'[72] Indeed, Miss Marple's ability to see the actual truth, rather than the truth as presented to her, is of crucial importance to the solving of this case. She despairs that 'none of these young people ever stop to *think*. They really don't examine the facts.' Nevertheless,

Pan switched to a photo cover in 1978.

Miss Marple is also driven by her instinctive feeling that the dead woman's husband had wanted to murder her, despite his excellent alibi, and she resolves to set a trap, which is so often a requirement of Miss Marple mysteries, as she relies on human nature rather than evidence that would stand up in court. She is also pragmatic, and unsympathetic, when it comes to the murder victim, wondering if it may have been 'better for her to die while life was still happy'.

A good old-fashioned poisoning is Dolly Bantry's case for the group, in 'The Herb of Death'. Sir Henry Clithering insists that all six guests must tell a story, and teasingly refers to 'Mrs B' as 'Scheherazade', the storyteller who frames *One Thousand and One Nights*, although Dolly objects to both names. She also struggles to tell her story, and so it is the responsibility of other guests to ask about the events that led to a person dying of digitalis poisoning, apparently as a result of foxgloves accidentally being used in the stuffing served at dinner. When Miss Marple states that the cook 'must have been a very stupid woman', it initially sounds like a harsh judgment, but of course what she really means is that the likelihood of such a poisoning being accidental was very low. The discussion also allows the guests

A rainbow and a padlock on the 1981 Fontana paperback.

to share different experiences, as Jane Helier refers to 'SA', or sex appeal. Miss Marple knows the concept but not the name, as in her day it was called 'having the come hither in your eye', lest we forget how much the world changed in the early twentieth century.

Meanwhile, it isn't obvious how sophisticated 'The Affair at the Bungalow' is until the story is over, as Jane Helier recounts a story of a mystery that she claims happened to someone else, but those present assume that it actually happened to

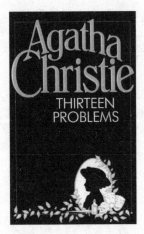
No 'The' on the 1986
Collins library edition.

her. By the end of the evening Miss Marple will have made a further deduction that serves as a reminder never to underestimate Christie's female characters. The tale concerns an apparent theft of jewels and cases of mistaken (or perhaps double) identities, in what seems to be a somewhat complicated plan. Dolly Bantry has read enough detective fiction to think that she can work out what happened, as surely the jewels were stolen by their owner. Such a solution certainly would not be without precedence in the world of Agatha Christie, but the truth is more surprising. As everyone says their goodbyes following the resolution, Jane Helier finally starts to understand the power of Miss Marple, who had earlier warned that 'women must stick together'.

The Thirteen Problems reaches its baker's dozen with the inclusion of a different type of story as its finale. In 'Death by Drowning', Sir Henry Clithering has returned to St Mary Mead, but this time there is no friendly telling of mysteries like a parlour game. Instead, he heeds the advice of Miss Marple regarding what initially seemed to be a suicide of a pregnant young woman; however, the evidence now points to murder. Miss Marple makes a game of this herself, however, as she writes down the name of the person whom she believes to be the murderer. Sir Henry investigates, having hoped for more data than this, but it is Miss Marple's knowledge of the village's schedules that helps him to move closer to identifying the culprit. This conceit of Miss Marple's works particularly well, as it allows the guilty party to remain in plain sight while the reader and Sir Henry cannot fail to be convinced that another person must have committed the crime. Miss Marple's understanding of relationships indicates just how much she sees and knows without being told, in a mystery that Sir Henry initially describes as being like a Victorian melodrama.

Christie's notebooks reveal that she had considered using real-life fellow mystery writers as guests who might meet and solve mysteries, and as this possibility is noted under the heading of '1931', this raises the prospect that she was planning a third set of mysteries in this mould. Her notes suggest 'Mr Wills Crofts and wife, Mr Bentley, Miss Sayers and husband …' Christie had worked with E. C. Bentley and Dorothy L. Sayers on the BBC radio serial *Behind the Screen* in 1930 (Christie contributed the second episode, 'Something is Missing'), and Freeman Wills Crofts had then been among the writers who joined for the follow-up, *The Scoop*, in 1931 (for which Christie wrote the instalments 'The Man with the Scar' and 'The Strange Behaviour of Mr Potts').[73] Nothing came of this idea. Another possibility was the title *Thirteen for Dinner*, which was later used for the American publication of the 1933 Poirot novel better known as *Lord Edgware Dies*.[74]

Another blue poison bottle on the 1988 Fontana cover.

Around this time, Christie was the victim of a crime of her own, which might seem to have been plucked out of one of her short stories. Her house at 47 Campden Street, London, was broken into in October 1931, although she was letting out the property at the time. Nothing of Christie's was taken, and a tin case of the tenants' letters was found by the police in Caledonian Road, but some jewellery and clothes were stolen. One of the residents decided to blame her charwoman, as she used to entrust her with any precious items when away, but hadn't done so on this occasion. It isn't clear why this would be the charwoman's fault. 'Aren't people mad?!' wondered Christie's secretary Charlotte Fisher after relaying the story.[75]

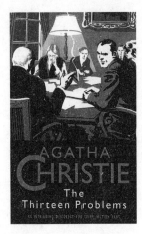

The Club around the table again in 1996, with art by Andrew Davidson.

Although *The Thirteen Problems* contains short stories that had already been published over the course of the previous four-and-a-half years (most of which pre-dated *The Murder at the Vicarage*), when it joined the Collins Crime Club it was seen by many reviewers as the second outing for Miss Marple. Miss Marple's skills were already so well known that the *Edinburgh Evening News* commented that 'Almost needless to say, Miss Marples [sic] triumphs again', and that Christie 'has excelled herself in the presentation of this series of mysteries: yet, although one is enthralled by their ingenious character, nothing but admiration can be expressed for the skilful pen sketches of the group of friends. Each is a type to be studied. *The Thirteen Problems* is a book to be thoroughly commended.'[76] At the other end of the country, the *Western Morning News and Daily Gazette* noted the Cornish connection, pointing out that 'more than once [Christie] makes use of local superstitions.'[77] The *Daily Herald* reviewer confessed that 'I've grown tired lately of this author's star turn, Ze Great Poirot – and so, I fancy, has Mrs Christie herself', as he welcomed the new style of detective.[78] When it came to favourite stories, reviewers' opinions differed. For the *Manchester Guardian*, 'Death by Drowning' and 'A Christmas Tragedy' were 'in their own class brilliant but somehow one feels both that one has been cheated, as if the dinner stopped at the hors d'oeuvre, and that the short story hardly shows Mrs Christie at her best. Or is it simply that one regrets the disappearance of Hercule Poirot?'[79] New Jersey's *Courier-Post* also considered 'Death by Drowning' to be 'probably the best yarn of all … a good puzzler for dexterous minds', alongside 'The Idol House of Astarte', 'if you like the kind of stuff which breathes spells from long ago'.[80] The latter story was not as well received by the *Times Literary Supplement*, which thought it was 'perhaps ornamented with too much romantic detail', but the implementation of Miss Marple was welcomed:

> It is easy to invent an improbable detective, like this elderly spinster who has spent all her life in one village, but by no means so easy to make her detections plausible. Sometimes Miss Marple comes dangerously near those detectives with a remarkable and almost superhuman intuition who solve every mystery as if they knew the answer beforehand, but this is not often, and Mrs Christie shows great skill in adapting her problems so that she can find analogies in Miss Marple's surroundings.[81]

In the United States this collection was released in 1933 under the title *The Tuesday Club Murders*, which for modern readers may feel like a direct influence on the phenomenally successful Richard Osman mystery novel of 2020, *The Thursday Murder Club*. However, Osman clarifies that 'It was honestly a coincidence', and that 'I hadn't heard of *The Tuesday Club Murders* until after publication. I love it, though. Feels like an unconscious tribute.'[82] Christie's publishers decided to make the most of this coincidence, and, in 2021, released a special hardback edition of the collection under its American title, with the strapline 'The Original Weekday Murder Club', which Osman noted with good humour.

A cheeky British reissue with the US title (2021).

Two decades after *The Thirteen Problems*' first publication, Christie indicated that she now felt that Miss Marple 'actually rivals Hercule Poirot in popularity. I get about an equal number of letters, one lot saying: "I wish you would always have Miss Marple and not Poirot," and the other "I wish you would have Poirot and not Miss Marple." I myself incline to her side. I think, that she is at her best in the solving of *short* problems; they suit her more intimate style. Poirot, on the other hand, insists on a full length book to display his talents.'[83] For Christie, *The Thirteen Problems* contains 'the real essence of Miss Marple for those who like her.'

'Miss Marple Tells a Story'
(Short Story for Radio, 1934)

At the turn of the 1930s, Agatha Christie had something of a burgeoning relationship with the BBC, which had begun its radio broadcasts in 1922. Christie consented to take part in two mystery serials, written by members of the Detection Club to raise money for their society. Dorothy L. Sayers co-ordinated the projects, with the first, *Behind the Screen*, transmitted in 1930, followed by *The Scoop* the next year. By this point, Sayers was growing weary of dealing with the BBC, especially as the realities of writing for a different medium started to sink in. This meant that there were many minor but time-consuming changes needed to be made to the submitted chapters, which were read aloud by their authors, including Christie.

ABOVE: Gladys Young, photographed here in 1960 for *Desert Island Discs*.

The BBC continued to like the idea of broadcasting mysteries on the radio, however, and a new book inspired J. R. Ackerley, the corporation's head of talks, to approach the author again.

In September 1932, Ackerley wrote to Christie to say that he had read and enjoyed *The Thirteen Problems* and wondered if she would be willing to write similarly conversational short mysteries for the radio, but this time with the stories played entirely through dialogue and performed like an audio play. Ackerley was particularly keen to see Miss Marple solve the mysteries but didn't want to have simple adaptations of the existing short stories, as he preferred new content.[84] Nevertheless, the suggested fee of 150 guineas (increased from 100) was not enough, despite Ackerley's pleading.[85] Christie was unmoved: 'The truth of the matter is I hate writing short things and they really are <u>not</u> profitable. I don't mind an odd one now and again, but the energy to devise a series is much better employed in writing a couple of books. So there it is!'.[86] Never one to be deterred, Ackerley appealed to Christie again in May 1933. She declined once more.

Despite her steadfast refusal to write a new series, Christie did eventually agree to write 'an odd one' in February 1934, although not before a great deal of negotiation over her fee. Ackerley insisted that thirty guineas was the most the corporation could pay, well below the £50 Christie wanted, but she reluctantly agreed.[87] A pencil mark on Christie's letter of agreement sums up the BBC's response to finally pinning down the author: 'Hooray!'[88] Christie asked for guidance on the story, and Ackerley responded that the key was that the emphasis should be on 'story telling', as he encouraged Christie to try to avoid using quoted speech.[89] Christie duly wrote a story called 'In the Mirror', soon renamed 'In a Glass Darkly', which she sent to the BBC in March, to be broadcast on 6 April. Unfortunately, this supernatural tale of a premonition of murder (featuring none of Christie's regular characters) was not considered to be suitable, even though it had already been placed in the provisional schedules. As a result, the transmission was delayed while Christie wrote a new story, and she agreed to make use of Miss Marple if possible.[90] Given the shortness of time available, Ackerley considered the possibility of a reworked version of the short story 'The Tuesday Night Club' being read out. The fact that Ackerley had impressed upon Christie the importance of it being a conversational story perhaps explains why Christie plumped for the prosaic 'Miss Marple Tells a Story' as a name for her new mystery.

For many years it has been generally accepted that Christie herself read out the story on air, but this was not the case. This claim seems to be a case of crossed wires within the BBC, given the fact that Christie was pencilled in to be the reader of 'In a Glass Darkly' before that broadcast was cancelled. The *Radio Times* did not name her as the reader of 'Miss Marple Tells a Story' at the time, but made the claim three years later

Miss Marple telling the story in its first print appearance in *Home Journal* (1935).

Gladys Young was famous for having appeared in the world's first television play, 'The Man with a Flower in his Mouth' by Pirandello (1930).

when it stated that she read the story as well as her contributions to *Behind the Curtain* and *The Scoop* (which we know she did in fact read out).[91] In a letter to Christie on 20 April 1934, Ackerley mentions the problems that their chosen reader had been having with one aspect of the story during rehearsals, which he asks Christie to clarify.[92] Confirmation that Christie did not read the story on air is in the BBC's Programme as Broadcast documents (an important official record of precisely what was transmitted and when), which reveal that the reader was in fact Gladys Young. Born in 1887, Young was a regular on radio, with her other roles including Lady Bracknell in *The Importance of Being Earnest* in 1953, and the part of Mrs Boyle in the original 1947 BBC Light Programme production of Christie's *Three Blind Mice*, the story that became *The Mousetrap*. Young read 'Miss Marple Tells a Story' on the BBC National Programme on 11 May 1934, and as the

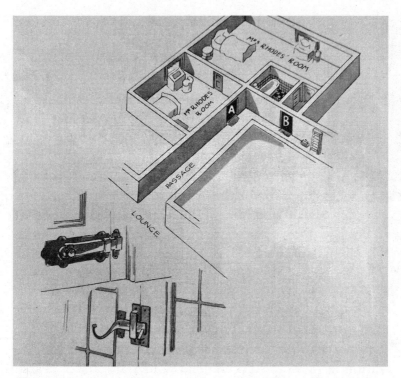

The room plan of the Rhodes' suite, the locked door and the latched window. 'Does it help you with your deductions?' asked *Home Journal* in 1935.

story is written in the first person this also means that Young was the first person to play Miss Marple.

Although a neat story in its own right, the hurried nature of its construction probably explains why the tale borrows from earlier Christie stories quite heavily at times. It opens with Miss Marple being paid a visit by Mr Petherick, the local solicitor seen in the first six of *The Thirteen Problems*. He brings with him a man sure to be arrested for murder, in what seems like a hopeless case, creating an opening reminiscent of Christie's short story 'The Witness for the Prosecution', which had been published as 'Traitor Hands' as early as 1925,

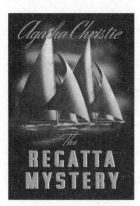

The story was published in Dodd Mead's 1939 collection *The Regatta Mystery*.

and would later become a hugely successful stage play. In 'Miss Marple Tells a Story', the apparently doomed man, Mr Rhodes, is the prime suspect for the murder of his wife. As in the early Poirot story 'Jewel Robbery at the Grand Metropolitan', a hotel's adjoining rooms and connecting doors provide both the mystery and means of this murder.

The only person with any apparent access to the room is the 'extraordinarily stupid, almost half-witted' maid, but Miss Marple knows better than to take such descriptions at face value. Although Miss Marple doesn't mention the story by name, she may well have made use of G. K. Chesterton's 'The Invisible Man' for the solving of this crime, which she finds 'remarkably simple'. More readers than usual may agree, but the story was written to be listened to rather than read, and so necessarily requires less concentration in order to work. When the mystery first appeared in print in *Home Journal* in May 1935 – as 'Behind Closed Doors' – the magazine helpfully included an excellent diagram of the adjoining rooms that doesn't necessarily aid the reader's deductions but does help with comprehension. Unfortunately, later printings of the story do not include any such illustration. In the United States the story was first collected within *The Regatta Mystery and Other Stories* in 1939, but the UK had to wait until 1979's oddball posthumous collection, the awkwardly titled *Miss Marple's 6 Final Cases and 2 Other Stories*. Even then, the book's editors were initially unaware of this story, as it had such a low profile, but they managed to sneak it in at the last minute.

By the end of the 1930s Miss Marple was starting to become a well-known figure, even though she had solved far fewer mysteries than Hercule Poirot. Nevertheless, she was occasionally referred to wistfully in articles and reviews ('Agatha Christie seems, alas, to have shelved Miss Marple', sighed a 1936 review of *The ABC Murders*) and was starting to become a point of reference that could be universally understood.[93] However, Christie's works were so successful this decade that Miss Marple is almost a footnote in her works. 1934 saw the publication of one of Christie's most famous titles, as Hercule Poirot solved a *Murder on the Orient Express*. Five years later *And Then There Were None* was published, a masterpiece of mystery that has gone on to be the best-selling crime novel of all time, with over 100 million copies sold. Christie's output

MISS MARPLE'S FINAL CASES

The murder depicted by Bill Bragg on HarperCollins' 2022 cover.

was prolific during this decade, with two or three books published every year, almost all of which became acknowledged classics. Nevertheless, Miss Marple was not fading into the background entirely. *The Murder at the Vicarage* was one of the titles under consideration for a potential film deal with MGM at around the same time, which would have netted Christie $7,500 for the title.[94] The deal fell through because of Christie's insistence that any of the films starring Poirot should depict the character as she wrote him, and in particular he should not have love affairs. 'Your masterly defeat of MGM's low schemes has vastly impressed the film industry!' wrote Edmund Cork, Christie's agent.[95] Christie knew what she wanted, and she knew what was important to her. She was always happy to stand her ground, whatever the temptation for money or other incentives. While she would reject the comparison, Christie's understated but solid determination was not unlike her own Miss Marple's dogged pursuit of the truth, at whatever cost.

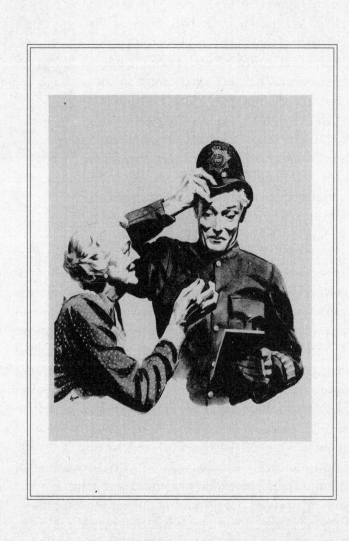

CHAPTER TWO:

THE

1940s

Although the latter half of the 1930s had seen little Miss Marple action while Christie focused her efforts elsewhere, the early 1940s saw a turnaround in the character's fortunes. In some parts of the United States she turned up in a new book featuring five of *The Thirteen Problems*, in a volume called *Mystery of the Blue Geranium and Other Tuesday Club Murders*. This was from Bantam Publications in California, and it was published early in the decade, likely for sale in newsagents and other non-book shops.[1] More significantly, Christie herself was working on more original material for the character. In part, this may be due to Miss Marple's timeless qualities feeling appropriate during the tumultuous war period. Christie had already been victim to one publisher's response to the new crisis

OPPOSITE: 'There's a pin in your tunic.' Miss Marple admonishes Constable Palk in the short story 'Tape-Measure Murder', published in *This Week* magazine and illustrated by Arthur Sarnoff (1941).

Mystery of the Blue Geranium and [four] other Tuesday Club Murders, issued by Bantam Books in c. 1941.

enveloping the world when *Collier's* magazine asked her to make the war more prominent for its serialisation of the Poirot novel *One, Two, Buckle My Shoe*. Then, later in 1940 she was asked to do precisely the opposite for a series of four short stories that *This Week* in the United States wanted for $1,500 apiece; no mention of the war was an 'absolute rule'.[2] Christie was given the opportunity to feature any detective she wished in these stories, including new inventions, and the fact that she chose Miss Marple indicates the fondness that she had for the character.[3]

It seems that Christie took some comfort from the old-fashioned ways of Miss Marple at what was obviously a difficult time. In 1942, Max became a volunteer reserve with the Royal Air Force based in North Africa, and Christie struggled with his absence as her attempts to join him in Cairo proved fruitless.[4] While her husband was away she turned to more practical matters and updated her will in case disaster struck. 'I cannot see why people are always so embarrassed by having to discuss anything to do with death,' she said. 'Dear Edmund Cork, my agent, always used to look most upset when I raised the question of "Yes, but supposing I should *die*?" But really the question of death is so important nowadays, that one has to discuss it.'[5] She decided to write two books that could be published posthumously, and informed Max and Rosalind of her decision. 'It will cheer you up,' she explained to them, 'when you come back from the funeral, or the Memorial Service, to think that you have got a couple of books, one belonging to each of you!' Of course, 'They said they would rather have *me*, and I said: "I should hope so, indeed!" And we all laughed a good deal.'[6] In the event, *Curtain: Poirot's Last Case* was published a few months before Christie's death, but the Miss Marple novel *Sleeping Murder* was indeed published posthumously, in October 1976.[7]

Christie was feeling restless at this point and was still hard at work on a variety of thriller and mystery titles, thirteen of which were published in the 1940s. These included Poirot investigating *Evil Under the Sun* in 1941 and *Five Little Pigs* in 1942, while Christie looked beyond her recurring detectives with the likes of historical murder mystery *Death Comes as the End* in 1945 and the classic *Crooked House* in 1949. The author also decided to give herself the additional challenge of writing two books at once, 'since one of the difficulties of writing a book is that it suddenly goes stale on you. Then you have to put it by, and do other things – but I had no other things to do. I had no wish to sit and brood. I believed that if I wrote two books, and alternated the writing of them, it would keep me fresh at the task.'[8] This 'freshness' is evident in Christie's choice of stories to write together. One, *N or M?*, features the return of Tommy and Tuppence, last seen in the 1920s and now a part of a spy thriller suited to wartime. The other novel is much more archetypal Christie, and takes place a long way from the war and any issues in the wider world. In it, Miss Marple returns as St Mary Mead contends with a new scandal: the discovery of a body in the library of Gossington Hall.

The Body in the Library
(Novel, 1942)

The Body in the Library was not the creation of a cliché by Agatha Christie; it is an example of her embracing an existing one. Christie had already played with the titular idea, identifying *The Body in the Library* as a novel written by her own fictional mystery writer Ariadne Oliver in the 1936 Poirot book *Cards on the Table*. Mrs Oliver bears more than a passing resemblance to Agatha Christie, and so perhaps this was a clue or even the impetus for her own story under this title that appeared a few years later, which she had been thinking about for some time. Christie explained that 'There

ABOVE LEFT: The first edition of *The Body in the Library*, designed by artist Leslie Stead, was a product of Collins' wartime austerity, with a reduced page count and a jacket printed in just two colours, black and red (1942). **ABOVE RIGHT:** The US first edition published by Dodd Mead (1942).

are certain clichés belonging to certain types of fiction. The "bold bad baronet" for melodrama, the "Body in the library" for the detective story. For several years I treasured the possibility of suitable "Variations on a well-known Theme".'[9] Christie was playing a game with herself here, as she aimed to put a new twist on an old cliché. It makes sense that she opted to do this while particularly bored due to the absence of Max, while also wishing to tell a story that rejected the realities of a country at war.

Wartime European edition published by Alfred Scherz's Phoenix imprint in Paris.

'I laid down for myself certain conditions,' Christie clarified. 'The library in question must be a highly orthodox and conventional library. The body, on the other hand, must be a wildly improbable and highly sensational body. Such were the terms of the problem, but for some years they remained as such, represented only by a few lines of writing in an exercise book.'[10] The library itself is indeed conventional, at least in the world of Christie, as it is owned by Miss Marple's friends Arthur and Dolly Bantry. Dolly's early morning dreaming about the vicar's wife in a bathing suit is interrupted by her maid, Mary, who cries out the immortal words: 'there's a body in the library'. Colonel Bantry is at first inclined to blame Dolly's recent reading, *The Clue of the Broken Match*, for what must be a misinterpretation of events. The Colonel states that, in this fictional story, 'Lord Edgbaston finds a beautiful blonde dead on the library hearthrug. Bodies are always being found in libraries in books. I've never known a case in real life.' And yet, there is indeed a dead young blonde woman in the Bantrys' library. This will soon become a local scandal, with Colonel Bantry at the centre of much gossip, as locals assume that some indiscretion on his part must have been the root cause for the crime. Those who know him best understand that this would not be in his nature, but nevertheless the Colonel is deeply troubled to see his good name impugned, and his resultant sadness is an effective theme in the book. Perhaps it was because the characters were pre-established that Christie felt bold enough to make more of the personal effect of a crime that, at least in part, has the hallmarks of a prank with devastating consequences. The slow ostracization of the Colonel leads to him shying away from his public duties, such as his work on the local council, while he concentrates on his own home and estate. It is a considerable relief to both him and the reader when the truth emerges.

Of course, it is Miss Marple who uncovers the real story that has led to this body in the library. She and Dolly have

The first US paperback from Pocket Books (1945).

forged a closer friendship since *The Thirteen Problems* (they are now on first-name terms), and she is the first person to be informed. 'Oh, I don't want comfort,' Dolly clarifies, when calling early in the morning. 'But you're so good at bodies.' Despite protesting that her mystery-solving has mostly been theoretical to this point, Miss Marple agrees to come to Gossington Hall to help. In part, Dolly is worried about the gossip that will soon engulf them, but most of all she is excited: 'It really *is* rather thrilling.' Miss Marple is given special access, whether the police like it or not, and in the process is reunited with Colonel Melchett and Inspector Slack, who investigated *The Murder at the Vicarage*, while Sir Henry Clithering also has a part to play. Upon seeing the victim, Miss Marple agrees with her friend that the scene of the crime somehow doesn't seem real. This is a good clue for attentive readers, although even Miss Marple struggles to find a relevant village parallel at the beginning of her investigation, much to Dolly's dismay.

Eventually the young woman is identified as Ruby Keene, who had been staying at the Majestic Hotel while working there as a dancer, helping out her injured cousin Josie Turner.[11] The coroner reports that eighteen-year-old Ruby was drugged and strangled, while an even younger female victim will be revealed before the end of the book, meaning this case is particularly brutal to young women. When one character is asked if the victim was pretty, we are told that the question is 'hard to answer from a view of the blue swollen face'. Christie was unapologetic about such choices, as she explained in a 1922 interview: 'My friends shake their heads and sigh that one so young – I am rather young, I admit – should refuse to dwell only on the seamy side of life; but as long as right triumphs in the end – and in my books it does – what does it matter? To tell you the truth, that is the only thing that gives me a twinge of remorse. Suppose I led the young and innocent to believe that the good always do come out on top, and the wicked end their days in misery or terror? They would find life so disappointing!'[12]

Italian edition published by Mondadori in 1948.

Miss Marple depicted on Biblioteca Ora's edition in Spain (1950).

The result of the murder is that St Mary Mead has 'the most exciting morning it had known for a long time'. The vicar and his wife, Griselda, make brief appearances, along with their son David. 'All the books say a child should be left alone as much as possible,' insists Griselda, and Miss Marple agrees. We also meet some of the local older ladies again, such as 'acidulated' Miss Wetherby, and Miss Hartnell. Soon, Miss Marple finds her village parallel, recalling when young Tommy Bond placed a frog in a clock to surprise his new schoolmistress. (Years earlier, Christie had recounted a similar tale as a

A very macabre 1952
Dutch edition from
H.J.W. Becht in Holland.

bedtime story for Rosalind, telling her daughter about the adventures of naughty Red Teddy, who one day put a frog in the teacher's pocket.)[13] One character wonders: 'Is the old lady a bit funny in the head?', but naturally there will be an explanation for this comparison when the solution is revealed. However, the journey to this solution is quite unusual for Agatha Christie. As many commentators have noted, there are almost as many investigators as there are suspects, with seven named members of the police force, plus Miss Marple. Christie made Conway Jefferson 'the pivot of the story' and then added a sprinkling rather than a surplus of connected characters. As she put it, 'In the manner of a cookery recipe add the following ingredients: a tennis pro, a young dancer, an artist, a girl guide, a dance hostess, etc., and serve up à la Miss Marple!'[14] The unusual nature of the novel, with its allusions to detective fiction cliché, is reinforced when one character mentions having procured autographs from several prominent detective story writers, including Christie herself.

The motive for the murder of Ruby Keene seems to be linked to the friendship she had with Conway Jefferson, who is resident at the hotel and not in the best of health. Indeed, we are informed that a sudden shock or fright could kill him, which is exactly the sort of thing dismissed as an unreliable method for murder in 'The Blue Geranium'. Conway was in the process of adopting Ruby and had already adapted his will to make her a major beneficiary, to the detriment of his son-in-law, Mark, and daughter-in-law, Adelaide, which inevitably casts suspicion on them. Conway was inspired by a real person, at least in part, as Christie remembered 'staying one summer for a few days at a fashionable hotel by the seaside I observed a family at one of the tables in the dining-room;

an elderly man … in a wheeled chair, and with him was a family party of a younger generation. Fortunately they left the next day, so that my imagination could get to work unhampered by any kind of knowledge. When people ask "Do you put real people in your books?" the answer is that, for me, it is quite impossible to write about anyone I know, or have ever spoken to, or indeed have even heard about! For some reason, it kills them for me stone dead. But I can take a "lay figure" and endow it with qualities and imaginings of my own.'[15] Other key characters include Raymond Starr, dancer and tennis pro at the hotel, and Basil Blake, a young man who works in the film industry and enjoys annoying the residents of St Mary Mead. He has rented a cottage on the outskirts of the village and uses it to gallivant with his blonde lover, Dinah Lee. Christie has fun with Blake, allowing him a heroic backstory (which results in a brief acknowledgment of the war), while also making him pay for his keenness to upset his neighbours.

One reason for the story's relative paucity of suspects is its unusually short length for an Agatha Christie novel, at little more than 50,000 words. If it had been up to Christie, this would have been the length of most of her novels, as she often had to introduce an extra murder or similar dramatic incident late in proceedings to get closer to the word-count stipulated by publishers. 'I don't like describing people or places,' she admitted. 'I just want to get on with the dialogue.' This was noted by several reviewers of this novel, and also explains her fondness for writing plays.[16] For Christie, 'a great deal of writing a novel is boring; it's a tiresome length, you have to go on for 60,000 or 70,000 words – 45,000 would be quite enough.'[17] In her autobiography, she clarified that 'I know this is

Pan Books' dramatic paperback cover from 1959.

A beautifully simple Crime Club library hardback from 1985.

One of twelve Christie paperbacks released by HarperCollins Children's Books in 1995, with art by Tom Connell.

considered by publishers as too short. Possibly readers feel themselves cheated if they pay their money and only get 50,000 words - so 60,000 or 70,000 are more acceptable.'[18]

The Body in the Library plays fair with its readers for the most part, although some have questioned the practicalities of the crime, including crime fiction writer P. D. James and the podcast *All About Agatha*.[19] These are reasonable critiques, and perhaps Christie underestimated the difficulties of at least one aspect of the murderer's methods, but readers who understand the world as crafted by Christie will still be satisfied with the final deductions. As ever, close attention should be paid to details, including evidence that may have been thrown away, which helps Miss Marple to work out the truth behind the murder. After all, we are told that Miss Marple has 'a mind that has plumbed the depths of human iniquity'. She is no longer presented as quite such a Victorian, and even slips into a puce silk evening gown at one point. Miss Marple admits to being a little snobbish in her attitudes, discussing what a girl 'of our class' would wear, but she is still aware of human nature in a more general sense, including the look that her maid would give when she wouldn't confess to eating some of her employer's cake. Nevertheless, despite enquiries at Somerset House, Miss Marple once more needs to set a trap to catch a killer, as evidence that will stand up in court is thin on the ground.

Although initially written alongside *N or M?*, *The Body in the Library* seems to have been delivered to her agent at least a few weeks after the other novel. By October 1940, Edmund Cork had read the book, liked it 'very much indeed', and expected it to be a success.[20] In the United States the *Saturday Evening Post* paid around $25,000 for the serialisation rights, although unfortunately for Christie the payment was held up due to her ongoing tax problems with the federal authorities. (The early 1940s saw the beginning of a long-running disagreement about the way in which Christie's earnings in the United States should be taxed, as she was an author based in the United Kingdom. This was an issue that would not be fully resolved for many years and caused the author much anxiety.) The magazine printed the story across seven parts in May and June 1941 and, as was typical for seriali-

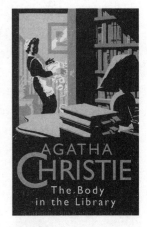

The Body in the Library launched HarperCollins' adult paperback range, also in 1995.

sation, some changes were made, most significantly the entire removal of Chapter 10, which deals with the discovery of the burnt-out car. More unusually, the American book publication from Dodd Mead in February the following year also omitted this chapter. In the United States, this omission continued for further printings and subsequent paperbacks for decades, meaning that many readers on that side of the Atlantic will not have read the full version of the novel.[21] The reason for this is likely to be the same issue that affected the next Miss Marple novel, *The Moving Finger*, in a more substantial way. This was the difficulty of transporting multiple manuscripts between countries at a time of war, meaning that the manuscript used for the serialisation would later have to be reused for book, even though edits had been made.

In Britain, the novel was published in May 1942 (a full year after its American serialisation), but not before Christie objected to the original blurb offered by the publisher. 'I think a blurb ought to be aimed at arousing attention,' she complained, 'rather than just recapitulating the opening events of the book. I enclose a suggestion of my own as being more pro-vocative.'[22] Her publisher, Billy Collins, had initially suggested that the cover for the book was likely to be one using lettering for the cover, as with *N or M?*, due to an apparent difficulty in putting together a pictorial one owing to the war.[23] In the event, the cover is both pictorial and text based. It cleverly uses the outlines of book spines on shelves to boldly spell out the title, followed by the author's name in large letters; simply the name 'Agatha Christie' was enough to guarantee a bestseller by this point.

An abridged paperback for language schools from Penguin Readers in 2008.

Around this time *Coronet Magazine* in Chicago profiled Christie in an article called 'Merchants of Murder', as she had reached what they described as 'the top rung of a spooky ladder of success'.[24] Professionally, Christie was starting to move into a class of her own, coming off the back of a prolific 1930s with several more titles ready to go, including the two reserved for much later publication, and the possibility of keeping a third (*Towards Zero*, investigated by Superintendent Battle) in reserve until she needed it, although in the end it was published in 1944.

On the whole, the book was greeted warmly by reviewers, thanks to Christie's 'splendid and witty female character sketches' and one newspaper even claimed that 'Miss Marple is even more fascinating than M. Hercule Poirot'.[25] The welcoming back of Miss Marple herself – in only her second novel – was a recurring theme in the book's reception. The *New York Times* seemed particularly thrilled, claiming that 'every one who has met this quiet-spoken village sleuth of Agatha Christie's will welcome her again with delight.'[26] One Canadian newspaper particularly enjoyed the sight of an older lady outsmarting the local police, pointing out that 'after all, she is a woman and at the end of this excellent story will be found good and sufficient reasons why a woman's mind should function where the male variety would be completely at a loss.'[27] Closer to home, the *Times Literary Supplement* found it hard 'not to be impressed by old-maid logic. When Miss Marple says "The dress was all wrong," she is plainly observing facts hidden from the masculine eye – facts which are of a very lively interest.'[28] Reviewers were more divided on the merits of the mystery; while some declared it to be 'well up to her usual high standard' or even 'at her best', others were less sure.[29] In particular, long-time fan and reviewer of Christie's work Maurice Richardson, of *The Observer* in the UK, felt the story fell a 'long way below Miss Christie's best. Ingenious, of course, but interest is rather diffuse and the red herrings have lost their phosphorescence.'[30] Perhaps Christie was becoming a victim of her own success, as the *New York Times* felt that 'Although this is not the best of Agatha Christie's plots, the story is still in the upper brackets of excellence.'[31]

A nod to the first edition in 2007, with art by Julie Jenkins.

The book was of sufficient interest to novelist L. P. Hartley that he dedicated some of his column in *The Sketch* to a discussion of it, and Christie more generally.[32] Hartley was particularly interested in the problem of using characters as both clues in a puzzle and as people who could exist in the real world. He praised Christie ('she is so good at imitating the surface of life – what could be more lifelike than her dialogue?') but felt that, when the truth is revealed and characters are not necessarily who the reader felt they were, 'we feel slightly resentful of the trick'. Regarding *The Body in the Library*:

Looking back, we realise that, in this spate of words, there is many a sentence, standing out quite boldly, that should have put us on the right track; only the right track, alas! sets such a strain on our credulity … Ingenious as the plan was, the chances of its succeeding were infinitesimal … in real life I am sure that Miss Marple would not have been alone in discovering [the plan's flaw]. She keeps it to herself, which is just as well, otherwise we should have missed this imperfect, but still dazzling, example of Mrs Christie's virtuosity.[33]

This 'imperfect, but still dazzling' example of Christie has since gone on to be such a well-known story that it may have even supplanted the cliché that it was spoofing.

The Moving Finger
(Novel, 1943)

In March 1941, Christie's agent wrote to his American counterpart to pass on some good news: 'The next Christie story will be a perfectly sweet poison pen tragedy featuring Miss Marple'.[34] For Christie, this new book, *The Moving Finger*, was another 'pleasant challenge to put up a classic theme to oneself and see what one can do with it!', following her success along similar lines with *The Body in the Library*.[35] *The Moving Finger* takes its title from the *Rubáiyát of Omar Khayyám* ('The Moving Finger writes; and, having writ, Moves on …'), a nineteenth-century translation of Persian poems allegedly written centuries earlier by Omar Khayyam. Christie

ABOVE LEFT: The UK first edition of *The Moving Finger* with its striking spider's web motif (1943). **ABOVE RIGHT:** The British first edition was pre-empted by Dodd Mead's American hardback in 1942, with a cover by Henry Koerner.

An early Pan edition from 1948 with art by Reina Sington.

was clearly a fan of the work, as she referenced it several times across her career, including with the title of her unpublished first novel *Snow Upon the Desert*. Even without knowledge of this influence, it is certainly an evocative title, and the book does precisely what its name implies, as a roving finger of blame and suspicion is pointed at the residents of the country village Lymstock, which eventually leads to murder.

The story is told by airman Jerry Burton, who is resting in Lymstock with his sister Joanna while he recuperates after an accident. One morning he receives a vicious and anonymous letter accusing him and Joanna of being lovers, not siblings. This is obviously not the case, and the pair initially assume that they are being targeted as outsiders, but soon learn that almost everyone in the village seems to have received similarly unfounded poison-pen letters. This creates unease, but things then worsen when Mona Symmington, the wife of the local solicitor, appears to commit suicide after receiving a note casting doubt on the paternity of one of her children. Mystery readers are right to be cautious of apparent suicides, but the next death is unequivocally murder, as the Symmingtons' maid, Agnes, is found dead with a brutal head injury. The vicar's wife, Maud Dane Calthrop, then decides that something must be done and calls in an expert to solve the mystery – 'We want someone who knows a great deal about *wickedness*!', she declares – and Miss Marple is sent for.

When St Mary Mead's finest arrives, it is almost three-quarters of the way through the book, indicating that otherwise Miss Marple may have worked out the truth a little too quickly for a novel-length mystery, as she only features in about ten pages. Miss Marple is excited to have been called, though:

'We have so little to talk about in the country!',
she claims, despite her history of crime-solving.
She immediately equates the late Agnes with
her own current maid, Edith: 'Such a nice little
maid, and so willing, but sometimes just a *little*
slow to take in things.' Christie's feelings about
the relationship between employer and servant
were influenced by her own older relatives. 'They
worked their servants to the bone but took a lot of
care of them when they were ill,' she told an interviewer. 'If a girl had a rather disorganised baby [a
euphemism for an unplanned pregnancy outside
of marriage], granny would go and speak to the
young man. "Well, are you going to do the right
thing by Harriet?"'[36] Miss Marple's deductions

The first in a
succession of American
paperbacks published
by Avon (1948).

continue to rely on human nature, and include her pondering
that 'To commit a successful murder must be very much like
bringing off a conjuring trick.' This principle of misdirection
is one that both she and Christie will return to in *They Do It
with Mirrors* a decade later.

Agnes does not receive adequate protection from her
employer, and the result is one of the most memorably nasty
murders in the whole of Agatha Christie, as she is first hit on
the head, and then a kitchen skewer is inserted into the base
of her skull. There is still a definite segregation between the
apparent importance of the lives of servants and those who
employ them, although neither of the dead characters is particularly missed at the book's conclusion. A cold-hearted Jerry
contemplates the deaths of Mona Symmington and Agnes,
and decides to emphasise that 'Agnes's boy[friend] hadn't
been very fond of her', and 'what the hell? We've all got to
die sometime', before concluding that 'everything was for
the best in the best of possible worlds'. While Jerry's feelings
towards Agnes are a blasé dismissal of the importance of the

Avon retitled the book *The Case of the Moving Finger* in 1952.

Art Sussman's cover for Avon in 1957.

life of a servant, his feelings about the late Mona Symmington are more personal. Throughout the novel Jerry strikes up a friendship, and later romance, with Mrs Symmington's daughter from her first marriage, Megan Hunter. Although she is twenty years old, Megan is childlike in character, and not treated as an adult by her peers and family until she and Jerry fall in love. She was one of Christie's own favourite characters: 'If Megan walked into my room tomorrow I should recognize her at once and be delighted to see her,' she wrote. 'I am grateful to her for really becoming alive for me. I would also like to meet the Vicar's wife, but am afraid I never shall.'[37]

Elsewhere in the village is a further cast of characters who all provide either entertainment or suspicion. Owen Griffith, the local doctor, is sketched out as a love interest for Joanna, although there are some questions raised about him and his sister Aimée, especially when it is revealed that they had witnessed a similar poison-pen letter campaign when they lived in the north of England. Aimee is rightly bitter that she could have been a doctor, but her parents were unwilling to fund her studies as they had for her brother. There are also characters in the Symmington household who may be significant to the mystery, including Richard Symmington himself, the family's patriarch, as well as the governess Elsie Holland, who mysteriously does not receive a poison-pen letter.

For many modern readers, one of the most striking residents of the village is Mr Pye, who is brought to life through a series of clichés that make it clear that he is gay. Jerry describes him as 'an extremely ladylike plump little man,

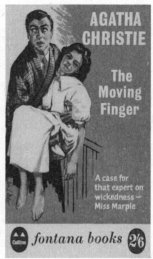

Collins' paperback imprint Fontana Books took over paperback rights from Pan for this 1961 release, with front cover by John L. Baker.

devoted to his petit point chairs, his Dresden shepherdesses and his collection of bric-à-brac.' Despite the sometimes cruel descriptions of him, Mr Pye seems to be quite a happy man, and he enjoys the company of the Burtons. However, his apparent 'ladylike' demeanour also means that he is enrolled in the cast of suspects when the police initially believe that the writers of the letters must be a woman. A typewriter is used for the envelopes of the letters (their contents being taken from a cannibalised old book), which makes identification of the individual responsible more difficult, although apparently they only used one finger, unlike Christie, who proudly told one interviewer that she used three fingers on each hand: 'most amateur typists can only use two', she boasted.[38]

Christie enjoyed making her 'contribution to the subject' of poison-pen letters, as she was interested in the psychology of such a campaign as well as the practicalities. 'How close a resemblance is there between them?' she wondered. 'Is the underlying motive nearly always the same? What scope does such material offer to a crime-minded person?'[39] Her contribution so impressed one reader that they were compelled to make contact with the author. Elbridge W. Stein of New York, an 'Examiner of Questioned Documents', complimented Christie on her discussion of motives for anonymous letters, and suggested to her a discussion of some interesting cases, although she doesn't appear to have taken him up on the offer.[40] She continued to return to the novel over the years, and as late as 1972 placed it in her top ten favourite books of her own. In 1966 it was one of the titles that she mentioned in her interview with Francis Wyndham, recalling that it 'has good misdirection. There's a trap set at the very beginning, and as arranged by the murderer you fall right in it.'[41]

AGATHA CHRISTIE
The Moving Finger

FONTANA BOOKS

An astonishingly photo-realistic painting by Tom Adams for Fontana in 1965.

Christie reflected that 'This is a book I found great pleasure in writing. I liked its cosy village atmosphere and characters. Exotic settings, I sometimes think, detract from the interest of the crime itself. For a crime to be interesting it should occur amongst people you yourself might meet any day.'[42] Her agents also liked it. Harold Ober, her American agent, felt that it 'seems to me one of the best she has done for a long time.'[43] Collier's magazine in the United States was happy to pay for serialisation rights (an important income stream), but they demanded more substantial changes than normal. It was standard practice for magazines and newspapers to edit novels for their readers, but in this case more changes were needed, particularly in order to move the action forward.[44] Christie agreed to undertake the changes herself ('I think I can deal with Poison Pen all right') and by mid-January 1942 she had condensed the first 103 pages of the typescript down to 71, with some minor additional material as well.[45] It was introduced as 'the story of a romance fostered by malice, overshadowed by murder, and haunted by mystery', with the budding relationship between Megan and Jerry emphasised throughout as its illustrations depicted Megan as a long-legged conventionally attractive woman dressed in the fashion of the day, rather than the childlike 'tall awkward girl' as described in the story.[46] Miss Marple did not feature in any of the illustrations.

The impact of the war meant that this editing had wider repercussions in the United States. In America, agent Harold Ober received a copy of the typescript at a time when sending material across the Atlantic was fraught with difficulties. In February he received two sets of notes that outlined revisions to be made, one apparently being for the novel (i.e., smaller typographical changes), and the more substantial revisions for the lucrative magazine deal, with serialisation set to begin the following month. In the days when reproduction of material was far from straightforward, this created difficulties as there now needed to be two different versions of the story, but Ober had only one typescript. The result is one of the oddest mysteries that international Agatha Christie fans have uncovered over the years, which is that the *Collier's* version of the mystery was then used as

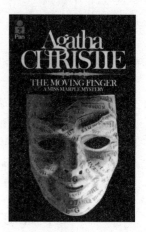

One of a short-lived range of Pan 'double-dagger' paperbacks in 1982.

the basis for the United States' book edition of *The Moving Finger*, meaning that it reads differently from the original version that was printed elsewhere, as well as being substantially shorter.

Christie fans in the United States could read the story quite some time before those in her home country. The American Dodd Mead edition was published in July 1942, with the British Collins Crime Club joining it some eleven months

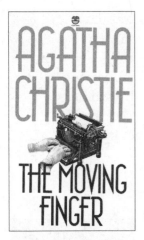

Anticipating Christie's centenary, Fontana repackaged the entire canon in paperback (1988).

later, in June 1943. The Collins cover depicts relevant objects caught in a spider's web, a reflection that, in December 1942, Christie had suggested either *The Spider's Web* or *The Tangled Web* for the British publication, but the former had been used for another recent book (and would later be used by Christie for an unrelated play), and the publishers didn't like the latter.[47] The British book used Christie's original text, although the 1953 Penguin edition erroneously used the shorter American version.[48] Difficulties of war impacted on publication, and like other books from this era, the novel was published across fewer pages due to paper shortages. This may have also accounted for malaise among magazines when it came to serialisations in the UK, as Amalgamated Press paid a paltry £300 to publish it in its magazine *Woman's Pictorial* in October and November 1942.[49]

In *The Sketch*, L. P. Hartley greeted the publication of the novel with some further ruminations on Agatha Christie. Picking up on Miss Marple's comment about misdirection, he pointed out that Christie did the same. 'There are quite a number of ladies in Lymstock . . . [but] we are too busy enjoying their company and their pointful conversation to be as alert as we might be,' he believed. He felt that the conclusion came:

as a surprise indeed, but not as a shock, and not with a sense of climax. We had found it so interesting to look in the wrong direction that we slightly resent being re-orientated, even in the service of justice. As regards dialogue and characterisation, *The Moving Finger* takes a high place among Mrs Christie's stories. The detective element, cleverly managed as it is, is a little disappointing. But then, in a conjuring trick, it is the illusion of magic that fascinates us, rather than the means by which the illusion is produced.[50]

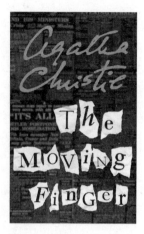

The Moving Finger was generally well received by critics. The *Oakland Tribune* felt that 'After reading this the fans will agree again that Agatha Christie never lets her readers down. Her astounding resourcefulness shows no strain.'[51] Other North American newspapers were equally pleased for the most part, with one being wowed by how Miss Marple 'unravelled the many twisted lines of this case by applying her knowledge, and prevented the wrong person from suffering horribly, makes an amazing story.

The 2006 paperback design by Nick Castle from HarperCollins.

Christie has again written one of those astonishing detective stories for which she has long been noted.'[52] The *New York Times* found it to be 'one of the better productions by a writer whose work is always good', while a Pennsylvania newspaper insisted that 'it is a strong-willed person indeed who will be able to leave this novel unfinished once he has started to read it.'[53] One critic was less pleased with the return of Miss Marple, however: 'Agatha Christie forsakes for once her delightful M. Poirot and foists upon us a rather tiresome elderly female detective whom she obviously cherishes', grumbled *The Courier Journal*, which at least admitted that the plot was 'sound and smoothly planned'.[54] For Montreal's *The Gazette*, there was high praise:

> Her picture of village life as seen through Jerry Burton's eyes is brilliant, her sketches of village character so true that the doctor, the lawyer and the rector and the others walk through her pages in the flesh, with their virtues and their foibles, their major and their minor tragedies and

their gossiping tongues. More still, there is romance. It touches the Burtons, brother and sister, and gives to *The Moving Finger* a charm which lifts the story to a plane rarely reached in mystery fiction. Agatha Christie gets better as she goes on.[55]

When published in Britain, Maurice Richardson in *The Observer* conceded that 'Probably you will call Mrs Christie's double bluff, but this will only increase your pleasure.'[56] The *Times Literary Supplement* was particularly keen on the new novel, calling it a puzzle 'fit for experts', even if it questioned some of the characterisation of Jerry. Nevertheless, the review concluded that there 'has rarely been a detective story so likely to create an epidemic of self-inflicted kicks'.[57]

Although *The Moving Finger* is not one of the most famous Agatha Christie novels, it certainly has an atmosphere all of its own, as it places the machinations of village life above the mystery at times, which means that it lingers in the memory long after the villain's reasonably straightforward motivation is revealed. In her autobiography, Christie stated that *Crooked House* and *Ordeal by Innocence* were the novels that satisfied her best, but that, to her surprise, a recent re-reading revealed that 'another one I am really pleased with is *The Moving Finger*. It is a great test to re-read what one has written some seventeen or eighteen years later. One's view changes. Some do not stand the test of time, others do.'[58]

Murder at the Vicarage (Play)
(Stage Adaptation, 1949)

During the 1940s there started to be more interest in Miss Marple appearing beyond the printed page. Although Agatha Christie was always particularly protective over the character of Hercule Poirot, she was a little more relaxed when it came to her other sleuths. Christie's agent fielded queries about adaptations of works starring her private detective Parker Pyne and the mysterious Mr Quin, as well as several other stories, and by the 1950s there were frequent queries about Miss Marple. The 1940s had laid the foundations for further appearances, as she first cropped up on radio, and then made her stage debut.

ABOVE: Barbara Mullen was the first to play the role of Miss Marple in the original production which was produced at the Playhouse Theatre, London, on 16 December 1949.

This time, Miss Marple took to the airwaves in the United States, where the rise of commercial radio resulted in an appetite for strong, clearly plotted stories that could be translated to the medium. One programme requiring such stories was *Murder Clinic*, which adapted several of Christie's stories, including one of *The Thirteen Problems* in January 1943. 'Sleuthing takes on a lavender and old lace tinge when Aratha [sic] Christie's mystery yarn, "The Blue Geranium" is

dramatized on Mutual Don Lee's *Murder Clinic*', read one piece of publicity for the half-hour programme.[59] The producers were apparently proud of the 'touch of realism' provided by the casting of septuagenarian Vivia Ogden as Miss Marple. According to the newspapers, Miss Marple is 'a ringer for Whistler's Mother', and 'tackles all sorts of weird happenings, including wallpaper that changes colour, in order to prove her case and get her murderer!'[60] Unfortunately, no recording is known to survive.

Vivia Ogden was a silent movie star who subsequently found fame on American radio as 'Mother' in the 1930s series *The Wayside Cottage*.

Back at home, Christie started to show an interest in placing Miss Marple on stage. Perhaps this was because the small, domestic stories in which the character had mostly featured so far could work particularly well in the confines of a theatre, and they were certainly a contrast to Poirot's more frequently globetrotting adventures. According to John Curran, who has forensically interrogated Christie's almost indecipherable notebooks, Christie considered dramatising *The Moving Finger* at some point, although the plans don't seem to have got very far.[61] Julius Green, historian of Christie's stage plays, discovered that Christie also considered adapting *The Murder at the Vicarage* for the theatre as early as 1939, and wrote to producer Basil Dean to suggest the idea.[62] There are occasional mentions of a stage version of the novel over the next few years in Christie's agent's correspondence, but it's not clear if these references are to a script by Christie or a new venture by someone else. On Christmas Eve 1942, Edmund Cork told his client that there was 'no news yet' about *Murder at the Vicarage*, and in September 1944 let her know that '*Murder at the Vicarage* has fallen through again'.[63] A few years later a deal was made that would finally bring the story to the stage, as in 1948 writers Barbara Toy and Moie Charles proposed adapting the story. Christie readily agreed, with a licence issued at the end of 1948.[64]

In mid-1949 a script was sent to Christie, who liked it on the whole. Toy and Charles necessarily reduced the cast of characters and made some more subtle commentary in the novel more overt, while also ensuring that events were dramatic enough for a night in the theatre, which required changes to the denouement. Christie acknowledged that 'It still has the rather too cosy novelish atmosphere of "Let's sit down and wonder whodunnit" – but I never could see how that could be avoided in this particular book.'[65] More generally, she was concerned that the story itself required simplification, pointing to the business with the clock in the study as an example. In the novel, the clock (which is set to the wrong time) is an important part of the mystery's construction, but Christie rightly pointed out that you could not expect a theatre audience to make sense of it in the way a reader could. Christie also approved of the addition of 'a kind of duel' in the last act, which sees a battle of wits between Miss Marple and a villainous character ('excellent, and gives drama'). In addition, Christie wasn't keen on the apparent use of weedkiller, as she felt that everyone 'knows the symptoms of weedkiller far too well ... Suggest cyanide. Miss M. always has it handy for wasps nest (right time of year).' More minor points included the question of the right fruit for summer, which meant that Miss Marple's plums became raspberries.

MURDER
AT THE VICARAGE
AGATHA CHRISTIE

Dramatised by
MOIE CHARLES AND BARBARA TOY

SAMUEL FRENCH LIMITED

The playscript was
published by Samuel
French in January 1951.

In terms of characters, Christie suggested the shoring up of Lettice Protheroe in particular, who 'must be definitely shown to be a vicious child, not merely a vague one'. A perceptive dramatist, she also suggested adding more incident early in the story, and indeed the slowness of the first act was commented on by several reviewers when the play made it to the stage a few months later.[66] Christie suggested that Lawrence and Anne had 'a moment or two of passionate lovemaking in the first scene of all. It would give the audience the sensation of knowing something the Vicar doesn't (the play at present is, like the autobiographical book, rather a reflection of just what he knows)'. Finally, the story's originator insisted on the final moments being changed. 'I do not like Miss Marple's fainting at the end. It is, it really is, corny. Just done for the curtain – and absolutely untypical of her. No, that really cannot be.' Christie was not only protecting her creation, but also ensuring that the play did not slip into parody. In the revised version of the script, the story ends with Miss Marple calling Inspector Slack, perhaps with a little smugness, that she has solved the case, even if it has resulted in a gun-wielding culprit causing a new death.

The play *Murder at the Vicarage* (which dropped the definite article from the title) necessarily differentiates itself from the first-person book, and offers a heightened version of the story and broader characters, including Miss Marple. We can no longer be guided by the vicar's withering insight, and so must immediately recognise character types as presented to us, as without the vicar's commentary much of the nuance is lost. However, it is also a story that makes relatively little use of clues surrounding the central crime, meaning that it doesn't always feel like much of a mystery. The small-scale setting makes the story superficially suitable for the stage, but the fact remains that *The Murder at the Vicarage* as originally written is predominately a character study, and the production struggles under all its constraints.

Given the fact that thirty-five-year-old Barbara Mullen was cast as Miss Marple in this original production, it makes sense that the script describes the character as 'neat, and of uncertain years' although she is still elderly.[67] Her arrival is announced alongside the rice pudding, which gives a sense of her (lack of) status. In fact, those unacquainted with the character may consider her to be one of the most viable suspects, as the play adds the detail that Colonel Protheroe was to sell his houses in the village, including Miss Marple's cottage, which would be an excellent motive for murder. 'He laughed in my face and said I'd better make the best use of my garden whilst I had it,' relays a shocked Miss Marple. St Mary Mead's finest really hits her stride when the police arrive, as she 'smiles smugly at knowing the correct procedure' when interviewed by the Inspector. Of course, she is inevitably over-looked, which she complains about: 'you gentlemen are always so dominating that it's almost impossible to get a word in edgeways'. Close readers of Christie's original Miss Marple stories may let out a small cheer when they hear a reference to the enduring mystery of the missing shrimps.[68] Her appearances are not always greeted warmly, just as in the original novel: 'All spinsters should be put away at fifty,' complains one character, with another calling her an 'old busybody'.

The investigation into the murder of Colonel Protheroe is complicated by the legion of enemies that he managed to accumulate. Even the curate Ronald Hawes exclaims: 'So there is righteousness in the world after all', once it is clear that the Colonel is dead. Another surprise for audiences may be the hints of nostalgia for wartime, as mentioned by Griselda. This play is set in 'the present time' of 1949, a world away

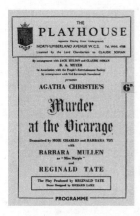

The programme for the 1949–50 London run.

from the Britain of twenty years earlier, when the novel was written. The path to identifying the person or persons responsible is so unclear that at one point a character responsible for at least part of the crime practically boasts of the fact: 'It certainly does seem to be a beautifully thought-out crime. No clues – nothing.' Thankfully Miss Marple is not deterred. 'The Inspector and I work on different lines,' she points out. 'He looks for clues in facts – while I look for them in human nature.'

The play opened in Northampton on 17 October 1949, directed by Reginald Tate, who also played Lawrence Redding, and who is probably best remembered for originating the part of Bernard Quatermass in the 1953 BBC television serial *The Quatermass Experiment*. Christie was in attendance for the premiere, and in later years she indicated some regret about allowing others to adapt her work. 'It seemed to me that the adaptations of my books to the stage failed mainly because they stuck far too closely to the original book,' she felt. 'A detective story is particularly unlike a play, and so is far more difficult to adapt than an ordinary book. It has such an intricate plot, and usually so *many* characters and false clues, that the thing is bound to become confusing and overladen.'[69] Christie, then, understood that adaptations of her work required changes, rather than a slavish adherence to the original plotting, in order for the story to work for a new medium; fidelity was not her primary concern. The play transferred to the Playhouse Theatre in London's West End on 16 December 1949, where it received a mixed but mostly positive reception.[70] By January 1950, Edmund Cork reported that it was doing better than most 'straight plays', and there was a suggestion that the theatre's stage could even be used to host a party to say farewell to Christie before her next trip to the

Middle East with Max.[71] However, a few months later Cork had to report what he called 'an ignominious conclusion', when the play closed at the beginning of April 1950, but it was at least a long-enough run for it to be of interest to those staging amateur productions.[72]

Perhaps surprisingly, the fact that Mullen was half the age of the character she was playing did not present much of an issue for many critics, although Christie was privately unhappy. 'I've had to put up with several plays and films that I *hate* to have been associated with my name,' she wrote in 1971. 'I hated *Murder at the Vicarage* and Miss Marple of twenty odd [sic] – and several of the "adapted" plays from my books.'[73]

The programme from London's Savoy Theatre, 1975–76.

Nevertheless, the play certainly didn't seem to do Christie any harm, and one critic argued that 'Without Miss Mullen, *Murder at the Vicarage* would not provide even a light evening's entertainment.'[74] *The Observer*'s Ian Brown felt that the story was 'neatly knit together and tied up for the stage', although he had some sympathy for the apparently loathed victim: 'The poor man was living with an unfaithful wife and an odious daughter in a village which had a half-demented curate, a nosy spinster, a battle-cruiserish memsahib, and a glib, philandering artist, very glossy and gay in his gent's Bohemian shirtings. Perhaps the Colonel was better out of it.' Mullen and Tate were both praised, and it was felt that their performances gave a 'West End quality to a production otherwise on a less exalted level'.[75]

W. A. Wilcox in the *Sunday Dispatch* was less keen, drawing attention to 'a long and rather dull session of chattering and twittering'. Wilcox was also an early advocate of the idea of a 'Dark Marple', arguing that 'I don't believe "X" did it. I think it was Miss Marple'![76] W. A. Darlington in the *Daily Telegraph*

Avril Angers took over from Barbara Mullen when the play transferred to London's Fortune Theatre in 1976.

was one of the critics who was confused by Mullen's casting. 'The mystery for me was why Barbara Mullen wanted to play Miss Marple,' he wrote. 'Throughout she was obviously a young woman acting on [sic] old one. Walk, gestures, voice were all careful imitations, and never seemed anything else. So why?'[77] Finally, *The Stage* considered the characters to be the real weak link. 'The figures in the play are little more than pawns on the criminological chess-board, and the dialogue rarely achieves any genuine dramatic quality,' stated the reviewer, who also found Miss Marple 'irritating' (which she is in this play, on occasion), and felt that it would be good entertainment strictly for those who were not regular theatre-goers.[78]

Later developments showed that Cork was right about the play's longevity among amateur and smaller theatrical groups. *Murder at the Vicarage* has been performed many times over the years, although Christie 'did not consider that any of the dramatizations [of her novels] were in any sense my plays'.[79] Nevertheless, the play was even revived in the West End in the 1970s, with Barbara Mullen reprising the role of Miss Marple. She was now, finally, the right age for the character.[80]

The 1940s saw some more intense reflection on the types of crimes considered to be typically popular both within English detective fiction and the British press, which had become increasingly obsessed with crime in order to satisfy its bloodthirsty readers. According to George Orwell in his 1946 essay 'Decline of the English Murder', a typical scenario for admirers of classic crime would be 'Sunday afternoon, preferably before the war'. Orwell considered what might be described as the 'perfect' murder for the readers of popular newspapers (and, surely, also popular fiction). 'The murderer should be a little man of the professional class,' Orwell claimed, who should also live in the suburbs and plan his crime to perfection, ideally in order to hide a less palatable truth, such as a confession of adultery. The murderer should live in a semi-detached house, to enable nosy neighbours (of the Miss Marple type?), and of course the murderer will also 'slip up', due to a tiny detail (that would no doubt be noticed by Christie's detectives).[81] In 1944, *The Big Sleep* author Raymond Chandler was less warmly nostalgic for what might be called 'cosy crime', even when it is vicious and brutal. His essay 'The Simple Art of Murder' revels in barbed compliments, such as 'The English may not always be the best writers in the world, but they are incomparably the best dull writers', and that *Murder on the Orient Express*'s solution 'is guaranteed to knock the keenest mind for a loop. Only a halfwit could guess it.'[82] Chandler helped to establish that there was a particular, almost indefinable, style to then-contemporary detective fiction, one which the readers readily accepted without thinking. For Chandler, these books 'do not really come off intellectually as problems, and they do not come off artistically as fiction. They are too contrived, and too little aware of what goes on in the world.' Such complaints of artifice, including an alleged depiction of England that never truly existed, have been frequently levelled at Christie and some of her contemporaries, but they are not always well-founded.[83] The fact remains that the continuing popularity of Christie's works over a century after her debut novel shows that, while readers may well notice the artifice of these stories, this helps rather than hinders their enjoyment. Arguably, the escapist, entertaining but dangerous world of St Mary Mead invites readers back time and time again precisely because of its intangible link with 'the real world' that we are otherwise forced to occupy.

10, Downing Street,
Whitehall.

21st April, 1950

 Fifty books! Many of them have beguiled and
made agreeable my leisure. I admire and delight in
the ingenuity of Agatha Christie's mind and in her
capacity to keep a secret until she is ready to
divulge it. And I admire, also, another of her
qualities, one that is not always possessed by
those who produce detective stories, her ability
clearly and simply to write the English language
 I am looking forward to the next fifty books.

C. R. Attlee

CHAPTER THREE

THE
1950s

A lthough myriad critics and readers had enjoyed the exploits of Miss Marple since her inception, by the end of the 1940s the character had featured in only three published novels and fewer than twenty short stories. Her appearances elsewhere had been irregular; the stage production of *Murder at the Vicarage* was probably the most prominent, but was hardly a runaway success, while she had only twice appeared on the radio. However, the 1950s saw Miss Marple become an even more prominent part of the world of Agatha Christie.

Not only did 1950 see the publication of a new Miss Marple novel, but in the United States she was also one of the stars of

OPPOSITE: It's 1950, and Agatha's 50th book, *A Murder is Announced*, is celebrated by her publishers, who released this tribute from the British Prime Minister, Clement Attlee.

The cover of the promotional leaflet for *A Murder is Announced*, which demonstrates how a combination of UK and US editions were needed to achieve the final tally.

a new collection of short stories, *Three Blind Mice*. Four Miss Marple tales that had been penned in the early 1940s found a home here, and in Britain they were later collected in 1979's *Miss Marple's Final Cases*.[1] *Three Blind Mice* (which is longer than a standard short story) is based on the radio play that became *The Mousetrap*, and it remains uncollected in Britain, while Mr Quin's 'The Love Detectives' was also uncollected in Christie's home country for many years due to its similarities to *The Murder at the Vicarage*. Nevertheless, with the addition of a few Poirot short mysteries, it's a good if slightly unusual collection that was well received by many, with the *Chicago Sunday Tribune* enjoying the fact that the book featured stories from three of Christie's star detectives, including 'acid-tongued little Miss Marple', a curious description of the tall and usually mild-mannered lady.[2] The *Hartford Courant* was less sure, feeling that 'the plotting is as slick as ever, but in the narrow space of more demanding forms, settings and characters suffer. The stories are thin, more like technical exercises than well-rounded yarns.'[3] With the star attraction of the title story unavailable to Collins, and a general feeling at the British publisher that Christie's older short stories were weaker and could do harm to her reputation, this collection did not make it across the Atlantic.

Any such qualms were not an indication of waning interest in either Agatha Christie or Miss Marple, though. The new decade would see Miss Marple stretch even further from the page as she reached the world of television, as well as reappearing on BBC radio, while the number of novels featuring her would more than double, to seven. However, Christie herself was starting to become more interested in the world of theatre than more prose. Although she continued to publish at least one new mystery novel a year, she much preferred writing for the stage, buoyed by the ongoing success of *The Mousetrap*, which premiered in 1952 and has run ever since, while other stage successes this decade included *Witness for the Prosecution* (1954) and *Spider's Web* (1955). When Christie did write books, Miss Marple was now the detective in a higher proportion of titles than ever before. Appropriately for a character who would find fame in her later decades, it took a considerable number of years for Miss Marple to really come into her own, but it would be worth the wait.

An oddly familiar cover for *The Mousetrap* when the 1978 script book was first released in paperback by Bantam (1981) – Tom Adams' painting for *They Do It with Mirrors!*

A Murder is Announced
(Novel, 1950)

In August 1948, Agatha Christie wrote to Edmund Cork and advised him of her current plans. Christie's thoughts for the future had the air of reluctance, given that she hadn't done any major writing that year, but she seemed happy to continue this ongoing holiday from murder, as she instead enjoyed her time with Max. 'I think – if I ever do settle down to write,' she told Cork, 'it will be a Miss Marple again.'[4] Christie had got over her earlier reluctance to use Poirot, but at around this time he was no longer the star attraction that he once had been in the all-important magazine market. Besides,

ABOVE LEFT: *A Murder is Announced* included a rare tagline on the jacket, making the most of this being Agatha Christie's fiftieth book (1950). **ABOVE RIGHT:** Dodd Mead went further: 'Agatha Christie's 50th mystery novel', they declared, with accolades by Ellery Queen and John Dickson Carr (1950).

Miss Marple's intuition-led detection meant that she tended to solve mysteries that required less complicated planning and placement of clues. A Miss Marple novel was therefore a perfect vehicle to ease Christie back into writing, and could supply a mystery of the type requested by the *Saturday Evening Post*: 'a story which is a good story without a murder, and then to add a murder'.[5] There is no doubt that *A Murder is Announced* is certainly this, as it stands tall as one of the very best Miss Marple novels.[6]

In Chipping Cleghorn an advertisement is placed in the local paper. 'A murder is announced,' it reads, 'and will take place on Friday, October 29th, at Little Paddocks at 6.30 p.m. Friends please accept this, the only intimation.' Understandably, this excites the interests of the locals, although judging by other newspaper headlines, the villagers seem to be quite casual about death, as nobody bats an eyelid that 'Twenty-three die of food poisoning in Seaside Hotel'. We witness several households' reactions over breakfast, most of which are excited by the prospect, in one way or another. Less impressed is the owner of Little Paddocks, Miss Blacklock. A sixty-year-old single woman who sports a choker of large fake pearls, Miss Blacklock seems resigned to being the recipient of a practical joke. She lives with her old school friend, Dora Bunner, as well as younger cousins Patrick and Julia Simmons, and lodger Phillipa Haymes, although as the story develops the reader is encouraged to question their true identities. As with the best Christies, it is nearly impossible for the reader to be sure if they have predicted a twist or fallen foul of a well-placed red herring.

On the advertised night, a selection of Miss Blacklock's friends and acquaintances make excuses to visit Little Paddocks, commenting on the central heating as they do so in what seems to be typical small talk. Then, the lights go out and a man bursts into the room where everyone has assembled, before a shot is fired, and the intruder ends up dead. The dead man is a local hotel worker originally from Switzerland, and the motive for the crime is difficult to decipher, but in fact eagle-eyed readers have been given two major clues before the end of the second chapter. Also important to the plot are the practicalities of how the murder could be committed in plain sight without the culprit being immediately identified, and in order to work this out Christie enacted the scenario with her neighbours in Wallingford, Oxfordshire.[7] Two more characters are also murdered before the end of the novel, both of whom are particularly likeable, meaning that their deaths have a strong impact.

A 'Thriller Book Club' edition from 1951.

Surprisingly, one of the least likeable characters is also the one with the most sympathetic back-story. Mitzi, housekeeper and cook at Little Paddocks, is a European refugee from the Second World War who is startled by any hint of violent behaviour. 'I do not wish to die!' she asserts. 'Already in Europe I escape. My family they all die – they are all killed – my mother, my little brother, my so sweet little niece – all, all they are killed.' Despite these tragic events, other characters are dismissive of Mitzi's feelings, and suspicious of her claims anyway. 'Yes, yes,' interrupts Miss Blacklock, when the murder of Mitzi's family is raised again, while others complain about her endlessly, and one even 'jokingly' sends her a postcard to say that the Gestapo is on her track. No doubt Christie intended to include Mitzi as some form of comic relief, but the intention falls flat, and her treatment reads as unusually mean and distasteful, especially as many characters are allowed to complain about 'foreigners' unchecked, which is similarly unusual for Christie. However, Mitzi does, at least, get to play out an important scene of bravery towards the end of the novel.

By this stage, Miss Marple's reputation precedes her among both members of the public and the police force, as Sir Henry Clithering suggests enlisting her help; he describes her to a colleague as 'just the finest detective God ever made. Natural genius cultivated in a suitable soil.' Miss Marple is excited to be contacted, and is described as having 'snow-white hair and a pink crinkled face and very soft innocent blue eyes, and she was heavily enmeshed in fleecy wool. Wool round her shoulders in the form of a lacy cape and wool that she was knitting and which turned out to be a baby's shawl.' Once she arrives in Chipping Cleghorn, Miss Marple is certainly well-placed to get the truth out of characters through both her usual questioning and a more careful examination of physical clues than she usually indulges in. She is unfazed by her role as detective. 'I can take care of myself,' she insists, marking her out as a more assertive and confident woman than the one who had been ignored during the 'Tuesday Night Club' meetings. In a characterful insight, Miss Marple also despairs that old age means that 'I've been alone for quite a long time now.' Her investigations include an examination of the doors at Little Paddocks, and a pair of lamps depicting a shepherd and shep-

Collins White Circle international paperback (1951).

herdess. Such attention to detail would be unfathomable to her creator, however. 'I think if you are an inventive person you often walk along thinking things in your head and you just don't recognise people,' confessed Christie in 1967. 'You could change everything round in this room and I shouldn't notice for days.'[8] Miss Marple also takes an active part in the story's resolution, dropping her voice to become 'quiet and remorseless' as she tells the story of how she laid a trap, in part by hiding in a broom cupboard ('Luckily I'm very thin') and, somewhat improbably and unnecessarily, by mimicking another character's voice.

Part of the plot concerns a medical operation of a type that a friend of Christie's had endured in Switzerland many years earlier. 'It will be a great ordeal for you, but if it succeeds it will make such a difference to your life that it will be worth anything you suffer,' Christie's mother had insisted, and it had indeed been a success.[9] Clues to the murderer's identity include the specific use of certain words, and even their spelling, which are essential to the deductions of both Miss Marple and the more alert reader. Christie and her publishers have struggled to control this aspect of the story over the years. Before publication, Christie responded to a copy of the typescript by noting that certain spellings and words were 'Very important', underlining that 'Plot depends on this'.[10] Although any issues were resolved in time for the 1950 publication, the book has been plagued by some unhelpful 'corrections' over the years, both to those points important to the plot, and the spelling of the name of the character Miss Hinchliffe, which occasionally gains an extra 'c' and becomes Hinchcliffe (with the latter spelling subsequently used for the screen adaptations of the novel).[11] As late as the 1980s, an attentive reader alerted Collins to the fact that the paperbacks then in print had also used incorrect spellings of significant clues. The printings reverted to the correct text for the next run, only for the incorrect spellings to then reappear, much to the frustration of the publisher.

An original typescript of *A Murder is Announced* survives, and demonstrates the extent of the changes made by Christie once a full draft of her novels had been written. Almost every page is filled with extra details and changes to

Fontana's paperback from 1953, with artwork by John Rose.

character names and chapter titles. On the first page alone, the novel's title is changed from *A Murder has been Arranged* to *A Murder is Announced*, with the first chapter title offered as 'A Murder has been announced', which is then crossed out.[12] Even the paperboy's name is changed from Johnnie Turtle to Johnnie Butt, while the village of Chipping Barnet becomes Chipping Cleghorn. Another option, Chipping Burton, was dismissed as being too similar to the real-life Chipping Norton, and Christie wasn't sure if there might be a real Chipping Burton anyway (although there isn't).[13] 'Anna' also became Julia, Swiss hotel worker Rene Duchamps ('Too French') became Rudi Scherz after Rudi Wiener was considered, while

Pan Books also published a paperback, with art by John Keay (1958).

Inspector Craddock replaced Inspector Hudson ('Too many H names?'), with Inspector Cary sketched out as a possible alternative.[14] This typescript also includes a slightly different advert in the paper, which is not only phrased differently but offers an earlier date and time. This was probably changed because Christie wanted the central heating to be deployed and the lights to be on when guests arrived, and so the later (and colder) the better. The original advert read: 'A murder has been arranged and will take place on Friday Oct 13th at Little Paddocks at 6.p.m. Friends please accept this, the only intimation.' Finally, Christie wondered if she should include a plan of the drawing room. 'Or is it clear?' she asked herself. In the end, she must have thought so as such an illustration does not feature in the final novel.

The novel was gratefully received by Christie's agents and publishers. 'I have just read *A Murder is Announced* and enjoyed it immensely,' Billy Collins wrote to her. 'I thought it was full of fun and one of your most ingenious stories

Miss Marple in the *Daily News* serial on 3 May 1950.

too.'[15] It was fortunate that Christie's new book was indeed one of her best, as its publication ended up being unusually important. The novel was finished as Christie's contracts with publishers Dodd Mead in the United States and Collins in Britain were to be renewed, and as well as discussions about the financial terms (Christie already received a deal that was more generous than almost any other author in the United States, with 20% of royalties, well above the country's usual top rate of 15%), there was an insistence that more effort needed to be put into publicising Christie's work. During these negotiations Christie was typically detached, simply trusting that Edmund Cork would do his best for her; she seemed more interested when asking him to place a bet for the Grand National on her behalf. Christie's chosen horse, Shagreen, fell at the twenty-third fence, but her own career continued apace. Writing from the British School of Archaeology in Baghdad, she confessed that 'I really felt very ill for the first fortnight out here. Lay in bed and groaned.' There was good news, however: 'I feel very well now, and the enforced meditation is giving me heaps of brilliant ideas for books.'[16]

Christie's agents got their wish for more publicity for her works, which meant that there were two important developments for *A Murder is Announced*. Firstly, the British serialisation of the story in the *Daily Express* was brought forward to February and March 1950 to support the West End run of the play *Murder at the Vicarage*.[17] But more significantly, Christie's publishers agreed that more needed to be done to publicise and celebrate her work, and Cork wrote to Christie in February to inform (and, perhaps, warn) the publicity-shy author that 'Collins are planning to bring out *A Murder is Announced* on June 5th, and they are proposing parties and lots of publicity to celebrate the happy event if you are feeling strong enough.'[18] Cork wrote a couple of weeks later that Collins 'have jolly well got to settle it pretty soon, as they are going ahead with terrific plans for the promotion of *A Murder is Announced*', as some questionable arithmetic meant that it was now being considered to be Christie's fiftieth book, giving a reason for a decent publicity drive at a time of important negotiations. This number was reached by including the likes of *The Regatta Mystery*, an American-only short story collection, while many pieces of attendant publicity would even erroneously refer to *A Murder is Announced* as either Christie's fiftieth novel or fiftieth thriller,

Harry Bennett's cover for Cardinal in the US.

neither of which is correct. Nevertheless, it became a suitable reason to explain her publishers' sudden interest in keeping Christie's agents happy – and sales buoyant – just when they needed her to sign on the dotted line.

In the United States, Dodd Mead even put 'Agatha Christie's 50th Mystery Novel' in large text on the cover of their first edition, which depicted a woman's screaming face in the midst of a pile of Christie titles, while they also agreed to expand their promotion of at least the next three or four Christie books, spending twice the usual amount in advertising.[19] In Britain, Collins' cover featured a simple clockface, and the note that 'For the 50th time the Queen of Detection defies her readers'. The first cover design had been rejected, and there was no time for Christie to approve this cover before the June publication, as she was in Iraq, but Cork assured her that it was 'quite unobjectionable', 'quite dignified' and featured 'no silly hooded figures'.[20] The book is dedicated to 'To Ralph and Anne Newman, at whose house I first tasted "Delicious Death"!', a reference to a particularly indulgent chocolate cake that is the centrepiece to one character's ultimately ill-fated birthday party. The precise details of the cake have long fascinated readers, and in 2010 an 'official' recipe was revealed by Jane Asher as part of celebrations for the 120th anniversary of Christie's birth.[21]

A Murder is Announced is a Christie title that has been particularly frequently commented upon by observers of Christie's work, including those who have found their own success in the world of crime fiction. A few years after publication, Christie argued that she specialised in 'murders of quiet, domestic interest. Give me a nice deadly phial to play with and I am happy.'[22] Although the initial murder may seem a violent one, quiet domesticity is an important element of the crime, in which the murderer will do anything to keep their happy life, even if it means a vicious death for others. The scale of motive remains reasonably small and straightforward. There is no international conspiracy to explain murder here, just a desire to maintain the status quo. After Christie's death, crime writer and critic H. R. F. Keating argued that she 'wrote about the generally accepted image of England so that Americans and people all over the world were delighted and in a way I really think [that] was one of her secrets. She handled her stock responses perfectly. She, being an ordinary person, thought in these terms and therefore produced books which ordinary people all over the world like and want to read.'[23] P. D. James was less complimentary, feeling that 'this story demonstrates both her strength and her weakness'.[24] James claimed that Christie's 'style is neither original nor elegant but it is workmanlike', and that 'Above all she is a literary conjuror who

Tom Adams' first cover for the book in 1963.

Ian Robinson painted Fontana's 1969 cover.

places her pasteboard characters face downwards and shuffles them with practised cunning.'[25] Damning with the faintest praise, James also argued that 'Perhaps her greatest strength was that she never overstepped the limits of her talent.'[26]

The contemporary reaction to *A Murder is Announced* was warm and celebratory, as befitted the publicity surrounding its publication. 'Here is a super-smooth Christie', felt the *New York Times Book Review*. 'Like so many of Miss Christie's quiet feats of magic, this one begins on a grotesque note ... It goes without saying that most readers will guess in vain, though the author lays her facts scrupulously on the line, with an assortment of her famous red herrings, all beautifully marinated.'[27] The *Times Literary Supplement* particularly applauded Christie's use of clues:

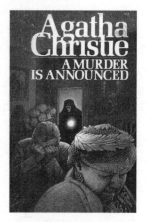

Tom Adams' second cover for Pocket Books in the US (1972).

> The plot is as ingenious as ever, the writing more careful, the dialogue both wise and witty; While suspense is engendered from the very start, and maintained skilfully until the final revelation: it will be a clever reader indeed who anticipates this, and though Miss Christie is as usual scrupulously fair in scattering her clues, close attention to the text is necessary if the correct solution of the mystery is to be arrived at before the astute Miss Marple unmasks the culprit.[28]

Others felt that the novel was 'well up to par, although it may not be such a consummately woven and baffling mystery as a few of its predecessors' and 'one of her very best'.[29] The *Manchester Evening News* commended Christie's 'fertile capacity for tying the reader up in knots is

Tom Adams' third cover, Fontana 1980.

as vigorously at work in this 50th crime novel as it was in the first', while *The New Statesman* warned that 'Never has it been so important to follow Mrs Christie's artless prose word by word … *A Murder is Announced* is a heady wine that will stand comparison with the Christies of any but the best vintage years.'[30] Maurice Richardson in *The Observer* agreed that it was 'Not quite one of her top-notchers, but very smooth entertainment.'[31] *The Sunday Times* pointed out that while 'Connoisseurs may find it not quite up to her very best … look what her very best was!'[32]

The biggest critical controversy was not in terms of reception, but the unwise decision of George Malcolm Thomson of London's *Evening Standard* to casually reveal the identity of the murderer in his brief review. This resulted in a rebuke from many readers and became an ongoing argument that reappeared in the newspaper for several days afterwards, with many letters decrying his choice to 'ruin' the book for many. Thomson was unapologetic: 'Why should a detective novel be treated differently from any other kind of fiction?'

Delicious Death featured on Fontana's 1982 cover.

he wrote in response, arguing that a 'competent' novelist like Agatha Christie did not need to rely on 'surprise and mental confusion'.[33] He also insisted that strong sales of the book meant that his review had done no financial harm, although members of the trade in *The Bookseller* argued differently, and claimed that some were not buying the book because they knew the killer's identity.[34] The *Evening Standard* revealed that only one in ten letters on the subject supported Thomson, who doubled down on his decision. 'The detective writers who have rushed to the support of Agatha Christie should keep their muddled reasoning for their novels,' he wrote, although few (if any) of Thomson's critic contemporaries supported him. In *The Tatler*, Paul Holt wrote of Thomson that 'You do not play fair.'[35]

Agatha Christie even found herself making a public statement on Thomson's reveal, when she attended a party at the Ritz to celebrate the publication of *A Murder is Announced* on 8 June, shortly after the review's publication. 'That sort of thing is what is known as not playing the game,' she told a reporter. 'I should never read a thriller if I knew what was going to happen before I began.'[36] Other guests at the party included publisher and friend Billy Collins, who confessed that he knew Christie's aversion to giving away too much information as she had chastised him about blurbs doing precisely that. Barbara Mullen also appeared, fresh from

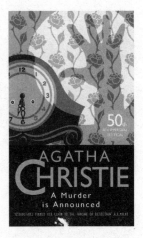

In 2000, HarperCollins published a hardback for the 50th anniversary of the 50th book.

playing Miss Marple in *Murder at the Vicarage* on stage, as did Ngaio Marsh, a fellow Queen of Crime. There was a cake featuring Poirot adorned with fifty candles, which Christie blew out in only three puffs. She then apologised to a reporter, with a quip that 'I'm sorry, but I really don't know how many I've killed off, but it must have been a simply appalling number.'[37] Christie even smiled for the cameras, despite having recently complained that a new official photo made her look ten years older than she was. This was all despite her shyness, and she later explained that she felt strongly that public appearances were 'not part of an author's life. If you act, or if you are an M.P. or a public spirited woman who sits on committees, then you are a part of it.'[38]

The celebrations resulted in a great deal of publicity, including a small pamphlet that was distributed to some of those in the book trade and press, which proclaimed that Christie had 'Made more money out of murder than any woman since Lucrezia Borgia', while including endorsements from the

A new series of Miss Marple covers in 2002 with photography by Jeff Cottenden.

likes of the Prime Minister, Clement Attlee, who wrote that 'I admire and delight in the ingenuity of Agatha Christie's mind and in her capacity to keep a secret until she is ready to divulge it. And I admire, also, another of her qualities, one that is not always possessed by those who produce detective stories, her ability clearly and simply to write the English language. I am looking forward to the next 50 books.' Eden Phillpotts, the writer who had encouraged a young Agatha in her teenage years, offered 'Very cordial congratulations to Agatha and her publishers on the brilliant record here celebrated. I remember her early poems and very good they were until the renowned Poirot took charge of her and led to the triumphant records of a master "sleuth" and the vivid and distinguished manner in which they have always been reported. An old friend greets her with great regard.'

There were also several articles in the press celebrating Christie's achievement, and even some more personal tributes from those who knew her. Christianna Brand recalled that:

> Some time ago, at a gathering of detective story writers, I was approached by a foreign gentleman who begged me to introduce him to Agatha Christie; and, since Agatha Christie is the kindest and most unaffected person in the world about the granting of such favours, I accordingly presented him. She gave him her hand, murmured a few, doubtless not epoch-making, words and gracefully allowed him to dismiss himself. Luminous with gratification, he returned to me. 'I feel,' he said, 'that I have shaken hands with a queen.' He then rather spoilt the effect by saying: 'I am *oh*fully dronk!'

Drunk or sober, I also can recognise a queen when I see one … at her best, indeed, both king and queen, for at her best there is nobody quite to touch her. Others may excel, do excel, I think, in characterization, in choice and portrayal of background, in literary style; but the essence of a detective story is plot, and in plot she is absolutely unsurpassed … But she is not concerned with 'atmosphere' – only with plot. Her purpose is not to terrify, to charm, to amuse: it is to mystify, and to this intention all else is subservient.[39]

Brand's recollections were supplemented by a testimonial from Ex-Superintendent Robert Fabian, of *Fabian of the Yard* fame, while Margery Allingham had much to say in the *New York Times Book Review:*[40]

With her brilliant contemporary, Miss Dorothy Sayers, she has helped to mold a somewhat loose art form into a concrete shape and give it both life and a tradition. If Miss Sayers has presented the detective story with literary distinction, Agatha Christie has kept its hair short and its feet on the ground, and of the two writers she is probably in the purest sense of the term, the more intellectual. …

Her appeal is made directly to the honest human curiosity in all of us. The invitation she gives her readers is to listen to the details surrounding the perfectly horrid screams from the apartment next door. Her characters, slapped in with an easy charm which has grown sure with the years, are the people we each know best. They are the nice or nasty everyday folk who sit at our tables and borrow our lawn mowers or scowl at us mysteriously (and unfairly) in trains … After all, one never really knows one's neighbors, does

The *Chipping Cleghorn Gazette* on 2007's cover by Nick Castle.

Jane Asher's exclusive recipe for a murderous celebration cake

Jane Asher's recipe was widely promoted for the Agatha Christie 120th birthday celebrations in 2010.

one? Not quite. What about the fellow who is reading this article over your shoulder now?

When her hundredth book is published (on present form this should take place in the fall of '75) she will doubtless receive the 'family canonization' of other minor saints and take her place between Florence Nightingale and Grace Darling.[41]

Agatha Christie was certainly continuing to ride the crest of a wave of popularity. Her agents and publishers told her that *A Murder is Announced* sold better and faster than any of her books to that point (around 42,000 copies in the first two months), and then the next year her standalone thriller *They Came to Baghdad* managed to do even better, such was the momentum of her success.[42] In September 1950, Christie was sent a scrapbook to commemorate the celebratory events and press coverage from earlier in the year. It has been retained by her family, and it is a charming and almost emotional record of an extraordinary outpouring of love for a writer who simply enjoyed penning mystery novels. 'Everything in life is partly hard work and partly luck,' Christie claimed later. 'And luck is really the important thing. There are a lot of lucky things: you may win a large sum on a premium bond, or you may find that some publisher likes your book and when those things happen to you, well, then it is very encouraging and you go ahead with a feeling that there is a chance for you and that you can go on.'[43] As ever, Christie underplayed her exceptional talent, even when it was obvious to the rest of the world.

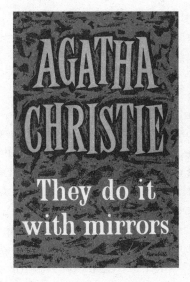

They Do It with Mirrors
(Novel, 1952)

They Do It with Mirrors is a novel that grapples with questions of how modern society should function, particularly in relation to criminal rehabilitation. Miss Marple becomes involved with such issues due to a request for help from one of her long-standing friends, Ruth Van Rydock, who is worried about her sister, Carrie Louise. Miss Marple remembers their youthful days in Italy:

> The pensionnat in Florence. Herself, the pink and white English girl from a Cathedral close. The two Martin girls,

ABOVE LEFT: Agatha Christie's name leapt out from an otherwise beige cover from Crime Club in 1952. **ABOVE RIGHT:** The American first edition published by Dodd Mead with another title change for the US market, *Murder with Mirrors* (1952).

Americans, exciting to the English girl because of their quaint ways of speech and their forthright manner and vitality. Ruth, tall, eager, on top of the world, Carrie Louise, small, dainty, wistful.

Although we haven't heard of the sisters before, the longevity of the friendships offers some insight into Miss Marple's life, especially when contrasted with her friends. After Italy, the three women soon moved in different circles, with Ruth living mostly in America but travelling frequently, and often seeing her old friend Jane as a result. A cosmopolitan woman, Ruth has refused to acquiesce to the demands of ageing: 'Do you think most people would guess, Jane, that you and I are practically the same age?' she asks, casually. 'Not for a moment, I'm sure,' reassures Miss Marple. 'I'm afraid, you know, that I look every minute of my age!' While we are in no doubt that Miss Marple may have the sharp mind of a younger woman, she most definitely appears to be a 'sweet old lady' by now, which Ruth Van Rydock is emphatically not. We are told that the young Miss Marple had been keen

The Fontana paperback of 1955.

to be a nurse (just as Christie had been in the First World War), although young Jane was going to undertake the Christian service of nursing people with leprosy. Ruth considered being a nun, but 'One gets over all that nonsense,' she clarifies. It turns out that she was happier to marry and divorce three times, building up her wealth along the way. Christie's own views on the function of women in society were not always progressive. 'The position of women, over the years, has definitely changed for the worse,' she claimed. 'We women have behaved like mugs. We have clamoured to be allowed to work as men work. Men, not being fools, have taken kindly to the idea.' For Christie, Victorian women had 'cleverly' established themselves as the 'weaker sex' but were now 'broadly on a par with the women of primitive tribes who toil in the fields all day ... whilst the gorgeous, ornamental male sweeps on ahead, unburdened save for one lethal weapon with which to defend his women. You've got to hand it to Victorian women; they got their menfolk where they wanted them.' These exterior appearances of frailty belying an inner steel certainly seems to have contributed to the characterisation of not only Miss Marple but also other older female characters. 'All my grandmothers' friends seem to me in retrospect singularly resilient and almost invariably successful in getting their own way,' Christie remembered. 'They were tough, self-willed, and remarkably well-read and well-informed.'[44]

Carrie Louise resides in England with her third husband, Lewis Serrocold and they live in a country mansion called Stonygates, adjacent to their own privately-run rehabilitation centre for young men. 'Juvenile Delinquency – that's what is the rage nowadays,' we hear, a topic about which Lewis Serrocold is apparently 'Crazy with enthusiasm!' Ruth asks Miss Marple to stay with Carrie Louise, using the pretence of poverty, as Ruth senses that something is wrong. Miss Marple is unfazed by the white lie that will get her through the gates of the house, even if it might appear embarrassing to others, as it seems to be such a plausible suggestion. She is a woman with little ego, even if it means wearing clothes that are shabbier than her custom when dropping in on a friend whom she had last seen in 1928. Miss Marple takes Ruth's concern seriously because of her own experiences of picking up on tiny troubling details that say so much, such as the woman who wore her Sunday hat the wrong way around, which it turns out was a sign that she had made a hurried escape from home that morning. The sense, in that instance, that something must be wrong was 'founded on *fact*', states Miss Marple.

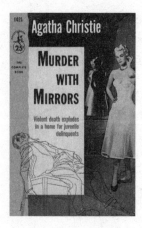

Pocket Books' 1955 paperback by Art Sussman.

Despite the strong presence of these 'juvenile delinquents', this is not a violent crime novel. Christie was more interested in characters and mystery than the brutal side of criminality. 'I don't find it very interesting,' she said. 'All that seems to happen is, first one side bashes the other side, and then the other side bashes the first one.'[45] The residents of the centre are mostly kept in the background, making it difficult for the reader to ascertain the extent to which they should be considered a threat. We are told that many of them are thugs; Gina (Carrie Louise's granddaughter) says that she likes these young men best. Gina is less keen on 'the queers', who are seen as mentally deficient, a stark reminder of how different the world was in the mid-twentieth century. 'Of course Lewis and [psychiatrist] Dr Maverick think they're *all* queers,' she goes on to say. 'I mean they think it's repressed desires and disordered home life and their mothers getting off with soldiers and all that. I don't really see it myself because some people have had awful home lives and yet have managed to turn out quite all right.' This claim goes almost unchallenged, but Miss Marple does not seem to be convinced. Christie was mainly interested in the origins of crime, and this period saw an expansion of analysis and treatment that asked questions of the perpetrators. In part, this was an attempt to uncover a pattern or explanation for criminal behaviour, which no doubt explains its inclusion here, even if it has dated badly.

As Carrie Louise is twice widowed (unlike her sister, who divorced all three of her husbands), she has a large extended family, which provides a good cast of suspects when Christian Gulbrandsen arrives and is soon murdered. He is the son of Carrie Louise's first husband and trustee of the charitable foundation behind the reform school. Gulbrandsen is murdered while everyone is distracted, first by an argument taking place, and then by the lights fusing (which is perhaps an unconscious call back to *A Murder is Announced*). The distracting argument occurs between Lewis Serrocold and Edgar Lawson, who is under the care of the reform centre and appears to be something of a fantasist. The supplied floorplan shows where each character appeared to be during the fateful moment and it is up to the reader, and Miss Marple, to work out if things are really as they appear. During the investigation, Gina returns to her old scapegoat: 'One of the queers did it,

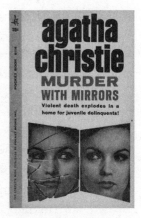

The 1962 photo cover from Pocket Books.

I should think,' she argues. 'The thug ones are really quite sensible. I mean they only cosh people so as to rob a till or get money or jewellery – not just for fun. But one of the queers – you know, what they call mentally maladjusted – might do it for fun, don't you think?' We shouldn't take her thoughts as an expression of Christie's own views, however, as Gina is characterised as unsympathetic and superficial. She puts great emphasis on her looks, feeling that they are the most important element of having power as a woman (almost the opposite to Christie's own views, and certainly unlike our own hero sleuth Miss Marple). Gina also ensures that her American husband, Walter Hudd, is fully aware that she can command the attention of other men, including some of those staying at Stonygates.

The book's title is a reference to the sleight of hand used by a magician or conjurer, and although the inclusion of the floor plan may make some readers wonder if the placement of a mirror will be significant, the story is not so literal. 'Misdirection, the conjurers call it,' clarifies Miss Marple. 'So clever, aren't they? And I never have known how they manage with a bowl of goldfish—because really that cannot fold up small, can it.' The fact that the title was not supposed to be taken literally didn't stop Christie's American publishers opting for the title *Murder with Mirrors*, which is eye-catching but inaccurate. Miss Marple muses on the connection to misdirection throughout the book and uses it to aid Inspector Curry's investigation into the murder. Curry has been forewarned about Miss Marple's deductive powers and is happy to use her skills to assist him in catching the murderer. The theatrical allusions come too close to home, however, when two more murders take place on stage (albeit not during a performance). These extra deaths are among the more obvious examples of Christie needing to find a way to drive a story's momentum when moving into the last act of the novel, and they do not have the impact nor narrative function that a murder usually receives in Christie's work.

And yet, if Christie were looking for a way to extend the plot so that she could reach her publisher's required word count, then it's odd that she didn't spend more pages on the denouement, which is sketched out in an unusually cursory manner. Once the solution is revealed, it appears that a great deal of action takes place, with a fatal dash to escape justice in what seems like an exciting scene. These events are recounted in a letter told across a mere one and a half pages, rather than being presented within the main narrative. Although Christie had used letters to explain elements of the plot before, most notably in *And Then There Were None*, there is usually a reason why it is needed. This is not the case in *They Do It with Mirrors*, as the letter is simply a summary of events seen by several people. Christie seemed unsure of the impact of the final section, as she asked her publisher to ensure that there was a clear chapter break after

One of Tom Adams' favourite paintings on this 1975 Fontana paperback.

the villain's name is revealed, in order to make it 'more dramatic'.[46] Happily, the book does return to possibly its strongest aspect in the epilogue, in which one character finds it difficult to imagine a young Jane, Ruth and Carrie Louise. 'It was all a long time ago …' concedes Miss Marple.

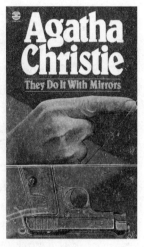

Fontana's 1984 artwork cover.

In early 1951 Christie returned to Baghdad with Max, travelling via Amsterdam, where she was bothered by journalists and even had a 'radio conversation' with one in order to get rid of them.[47] *They Do It with Mirrors* was sent to her agent before the couple left for their travels, along with the Poirot novel *Mrs McGinty's Dead.* Typed copies were made in the spring, and in the summer were sent to Christie for any corrections or altera-tions. Christie at this point produced a new sketch of the Great Hall floorplan at Stonygates (having lost the first one), which she insisted must be re-done by someone else for publication: 'I just can't draw!'[48] She did not always supply floorplans of houses in her books, but felt that, for this title, it was 'neces-sary, I think, so as to understand the set up'.[49]

August 1951 also saw the beginning of a conversation that would go on to be an important aspect of Agatha Christie's vis-ibility and longevity, as well as her workload. Mindful, as ever, of the very high levels of taxation that she faced at the time, and keen to ensure her family benefited from her success, Christie decided to gift the rights to some of her new works to others, including her only grandchild, Mathew Prichard. For Mathew, the gifts included not only *They Do It with Mirrors*, but more famously *The Mousetrap*, the play that would become a theatrical phenomenon. The move required a little legal manoeuvring, but the assignation of copyright was eventu-ally settled, and led to the unusual situation in which Agatha

Christie's new murder mystery novel was owned by a seven-year-old schoolboy. This meant that commercial decisions related to the title were decided not by Christie, but by her daughter, Rosalind Hicks, who controlled the copyright along with Edmund Cork until her son came of age.[50]

In America, Harold Ober felt that his client's new novel was unlikely to fare well with magazines. He considered it to be 'very slow – almost dull reading – up to Page 90. From there on it is an exciting story and extremely good Agatha Christie.'[51] However, he didn't believe that any magazine would be interested unless this early section was greatly condensed, and asked Cork if he thought Christie might allow an editor to do the work on her behalf, although he didn't want to worry her.[52] Ober was right, and the *Saturday Evening Post* swiftly declined the story, while supplying an extra bit of feedback regarding the character of American Walter Hudd, whom they declared to be 'the most incredible character they have ever encountered', and not in a positive way. 'You don't have to tell the author!' wrote Ober.[53] Cork passed on the gist of the feelings

Cosmopolitan's header for the serial illustrated by Joe Bowler.

One of George Ditton's detailed paintings for the *John Bull* serialisation (1952).

to Christie, who seemed unfazed but wanted to ensure that the characters were made clear to the readers of the novel and was happy to let an editor reduce the early part of the book for serialisation if needed. Cork also suggested that 'if it would save anyone's feelings, the young American could quite easily be an Australian!!'[54]

The beginning of the 1950s also saw a more formal emergence of the concept of 'A Christie for Christmas', a strategy where a title would be published in order to specifically appeal to the Christmas market. In earlier decades it had not been unusual for Christie to publish more than one book a year, especially in the 1930s, but 1953 would be the final year in which more than one Christie mystery novel was published.[55] In time it became clear that releasing these novels for the Christmas market was an important commercial decision; after all, her books made for a perfect present. Collins argued that well-timed publication could result in the sale of an extra fifteen to twenty thousand copies, and so it was decided that *They Do It with Mirrors* should be aimed at Christmas shoppers.[56] As ever, the question of serialisations had to be confirmed before any assurances could be given, to make sure that any novel didn't tread on the toes of an agreement with a magazine or newspaper serialising the story. In the end, this was fairly straightforward. Harold Ober struggled to sell the story to any of the better-paying magazines in the United States, but *Cosmopolitan* paid $7,500 to run an edited version in their April 1952 issue. This version of the story presented a sharper opening for magazine readers, beginning with Miss Marple's arrival at Market Kindle (as per the novel's third chapter), before summarising the conversation that led her there. *Cosmopolitan* paid less than half the amount offered by *Collier's* for the more popular novels, but $500 more than the *Chicago Tribune* paid for the Poirot mystery *Mrs McGinty's Dead* the same year, meaning that Miss Marple beat Christie's first detective, a certain Belgian, by a whisker.[57] In Britain, Cork expected *Woman's Journal* to take the story, but it was *John Bull* that serialised an edited version of the story across six parts in April and May 1952. George Ditton's illustrations in *John Bull* did a particularly good job of embellishing the story's atmosphere and character with colourful and lifelike images.

HarperCollins' paperback from 2007.

It was *Cosmopolitan* that initially decided to rename the story to *Murder with Mirrors*, and Dodd Mead then followed suit, reasoning that keeping the title would help sales.[58] The American version of the novel was also the first to see print in September 1952, because Collins wanted to keep back the publication, initially to December, then early November, before settling on 17 November.[59] The simple text-based cover meant that there was no need for discussions (or arguments) with the author, while the blurb set up the essence of the story without giving too much away.

Reviews for the book were generally positive (Christie 'has few peers and no superiors', said one), even if this wasn't felt to be one of her very best.[60] Commendations were a little vague: 'clear, slick and smooth' said another.[61] For others it was 'another fine Christie mystery' and 'a bright story'.[62] The understated but positive reaction was perhaps best summarised by *Punch*, which declared the book's puzzle to be 'only fairish by Christie standards, ingenious by others'.[63] Francis Iles in *The Sunday Times* marvelled that Christie was able to introduce a plot 'as ingenious as ever, and a new set of characters who are both interesting and convincing; and her writing still retains all its peculiar vivacity and freshness. How does she do it? Perhaps the actual identity of the criminal is not such a shock as usual, and the solution is just a little more contrived; but the surprises are there just the same.'[64] Maurice Richardson felt the opposite to Harold Ober, as in his *Observer* review he declared that 'First half is lively ... there is a marked decline in sprightliness later on, but half a shot is better than no dope.'[65]

Holly Macdonald's 2022 design, with art by Bill Bragg.

In Chicago, the *Tribune* wondered what the novel told the reader about post-war British identity. It picked up on Miss Marple's claim that 'Foreigners never can understand why we're so proud of Dunkirk. It's the sort of thing they'd prefer not to mention themselves. But we always seem to be almost embarrassed by a victory – and treat it as though it weren't quite nice to boast about it.' The newspaper was taken by Christie's insight, and stated that 'As social criticism, we assign this a very high mark.' Although the reviewer claimed to have 'guessed the villain inside of 20 pages', this is a significant example of Christie being treated as a writer of literature, and not simply a creator of puzzles. Christie's readers already knew that her insight into human nature rivalled Miss Marple's, and would no doubt welcome the observation that 'As an observer of social currents, she is unmatched.'[66]

The book was also picked up for comment on its societal themes as well as its puzzle construction by the *Oakland Tribune*:

> When Agatha Christie writes a detective story, it remains a detective story. Psychology, sociology, the marvels of science, symbolisms and ideologies are not allowed to steal the show, although she is quite capable of using any and all of these as contributory threads giving tone and colour to her overall pattern. In this instance, for example, she takes deceptively casual side swipes at the sociological question [of] whether in trying to adjust the misfits we are inclined to ignore the needs of the fit; the moral question of end justifying means; the philosophical question of whether the unworldly idealist may have a clearer view of reality than the aggressively disillusioned 'realist'.
>
> But these are sauce, adding piquancy to the main dish, whose ingredients are the tried, true and unbeatable combination of crime, clues and likely suspects.[67]

Indeed, *They Do It with Mirrors* is just one notable example of Christie writing stories that touch on wider themes, while still foregrounding the mystery and its detection. She was always much more than 'just' a constructor of puzzles.

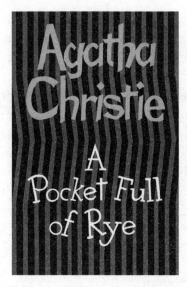

A Pocket Full of Rye
(Novel, 1953)

In early 1952, Christie was shocked to hear of the passing of King George VI, which occurred while she was in Baghdad. 'All my clothes are unfortunately rather lurid and I have to wear my one black dress in all weathers – the temperature having varied a great deal in the last ten days,' she lamented to Edmund Cork. Better news for Christie was that 'Typewriters seem to be flowing in Baghdad this year, so I have bought myself a portable Royal which I like very much – and which I hope will encourage me to be industrious??'[68] Unfortunately, she would suffer a more significant professional and personal setback later in the year when, just a few chapters into writing

ABOVE LEFT: Another simple yet effective graphic design of red and black stripes for the first Crime Club edition (1953). **ABOVE RIGHT:** 'A New Red Badge Mystery' declared the US dustjacket, as Dodd Mead sought to capitalise on the reputation its 24-year-old mystery imprint (1954).

POLVERE NEGLI OCCHI

di AGATHA CHRISTIE

Mondadori's strikingly graphic 1954 cover.

her new Miss Marple novel, she broke her wrist.

By the time of her injury, Christie had already sketched out the basis of *A Pocket Full of Rye* in her notebooks and had started to type them up.[69] For the author, much of the job of putting together her mysteries and other stories was done through thinking over ideas and plots that might not see print for years, or even decades. 'I still insist on being left entirely alone for a few hours every day,' she told an interviewer. 'You know how it is. An idea knocks about for months and you say, "It would be rather interesting if one day I could manage that."'[70] Christie was often asked about her method, and even though she did spend a great deal of time planning her mystery novels, she was always coy about the details. She claimed that:

> the disappointing truth is that I haven't much method. I type my own drafts on an ancient faithful machine that I've owned for years, and I find a dictaphone useful for short stories or for recasting an act of a play, not for the more complicated business of working out a novel. No, I think the real work is done in thinking out the development of your story and worrying about it until it comes right. That may take quite a while. Then when you've got all your materials together, as it were, all that remains is to find the time to write the thing.[71]

In *A Pocket Full of Rye*, the ideas included familial relationships and a murder linked to the nursery rhyme 'Sing a Song of Sixpence', and in early notes the plans for the book were intertwined with those of *They Do It with Mirrors*.[72] The story sees the murder of patriarch Rex (Latin for 'king') Fortescue in his office: '*The king was in his counting house counting out his money ...*', as the rhyme goes. It is discovered that the dead man had rye in his pocket, and subsequent murders continue the nursery-rhyme theme, with victims including a member of the domestic staff. Christie was aware that such characters were becoming increasingly anachronistic in post-war Britain, but she found them to be an important part of the household. 'One of the things I think I should miss most, if I were a child nowadays, would be the absence of servants,' she said. 'To a child they were the most colourful part of daily life.' Christie also recalled that 'Far from being slaves they were frequently tyrants. They "knew their place", as was said, but knowing their place meant not subservience but

The 1954 Pocket Books paperback combined a photo with art by James Meese.

pride, the pride of the professional.'[73] Housekeeper Mary Dove is an example of this sort of no-nonsense servant, as she runs the house with efficiency and even a little cunning. Miss Marple is inspired to pay a visit due to the circumstances of one her former maids, Gladys, and finds herself working with Inspector Neele to help solve the mystery.

There are certainly plenty of suspects for Rex's murder, as he ruled the family business with a rod of iron, and several characters might have had reason to wish him dead. These included his wife, Adele, his sons, Percival and Lancelot, and possibly an unknown individual linked to the Blackbird Mine in Africa, an abandoned project that seems to have cast a long shadow. Christie does a particularly good job of presenting clear characterisations from the first page, when we are shown the inner thoughts of one of Rex's employees, who struggles to work out precisely how to make the optimal cup of tea. Other memorable

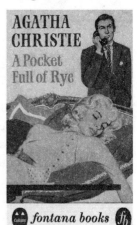

Fontana's 1958 paperback.

characters include the sharp-tongued religious fanatic Miss Ramsbottom, who becomes friendly with Miss Marple.

The novel provides some interesting commentary about characters and situations that unwittingly give an insight into Britain of the early 1950s. The panic that ensues after Rex Fortescue is found poisoned is partially linked to confusion about the then-new National Health Service, which was formed in 1948. Meanwhile, the rise of the working classes and women in the workplace leads to some clashing communication between characters, even down to the question of telephone manner and accents. As a result, Neele's straightforward style puts some noses out of joint, while Sergeant Hay is not at all attuned to culture matters, even when it is as well-known as *Alice in Wonderland*. 'Third programme stuff', he dismisses, referring to the more highbrow radio station that later became BBC Radio 3. Nevertheless, the novel exists in a world of wealth, foie gras sandwiches and all.

A Pocket Full Of Rye

Seventies glamour by Robert Schulz for Pocket Books (1973).

Elsewhere, a poisoning reminiscent of one of *The Thirteen Problems* is mentioned and may be part of a solution, while Christie laces her storytelling with a great deal of atmosphere alongside wit and social commentary. This is necessary because the characters are an unusually unlikable bunch, and so Christie needs to deploy further devices to keep the reader engaged. They also serve as a direct contrast to the now much softer Miss Marple, who is even described as 'fluffy' when approaching the 'fortress' of the Fortescues' house. Miss Marple correctly works out that the murderer is a particularly cruel person, whose actions work to humiliate one victim in particular. In the book's final pages, Miss Marple receives a posthumous confirmation of one character's sad circumstances that led to their murder, and the reader cannot help but be moved, especially as the credulous victim stood out so strongly compared to the machinations of the Fortescues. 'This is a wicked murderer,' Miss Marple tells Inspector Neele, 'and the wicked should not go unpunished.' Miss Marple does all that she can to ensure that they do not.

In September 1952 both Christie and Cork were battling with the question of what to do about the author's 'wretchedly tiresome' wrist injury.[74] Having initially accepted that time for it to heal was needed, the decision was soon made that Christie could use a dictating machine to finish the book. She was duly sent a 'Dictaphone Time-Master', which was apparently the best available, and cost £130 (equivalent to over £3,000 in 2024).[75] The output would then be transcribed by one of the company's agents, and Christie soon got the hang of things despite inadvertently damaging some early recordings. By the following decade, Christie was routinely dictating her novels. Cork also noted that one drawback of the machine was that it would not work with the DC electricity supply used at her house, Greenway, in Devon, which she and Max had purchased in 1938. This implies that Christie may have done some writing there, although she didn't do any substantial work at the house, as it was her holiday home.[76] Christie soon got used to the new way of writing, and sent off the first three dictated chapters (seven to nine) at the beginning of October, as she was clearly working as efficiently as ever.

At this stage of her life and career, Christie started to turn to her family for reassurance, although not necessarily for advice. She claimed that Max was 'made to' read her novels and that she would show him the first chapter once done.[77] She confessed that it was easy to put off the process of actually writing the novel, and that generally she didn't like to discuss much about her work until it was done. 'I find the moment

Agatha Christie
A Pocket Full of Rye

Tom Adams'
decomposed blackbird
art in 1975.

Agatha Christie
A Pocketful of Rye

Mistitled by Fontana in 1984 as *A Pocketful of Rye*, with art by Martin Baker.

you've talked about a thing you're rather dissatisfied with it,' she said.[78] In the case of *A Pocket Full of Rye*, Mathew Prichard has a strong memory of being present when the new novel was read aloud to the family by his grandmother, whom he called Nima.

I remember the year when Nima read us a chapter or two of *A Pocket Full of Rye* after dinner each night. I can remember the game as if it were yesterday. All the family sitting round the drawing-room at Greenway, coffee cups empty on the tray, a little cigar smoke rising from my grandfather's cigar, mauve chintzy covers set on the chairs and a piano in the corner of the room. Nima sat in a deep chair with a light directly above her and spectacles, a strange butterfly shape, were pushed slightly forward. After every session, except the first two or three, we were all invited to guess the identity of the murderer.

Two reactions I remember clearly: my grandfather Max usually finished his cigar and went to sleep during the reading, waking up with a start when we were all guessing. He then consistently and obstinately plumped for the most unlikely and impossible suspect and went to sleep again. My mother, on the other hand, maintained the solution was, of course, crystal clear to anyone with a grain of intelligence and that the plot was so transparent that it was hardly worth inflicting it on the public. However, she was not prepared to be more explicit. There was, of course, a serious purpose behind these highly enjoyable occasions. Nima was anxious to try out her book on a live audience which enabled her to test its plausibility and its plot. Needless to say Max and my mother in their wholly different ways guessed correctly and infuriated the rest of us![79]

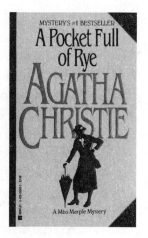

Christie agreed that 'I can't often put anything over on my daughter' and didn't really mind if her family members did guess correctly.[80] Two decades later, in what would be her final interview, Christie recalled that 'it was rather a good game'.[81]

By February 1953 a full draft of *A Pocket Full of Rye* was being typed up and sent to Christie while she and Max journeyed to Syria through Europe. They visited Paris and then Rome,

Berkley's 1991 paperback with a striking silhouette.

where they contracted 'flu. 'Why do these things have to happen when you go abroad to enjoy yourself?' she pondered. She then received both pleasant and unwanted arrivals, as an 'enormous bouquet of red roses arrived in my room in Rome and cheered the sufferer up, so that I had graciously to consent to an interview, so three young men arrived with a selection of cameras and I whispered hoarsely to them in French – their French was also a little sketchy, so goodness knows what I've actually said. The hotel was absolutely thick with Cardinals and magenta sashes and pectoral crosses. Max and I probably breathed over a Cardinal in the lift and hence the cause of the Pope's flu.'[82] Once in Syria, Christie enjoyed the mild winter and, as she pointedly told her agent, 'spent most days sitting on the balcony in the sun recovering from OVERWORK!'[83]

Christie had always taken a strong interest in her husband's work, and she used *A Pocket Full of Rye* to benefit the British School of Archaeology in Iraq, which led to a complicated arrangement. The school was gifted the copyright to the book, which was then purchased by Edmund Cork himself, who found that he needed to set up a company in order for the move to be financially expedient. This awkwardness was the result of Christie trying to ensure that the royalties from her books could benefit her family while not adding to any individual's tax burden. The difficulties of the arrangement for *A Pocket Full of Rye* kickstarted discussions about possibly setting up a company in Christie's name to make her tax and gifting arrangements easier in the future. This led to the creation of Agatha Christie Ltd in 1955, although the author initially thought that it 'just seems too difficult for words'.[84] Because Cork was now so closely involved with the book, he asked his American counterpart to give his own views on its quality: 'I don't know whether American children sing "sing a song of sixpence, pocketful of rye",' he confessed.[85] Harold Ober replied that he thought the story was likely to do well as a novel but would struggle to find a home for serialisation due to the lack of sympathetic characters. He also judged the

The king was in his counting house...

1996 children's edition with nursery rhyme cover.

use of the nursery rhyme to be 'far fetched', and thought that the ending needed work in order to make it more convincing, as he wasn't sure that Christie had played fair.[86] Christie did make alterations to the end of the novel, snipping out an epilogue as she felt it was anticlimactic, but it's not clear if any other changes were made in line with Ober's comments.[87]

Cork told Christie that he thought the novel was 'awfully good', and that 'with polishing it might become quite superlative!'[88] Once again, Collins requested that the book be finished in time for the all-important Christmas market. Christie had other preoccupations while she completed the final corrections, including

the impending celebrations for the coronation of Queen Elizabeth II. Cork managed to
obtain seats for her at 145 Piccadilly (the site
of the Queen's childhood residence, destroyed
in the war), including a 'scrumptious lunch in
the marquee' for Christie and her guests, who
included her grandson Mathew.[89] Some seventy
years later, Mathew still recalls the 'great day'
spent with his grandmother and Max, as they
watched the Queen pass by in the Gold State
Coach.[90]

Christie decided to dedicate the book to Bruce
Ingram, who had published many of her early
short stories in *The Sketch*. Collins were happy to
receive and publish the new novel, and their reader's report
by George Hardinge noted the 'exotic element' of the nursery
rhyme. Hardinge felt that:

A clothes peg on HC's
2002 photo cover by
Jeff Cottenden.

> It should, I think, be possible to name the murderer with
> certainty by keeping a very close eye on the motives and
> disregarding means and opportunity (which do not work
> too well), but I must admit I failed to do so. It can, therefore,
> be defined as a fair-play murder story, although the means
> adopted for the first murder is so far-fetched as slightly to
> strain even that special standard of plausibility which Mrs
> Christie has virtually created among her many readers.
>
> The solution, therefore, although surprising and ade-
> quate, does not make one kick oneself for one's own stupid-
> ity as it has done in the very best Christies.
>
> There is no standard of comparison except her own
> books. I rate this a 'good' Christie, not among the very best
> such as *Lady Edgware Dies* [sic] or as good as *The Blue Train
> Murders* [sic] but holding quite an honourable place in that
> large and distinguished field. It is highly readable, exciting,

A rejected HarperCollins cover design from 2008.

The published version from 2008.

baffling, and intelligent; it is plotted and handled with a skill which makes most current detective fiction look like the work of clumsy beginners.[91]

Christie offered some final corrections to Collins, and approved a blurb that the publisher hoped would not give too much away. Billy Collins himself wrote to Christie to say that 'Everyone who has read advanced proofs of *A Pocket Full of Rye* is very keen on it. I hope maybe you are writing another one now.'[92] Nevertheless, Ober was correct that the top-paying magazines did not pick up *A Pocket Full of Rye*, although the *Chicago Tribune* did pay $7,000 for the rights, with their serialisation beginning in January 1954. This meant that the Dodd Mead publication of the novel in the United States had to be delayed until March that year. In Britain, the *Daily Express* serialised the novel, printing an abridged version in September and October 1953. Meanwhile, Christie started a new contract with Collins, giving her a £2,000 advance for each book and a 20% royalty. Ready for Christmas, the novel was in British bookshops from 9 November 1953, with a colourful text-based cover. When Cork wrote to Christie with the news, he reminded her of the 'magnanimity' of donating the book's copyright to benefit the School of Archaeology. 'If you don't get a Dame-dom there is no justice left in the world.'[93] In *The Observer*, Maurice Richardson agreed, apparently coming to the same conclusion independently, even if the novel wasn't one of his favourites: 'Not quite so stunning as some of Mrs Christie's criminal assaults upon her readers; the souffle rises all right, but the red herrings aren't quite nifty enough. But how well she nearly always writes, the dear decadent old death trafficker; they ought to make her a Dame or a D. Litt.'[94]

At one point in *A Pocket Full of Rye*, Inspector Neele exclaims that 'I simply can't swallow this nursery rhyme business', and some critics agreed. Certainly, the novel is one of the less convincing uses of a device that Christie had drawn on for decades, and it would be the last time that she placed a nursery rhyme in one of her novels so prominently. 'The author appears a little too affectionately to her nursery rhyme analogy, appearing to have a curious need of some such balustrade to hold onto,' stated *The Sketch*'s reviewer, G. B. Stern.[95] However, there were plaudits aplenty, even with some reservations. The *Manchester Guardian* judged it to be 'almost up to her best standard', although it wondered whether Miss Marple was needed.[96] Regional newspapers on both sides of the Atlantic saw the book as evidence that Christie was maintaining her reign as Queen of Crime. One stated that 'There are no flaws in logic. It is the emotional trick of snaring your affections to pull you off trail that make you cry, "No fair". This may leave you with a pocketful of wry.'[97]

Christie was certainly demonstrating that as an author she could be both reliable and surprising. While it is questionable if the *Times Literary Supplement*'s conclusion that 'It is a pleasure to read an author so nicely conscious of the limitations of what she is attempting' is supposed to be a compliment, it does in fact encapsulate the essence of Christie's success.[98] By this point in her career she could still offer new stories such as *A Pocket Full of Rye* that feel both familiar and yet fresh. Her confidence as a writer had grown substantially over the years, and she could juggle her passion for some projects (particularly those in the theatre) with the day-to-day job of penning a new Miss Marple mystery or similar. Agatha Christie was in charge of her own destiny.

Miss Marple on Radio and Television in the 1950s

During Agatha Christie's lifetime, there was only one full-cast adaptation of a Miss Marple story on British radio, but this was not because of any lack of interest from the BBC.[99] Christie disliked adaptations generally, although she consented to 'single voice' readings of her stories. These were a success for the BBC, which often placed them within its *Woman's Hour* programming. In this era, titles included the Miss Marple mysteries *The Moving Finger* in 1955 (read by James McKechnie), *A Murder is Announced* in 1955, and *They Do It with Mirrors* in 1956 (both read by Mary Wimbush). Futile attempts were made to produce full dramatisations of more

ABOVE: Gracie Fields as Miss Marple (left) in Showcase Productions' *A Murder is Announced*, which aired on 30 December 1956. Roger Moore as Patrick Simmons and Jessica Tandy as Letitia Blacklock.

stories, including *The Moving Finger* (suggested in both 1953 and 1957), *The Thirteen Problems* (1955), *4.50 from Paddington* (1958), *A Murder is Announced* (1961), and both the novel and play version of *[The] Murder at the Vicarage* (1965 and 1966 respectively). Even an attempt to adapt the single short story 'The Idol House of Astarte' in 1970 was declined by Christie's agents. In part this was because not only did Christie not approve, but they also complicated the rights situations for more lucrative motion picture deals.

An exception was made in 1956, when the BBC's radio station The Light Programme put together a festival celebrating the work of Agatha Christie. Similar festivals had taken place for J. B. Priestley and W. Somerset Maugham, and although the BBC felt that there were names of 'greater academic distinction' than Christie, those involved managed to overcome their snobbery when it was acknowledged that she was suitable for the radio station's audience.[100] The festival's emphasis tended to be on Christie's other leading detective, Hercule Poirot, but Miss Marple made an appearance in an adaptation of 'Death by Drowning', the last of *The Thirteen Problems*. The play was recorded on 22 December 1955, following rehearsals the previous day, and was first broadcast on Sunday, 19 February 1956, at 5.30pm, just after a repeat of the most recent edition of popular comedy *Hancock's Half Hour*. Star billing was given to Milton Rosmer as Sir Henry Clithering, who had just finished touring in *Witness for the Prosecution*. A prolific actor, with many film roles, as well as film directing experience, to his name, he had replaced John Turnbull at a late stage; Turnbull may well have been in ill-health, as he died only four days after the play was transmitted. Anthony Woodruff played Colonel Bantry (doubling as a police sergeant), while Miss Marple was played by Betty Hardy, who often played small but significant parts, including in long-running soap opera *Coronation Street*, in which she

Betty Hardy was Miss Marple in BBC radio's *Death by Drowning*, broadcast in 1956..

took on the part of Mission Hall cleaner Clara Midgeley while Ena Sharples was away in 1965.[101]

As the billing indicates, Anthony Aspinall's script foregrounds Sir Henry Clithering rather than Miss Marple, just as the original short story had done. Sir Henry even introduces the story, as he tells the tale of his visit to the Bantrys, and when Miss Marple arrives she is referred to as 'our famous Miss Marple', and someone who is respected by both men. A recording of the play is not known to survive, but the script demonstrates that it stuck closely to the original story, and the *Edinburgh Evening News* felt that Betty Hardy played Miss Marple well.[102] Nevertheless, Christie and Cork were unhappy with the production, and tried to have a 1957 repeat of it cancelled, although they were unsuccessful. It is possible that this was one of the productions that Christie was referring to when, in spring 1956, she wrote to Cork from Nimrud to say that 'I hear from one or two sources that some dreadful things of mine have been done on the wireless. Adaptations of stories? Or just based on them. Very bad, I understand, and "bad for my reputation"'.[103] And yet it was acknowledged that the festival would 'help the Trade' when it came to Agatha Christie.[104]

In the United States, it was television that was causing many a headache for Edmund Cork and Harold Ober. In the medium's early years, television productions were mostly performed live, but by 1949 the situation was changing and recordings were being made to distribute to other stations. Film companies argued that this was a contravention of their own rights to authors' works, creating a great deal of debate. As Cork told Christie, the pre-recording of material could well have prevented the broadcast of the unfortunate gaffe that afflicted a 1949 BBC performance of *And Then There Were*

None (in which the General was seen walking off set after he had 'died'), but the legal complications still made live broadcasts preferable on the whole.[105] In the 1950s there were several attempts to bring Miss Marple to television, but only one came to fruition. Asked about the idea in principle, Cork told Ober that, as with Poirot, Christie felt that Miss Marple should not be seen on television, for fear of destroying the 'good will' of readers who had conjured up their own idea of the character.[106] As Cork explained, Christie's objections had an 'emotional quality', against which it was difficult to argue.

Nevertheless, Christie's objections did not deter prospective producers. Only a few months later, Ober was approached by television producer Winston O'Keefe, who wished to cast Fay Bainter as Miss Marple in a new series. Bainter had won an Academy Award for *Jezebel* in 1938, and O'Keefe was looking for a new suitable project for her. O'Keefe was anxious to have the chance to bring Miss Marple to television, and Ober wondered 'if we agreed to insist that the proper person portray Miss Marple and that the stories and characters were handled in a dignified way that would in no way harm Mrs Mallowan's stories, do you think she would change her mind?'[107] Ober was under pressure when it came to trying to find a way to use Christie's properties for television in some way, and followed up his note to Cork by arguing that 'I do not think that [Christie] need have the worries about Miss Marple that she has for Poirot. Marple doesn't have the wide audiences that Poirot commands, and there is the fact that it would be easier for a television producer to come nearer to a sympathetic conception of Marple then it would be to handle Poirot in the way we'd like to see him done (if this should ever happen).'[108]

In March 1951, Ober let Cork know that plans for any series would have to be changed to an American woman, with a 'Cape Cod background', which he insisted would be sympathetic to the original character. More troubling was the realisation that there were relatively few Miss Marple stories, and so 'almost entirely new "situations" will have to be created. What we will have will be essentially Miss Christie's name and the name Miss Marple. The fundamental, basic thinking – put into an entirely new setting.'[109] Any series would pay Christie $150 per episode for the first year, rising to $250 the year after, although her tax situation in American meant that actually extracting this money would not be straightforward.[110] Surprisingly, Cork initially replied saying that he thought Christie would agree to the plans once she learned of them (she was in Iraq at the time).[111]

By early 1952, Christie was still averse to television in general, and particularly the appearance of either Poirot or Miss Marple, although a potential (but unmade) production starring Robert Emhardt as Parker Pyne was approved.[112] By now, more than a year had passed since O'Keefe first proposed his Miss Marple series, and Ober was fed up with new clauses in a potential contract and the contradictory statements from Cork regarding whether Miss Marple could be used or not. Ober had let O'Keefe know that Miss Marple was available in good faith, and while he was happy for the deal to be cancelled due to the actions of the producer's lawyers, he objected to being told that Miss Marple was unavailable after all. 'If we have to withdraw Miss Marple now, the news will spread that we have backed down on our word,' he told Cork, 'and we feel that it would be embarrassing. If Miss Marple is done on television, Mrs Mallowan will never see the show, she won't be bothered by any possible adverse criticism (although you understand we would try to get the best production we can).'[113] Mindful of the upset, Cork proposed to use his Power of Attorney over Christie's affairs to initially authorise the deal, as he felt sure that he could get Christie to agree, despite her previous opposition, although Ober was reminded that 'Poirot, of course, is still sacrosanct!'[114]

Christie would have been grateful that O'Keefe's series did not materialise, and once the deal collapsed, Ober told prospective producers that Miss Marple was not available for television. However, in February 1954 a new proposal was intriguing enough that he revisited the conversation. This time, it was the name Peggy Wood that aroused interest. Wood is perhaps now best known as the Mother Abbess in 1965's *The Sound of Music*, but at the time she was famous as the matriarch in the popular family drama *Mama*, which had been running on television since 1949. Along with *Mama* producer Carol Irwin, Wood wished to develop a Miss Marple series, and Ober was positive about its prospects.[115] This potential project rumbled along in the background for a few years, even while Ober was fielding other approaches about Christie's characters, including another attempt to bring Parker Pyne to the screen, as well as a potential anthology series.[116] By mid-1955 Wood was still interested enough to request a meeting with Christie when she was next in London, although her plans changed and nothing was arranged.[117] Nevertheless, both Wood and her lawyer continued to make occasional contact about a potential Miss Marple series, but they would soon be beaten to the punch.

In October 1956, Cork agreed to allow American network NBC to broadcast an adaptation of *A Murder is Announced*, for which they paid a premium price. As a one-off live production, this seems to have been less objectionable than an ongoing series, and notably the adaptation kept the British setting and cast British actors.[118] Adapted by William Templeton, the hour-long drama was broadcast live on 30 December 1956 and cast Jessica Tandy as Letitia Blacklock and Roger Moore as Patrick, both of whom were billed above well-known British entertainer Gracie Fields, who became the first person to play Miss Marple on screen. The adaptation opens with the placing of the advertisement in the

Gracie Fields and Roger Moore.

paper ('Oh, I don't think we can publish anything like this!' reacts the woman at the newspaper's desk), with its wording borrowing one of Christie's working titles for the novel as it now reads:

> A murder has been arranged and it will take place on Friday October the 29th at Shendon House, at 6.30pm. Friends please accept this, the only invitation.

Much of the production takes place at Miss Blacklock's residence, and generally follows the structure of the novel, although with a significant reduction in characters. For example, Patrick is no longer accompanied by his sister Julia, while Colonel Easterbrook (now Colonel Harrison) attends the house alone. Hinchcliffe (Pat Nye) and Murgatroyd (Josephine Brown) remain present, as do Dora (Betty Sinclair) and Mitzi (Christiane Felsmann), the latter being markedly steelier and less hysterical than the character in the novel, while Dora is also notably more sensible.[119]

When Miss Marple arrives, she is clearly a strong and

no-nonsense woman, played with a Scottish accent. Described as 'an extraordinary old gossip' by the inspector, she is forthright and keen to solve the crime. The condensing of the events means that Miss Marple seems to spend less time simply observing, as she is happy to take an active part in the investigation. When she attends a party at Letitia's house, Miss Marple even dons her glasses so that she can take a close look around. She seems physically strong, wearing a simple black dress, and is certainly a force of nature. Jessica Tandy gives an assured performance in what is essentially the main role, while Miss Murgatroyd and Miss Hinchcliffe (coded as a lesbian couple in Christie's novel) are particularly full of personality. Murgatroyd provides some welcome comic relief, before a moment of pathos late in the production.

The production is generally an accomplished one, and despite the potential issues with any live production, there are only a few stumbled lines, most notably made by Malcolm Keen playing the unnamed inspector. The adaptation retains three murders, although the final victim is changed, and this means that there is a great deal of action to cover in one hour (including commercials).[120] The reduction of characters means that suspicion must be cast in different directions. Moore's suave Patrick remains suspicious, but even the bumbling Murgatroyd is marked out as a potential murderer. By the end of the hour, Miss Marple has carefully explained her final trap, although it isn't needed, as the murderer confesses. 'I didn't mean to hurt anyone,' they repeat, which is certainly a questionable claim.

Although a very good story and a perfectly serviceable production, this adaptation of A Murder is Announced suffers from its fast pace. There is no time to consider the background to the mystery and the subsequent clues, while the strong characterisation of the book is inevitably reduced. For the Daily News, the production was 'a deft thriller' that 'came across as artfully contrived melodrama', with Fields' performance singled out as 'outstanding'.[121] The *Kansas City Star* was less enamoured, stating that it was 'as obvious as if the solution had also been announced'.[122] The *New York Times* also argued that the mystery 'was not whodunit, but rather why. Why, for example, did Jessica Tandy and Gracie Fields ever get involved in such an inferior melodrama?' For the reviewer, 'It was murder from beginning to end.'[123]

Harold Ober was proven right when he stated that Christie need never learn the details of any American television productions, as almost a month after transmission Cork mentioned the adaptation to her as a forthcoming event.[124] In Britain, nobody seemed to notice Miss Marple making her television debut across the Atlantic. Peggy Wood was still interested in a Miss Marple series as late as 1958, but by this point felt that she was too identifiable from *Mama* to take on the part herself, suggesting silent film star Lillian Gish instead.[125] This vague idea got no further, and soon there would be bigger plans for Miss Marple, which would move her on to the big screen.

4.50 from Paddington
(Novel, 1957)

In her sixty-seventh year, Agatha Christie was still managing to conjure up striking ideas inspired by real life that could grip the attention of any reader. In *4.50 from Paddington* she sets out a highly memorable and visual premise for a mystery when Mrs McGillicuddy returns from her Christmas shopping in London and finds herself dozing off on the train. When she awakes, another train has pulled alongside hers, and then, as Christie put it in her self-penned blurb for the book:

ABOVE LEFT: The UK first edition in black and red was another creation of Collins' in-house design team (1957). **ABOVE RIGHT:** Also in black and red, Dodd Mead's jacket with the book's exclamatory American title, *What Mrs McGillicuddy Saw!* (1957).

in a first class carriage of the second train, Mrs McGillicuddy sees, to her horror, a man strangling a woman … Then the second train gathers speed and vanishes into the night. Who was the woman? Who was the man who strangled her? And why is the body not found for so long? As Mrs McGillicuddy is going to stay with her old friend Miss Marple, you may be sure that these questions all get answered – in the end.

By the mid-1950s, Agatha Christie was the centre of attention whenever she published a new book or wrote a new play, whether she wanted to be or not. There were many requests for interviews, which she mostly refused as she kept to her routine of writing over winter before accompanying Max for his work early in the year, and then resting over summer while fielding any queries and perhaps formulating new ideas. In 1955 even *Vogue* magazine wanted Christie to tell them what Christmas present she would like to receive, but no doubt the mention of an accompanying photoshoot was enough to ensure that the author declined the request.[126] Meanwhile,

Cardinal paperback illustrated by Morgan Kane (1958).

Christie was climbing ever higher within the establishment, as the New Year's Honours for 1956 saw her made a CBE, although she still found some reason for complaint. 'The worst of a CBE seems to be the amount of congratulations you have to answer,' she wrote to Edmund Cork, 'many from people one hardly knows!'[127] Christie was amused to note that one Iraqi newspaper saw fit to promote her to Dame, fifteen years ahead of the fact.[128] 'Well Edmund, how do you feel in 1956?' she asked her agent. Referring to the fact that she now received a salary from Agatha Christie Ltd, she continued: 'As an employed wage slave I feel fine – but not at all like work.

Idleness for me!'[129] The author was writing from Tripoli in Libya, where she also happened to see *Murder at the Vicarage*'s stage dramatist Barbara Toy, who was apparently looking happy. While Christie may have felt idle, she continued to work on her projects, including the new Miss Marple novel that she delivered to her agent in February 1957. 'We think it is rather a good one,' said Edmund Cork upon reading it, in a letter to his American equivalent, and it has certainly gone on to become one of Christie's best-known novels.[130]

After its attention-grabbing opening, *4.50 from Paddington* settles into more conventional ground, although unusually for a Christie, we know that the murderer is a man from the beginning. This results in a novel in which almost all the female characters are sleuths of some kind, while the men remain suspects. After a little detection of her own, Miss Marple believes that the now-missing body of the woman who Mrs McGillicuddy saw strangled may be located in the grounds of Rutherford Hall, to which the train lines are adjacent. In typical fashion, Miss Marple is no-nonsense about the prospect of solving a murder, and isn't at all shocked to hear the descriptions of the victim's 'contorted face'. Instead, she is practical, realising that as the police will not do anything without evidence, she must investigate herself, although Miss Marple acknowledges that her advancing years mean that she cannot do as much active sleuthing as she wanted. In Christie's original typescript, it was revealed that Miss Marple is almost ninety years old, meaning that she was ageing only a little slower than the 'sixty-five to seventy'-year-old she originally envisaged in 1927. On the advice of Collins, it was decided that this revelation should be removed. 'Miss Marple's age had better be discreetly slurred over,' Christie concurred. 'She probably is ninety,

A 1959 Book Club jacket.

but we won't say so.'[131] Nevertheless, despite an instruction being sent to Harold Ober and Associates in the United States, the age remained in the American version of the book. 'I shall be ninety next year,' Miss Marple says in this original text, and when another character tries to correct her ('Eighty-seven'), she stands firm: 'You young people don't know best about everything.'[132]

Miss Marple is well-known to locals as 'fluffy and dithery in appearance, but inwardly as sharp and shrewd as they make them'. Her advancing years are taking a toll, however, and so she draws up her own reasoning for why she may be well-placed to solve this crime, including her experience of life and human nature, as well as friends and family whose expertise in crime, railways and maps may well help her. Nevertheless, she knows that she needs help, as she is 'old and tired', and so calls on Lucy Eyelesbarrow, a thirty-two-year-old domestic worker extraordinaire. Lucy is a curious character: a scholar, with a First in Mathematics from Oxford University, she

The Fontana paperback was notable for its back cover (1960).

decided against a career in academia in favour of becoming an exceptionally accomplished if rather improbable domestic worker who picks and chooses profitable short-term contracts. Intrigued by Miss Marple's mystery, Lucy agrees to take up a position at Rutherford Hall, where she will try to find both the missing body and any other clues.

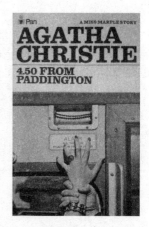

A 1976 Pan Books cover.

At the Hall, Lucy finds a dysfunctional family starting to congregate for Christmas. Luther Crackenthorpe is the grumpy patriarch, but has little access to the bulk of the family money due to disagreements with his late father, who left it in trust; when Luther dies, the capital will be split between his children. There is some question about his health due to regular visits from local Dr Quimper, who also seems to have designs on Luther's daughter, Emma. Crackenthorpe's other visiting children include Cedric, who 'Paints pictures in foreign parts'; Harold, who works in the city; and Alfred, who is 'a bit of a black sheep'. Eldest son Edmund died in the Second World War, while other daughter Edith also passed away and is survived by her husband, Bryan Eastley, who is also visiting with their son, Alexander. Lucy uses golf practice as a cover for her investigations, and we learn that society is continuing to change. There are constant complaints about the cost of running Rutherford Hall, for example; as J. C. Bernthal has pointed out, this is not a nostalgic country house mystery.[133] The creep of new housing developments is also mentioned dismissively by bad-tempered Luther Crackenthorpe. 'Nowhere to walk outside this place,' he complains. 'Nothing but pavements and miserable little band boxes of houses.' Nevertheless, Lucy finds what she needs: a broken thorn and powder compact, indicating that the body may have been thrown from the train after all. After more

'I thought it much wiser to find the body first,' Miss Marple advises Inspector Craddock, illustrated by K. J. Petts for the UK serial in *John Bull* magazine (1957)

investigations, she finds the dead woman in a sarcophagus located in a barn.

The discovery of the body confirms Mrs McGillicuddy's account, and the subsequent return of Inspector Craddock from *A Murder is Announced* means that Miss Marple is taken seriously at last. The dead woman's identity remains a mystery until the very end (and we never even learn her real name); as John Curran discovered, even in her notebooks Christie seemed unsure exactly who the victim would end up being.[134] As it turns out, this hardly seems to matter because Miss Marple arrives at the solution through instinct rather than facts and clues. For mystery readers this can be frustrating, but Christie was never in any doubt that instinct was Miss Marple's main weapon against wickedness. As she wrote in 1928, 'A "woman's instinct" is in any case a very debatable thing. We use the phrase glibly enough, but when we come down to facts, what, after all, does it mean? Shorn of all glamour, I think it comes down to this – women prefer short cuts! They prefer the inspired guess to the more laborious process of solid reasoning. And, of course, the inspired guess is often right.'[135] Certainly it is an 'inspired guess' that leads Miss Marple to set a trap that even she acknowledges has its flaws. However, chance opportunities do occur in real life, and two years after publication, Christie even received a letter from an Australian school teacher, headed 'AMAZING COINCIDENCES', which outlined that she once had a pupil identify a miscreant from just their back, just as occurs in *4.50 from Paddington*. She offered a further example of a coincidence should Christie wish to make use of it, which concerned the murder of her cousin on a sheep ranch, with the murderer having been inspired by a 'fool proof' murder described by author Arthur Upfield in a talk that he attended.[136] Christie politely thanked her for her letter.

Fontana's 1984 cover by Martin Baker.

Once the murderer is identified, the elderly Miss Marple deftly escapes from his hands, quite literally. Of course, there is also a happy ending of sorts for Lucy Eyelesbarrow, who has found love among her admirers at Rutherford Hall, although the reader will have to decide for themselves precisely who the object of her affection is. Miss Marple then reflects on the murderer's fate, and claims that capital punishment had been abolished, although in fact it was still the subject of debate and this would not happen until 1969, with the last hangings occurring in 1965. Miss Marple's thoughts on capital punishment were to become the subject of a column in the *Guardian*

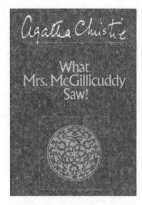

A hardback from Dodd Mead's 'Winterbrook Edition' series (1987).

by then-Lord Altrincham (later simply John Grigg, after he renounced the title) in 1962, entitled 'Goodbye to the Gallows':

> Agatha Christie published *4.50 from Paddington* in 1957, and when writing it she must have thought the death penalty was on the way out. After the murderer has been discovered (and I cannot forbear to mention that I managed to spot him) the author puts these words into the mouth of Miss Marple: 'Everything he did was bold and audacious and cruel and greedy, and I am really very, very sorry that they have abolished capital punishment because I do feel that if there is anyone who ought to hang it's ...'
>
> But Miss Marple could derive little comfort from the Homicide Act, because the cool and calculating murderer would never be deterred by it. He would only need to choose his method with care, so that the crime, even if it were pinned to him, would be 'capital murder' within the meaning of the Act. The gallows is a piece of medieval furniture completely out of place in a civilised modern society. When it has gone the way of the rack and the block those who now firmly believe in it will soon be wondering why it was retained for so long.[137]

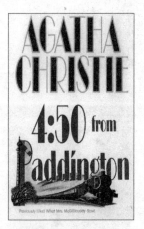

'Mrs McGillicuddy' was retired from the covers when the American and British book titles were aligned in 1992 and Harper Mystery began publishing the paperbacks.

Over the next decade Christie became more concerned about what she saw as the decline of law and order, and the lack of appropriate punishment for criminals. 'It frightens me that nobody seems to care about the innocent,' she wrote. 'Nobody seems to go through the *agony* of the *victim* – they are only full of pity for the young killer, because of his youth. Why should they not execute him? We have taken the lives of wolves, in this country; we didn't try to teach the wolf to lie down with the lamb – I doubt really if we could have. We hunted down the wild boar in the mountains before he came down and killed the children by the brook. Those were our enemies – and we destroyed them.'[138]

When the typescript for the novel was delivered to her agents, it bore the title *4.54 from Paddington*. The book would go through many titles before publication, with Christie herself wondering about different times and stations, at one point even suggesting that 'Padderloo' should be the name of the terminus (mixing Paddington and Waterloo stations), just in case a resident of a large country estate half-an-hour from Paddington should be upset about being impli-

Paddington's famous clock on one of HarperCollins' relaunch titles in 1995.

cated in the fictional crime.[139] The name *Eyewitness to Murder* was suggested by both Christie and her American agents independently, and this (or *Eyewitness to Death*) was fixed as a potential American title for some time. For the British title, Christie agreed that '*4.50 from Paddington*, or even *5 o'clock from Paddington* is a better title. I put 4.54 because there is actually no train at that time, and I thought people might write and say "but the 4.40 (or whatever it was) goes to Weston Super Mare." If that doesn't matter, I'm agreeable to any time for the train – the others to be altered to fit the time sequence.'[140]

Christie's British publishers, Collins, were pleased to read her new novel. The reader's report stated that 'This seems to me to be rather a good Christie, certainly an improvement on [her most recently published novel] *Dead Man's Folly*, though it must sadly be confessed that the brilliant ingenuity of the early books is absent. But she is as skilful as ever.' The reader did sound one note of caution:

* * *

It seems to me that this solution is not quite as surprising as it ought to be and, what is more, that it is not quite fair because unless I am being very stupid I cannot see how anyone could have known the murderer's motive and the opportunities for everyone to commit the three crimes are pretty well equal. I think this may be picked up on by hostile reviewers but they should really be disarmed by the wonderful beginning and Mrs Christie's wonderful readability and technique. Miss Marple is the horried [sic] old thing she always is but Lucy Eyelesbarrow is a splendid character and I did wonder whether perhaps she is being groomed to succeed either Poirot or Miss Marple in the Christie canon.

I certainly enjoyed reading this and I think we need have no fear about its failing to do as well as the other Agatha Christies.[141]

What horrible truth does the box hold?

Read Agatha Christie's *new mystery story*

"EYEWITNESS TO DEATH"

An elderly woman insists that a murder has been committed. The authorities won't believe her. They can find no body.

Did her imagination play tricks on her? Or did she really see a woman being strangled to death? A coffin-shaped stone box holds the answer.

For mystery at its best, be sure to read "Eyewitness to Death," the latest story by Agatha Christie, world famous writer. This never-before-published novel starts exclusively in Sunday's

Chicago Sunday Tribune
WORLD'S GREATEST NEWSPAPER

An advert for the American newspaper serial from 25 October 1957.

Across the Atlantic, Harold Ober felt that the novel was 'one of her very good ones', although he was having difficulties with selling it to the highest-paying magazines, such as the *Saturday Evening Post*, as the serial market had 'gone to pieces' for detective fiction.[142] This was unlucky for Christie, as, whether consciously or not, she had created exactly the sort of mystery that her American publishers in particular wanted: a strong opening hook, with a spectacular murder early on, and then a story with elements of romance focusing on an interesting young female character. In the end, the *Chicago Tribune* offered $7,500, and published it from October to December 1957. Although the newspaper called

HarperCollins' paperback by Julie Jenkins (2007).

the story *Eyewitness to Death*, Dodd Mead decided on a new title for their publication of the novel in the United States in November 1957, opting for the somewhat dramatic *What Mrs McGillicuddy Saw!*, while they also retained the train's original departure time of 4.54 in the text. In Britain, Christie asked her publishers to show some restraint in their description of the author on the dustjacket: 'Too much fatuous praise I am sure annoys readers.'[143]

Once the main queries had been dealt with, Christie went off on her travels again, including a return to Nimrud. She complained to Cork that because of the way that books were sent to her, customs authorities were keeping hold of them, 'listening in case they tick! and satisfied that it's not a bomb, then suspect it of being Communist propaganda, and then someone has to go and clear it.'[144] By May 1957, she and Max had moved on to the United States, visiting New York, Harvard and the Grand Canyon, from where she wrote to Cork that she was 'Enjoying myself terrifically – in fact couldn't be enjoying myself more! Must do all this again!',

One of a quartet of railway-themed hardbacks designed by Neil Gower (2018).

despite her aversion to some of the travel logistics: 'I hate flying'.[145]

In Britain, the novel was published on 4 November 1957, which was perfect timing for the Christmas market and complemented by the seasonal setting of the book. This was not before a last-minute crisis, in which some sloppily put-together proof pages made it to Christie, much to the embarrassment of Collins, which apologised profusely.[146] A few reviews highlighted disappointment at the mystery's solution, with one feeling that 'The story is not one of Mrs Christie's best – there is none of her usual skilful giving the reader the vital clue while distracting his attention, and the choice of culprit seems almost arbitrary', and another that 'This is wonderful entertainment, though a little resentment may be felt at the ending.'[147] Francis Iles in the *Guardian* was keen to praise Christie generally, although for him this novel fell short:

> I have only pity for those poor souls who cannot enjoy the sprightly stories of Agatha Christie; but though sprightliness is not the least of this remarkable writer's qualities, there is another that we look for in her, and that is detection: genuine, steady, logical detection, taking a step by step nearer to the heart of the mystery. Unfortunately it is this quality that is missing in *4.50 from Paddington*. The police never seem to find out a single thing, and even Miss Marples [sic] lies low and says nuffin' to the point until the final dramatic exposure. There is the usual small gallery of interesting and perfectly credible characters, and nothing could be easier to read. But please, Mrs Christie, a little more of that incomparable detection next time.[148]

Several reviewers also highlighted the character of Lucy Eyelesbarrow as an interesting one, as well as a potential new sleuth for Christie, although she did not reappear, despite being the type of younger detective that the author wished she had invented early in her career. The *Western Mail* felt that 'Miss Christie, who I believe hates the sight and sound of Hercule Poirot, is obviously on the point of killing off Miss Marple, and switching to Lucy Eyelesbarrow.'[149] Meanwhile, *The Tatler* had more practical advice for readers: 'Only one warning: if *4.50 from Paddington* is read by you in the course of a train journey, it may make you nervous of looking out the window.'[150]

An illustration for the *Eyewitness to Death* serial (1957).

The 1950s saw Agatha Christie become consistent in her work routine, which satisfied the company that bore her name, as well as her long-time publishers and agents. But as she moved into old age, so the meaning of the name 'Agatha Christie' moved beyond her writings. The increased interest in her work meant that it was only a matter of time before a more substantial deal would be struck to enable screen adaptations of Christie's work, especially in the wake of the critical and financial success of Billy Wilder's *Witness for the Prosecution* (1957). Soon, Christie would find that control over some of her characters and stories would start to slip from her grasp.

CHAPTER FOUR:

THE
1960s

n some ways, the 1960s was Agatha Christie's most successful decade. Although many of her best-known novels were published from the 1920s to the 1940s (and adaptations are often set in the same period as a result), the 1960s saw the author's formidable success continuing to grow apace with her keenly awaited 'Christie for Christmas' each year. But it was not just her new novels that allowed her to scale new heights of popularity, as UNESCO declared Christie to be the world's best-selling and most widely-translated novelist. Meanwhile, a new arrangement with the film studio Metro-Goldwyn-Mayer meant that there was now a concerted effort to translate a number of her

OPPOSITE: *Murder She Said* was the first Miss Marple film starring Margaret Rutherford, released in 1961, but in France and elsewhere the movie retained the title of the book on which it was based.

The icon for the *Swinging Christies* podcast, designed by Bartlett Studio (2024).

works to both the big and small screen, and Miss Marple would be the most notable recipient of this boost in publicity. Crucially, Christie continued to situate her stories in the present day, even as society changed. This meant that the Swinging Sixties was most definitely a character of its own in some of her later work, most notably the Poirot mystery *Third Girl* in 1966, while longing for a lost past is a central theme of the Miss Marple novel *At Bertram's Hotel* a year earlier.

For Agatha Christie, the main aim of the 1960s, it seems, was to avoid stress and not get too bogged down with work. 'I hope 1960 has opened auspiciously for you – and not too many bothers,' she wrote to Cork from Sri Lanka in January 1960.[1] Unfortunately for her, the following decade would not be without its 'bothers', with developments that would cause the author great distress, even as her popularity continued to grow.

'Greenshaw's Folly'

(Short Story, collected in *The Adventure of the Christmas Pudding and a Selection of Entrées*, 1960)

Although Miss Marple made her debut in a short story, by the 1950s the form was losing its appeal for authors, as the previously lucrative magazines turned elsewhere for content as fiction fell out of fashion among their readers. Nevertheless, Miss Marple's earlier adventures remained in print and widely read; in June 1960, a school in Nairobi even wrote to the author to ask if they could set up their own 'Tuesday Night

ABOVE LEFT: 'Greenshaw's Folly' first appeared in book form in Crime Club's *The Adventure of the Christmas Pudding and a Selection of Entrées* (1960). ABOVE RIGHT: The story's first US book appearance was in Dodd Mead's collection *Double Sin and Other Stories* (1961).

'The Greenshore Folly' finally saw print in 2016 with a new cover by 88-year-old Tom Adams.

Club': her agents had no objection.[2] In Britain, the same month saw final confirmation that, for once, Agatha Christie would not have a new 'Christie for Christmas' ready for her publishers in time for the festive season, largely because of her theatrical commitments as well as time spent on a trip to India that year.[3] This came as no surprise, as the author had been involved in a plan to put together a new collection of older and revised short stories for publication towards the end of the year, and suggested several titles, including two starring Miss Marple: 'The Case of the Perfect Maid' and 'Greenshaw's Folly'.[4] Only the latter featured in the final collection, which was eventually called *The Adventure of the Christmas Pudding and a Selection of Entrées* (to give it is full title), comprised of five Poirot mysteries topped off with this single Miss Marple story.[5]

'Greenshaw's Folly' was first published in both Canada and Great Britain just a few years earlier, in 1956, and its genesis is one of the most convoluted of any Christie story. In November 1954, Edmund Cork wrote to Exeter's Diocesan Board of Finance with an offer from Agatha Christie regarding her local church in Churston Ferrers, Devon, near to Greenway. Christie had decided that she wished to fund a new stained glass window for the church, and mindful of the tax difficulties of cash gifts, suggested that she donate a story (and its proceeds) to the church.[6] Christie explained this gesture in her autobiography: 'It is a beautiful little church and the plain glass east window always gaped at me like a gap in teeth,' she wrote. 'I looked at it every Sunday and used to think how lovely it would look in pale colours.'[7]

The Diocese's solicitors responded to Cork's letter outlining the likely cost of around £1,250, at which point it was confirmed that the gifted story would be called 'The Greenshore Folly'.[8] Local artist James Paterson duly sketched out a design in consultation with a local clergyman, which he sent to Christie in December 1954, but although the author liked the colours, she had issues with the design.[9] Christie's 'serious objection' was that 'it is not a window of happiness or of thanksgiving'; both the designer and Diocese expected an east-facing window to be of the crucifixion. Christie considered it to be 'a very fine design but terribly grim!' Instead, she wanted 'a happy window, embodying the goodness of God, not His suffering', ideally illustrating Psalm 23's 'The Lord is my Shepherd'; two decades later, the same Psalm would be read at Christie's funeral, at her own request.[10] Following this feedback, a new design was sent to Christie, as well as a sketch of the stained-glass window that had been erected in Southbourne Church, West Sussex, in honour of her grandfather, Nathaniel Frary Miller, presumably to serve as inspiration. A new design was completed in May 1955, and once Christie was happy, she also advised on her preferred inscription, which included 'Surely goodness and mercy shall follow me all the days of my life'.[11]

Having established the details of the window, thoughts turned to selling 'The Greenshore Folly' in order to fund it. For this story, Christie had made use of her most famous detective, placing Hercule Poirot in a novella-length mystery that saw the murder of a girl in the grounds of a house clearly inspired by Greenway, resulting in a neat link between the story and the gift, but there was an unexpected problem. 'The Greenshore Folly' was too long to be sold as a short story but not long enough to be serialised like a novel. In May 1955, *Cosmopolitan* magazine in the United States rejected it unless the ending were revised; Cork suggested Christie might undertake the revisions considering the story's importance, but this didn't happen.[12] A ray of hope then arrived in the

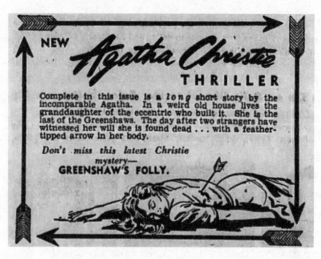

Advertisement for the 1959 serial.

form of *This Week* magazine's Stewart Beach, who had been desperate to secure a suitable Christie story. Unfortunately, the mystery's length put off both him and the *Chicago Tribune*.[13] Christie's philanthropic gesture was soon nicknamed 'the blood-stained window' by her agents, a reflection of the murderous difficulties it was causing them. In July, Christie withdrew 'The Greenshore Folly' and planned to write a new story to be sold instead. This original version of the story did not disappear, however, as Christie reworked the mystery to become *Dead Man's Folly*, a novel published the following year. The original novella-length version was eventually published in 2013 as *Hercule Poirot and the Greenshore Folly*.

Although Stewart Beach could not accept the original 'The Greenshore Folly', he outlined what he required from any new story from Christie, requesting a new 7,000-word mystery for which he would pay $3,500.[14] Christie set to work right away. For legal reasons Christie's replacement story could not have an entirely new title, although it was modified to 'Greenshaw's Folly'. In every other respect, it is a completely new mystery, this time featuring Miss Marple, who is visiting Raymond and Joan West when she hears of a local murder. 'Greenshaw's Folly' is the name of a house that curiously mixes Indian, French and Italian architecture, and it is local to the Wests. Raymond decides to show the unusual building to his friend Horace Bindler, a literary critic. They meet the house's owner, Miss Greenshaw, and her staff: housekeeper Mrs Cresswell and the young gardener, Alfred. The two guests are then asked to witness Miss Greenshaw's will, and they go on to volunteer the services of Joan West's niece, Louise, to help edit the diaries of Miss Greenshaw's grandfather, Nathaniel. One day shortly after, Louise is shocked to hear a scream from the gardens and sees that Miss Greenshaw has been impaled by an arrow. Both Louise and Mrs Cresswell are locked in their rooms and so cannot assist, and when the police finally arrive, Miss Greenshaw is dead.

The original typescript of 'Greenshaw's Folly' survives, and it shows how Christie worked hard to try to balance the clues properly. This early version had Miss Greenshaw attacked with a spade rather than an arrow, while various mentions of the police are reduced and reworked, possibly to both play fair with the associated clues while also preventing the reader from solving the case too easily. Christie also deleted details about Nathaniel Greenshaw's diary, including the 'personal charm of a barmaid in the neighbouring town'.[15] Additionally, Miss Marple originally had more ruminations about Mr Naysmith, a man she knew who liked to give false impressions just for the fun of it. In response, Inspector Welch dismisses her as 'batty'.[16]

The country house setting also allows the author to hark back to times past, especially when it comes to the reduced staff on display, as Horace Bindler remembers the housemaids and parlour maids of his youth, while also curiously yearning for a body in the library. This time, Christie does

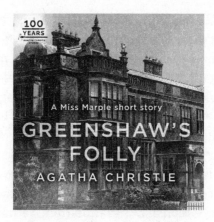

A 2020 audiobook cover for the story, designed by Holly Macdonald.

not oblige, but Miss Marple is never far away. 'Some commit murder, some get mixed up in murders, others have murder thrust upon them,' reflects Raymond. 'My Aunt Jane comes into the third category.' Raymond is little changed in many ways, but we are told that the topics of his books have softened somewhat as he moves into middle age, while the breakdown of Louise's marriage is not considered a scandal any longer, as it would have been when Miss Marple first appeared in print. The final solution may not be wholly practical, but the story is no less entertaining for it, and it is a delight to see Miss Marple in another short story; this was the final one that Christie penned for her.

Christie sent the new story to Cork just a month after it had been requested, and Cork passed it on to Dorothy Olding in the United States, who was now Christie's agent in America following the death of Harold Ober in October 1959; Olding had previously handled Christie's work when Ober was ill earlier in the decade, and so this was a smooth transition. Olding was immediately concerned, as she felt that in this mystery Miss Marple was 'smart beyond words' and made deductions too quickly and easily.[17] Beach had his own reservations, as he believed that the first half of the story did not have enough suspense, and he suggested swapping out Horace Bindler for Miss Marple, allowing her to play a more active part in the early part of the story. He requested more growing menace and suggested that Louise realising that she is locked in her room could be a suitable cliffhanger.[18] Christie did not agree to the proposed changes, and had not been informed that the story was supposed to be suitable for publication in two parts, meaning that any revisions would have to be substantial.[19] *Collier's* magazine then declined the story as well.

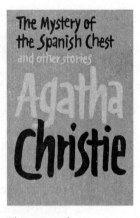

The original unpublished design for the UK collection sported a different title (1960).

By February 1956 Christie was becoming restless, writing that 'the one thing I want to know is how Greenshaw's Folly is faring? Because I want that window done and in before I die! If you can't sell it as it is – I could alter it – a fag – but possible'.[20] Cork now suggested the option of last resort: Agatha Christie Ltd itself would buy the story from the Exeter Diocese for £1,000, which would allow the company's cash to flow directly to the church. Cork also noted with some amusement that *Collier's* magazine had paid some $17,500 for *Dead Man's Folly*, which they then decided to edit, having earlier turned down the much cheaper and shorter version of the mystery. Although Christie felt that the failure to sell the story was 'very humiliating', she conceded that selling the rights to the company was the right thing to do.[21] In Britain, the story was published by the *Daily Mail*, which printed it in December 1956 with striking illustrations by Leslie Caswell, a month after it had debuted in Toronto's *Star Weekly*, which paid $1,000 for the rights.

For Christie, the important thing was that the story had indeed resulted in her beloved stained-glass window. 'I love it and enjoy looking at it on Sundays,' she wrote. 'Mr Patterson

[sic] has made a fine window. It will, I think, stand the test of the centuries because it is simple. I am both proud and humble that I have been permitted to offer it with the proceeds of my work.'[22]

The 24 October 1960 publication of *The Adventure of the Christmas Pudding* collection in Britain came little more than a month after Christie's seventieth birthday, and thankfully the author didn't seem to spot that her character was referred to as 'Miss Marples' on the dustjacket of the first edition. Inevitably, Christie's birthday coincided with media requests from around the world – 'Naturally no!', she wrote to Cork.[23] She was a little more interested in an invitation to participate in a Japanese International Mystery Writers Club, however. 'Though not wishing to take an active part in anything of this kind it might be a good excuse for a journey to Japan!' she confessed.[24] She enjoyed her milestone birthday 'and hardly felt my age!!! (Rich hot lobster for dinner!)'[25] Because the United States had its own short story collections, *The Adventure of the Christmas Pudding* was not published there. Instead, an omnibus edition called *Murder Preferred* was released, which collected the novels *One, Two, Buckle My Shoe* (published as *The Patriotic Murders*), *Five Little Pigs* (*Murder in Retrospect*) and *A Murder is Announced*. The following year, 'Greenshaw's Folly' appeared alongside another Miss Marple short story, 'Sanctuary', in the United States collection *Double Sin and Other Stories*. From 1961 onwards, Christie resumed her regular schedule and published a new novel every year until *Postern of Fate* in 1973, the last mystery that she wrote.

Murder She Said
(Film, 1961)

In the late 1950s, serious discussions were had with the film studio Metro-Goldwyn-Mayer concerning the rights to adapt many of Agatha Christie's works for television. Christie's publisher, Billy Collins, brought together Agatha Christie Ltd and the head of MGM's British division, producer Lawrence ('Larry') P. Bachmann, and between them they then tried to come to an arrangement, all while fending off demands from legal representatives from both parties who struggled with the convoluted nature of the deal. The final contract would have ramifications for decades, and significantly affect both Christie and her daughter, Rosalind.

In early 1960 a basic agreement in principle had been made,

ABOVE: Not 'Paddington' or 'McGillicuddy', but in 1961 it was *Murder She Said*.

Fontana's first tie-in book cover for an Agatha Christie book (1961).

Cardinal Books also published a US tie-in paperback.

and crucially for Christie it excluded some novels that she potentially wished to dramatise for the stage one day, as well as those that had already been adapted for the theatre. The titles 'reserved' for potential dramatisation by Christie included Miss Marple in *A Murder is Announced* and *The Moving Finger*; the Poirot novels *Cards on the Table*, *Murder on the Orient Express*, *Evil Under the Sun* and *Three Act Tragedy*; and the standalone mysteries *Crooked House*, *Sparkling Cyanide* and *Murder is Easy*. Otherwise, most Christie mystery novels and short stories were included, although it excluded those not owned by her, including *A Pocket Full of Rye* and *They Do It with Mirrors*. At this stage, MGM were only envisaging a deal that would cover television (particularly in the United States), and one of the first thoughts was for an anthology-style series with Christie's name as the big attraction, rather than one of her sleuths.

Christie remained both indifferent and resigned to the news as it was relayed to her, as lawyers squabbled over registrations of copyright for decades-old stories, which necessitated trips to the Library of Congress to confirm details. The contract reached its seventh draft by January 1960, while Edmund Cork enlisted the help of expensive solicitors and had 'a very strenuous time' trying to iron out the details, mindful that 'there will be a lot of broken hearts if it goes wrong'.[26] Christie replied to her agent's update while staying at the Taj Mahal Hotel in Mumbai, where she was enjoying 'peace, perfect peace', while acknowledging that 'I hope there won't be "broken hearts" over this MGM agreement – but what will be – will be! And what one

A Belgian lobby card featuring James Robertson Justice.

loses in cash one may gain in absence of worry. But don't break your heart over it, Edmund dear.'[27] His heart may not have been broken, but the following month Cork told Rosalind that 'This MGM deal has almost destroyed me'.[28] Nevertheless, the end of the month saw confirmation that MGM had decided to go ahead with the agreement, and the contracts were signed. Rosalind's husband, Anthony Hicks, confessed that he was starting to feel optimistic at last, and for a while he was right to do so, as in March MGM made their first payment to Agatha Christie Ltd for $75,000 (£26,732 0s 3d).[29] The deal was on, but there had been one significant last-minute amendment: although MGM were mainly interested in television, they had suddenly become concerned that any cinema films from Christie's works might prove to be an unwelcome rival to their own productions. It was then decided that the deal would cover theatrical films as well as television, although at the time nobody expected to exploit this clause. This would soon change.

For a while MGM concentrated on putting together both a

general Agatha Christie series of mysteries for television, and a programme starring Miss Marple. This was a nuisance for Cork, as he had to comb through paperwork relating to earlier adaptations. MGM were permitted to choose forty titles from the approved list of Christie stories covered by the contract, and they turned their attention to Miss Marple first of all, perhaps because of the potential international appeal of her quintessential Englishness.[30] By April, there were two scripts for the Miss Marple series ready to show Christie, while

A French poster with a collage of the principal cast.

plans continued apace for a Poirot pilot starring José Ferrer. The Poirot programme was eventually shown in April 1962, although with Martin Gabel playing the Belgian detective, and it was not picked up for a series. Nevertheless, this was further than Miss Marple got when it came to small-screen adventures with MGM, as later in 1960 thoughts turned to a big-screen debut for the character. By this time the press had started to pick up on the news, and the *News Chronicle* even declared that the contract 'will make her the richest woman writer in the world', claiming that she would receive around £1,000,000. This was not the case, and a figure in that region could only be reached if the contract were extended repeatedly and became a considerable success.[31] In response to a reporter, Christie insisted that 'Nothing has been put on the dotted line yet. This has been blowing up for some time. Discuss it with my agent.' Cork was similarly coy, even though the contract had indeed been agreed, but Bachmann was keener to speak. 'The deal with Mrs Christie was arranged on my initiative,' he boasted. 'We hope to get several TV series from them. We are counting on her to help with the preparation of the material, since she has a wonderful power of analysis, but we have made no agreement about future work.'[32]

There was little apparent movement over the summer ('There are daily roars from the MGM lion, but not more hard news yet,' Cork told Anthony Hicks), until a script arrived for Christie at Greenway.[33] This was for a cinema film rather than a television series, and was an adaptation of *4.50 from Paddington*, one of Miss Marple's more recent cases. No doubt the attention-grabbing and highly visual opening, combined with the appeal of the English country house for international markets, made this a good bet for MGM's European division.

Initially, MGM considered some 'sophisticated American minxes' to play Miss Marple, indicat-ing the extent to which they were willing to make changes for potential commercial gain, but by the end of the year there was only one name in mind: Margaret Rutherford.[34] A respected actor specialising in quirky character parts, Rutherford initially resisted the advances of MGM due to her aversion to using crime for entertainment. In part, this was due to her sad and difficult early family life, which saw her grandfather mur-dered by her own father, and then the suicide of her mother. 'Possibly the person who did most to convince me that Miss Marple was in fact a very fine woman and definitely on the right track was the

A Spanish tie-in paperback (1961).

director, George Pollock,' Rutherford later remembered. 'He persuaded me that Miss Marple was not so much concerned with crime, even though she was an indomitable sleuth always one stage ahead of the police, but that she was more involved in a game - like chess - a game of solving problems, rather than of murder.' Rutherford considered this argument, and after reading the script discussed the role with her husband, fellow actor Stringer Davis. 'We both agreed - Miss Marple was undoubtedly a good woman and helped people. It was on Christmas Day 1960 that I finally took the plunge and

A Danish poster for the film.

A Danish flyer promoting the film.

phoned George with my answer: "Yes, I will be Miss Marple." He seemed delighted and said that it was his best Christmas present!'[35] It's likely that Rutherford was also keen on the fee, of £16,000 for a single film with the possibility of more to come, as she struggled to manage her finances and needed money at the time.[36]

This script was initially called *Meet Miss Marple* (emphasising her introduction as a potentially recurring character), but by the end of production it had become *Murder She Said* (which emphasised the crime to be solved instead).[37] Production commenced at Borehamwood Studios on 31 January 1961, with location work including Denham in Buckinghamshire (standing in for Milchester, Miss Marple's home village in this film), Radnor Hall in Hertfordshire (as Ackenthorpe Hall, renamed from the book's Rutherford Hall, no doubt due to the coincidence of the star's name), and – of course – Paddington station in London for the opening sequence. Cork told Christie the news, and the author seemed happy enough with the details, although she maintained little interest in what MGM were doing as she considered it to be a business arrangement to be dealt with by the company, rather than herself.

Margaret Rutherford 'wanted my audiences to feel the credibility of Miss Marple so I carefully chose the kind of clothes that I myself would wear', which included practical items as well as more flamboyant pieces of costume, such as her memorable cape and hats. 'There was a dear little blob of a deer-stalker hat that I did take a fancy to, and Stringer has his own version of it hanging in the cupboard today,' she

un capolavoro di AGATHA CHRISTIE

ASSASSINIO SUL TRENO

Appealing to 1961 Italian cinema audiences with heightened peril.

remembered.[38] The script, by David Pursall and Jack Seddon, also makes changes to Miss Marple that needed to be reflected in her appearance. In their adaptation, Miss Marple takes a much more active part in proceedings, and replaces both Mrs McGillicuddy and Lucy Eyelesbarrow, which means that she must also dress up in a maid's outfit while going undercover at Ackenthorpe Hall, before going golfing as part of her investigation. In one memorable disguise, Miss Marple even goes undercover as a track layer for the railways while she looks for clues. 'The scene was filmed at the local train crossing near Gerrard's Cross and George Pollock assured me that he had double checked that in fact no trains would come during shooting,' remembered Rutherford. 'I had enough worries without that to cope with.'[39] These extra identities

An Italian tie-in book
cover from Mondadori
(1979).

for Miss Marple mean that she is quite unlike the character as established by Christie, who certainly would not poke her tongue out at passing children, as Rutherford's Miss Marple does. The scriptwriters were unapologetic about their decisions. 'The Miss Marple of the books struck me as snobbish, unkind and cold, with a stealthy, almost reptilian eye,' claimed Jack Seddon several years later. 'The intention with the screen Miss Marple was to create a person of warmth and gusto and, as portrayed by the late Margaret Rutherford, it seems this intention was achieved.'[40]

Joining Margaret Rutherford in the cast is her husband, playing local librarian Mr Stringer, who is happy to be a sounding board for Miss Marple. Other cast members include faces that were either already familiar or would become so, including Peter Butterworth, Richard Briers, and Joan Hickson, who would take on the part of Miss Marple herself more than two decades later. Dr Quimper is played by Arthur Kennedy, who was the token American actor so often required by the big film studios, while Australian Charles 'Bud' Tingwell makes his first appearance as Inspector Craddock; he would return for the three sequels. However, Rutherford's most memorable co-star is undoubtedly James Robertson Justice as Ackenthorpe himself. Justice displays a great deal of grouchy personality when playing the part, which makes him an ideal sparring partner for Rutherford's bold Miss Marple. Although he initially complains that 'A plainer Jane I've never set eyes on in my life', by the end of the film Ackenthorpe is ready to propose marriage to Miss Marple. 'Who on earth would have you?' he argues, when she turns him down, as she is reunited with Mr Stringer.

Justice's energetic performance in the film is particularly

welcome, seeing as Ackenthorpe's family are such an uninspiring bunch. When the brothers arrive midway through the film, there is little chance for the audience to either get to know about them nor care about them, and the film starts to meander after its promising opening. It is particularly unfortunate that these family members are so uninteresting that, when two of them are murdered in the film's final act, audiences may struggle to remember who they were. The film was tailored to acquire a family-friendly certificate from censors, and so there is little in the way of detail when it comes to murder, but Miss Marple's new placement at Ackenthorpe Hall allows her to be in more direct danger, as she is surely associating with a murderer. Occasionally there is a creepily effective atmosphere, particularly the discovery of the third body on a dark and stormy night, but the memorably jaunty music from Ron Goodwin is never far away to lighten the mood.

The advertising emphasised the fun nature of the investigation, with exhibitors encouraged to run their own 'Guess the Murderer' competition. Meanwhile, the trailer opens with both earlier titles of the story ('This is the *4.50 from Paddington ... Meet Miss Marple*') before Miss Marple addresses the audience directly, following the murderous scene out of her window. 'Now you saw that, didn't you?' she cries, pointing directly at the camera. 'Do you think anyone will believe us?' When the ticket inspector is indeed suspicious, she implores him to 'ask them, they saw it happen', pointing at the audience once more. 'What did I tell you?' she asks us. 'Nobody's going to believe us.' Clips then included lighter moments from the film, such as Miss Marple asking for a 'leg up' from Mr Stringer, as well as some more atmospheric sequences. 'Only

A Swedish cover from Bonniers with art by Adrian Purkis (1980).

Agatha Christie,' we are told, 'can mix murder and mirth with such hilarious abandon', although the original novel did no such thing. Nevertheless, it is quite clear that this film is not designed to be taken too seriously. Once Miss Marple helps to catch a murderer, she promptly faints, which is something that Christie had dismissed as 'corny' when it was suggested for the play of *Murder at the Vicarage* over a decade earlier.

The film was released in September 1961, and proved to be one of MGM's biggest successes of the year: a few months later it was on course to make more than £100,000 in profit, following production costs of £123,073.[41] Christie saw an early preview of the film in London, and then once again when her local cinema in Devon was chosen to host an early screening in order to test the market before its wider release. She explained her reaction in a letter to Cork:

> Frankly, it's pretty poor! I thought so that evening in London, but I couldn't say so before Margaret Rutherford, especially as she herself was so good – I thought it might seem better if seen in a real cinema with people – But no, definitely not.
>
> As my eldest nephew said to me in a sad voice as we left 'It wasn't very exciting was it?' And I really couldn't have agreed with him more – none of us thought much of it. The truth is there is no sustained interest – it's muddling with a lot of brothers turning up in the middle, and no kind of suspense, or feeling of things happening.
>
> It was a difficult book to choose and I always wondered why they did – and I do think it's a bad script ... I also think it's badly produced – and its photography isn't good – very poor by modern standards of films. MGM ought to be able to do better than that, it might have been rather better on television. The best things about it are excellent character studies by [Rutherford] and her husband and J Justice, but

as they haven't much to do with the plot – another kind of plot might have suited them better!!!

There's no doubt about it. I have been spared a good deal by keeping aloof from films, etc. [*And Then There Were None*] was bad – *Spider's Web* moderate – only *Witness* [*for the Prosecution*] was good.[42]

Christie also clarified in a postscript that Cork should not 'think I'm upset by *Murder She Said*. I'm not. It's more or less what I expected, all along.' It is interesting that at this point Christie praises Rutherford's performance as a highlight, when she would later come to criticise it. A few years later, a letter from Christie to Bachmann reinforced the fact that she understood that some changes would be necessary when bringing Miss Marple to the screen. 'I do recognise that you were within your rights to adapt them fairly freely, as you did in *Murder She Said*,' she wrote. 'But at least that satisfied basic requirements, in that it was recognisable as the same fundamental story … and I realised that Miss Marple had to take a more central part. Whether I liked it or not, was my headache! The thriller aspect suffered, but Margaret Rutherford, though not much like Miss Marple, gave a most enjoyable performance.'[43]

Christie's initial thoughts on Rutherford were echoed by many film critics, who mostly received *Murder She Said* warmly. In *Kinematograph Weekly*, the film was described as 'Ingenious', with the plot 'skilfully handled by Margaret Rutherford, whose sense of humour cleverly offsets the eerie. There are laughs and thrills galore, and a neat in-the-nick-of-time twist ending.'[44] The *Illustrated London News* similarly considered it to be 'a joy. Snorting, severe, permanently indignant yet permanently dignified, she is anyone's idea of an English great-aunt.'[45] Across the Atlantic, the *San Francisco Examiner* thought the ending of the film was a disappointment, and bemoaned the inclusion of an American in the

The film title was reused for a book of Miss Marple quotations in 2019, edited by Tony Medawar.

'crisply British' film, but otherwise indicated that the movie had potential for international appeal as a 'sometimes witty, occasionally eerie' story through which Rutherford sailed 'like a majestic battleship'.[46] For the *Detroit Free Press* it was simply 'wonderfully suspenseful, funny and entertaining ... It will probably create a new mob of Agatha Christie fans, too; not that she needs them.'[47] In her autobiography, Rutherford explained that she was relieved by the reaction. 'At least I felt that I had not let Miss Christie down,' she said. 'This delightful woman came down to see me on the set and when we met face to face we instantly clicked.'[48]

Murder She Said did well enough that plans for subsequent productions were immediately put in motion. MGM were keen to extend their contract with Agatha Christie Ltd (with a further payment of $50,000), and were still considering a television series for Miss Marple, likely to be filmed in Britain.[49] However, in the end Miss Marple would return to the big screen in 1963 – but, this time, she would not be solving one of her own mysteries.

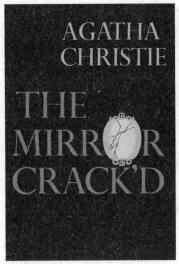

The Mirror Crack'd from Side to Side
(Novel, 1962)

While the precise details of Miss Marple's age were removed from 1957's *4.50 from Paddington*, by the 1960s time has most definitely marched on for both the character and her world. The beginning of *The Mirror Crack'd from Side to Side* deals with a changing Britain as well as Miss Marple's increasing age, as the elderly sleuth sadly surveys her garden, to which she can no longer attend properly. 'One had to face the fact: St Mary Mead was *not* the place it had been,' Christie acknowledges, 'but what one really meant was the simple fact that one was growing old.' Many of the characters whom we had got to know in *The Murder at the Vicarage* and other early Miss Marple

ABOVE LEFT: The Crime Club Choice title for November 1962 was printed in bright green from side to side. **ABOVE RIGHT:** The US first edition from Dodd Mead with its truncated title wore a more sober black jacket (1963).

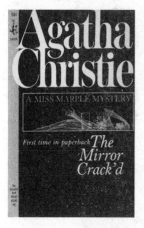

Pocket Books'
paperback (1964).

mysteries have now moved or died; both Colonel Bantry and Miss Wetherby have now 'passed on', although Miss Hartnell is still around, 'fighting progress to the last gasp'.

At this point in her career Christie was regularly dictating her work rather than typing it up, and this probably explains why this scene-setting is so lengthy. What might have been a few typed lines becomes something more personal, which seems to have really resonated with the author now that she was in her seventies, including such diversions as the naming of new roads ('why everything had to be called a Close she couldn't imagine').[50] Such nostalgia was less specific and more limited in earlier Miss Marple adventures, but the passage of time meant that Christie was now much closer in age to her creation than she had been when writing 'The Tuesday Night Club' in her mid-30s. But although Christie and Miss Marple are both nostalgic, they are not conservative about the future. Nevertheless, Christie was a little pessimistic, particularly about crime in the real world. 'I wouldn't like to live alone in the country,' she said. 'You get a great deal deafer and blinder as you get older and you have less warning, you're more startled than you used to be.'[51] As the presence of a 'glittering' new supermarket demonstrates, St Mary Mead is no longer the quiet country idyll that it once was. Fittingly, the most significant development in the village is known as 'the Development'. This new housing estate 'had an entity of its own, and a capital letter', and allows village life to somewhat catch up with the modern day, as she found it in 1962. 'And why not?' Miss Marple asks herself. 'The houses were necessary, and they were very well built.'

For Miss Marple, one advantage of the Development is that it is a potential source of new domestic staff, and she employs

Cherry Baker from the new estate to assist her around the house, which in turn helps Cherry to pay for her hire-purchase agreements, to her employer's quiet horror. This arrangement is more casual than the parlourmaids of the past, and Christie confessed that 'you rather miss servants. They always had an interesting part to play in books and could be really important characters: you just can't get the effect with daily helpers.'[52] Nevertheless, this more modern arrangement works well, and certainly Miss Marple prefers the company of Cherry to that of the dreaded Miss Knight, who has been sent by Raymond to aid his aunt in her recovery from bronchitis. When Miss Knight causes Miss Marple to drop a stitch in the middle of a patronising conversation, she is sent out to buy an unnecessary item from the farthest shop possible.

Unfortunately for Miss Marple, her foray into the Development results in misfortune. While she wanders through the new housing estate observing 'terribly depraved' young people, with 'sinister' looking boys and trousered girls, she stumbles and hurts herself, so is forced to rest at home while she recovers. The ramifications of this are twofold: firstly, she is forced to endure the company of Miss Knight for even longer, although Miss Marple takes enough of a shine to Cherry that both she and her husband are invited to move in with her by the end of the book. Secondly, her lack of mobility means that she misses out on an exciting new social event, which is a fête at Gossington Hall. However, this is not to be hosted by Dolly Bantry, who now resides in the lodge on the grounds, having sold the grand house some years earlier following the death of her husband at some point since *The Body in the Library* two decades earlier. Although local rumours had suggested

Tom Adams' 1965 cover, one of his own favourites, featured a figure based on a painting of the Lady of Shalott by the Victorian painter John William Waterhouse.

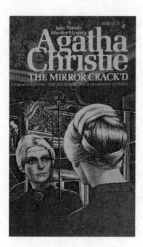

Tom Adams' cover for Pocket Books' American paperback range (1972).

that Charlie Chaplin would be the Hall's newest owner, it is film star Marina Gregg who buys it, and moves in with her fifth husband, movie producer Jason Rudd, following extensive renovations. The fête is being held to raise funds for St John Ambulance (and satisfy nosy locals), but disaster strikes when Development resident Heather Badcock is poisoned, having drunk a cocktail intended for Marina. Luckily for justice, Miss Marple has been prescribed 'a nice juicy murder' by her doctor, and so she sets out to catch a killer, even while she's forced to stay at home.

Inspector Craddock is soon assigned to the case, having earlier investigated the murder at Little Paddocks. He willingly works with Miss Marple (who he initially fears may have died since the events of *A Murder is Announced*), whom he now calls 'Aunty' in a sign of affection. There are plenty of strong characters for the reader to meet, although few are particularly likable, and the mystery itself will not confound any seasoned reader of detective fiction. The title draws on the Tennyson poem 'The Lady of Shalott' ('Out flew the web and floated wide / The mirror crack'd from side to side / "The curse is come upon me," cried / The Lady of Shalott'), and it ties in with a 'frozen' look of 'doom' seen on the face of Marina Gregg before Heather Badcock's murder, which may be significant to solving the case. Before the end of the novel there will be two more murders, while a final twist concerning a past relationship between two characters is both poorly signposted and unnecessary.

In general, the book has an unfortunate lack of precision, even while being a highly readable mystery. This is notable in the pharmacological description of the poison that kills the first victim, which a younger Christie would have been keen to be specific about, but here is described somewhat sloppily as 'hy-ethyl-dexyl-barbo-quinde-lorytate, or, let us be frank, some such name'. Despite the fictitious name of this poison (itself unusual for Christie), she still preferred the method to other murder weapons. 'What's difficult is having a very clear way of murdering people,' she said later. 'Going into the subject of firearms is very difficult for an unsophisticated woman: you can always rely on a dull blow on the head, no magic needed for that. Atomic scientists tell me they have very clever ways, but they're so difficult only an atomic scientist could do it.'[53] Poison enabled an array of characters to fall under suspicion, none of whom would require any specialist knowledge, creating the best array of suspects.

Christie first signalled that she would begin work on the novel in August 1961, when she informed Edmund Cork that she intended to write her new book over winter. By this stage of her career, Christie was given free rein when it came to deciding on the nature of her novels and any featured detectives, but Miss Marple seemed to be finding favour with the author around this time, as she would put her in three novels across the next four years. She later declared that, compared to Hercule Poirot, 'Miss Marple is really much more fun, a less artificial character and easier to introduce', something that is helped by her inherently anachronistic nature, as the elderly Miss Marple always exists a little outside of modern society, whether it is the 1920s or the 1970s.[54]

Christie completed her draft of the novel in March 1962, but unusually there were problems almost immediately. She was tired after the exertion of writing and retreated to Greenway to recuperate, even though she was mindful that the text needed more changes; this delay meant that there was no guarantee that the book could be a Christie for Christmas for 1962.[55] A decade later, she explained that 'I think that concentration makes you tired,':

You may have got your plot ready and your characters – you can't do anything until you have thought of the characters and you can feel they are real to you. Not necessarily to anyone else but real to you, and you can go walking about the garden with them or down the street and you are talking to Mabel so and so, or Miss Marple is having some sort of trouble with her garden and perhaps her broad beans haven't come up properly this year, and you can feel it all happening … When you write a book you get very tired. I should say about a little after three-quarters of the way through. You begin to feel that this book is no good, I am sure. You will have to read it again to see if it has gone wrong anywhere. You know perfectly well where your stories are going, but when you feel it has nearly got there, it is as though you were running into Paddington Station and you think, very soon I am going to finish.[56]

However, *The Mirror Crack'd from Side to Side* had a significant issue, which was first raised by Dorothy Olding in

America, who revealed that she immediately worked out the nature of the entire story (including its solution) after the first murder, and was concerned that she would not be alone.[57] Olding sent the story to the *Ladies' Home Journal* in the hope that they might pick it up for serialisation, but her fears were well founded. The magazine responded that they were 'desperately sorry' not to be able to buy the story, but confessed that all six editors who had read it immediately worked out the murderer's identity and motive.[58] Although changes could be made to fix the issue, the characters were not engaging enough for them to pursue any serialisation, although Miss Marple was described as 'purely wonderful'.

A licence to Penguin resulted in this 1975 photo cover.

At Collins, a similar tale was unfolding. For the first time in her career, her publisher had serious concerns that the mystery elements of a Christie novel might be unsatisfying for readers. George Hardinge (who had for many years prepared the initial Collins reader reports on Christie's works and became Lord Hardinge in May 1960) felt compelled to write to Billy Collins himself after reading it, raising his concerns about:

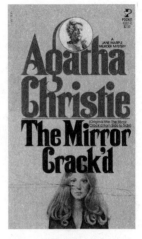

Pocket Books 1981, incorporating a Miss Marple portrait in the series design.

> a serious flaw in this book. For this reason, I think it very important that you or Mr Smith should read it personally to see whether I have made a mistake or am exaggerating ... The fact is that I saw through the trick as a very early stage in the book and even worked out before the murder who would be killed and by whom and why. To the end I hoped I had been taken in by a red herring, but this proved not to be the case. If this view is borne out, it will be a very difficult point to take up with Agatha Christie yet I think it would be very damaging to leave it and to hope that all will be well. I believe that with her ingenuity there might be no great difficulty in eliminating the flaw ... Apart from this awful snag, the book is of the usual shrewdness and high standard.[59]

Christie was always concerned about clues in her books and wished to be scrupulously fair to her readers. She bemoaned 'false clues' set by other crime writers, proudly claiming that 'I never cheat'.[60] Her fairness was doing her work a disservice here, as Billy Collins agreed with Hardinge that the book needed remedial work before it could be published, not just because of the solvability of the case, but also a perception that some readers may be sensitive to its details.[61] Cork wrote

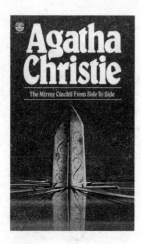

1980s artwork on Fontana's paperback (1984).

to Christie, asking that many of the early clues be removed. The result was that a precise but important detail was deleted throughout the bulk of the book, and now made a very late first appearance, at the beginning of Chapter Twenty-Two.[62] Harding praised Christie's 'extremely skilful' editing, while acknowledging that it 'does come very close to cheating', but 'it is still going to make the book more enjoyable to read for most people.'[63] Christie was less sure: 'I can't help feeling it's cheating this time – and not quite fair.'[64]

It then took a while for a final title to be decided upon; Billy Collins preferred *The Mirror Crack'd from Side to Side*, while Lord Hardinge preferred a shortened *The Mirror Crack'd*; in the end, the former title would be used in Britain, with the latter in the United States.[65] There was by this point a general agreement that titles should remain the same for book publication internationally, although Christie approved of one (ultimately abandoned) suggestion for the American publication: *The Look of Doom*. American women's magazines still proved particularly anxious, however, about some aspects of the story that they felt may upset their readers, which ruled it out for them, and final proofs were received in August 1962, just in time for a Christmas publication.[66] By this point Christie's American agents had made Cork and Christie aware of a real-life link between Marina Gregg and the movie star Gene Tierney. Both actors shared a similarly sad circumstance, but Cork insisted that Tierney's story was little-known in Britain.[67] Some time after publication, however, one fan from Seattle wrote an indignant letter to Christie, accusing her of thoughtlessness, that she appeared to be using Tierney's tragedy as a plot device. Cork's office responded that Christie had not been aware of Tierney's story: 'This may sound incredible to you, but it is a fact, and it was not until after the book was published that she learned of this coincidence.'[68]

The book was published on 12 November 1962 in Britain, following a fair complaint from Christie about the draft blurb ('after having published my books for about thirty odd years my publishers ought to know how to spell Miss Marple's village – St Mary Mead, not Meade'), and a suggestion from the author that the title be arranged diagonally.[69] Cork was starting to feel positive now that the corrections had been made, although there were still some queries to resolve, as Dolly Bantry's misquoting of Tennyson caused confusion. In America, the book didn't arrive on bookshelves until September 1963, and the *Chicago Tribune* and the *Daily Express* both made offers to serialise the story.

THE MIRROR CRACK'D FROM SIDE TO SIDE

The 2022 UK cover by Bill Bragg.

Commercially, *The Mirror Crack'd from Side to Side* did very well, topping the bestseller lists in Britain for several weeks. The critical reception was a little more mixed than usual, mostly because some reviewers spotted the solution quite quickly, even after the revisions. 'Ingenious but derivative,' stated the *Montreal Star*; 'I guessed in the second chapter'.[70] In Australia, Sydney's *The Age* pondered the question of Christie's enduring appeal in terms that were initially dismissive:

What is Agatha Christie's secret? She is a naïve crime writer, makes funny little mistakes, has none of the technical competence that comes of attending schools of creative writing. Yet who has been more popular over a generation? And who more deservedly? These questions are raised in the inquiring mind by reading her excellent latest novel *The Mirror Crack'd from Side to Side*. The answer to them might be that all her people are real. They are not great, subtle portraits, but they are pleasant little vignettes of flesh-and-blood men and women, drawn by a nice woman with a shrewd eye. She is much better when, as in this case, she is writing about her elderly spinster detective, Miss Marple, than when she is trying to make something human and interesting out of her grotesque cardboard creation, Hercule Poirot.[71]

The review also noted Christie's 'shrewd commentaries on modern life', an element that can be forgotten by more casual readers who do not see how Christie changed with the times. The *Times Literary Supplement* similarly commended Christie on her successful career upon the publication of this novel, albeit laced with criticism. 'Agatha Christie deserves her fame,' the review read. 'Her writing is abominably careless, her formula hopelessly out of date; but, forty-two years after her criminal debut, she still offers an incomparably readable, skilful and amusing detective story.'[72] More straightforwardly, for the *Daily News* the novel showed that 'Once again Agatha Christie demonstrates that in the field of the crime novel her achievement is unique and justifies her pre-eminence among the world's mystery writers.'[73]

For the book's dedication, Christie decided to pay tribute to the Miss Marple of the silver screen: 'To Margaret Rutherford, in admiration'. Rutherford was thrilled with the dedication and penned a lengthy letter to Christie as a result, written in green ink. The actor called the dedication an 'honour', and 'one of the proudest moments of my life ... I am glad you were really so pleased with my performance, as no one but yourself really knows what Miss Marple is like. I just put myself in her hands, with faith, and let her do the rest. And very happy she made me!'[74] Rutherford finished her letter by wondering if this new book would be MGM's next Miss Marple film, but, instead, Miss Marple was transported into a scenario that would exasperate her creator.

Murder at the Gallop
(Film, 1963)

In 1974 Agatha Christie gave her final interview, shortly in advance of the release of the star-studded film of *Murder on the Orient Express*, which starred Albert Finney as Poirot. The questions from her interviewer, Lord Snowdon, inevitably turned to adaptations of her work. Christie particularly recalled one Margaret Rutherford film from over a decade earlier. 'The second film they made at a livery stable,' Christie explained. 'Now [is there] anything more impossible than [Miss Marple] at a livery stable. I mean, *horses* – you feel it's impossible.'[75] Impossible or not, this is where Miss Marple's next cinematic adventure would take place, in an adaptation of *After the Funeral*, a novel that featured Hercule Poirot as the detective.

ABOVE: The principal poster accentuated the comedy element in the new film.

The choice of title for MGM's next adaptation had taken some time to decide upon. In August 1961, MGM offered $25,000 and half the profits in exchange for the rights to make a film of *Death on the Nile*, which was one of the 'reserved' titles not included in their umbrella deal. While this was considered 'pretty tempting', it came with its own complications due to taxation, which eventually ruled it out. It's not clear if the intention was for *Nile* to be transformed into a Miss Marple story, or if it would remain investigated by Poirot, or even Canon Pennefather from Christie's stage adaptation *Murder on the Nile*. Anthony Hicks suggested *Murder in Mesopotamia* as an alternative ('pretend the Nile is the Tigris!'), while Christie suggested *Death Comes as the End* (set in Ancient Egypt) or one of the 'Tuesday Night Club' Miss Marple stories.[76] In fact, Cork had already suggested *Death Comes as the End* to Lawrence P. Bachmann, but the producer remained wedded to *Death on the Nile*, at least until early the following year, when he wrote to Christie after a trip to Egypt. Bachmann had enjoyed reading the historical mystery on his travels, and complimented Christie on its 'splendid story, excellent characterisations and fascinating use of the historical background'.[77] Nevertheless, MGM did not make a film of the story, and as of 2024, *Death Comes at the End* remains one of the very few Christie novels never to have been adapted for the screen.

Flora Robson, Robert Morley and Margaret Rutherford star in
Murder at the Gallop
M.G.M.'s hilarious new thriller based on
AGATHA CHRISTIE'S
AFTER THE FUNERAL

fontana books   3'6

Fontana's 1963 book cover made no mention of Hercule Poirot.

Discussions with MGM were so slow that there was talk of terminating the deal, much to Bachmann's displeasure, but there was also a feeling that the success of *Murder She Said* on both sides of the Atlantic indicated that successful films could be made in Britain, rather than Hollywood. One issue was that the deal had originally been envisaged as one primarily for

A dramatic poster for the French release.

television, but the 'rather flat' Poirot pilot episode did not seem to please anyone, although Charles Boyer was now keen to play the fastidious Belgian in his next screen adventure.[78] Talk of a Miss Marple television series had dissipated, but a potential anthology programme fronted by a 'very famous' star remained a possibility.[79] Correspondence ambled along, until by the end of the year it was revealed that the contract would indeed be renewed, and the next project in front of the cameras would be *Murder at the Gallop*, with Margaret Rutherford returning as Miss Marple and production scheduled to begin on 31 December 1962.

Murder at the Gallop places Miss Marple into *After the Funeral* and runs at a briskly paced eighty minutes. It retains only some of the core elements of the original novel, and instead

A more comedic French poster.

uses its screen time to show off the talents of both Rutherford and Miss Marple. During her investigations we see her do everything from riding both a horse and a bicycle to snooping at windows (while balanced precariously), and appearing to nearly have a heart attack while dancing the Twist with Mr Stringer. Agatha Christie's Miss Marple may not have done these things, but they are still entertaining to see on screen. As with the previous film, Miss Marple is an active presence in the story, as she witnesses key moments following the death of the wealthy Mr Enderby Sr, and then that of the little-known Aunt Cora. Alongside Mr Stringer, she is again reunited with Inspector Craddock, played by Charles Tingwell, who should know better than to dismiss Miss Marple's concerns: 'you will hear from me again when my case is completed', she assures him. We also see Miss Marple take part in village life, which is picture-postcard appropriate for an American film studio;

unlike in Christie's most recent Miss Marple novel, there is no new housing estate here. New cast members include Flora Robson as Miss Gilchrist and Robert Morley as Hector Enderby, and Morley would soon take on the role of Captain Hastings too, in MGM's *The Alphabet Murders*, in 1965.

George Pollock returned to direct this second film outing for Miss Marple, with a script by James P. Kavanagh, who mostly wrote for American television. His reworking of the story shows Miss Marple moving from location to location as she finds clues, the first of which is a piece of mud that must match a riding boot of one of the suspects. It is revealed that Mr Enderby died from fright, perhaps due to a fear of cats.[80] Even Agatha Christie herself has a role to play, with another acknowledgement of her as a real writer in this fictional world. 'Surely inspector, you have read Agatha Christie's remarkable novel *The Ninth Life*?' asks Miss Marple of Craddock. Of course, there is no such Christie novel by that name in the real world. 'Agatha Christie should be compulsory reading for the police force,' she argues. Craddock is played as a lighter character here than in the earlier film, at ease with Miss Marple's own detecting, which includes the infamous infiltration of the local riding school. The sight of Rutherford in the saddle remains an incongruous one, which was exploited mercilessly for the advertising material, even though most of the shots in the film use a double rather than the actor herself. Miss Marple also finds herself on the receiving end of a proposal from a leading man at the end of the film again, although this time the suggestion is more of a working arrangement.

In London, *Murder at the Gallop* was released in May 1963, with the *Daily Mail* calling it 'Unbelievably enjoyable', as it joined another

'The funniest woman alive' screamed the advertising.

The German film kept *After the Funeral*'s German book title, literally 'Bouquet of Fake Flowers'

chorus that declared Rutherford not only delightful in her own right but, for many, perfectly cast in the role of Miss Marple.[81] As with earlier reviews, her physicality was repeatedly referred to, with the *Daily Express* claiming that 'While she is around, the film doesn't need any sets. Close-ups of her fantastic face are all that is necessary.'[82] Rutherford was also complimented when the film was released in the United States at various points across the year, first in New York in June, where the *New York Times* felt that the picture 'moves slowly and without much fuss or feathers, but it holds the pace of one of those nice mystery fictions that are good for reading yourself to sleep.'[83] Other critics were also less keen on the film than its star: 'The film is all Maggie's,' said one. 'The tone is one of such understatement and low-key humour that *Murder at the Gallop* often bogs down. It suffers most, however, whenever Maggie is off camera, which, fortunately, is seldom.'[84] One reviewer called Rutherford's performance 'sheer genius', while another was clear about where the attraction for the film lay: 'It's a Rutherford show, for Rutherford fans.'[85]

Christie did not rush to see the film for herself, and initially relied upon the opinions of friends who saw it before her. They told her that 'Margaret R gave a splendid performance – but [the] story had become incredibly silly – nothing like the book – and why Miss Marple in a Poirot book anyway?'[86] This repurposing of a Poirot story for Miss Marple would rankle with Christie for some time, but the truth of the matter was that there was only one other Miss Marple novel available to MGM: *The Body in the Library*. The others were either not owned by Agatha Christie Ltd or were in the list of 'reserved' titles.[87] Nevertheless, this contributed to the breaking down of her working relationship with Bachmann. There were further

An alternative poster for cinema's latest 'Mustseeit' movie.

signs that MGM were pushing their luck when it came to their use of Christie's properties when they asked for permission to move *Murder on the Orient Express* from the list of 'reserved' titles, so that they could adapt the story for the screen. Cork believed that this would be 'disastrous' and Christie agreed.[88] 'No,' she wrote, 'MGM must do without it – they have plenty of other material. *Orient Express* took a lot of careful planning and technique – and to have possibly transferred to a rollicking farce with Miss Marple projected into it and possibly acting as the engine driver – though great fun, no doubt, would be somewhat harmful to my reputation!'[89]

Oblivious to the author's increasing disquiet towards MGM, Bachmann wrote to Christie with the good news that *Murder at the Gallop* had broken records at a New York cinema, while he planned to start on an adaptation of *Mrs McGinty's Dead* shortly (another Poirot novel that would be repurposed for Miss Marple).[90] Christie responded that 'I am glad to hear it is doing well', before factually stating without opinion that 'I did go to see it in London.' The author then sounded one note of caution: 'Don't kill Margaret Rutherford by making her embrace too many outdoor sports.'[91] Christie and her daughter Rosalind were dismayed by the knock-on effects of Miss Marple's appearance in a Poirot story, as publicity stills of Rutherford were used on the cover of a new British paperback edition of *After the Funeral*. Rosalind considered this to be 'most misleading and unfair' and sought an assurance from Billy Collins that it would not happen again.[92]

Over the course of the next year, Christie would become increasingly distressed about MGM's treatment of her works and characters, and in 1964 she wrote a letter to Bachmann in which (amongst other things) she outlined her issues with this film. 'In *Murder at the Gallop*, I consider you went too far', she wrote:

> The basic plot, though labelled as adapted from it, was not the least like *After the Funeral*. Miss Marple galloping about on horses was ludicrously unlike the original Miss Marple. But worst of all, she was never in that book at all – it was a Poirot one. This led to a very awkward result for me, since my publishers put on the market *After the Funeral* in a cheap edition with a notice outside advertising it, not as a Poirot book, but conveying that it was a Miss Marple one, and suggesting that a purchaser would find the book to be the same story as the film.
>
> I do not think that you should allow yourself to distort a book you adapt to that extent.[93]

Nevertheless, Rutherford's Miss Marple remained popular with audiences, and would find herself in increasingly far-fetched scenarios before the relationship between Christie and MGM disintegrated only a short time later. Christie had discovered that Miss Marple was now an entity over which she no longer had exclusive control.

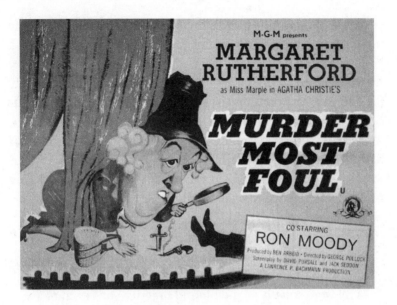

Murder Most Foul
(Film, 1964)

In April 1963, Agatha Christie responded to a journalist who had recently interviewed Margaret Rutherford about Miss Marple, and wanted to hear a few words from the character's creator. A few words were all he received, as Christie gave the briefest of responses to his questions. Why have an old lady as a detective, he wondered: 'No particular reason', was Christie's reply. Was Miss Marple based on a particular person? No, Christie claimed, she was 'A fairly typical old lady of an old fashioned type.' Margaret Rutherford was 'Suggested by MGM', and the advice Christie gave to her was simply 'None'. As for any future Miss Marple plans: 'Indefinitely,

ABOVE: *Murder Most Foul* adopted a quotation from Shakespeare for its title that distributors in other countries would find it hard to translate...

yes.'[94] Christie would soon work on back-to-back Miss Marple novels, and in part this seems to have been borne out of a keenness to wrestle back the public image of the character from the films that had become so popular. Unfortunately for Christie, the complaints that she had about *Murder at the Gallop* would only be magnified by the next two pictures.

Despite Margaret Rutherford's initial misgivings, the actor had, by this time, started to embrace the part of Miss Marple. Speaking to Elspeth Grant in an interview the following month, Rutherford revealed that:

> I regard Miss Marple as an extremely capable woman, able to turn her hand to anything – so naturally in playing her I wanted to do the chores, the washing up, cooking and so on as if I were equally adaptable and practical, or I would have been letting her down. I think Jane Marple is one of the most striking characters Agatha Christie has ever created. I very much admire her and I am honoured to play her. She is not interested in crime for its own sake and she is not an avenger: she believes in the sanctity of human life. She is with the forces of Light against the forces of Darkness – and it is in this spirit that she seeks to illuminate the sombre mysteries upon which she stumbles. She is for Truth – that is why she is so important.

'*Murder on Stage*' in Italy.

Rutherford hadn't entirely lost sight of her initial issues with the murder mystery genre, however, as the actor revealed that she had been asked to perform in an Agatha Christie play, 'but they all have such tremendously long runs and I couldn't bear to be associated with crime for any length of time – it is so very, very depressing.'[95]

Nevertheless, by 1963 it seemed likely that there would be a long run of Miss Marple pictures, with the next, *Murder Most Foul*, budgeted at £148,000. The film saw the return of screenwriters David Pursall and Jack Seddon and director George Pollock, and was this time based on yet another Poirot novel, *Mrs McGinty's Dead*. Christie was unimpressed that Miss Marple would be solving a Poirot mystery again. 'Have you got to use all the Poirot books for featuring [sic] Miss Marple?' she asked Bachmann. Seemingly unaware that *The Body in the Library* was the only Miss Marple novel available to MGM, Christie continued: 'It seems odd when you have so many Marple books! It involves me

'The Lady Detective Takes to the Stage' in French.

in a lot of correspondents who write to me pointing out that Miss Marple was never in that book. As the story is not going to be anything like the book anyway it seems unnecessary.'[96] The producer was sympathetic, and promised Christie that this would be avoided in future. Unfortunately, neither the author nor her agent understood the ramifications of this, as Bachmann was signalling his intent to create entirely new mysteries for Miss Marple, if he couldn't repurpose other Christie novels that he felt were suitable for MGM's preferred mixture of action, comedy and mystery.[97] Christie was also unhappy with the change of title, which she had ridiculed almost forty years earlier in her short story 'Mr Eastwood's Adventure', in which an aspiring writer despairs that his editor may 'alter the title and call it something rotten, like *Murder Most Foul*'. The title comes from *Hamlet*, but even Shakespeare-loving Christie felt that it was a cliché too far: she asked her agent if he could 'imagine a triter title'. The film's name was the least of her concerns anyway, such was her lack of confidence in the quality of MGM's productions: 'I wish they weren't doing *Mrs McGinty*. It's one of my best books.'[98]

Murder Most Foul retains some of the key aspects of *Mrs*

Miss Marple *'in the Spotlight'* in this dual-language poster from Belgium.

McGinty's Dead (including a crucial language clue that leads to the murderer) while extensively reworking the surrounding story to make it more suitable for Rutherford's boisterous Miss Marple. The film opens with a surprisingly gruesome silhouette of the hanging body of Mrs McGinty, and the police's discovery of a man apparently responsible – her lodger, Harold Taylor. In the original novel, Poirot sets out to prove the innocence of Mrs McGinty's lodger, and Miss Marple does the same here, albeit in a more direct way. Placed on the jury of Taylor's trial, Miss Marple annoys the judge first with her loud knitting, and then her refusal to find the man guilty. She then sets out to locate the real killer, and in the meantime finds that Mrs McGinty had a theatrical background, where the motive for her murder may be found, and so Miss Marple signs up to be a part of the theatrical company.[99]

Inspector Craddock and Mr Stringer appear again, and Stringer Davis later explained what he felt was his function in the film. 'In the books Agatha Christie could just write down what Miss Marple was thinking,' he said. 'But in the films she has to explain it to the audience, and the only way to do that was to have someone thoroughly dense for her to talk to in front of the camera. That's how Mr Stringer was born.'[100] Rutherford is also joined by the likes of Ron Moody, whose character, H. Driffold Cosgood, leads the theatre company (and is hopeful that Miss Marple may bankroll their next production), and a pair of young faces who would soon become more familiar to television viewers: James Bolam (later to become one of *The Likely Lads*) as actor Bill Hanson, and Francesca Annis (Tuppence in ITV's *Partners in Crime*) as his fiancée, Sheila Upward. Other characters include Eva McGonigall, played by Alison Seebohm, who appears to be in possession of the powers of premonition. No doubt included in order to add some atmosphere to what is otherwise a rather talky production, Eva nevertheless seems to have wandered in from a different picture.

Miss Marple continues to take centre stage, this time both figuratively and literally as Rutherford takes every opportunity to steal a scene, as befits the main attraction for much of the audience. She still gets her comedy moments, and there are even hints of the theme tune of sitcom *Steptoe and Son* when she accompanies a horse and cart in one scene. Miss Marple works everything out by the final reel, and there is no hiding her ostentatiousness during her investigations as she dons a sparkly cape just as proceedings are moving to a head. Despite her theatrics and varied background, it still comes as a bit of a surprise when Miss Marple wields a gun during her final face-off with the murderer, as we learn that she is a shooting champion (of course). Inspector Craddock fares less well, as he ends up in hospital, but he will be cheered by news of his promotion to Chief Inspector.

While production was underway, Christie and Cork were concerned more with the wider ramifications of the Miss Marple films than the content of the productions themselves. Most particularly, Christie wanted an assurance that Rutherford would not be featured on any tie-in paperback of *Mrs McGinty's Dead*. 'She feels strongly about this and we must show her the suggested wrapper for *Mrs McGinty's Dead* before going ahead. This is vital', read the notes of one meeting with Billy Collins.[101] In January 1964, Cork wrote to Rosalind to say that he had requested that any paperback should only have a 'dignified notice' about the film to

Margaret and Oscar!

'Four Women and a Murder': the original 1963 German release poster.

satisfy the book trade.[102] Rosalind was pleased with the news, and emphasised that pictures of Rutherford should not be used: 'Everyone I know has complained about the *Murder at the Gallop* edition – even our local manager at Smiths said it was most misleading.'[103] Collins agreed, and the Fontana paperback restricted mention of the film to its back cover, although some early editions of the paperback also mentioned it on a red sticker placed on the front cover.

Christie was not excited by the prospect of the film and outlined her annoyance in a letter to Bachmann in April 1964. 'Your practice seems to be to invite me to see a film after it is made. And what, I may ask, would be the point of protesting then?' she asked. 'However, you did know what I felt about the *Gallop* one! I've been dreading having to see *Murder Most Foul* … My general attitude is that I am prepared to suffer in silence up to a reasonable point.'[104] For Christie, MGM's approach had gone beyond 'reasonable' expectations; she always knew that her stories would need to be reworked for the cinema, but felt that they were now making changes that were excessive. Mindful of the importance of the author, Bachmann always responded courteously to Christie's letters, but he rarely agreed with them. A few years later he told an interviewer that 'I am not sure Miss Christie was right to complain, because she always said her stories were too slow and old-fashioned to film unless they were chopped and changed. I mean, you can't have the great detective holding up the action for three chapters while he lectures on crime.'[105]

In Britain, *Murder Most Foul* was released in different regions at different times, with the earliest reviews appearing in October 1964, while cinemas were encouraged to run a 'Spot the Murderer' contest, as well as a suggested painting competition, with a line drawing of Margaret Rutherford as Lady Justice providing the basis of any artistic endeavours. 'The genre is out of tune with the times of course, which could go a long way toward explaining its popularity,' argued *Films and Filming*. 'Part of the conceit is to pretend that the adventures of Miss Marple are happening now, while the pleasure is rooted in that aura of the middle distance ... It is all very neat and soothing; and so long as they keep it like this, Miss Marple must stay.'[106] On the whole Rutherford's performance was seen as a highlight in an otherwise quite flat production, with the *Daily Mail* bemoaning that 'This comedy-thriller is neither side-splittingly funny nor breathtakingly thrilling.'[107] In the United States, the film was released after *Murder Ahoy*, making this their fourth Miss Marple movie, and for some reviewers fatigue was starting to set in. The *Boston Globe* felt that 'invention is occasionally thin; a logical progression of clues turns into intricate confusion by the time half the story

'*Three Crimes – One Killer*': a Spanish lobby card.

'*That's What She Said*' from the Czech Republic, designed by Milos Reindl (1966).

is told', while for the *New York Times* 'familiarity breeds ennui'.[108] The *Montreal Star* did at least acknowledge the fans of Christie who were disappointed by the screen treatment of one of her most famous characters: 'The only moviegoers who might not enjoy *Murder Most Foul* are Agatha Christie devotees who simply cannot stomach Margaret Rutherford's delicious misrepresentation of dear, sweet little Miss Marple.'[109]

For Agatha Christie, the films of MGM were starting to become an annoyance, largely because audiences were understandably muddling up what was the work of Agatha Christie and the filmic inventions. 'None of the people are as I have described them,' she said in a later interview. 'She is not a gossiping spinster, elderly, in a village, at all. When I saw it done, the characters were not like the persons I thought of. It spoils it for me going to see it. Quite a lot of people like them, I mean, they really don't care ...'[110] Rutherford later recalled that 'It was not until sometime later that I heard in fact that Miss Christie was not terribly keen on me for the part. She had nothing against me as an actress, but she had based the character to some extent on a little aunt of hers who in no way resembled me physically. She pictured [Miss Marple] as a fragile, pink-and-white lady.'[111]

Unfortunately for Christie, more significant deviations from her work were on the horizon.

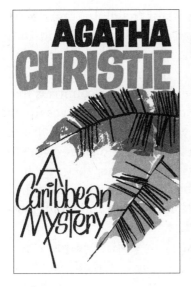

A Caribbean Mystery
(Novel, 1964)

Towards the end of *A Caribbean Mystery*, the wealthy and elderly Jason Rafiel asks a question of his accomplice in crime-solving, Miss Marple: 'How can you and I set about preventing a murder? You're about a hundred and I'm a broken-up old crock.' However, Miss Marple seems to have had a new lease of life thanks to the warmer climes. As the title indicates, the mystery novel takes place on the fictional Caribbean island of St Honoré, and is clearly inspired by the author's own travels. The book is dedicated to the architect John Cruikshank Rose, 'with happy memories of my visit to the West Indies' – a reminder of how much Christie enjoyed

ABOVE LEFT: Collins' Crime Club's striking UK jacket for *A Caribbean Mystery* (1964). **ABOVE RIGHT:** The US first edition published by Dodd Mead, also in white with a palm tree motif (1964).

Another Book Club,
another body (1964).

travelling to all parts of the globe. Over forty years earlier she had set out on her Grand Tour of the world with her first husband, Archie, and while that itinerary hadn't included the West Indies, the couple did visit other countries that were at the time under British rule, just as much of the Caribbean was. 'I am not sure that the people in the Overseas Dominions are going to like me,' she confessed at the time; 'they may find my love of crime objectionable, for I believe they have less tolerance than London and Londoners. It cannot be helped!'[112]

A Caribbean Mystery sees Miss Marple play a prominent part in proceedings, as she is actively involved in the investigation from the very beginning. She is taking a holiday courtesy of Raymond West, with her house being looked after in her absence by a gay man who is writing a book: 'surely even dear old Aunt Jane has heard of queers,' ponders Raymond. At the book's opening Miss Marple is being regaled by the retired Major Palgrave, who is telling her another of his stories. Even the hint of a murder mystery doesn't seem to be enough to make this tale worth hearing, but the Major's claim to have a photograph of a murderer piques the interest of Miss Marple. When the Major is soon found dead, Miss Marple wonders if he knew too much, and before long it seems clear that an established murderer is up to their old tricks again. Miss Marple is determined to catch the killer, although she'll be too late for at least another two victims. To these ends she is prepared to mislead others if it means that her investigation can continue unimpeded. For example, she lies about her reasons for wanting to recover the alleged photograph of the murderer from Major Palgrave's belongings. Miss Marple is still an understated observer, but the uncertain nature of the first murder means that she must initially act alone when it comes to some of her detection, as she is without her 'usual allies'.

Joining Miss Marple on the island are a selection of vivid characters, including some who may have dark secrets to reveal by the end of the novel. We meet Greg and Lucky Dyson, a married couple whose relationship seems inscrutable, as is that of Edward and Evelyn Hillingdon, who do not seem to love each other. There is also the outlandishly ageist Señora de Caspearo from Venezuela, while the Golden Palm Hotel is run by the hardworking Tim and Molly Kendal, along with staff including the maid Victoria Johnson. This is a book concerned with more mature adult relationships than young love, and there is a strong sense that many characters are simply maintaining the status quo for appearances' sake. Sex is mentioned, but romance is rarer. Instead, uneasy and manipulative relationships abound, while Miss Marple is perhaps reminded of her younger self when observing Mr Rafiel's secretary, Esther Walters: 'Miss Marple sighed, a sigh that any woman will give however old at what might be considered wasted opportunities. What was lacking in Esther had been called by so many names during Miss Marple's span of existence. "Not really attractive to me." "No SA." "Lacks Come-hither in her eye." Fair hair, good complexion, hazel eyes, quite a good figure, pleasant smile, but lacking that something that makes a man's head turn when he passes a woman in the street.' Now in her dotage, Miss Marple cannot help but wonder what might have been.

Miss Marple is conscious of her age and resents 'this calm assumption that everyone of advanced years was liable to die at any minute' following Major Palgrave's death. She seems both comfortable in herself while also a little

The first paperback from Fontana (1966).

Eye's front – the first Tom Adams cover from 1968.

Eye in the sky – Tom Adams, 1978.

unsure about how to navigate the modern world, including clothes, and so she sticks to grey lace. Despite being in a hotel with so many older guests, she is dismissed by many. Even Mr Rafiel states matter-of-factly that there is a pecking order when it comes to murder: 'Deaths of millionaires are scrutinised rather carefully, aren't they, unlike mere wives?' Even more of this dismissiveness was present in Christie's original typescript. A deleted section had Miss Marple's mind wandering when mulling over a conversation, which results in patronising sympathy from hotel resident Joan Prescott: 'poor old dear,' she thinks, 'must be well on in her seventies or even possibly in her eighties. Really it was wonderful that her faculties were as good as they were.'[113] Miss Marple also struggles with some modern greetings, as Mr Rafiel has to call 'Hi!' several times before she realises that he is trying to catch her attention. We may also sense some of Christie's sarcasm when it comes to idioms when Señora de Caspearo says of her children that 'I have three angels', which makes Miss Marple 'rather uncertain as to whether this meant that Señora de Caspearo's offspring were in Heaven or whether it merely referred to their characters'.

We learn a little more about Miss Marple's earlier life through some brief reminiscences, although a detailed biography continues to elude us. She has worked for the Armenian relief, where she witnessed an elderly clergyman succumb to some form of breakdown: 'They telephoned his wife and she came along at once and took him home in a cab, wrapped in a blanket'. She also recalls 'A young man she had met at a croquet party. He had seemed so nice – rather gay, almost Bohemian in his views. And then he had been unexpectedly warmly welcomed by her father. He had been suitable, eligible; he had been asked freely to the house more than once, and Miss Marple had found that, after all, he was *dull*. Very dull.' This story has elements in common with observations made by Christie in her autobiography, which she was working on at the time, and a similar story is told in the next Miss Marple novel, *At Bertram's Hotel*.

A Caribbean Mystery

Caribbean nudity! Robert Schulz art for Pocket Books (1973).

Of course, Miss Marple does indeed solve the mystery, despite Mr Rafiel's dismissiveness. In doing so, she earns his respect: 'So you're Nemesis, are you?' he asks, setting up an idea that would be picked up on by Christie and Miss Marple early in the next decade. 'Nemesis' is precisely what she is, although 'standing there in the moonlight, her head encased in a fluffy scarf of pale pink wool, [Miss Marple] looked as unlike a figure of Nemesis as it was possible to imagine.' Before Miss Marple can solve the mystery there will be more criminal activity on the island, including the death of a maid. In her later years Christie still liked many younger people when she met them, even if she disapproved of fashions and what she perceived to be violent trends. 'I have always found young people terribly nice to me,' she said, 'but there are some shockers about, of course'.[114] According to Christie, Miss Marple was also less sure about the cultural changes of the 1960s, including the Beatles. 'Miss Marple, I remember, never really liked the steel bands in the West Indies,' the author later recalled when asked what Miss Marple would think of the popular beat combo. 'She would, I feel, be upset and would deplore the wrecking of their vocal chords by over-production and would probably beg them to study voice production before it was too late.'[115]

The original notes for *A Caribbean Mystery* mention Hercule Poirot as a possible investigator, which perhaps makes more sense in some ways, as Poirot was known for his international travels, while this is the only time that Christie took Miss Marple out of her home country. These thoughts don't seem to have got very far, and Christie had no plans to include both detectives in the same mystery.[116] 'People never stop writing to me nowadays to suggest that Miss Marple and Hercule Poirot should meet – but *why* should they?' she argued. 'I am sure they would not enjoy it at all. Hercule Poirot, the complete egoist, would not like being taught his business by an elderly spinster lady. He was a professional sleuth, he would not be at home at all in Miss Marple's world. No, they are both *stars*, and they are stars in their own right. I shall not let them meet unless I feel a sudden and unexpected urge to do so.'[117] Christie had penned a Poirot novel the previous year, *The Clocks*, and had been unhappy that she hadn't had time to improve the story before publication. As a result, she gave herself plenty of time to work on *A Caribbean Mystery*, which was in a fairly advanced stage by November 1963.[118]

A red Cardinal was the basis for Fontana's 1985 cover.

Christie's original typescript survives, but the changes before publication were not extensive. Most notably, the cover calls the novel *Shadows in Sunlight*, with *A Caribbean Mystery* as a subtitle on the title page. The original title is evocative, but perhaps less direct than her publishers would like. There are also some minor changes to chapter titles, which are factual and short in any case ('Exit Victoria Johnson' is particularly perfunctory). New additions include some details of who may have been in Major Palgrave's line of sight when he was showing the photograph of an alleged murderer, while some repetition reinforcing its importance is removed. This includes a brief reconstruction of the scene by Miss Marple herself, while Tim Kendal is referred to as Tim Kelly. New material also includes the mention of the 'brides in the bath case' and some more explicit discussion of who Miss Marple suspects to be the murderer before she comes to the correct conclusion. One regrettable deletion is a perfect description of Miss Marple as she sets out to solve a murder: 'Armed with her knitting, and full of determination'.[119]

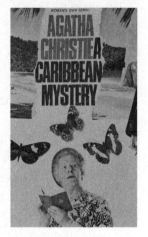

One of many pages in *Woman's Own* for its five-part serial in 1964.

Early 1964 was a busy time for the author, as her publishers had plans for an 'Agatha Christie Fortnight' in May, which would see displays of her books in shops all over the country and two million paperbacks sent to retailers. Collins were keen for Christie to help to publicise the event by going on television, but knew that the chances of her agreeing were slim; indeed, she declined.[120] Christie took her time with *A Caribbean Mystery*, and a typescript and corrections were received in May 1964. Dorothy Olding was positive about the 'very pleasant' novel and felt it had a good chance with magazines for serialisation, and asked Christie's British agents to pass on her best wishes and compliments for the novel, as well as those of one of Harold Ober & Associates' most famous clients. 'I'm sure I've told you that Jerry Salinger is a great fan of hers,' Olding wrote, 'and would love her to know this'.[121] 'Jerry' was better known as J. D. Salinger, the author of the seminal *The Catcher in the Rye*.

Unfortunately, Olding was wrong about the story's chances with magazines. It was declined by *Ladies Home Journal*,

Hilda Barry.

McCall's and *Good Housekeeping*, with the latter two both feeling that it was too 'straight' as a mystery, although one of the readers thought it was 'the best Miss Marple I've read in ages'.[122] Women's magazines tended to require a strong young female character, ideally featuring in a love story of some kind, and there was little of this in *A Caribbean Mystery*, which affected its chances. It was eventually picked up by the *Chicago Tribune* for $6,000, even though many newspapers generally did not take mystery serialisations any longer, while *Woman's Own* in Britain published the story for 4,000 guineas.[123] The magazine illustrated the story with specially-shot photographs, including the actor Hilda Barry as Miss Marple, and a general look that seemed to pay homage to the 1962 James Bond film debut, *Dr. No*.

At Collins, both Lord Hardinge and Billy Collins himself enjoyed the novel, with the former impressed by 'the way the pattern of murder is trailed in front of the reader, and yet even he is too dense to see the same pattern being repeated under his nose'.[124] The novel was published on 16 November 1964 in Britain, and September 1965 in the United States, where it was delayed while the still-important serialisation deal was worked out. The British cover was attractive and simple, with two colourful palm leaves framing the title, while inside there was an important disclaimer. Christie dictated a side-swipe at the MGM films on the title page of her original typescript:

Featuring MISS MARPLE
The Original Character as Created By Me

Christie then scrubbed out 'Me' (a quirk of the dictation process) replacing it with 'AGATHA CHRISTIE', and the book followed suit upon publication.

As was common with Christie, reviews of the book tended to take the opportunity to compare her latest efforts with earlier ones, as critics tried to detect signs of a weakening hold over the reading public. 'If the choice [of top crime fiction book] falls on Miss Agatha Christie it is because this serpent of old Nile shows almost her old deceiving skill in *A Caribbean Mystery*,' wrote Julian Symons in *The Sunday Times*:

An advert for the New York serialisation (1965).

> The marvel of Miss Christie is that, although her deceptions vary tremendously in form … her characters stay the same. An hour or two after reading we remember neither their names nor their nebulous occupations, and this is not surprising, since so many of them appear to have unlimited leisure. From one book to another their reality is purely that of suspects in a murder game, and it remains true today, as it was true thirty years ago, that there is no more cunning player of this game than Agatha Christie.[125]

Other critics found the clueing of the novel to be fair and even simplistic, but several confessed that they failed to solve the case anyway. 'Solution laughably simple, but will you guess it?' asked one, while another stated that 'The story is simply but fairly clued and the solution not too easily guessable.'[126] For long-term admirer Francis Iles in the *Guardian*, 'Mrs Agatha Christie has done it again. In *A Caribbean Mystery* she tells the reader explicitly what is going to happen; and yet when it does, nine out of ten will be taken completely by surprise – as I was. How *does* she do it?'[127] Maurice Richardson in *The Observer* complimented the book's characterisations, while others considered the book to be 'top drawer', with

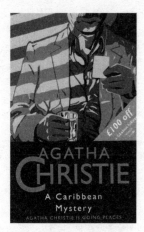

HarperCollins' cover, illustrated by Alun Edwards, here in a 1997 promotional edition with the travel agency Going Places.

some considering it to be more sophisticated than earlier efforts, and positive responses to the book's use of humour.[128] 'Agatha Christie writes with such disarming ease and simplicity that we sometimes fear unwary readers do not fully appreciate her narrative talents', argued one critic. 'But the truth is that she is one of our finest authors in any genre.'[129]

Following publication, Cork wrote to Christie to congratulate the author on her new book. 'Critics have got into the habit of taking your successes for granted, but even they have burst into song this time!' he wrote.[130] He also passed on good news about sales, with 46,000 copies already sold in Britain, only a week after publication. There was no sign of Agatha Christie's success flagging, and this meant that there would be more attempts to exploit her work in other commercial arenas. Most pressingly for Christie, Cork, and the Agatha Christie Ltd board, however, there would be one more Margaret Rutherford film for MGM, and once they saw the script they realised that they were going to have a battle on their hands.

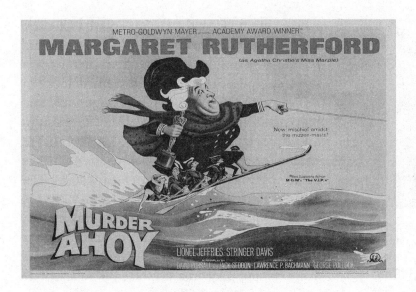

Murder Ahoy
(Film, 1964)

It is a curious fact that *Murder Ahoy*, a film that caused almost no ripples when first released in 1964, is in fact one of the most significant points of development when it comes to the world of Miss Marple, as it became the focus of wider questions about Christie's ownership of the character that she had created and nurtured.[131]

The MGM films were still making good money for Agatha Christie Ltd, guaranteeing an income of $75,000 per year, with an extra $25,000 for every production after the first two, and so further screen adventures were almost inevitable.[132] In March 1964, Patricia Cork (daughter of Edmund, with

ABOVE: The film poster depicted Margaret Rutherford clutching her Oscar, awarded earlier in the year of release for her role as the Duchess of Brighton in *The V.I.P.s* (1964).

A dramatic poster from Italy, where the campaign appears to have been less comedic.

whom she now worked) sent Agatha Christie the latest script, once more penned by the team of David Pursall and Jack Seddon. In her cover letter, she judged that the script seemed no better nor worse than the previous films, but noted that it was an original story.[133] This was the result of an ill-judged attempt by producer Lawrence P. Bachmann to avoid the complaints from Christie about putting Miss Marple in Poirot stories; he felt that an original screenplay would be the perfect solution. *Murder Ahoy* informs us that Miss Marple is descended from an important naval family, and she turns sleuth when she suspects foul play on a ship used to rehabilitate young criminals. Bachmann did not count on Christie's strength of opinion when it came to the use of her character. 'I return to you this farrago of nonsense!' wrote Christie to Patricia Cork by return of post.[134] 'Is it supposed to take place in the Navy with real Naval officers?!!' Christie was shocked not only by what she perceived to be the low quality of the script itself, but also the extent to which MGM were permitted to simply make use of Miss Marple as they saw fit, without Christie being given the power of veto. MGM were obliged to show her scripts and listen to feedback, but not to act on it. Christie underestimated her own star power when she then wondered:

> Why on earth can't MGM write their own scripts, engage Margaret Rutherford to play an old lady, 'Miss Sampson', have plenty of cheap fun and leave me and my creations out of it?
>
> The shock to me is to find that possibly MGM have the right to write these scripts of their own featuring my characters. That neither I or Rosalind seem to have known.

When Edmund talked to me a week or two ago, he mentioned this only as a suggestion on MGM's part, that we could refuse? Surely this must be so? Anthony seems to know nothing of it either.

Christie also drew comparisons with the popular television adventures of *Dr Finlay's Casebook*, based on the works of A. J. Cronin, in which she judged that the doctor was 'now entirely different' from the original books. 'I don't suppose there could be any greater misery for an author than to see their characters completely distorted,' she continued. 'After all, I have a reputation as an author. One isn't made an F.R.S.L [Fellow of the Royal Society of Literature], for nothing.' Christie found the (mis)use of her creation to be emotionally difficult. 'I really feel sick and ashamed of what I did when I joined up with MGM,' she wrote. 'It was my fault. One does things for money and one is wrong to do so – since one parts with one's literary integrity. Once one is in the trap one can't get out.' For the author, the script was confirmation of long-held fears about adaptations of her work. 'I held out until seventy but I fell in the end. IF they can write limitless scripts of their own, we've really had it. But I still hope that isn't true.'

un capolavoro di
AGATHA CHRISTIE

ASSASSINIO A BORDO

con MARGARET RUTHERFORD
LIONEL JEFFRIES · STRINGER DAVIS
regia di GEORGE POLLOCK
VIRACOLOR

Co-star Lionel Jeffries was painted into this poster.

The strength of Christie's reaction appears to have caught both MGM and her agent by surprise, which indicates that they hadn't really been paying attention to what she had been saying for many years. Nevertheless, Agatha Christie Ltd sprang into action in order to defend the author's interests. The company's solicitor argued that MGM had acted in bad faith, and felt that Christie had the right to withhold approval, but also pointed out to Patricia Cork that casting Rutherford as a similar character would simply mean that the company made no money from a film that was clearly based on Miss Marple.[135] One significant issue was that the script had been sent just weeks before production was due to start, and so there wasn't the time to rewrite it. Writing to Edmund Cork, Christie stated that 'I certainly cannot approve of this script since it entirely distorts the character of Miss Marple herself. In *Murder She Said* Miss Marple was still feasible, but in *Murder at the Gallop* besides introducing Miss Marple into what was a Poirot story and thereby distorting it completely, she was also utterly out of character and beginning to be quite unrecognisable.' This distortion of the character was an important point of principle for her creator, who was concerned about disappointed readers. Christie pointed out that Miss Marple 'has an established life, character, and personality. You cannot expect me to agree or to like the complete distortion of one of my favourite creations'. For Christie, the possibility of MGM writing their own scripts 'horrified and upset me more than I can say'.[136]

The pressures of the forthcoming production meant that an agreement needed to be made swiftly, and Rosalind wrote to Cork with details of one compromise: the addition of a caption at the beginning of the film, written in

consultation with Christie, which was placed below the screenplay writers' credit: 'Based on their interpretation of Agatha Christie's "Miss Marple"'. Rosalind acknowledged that 'I know my mother is upset but I doubt if I am any less so!', and felt that 'we have really let my mother down very badly over this whole deal'.[137] Anthony Hicks argued that both Christie herself and the company should have right of veto with MGM, a perspective that was argued for some time but dismissed as unworkable by MGM, at least in part because films were constantly rewritten and

The German poster.

re-edited up to the date of release, and so there could be no single 'authorised' version until it was too late to make any changes. Bachmann acknowledged the difficulties he caused, and wrote to Christie to apologise, calling the caption 'a most graceful and generous solution' along with a promise that nothing like this would happen again.[138]

Production was announced to the press at the end of March 1964, and two weeks later Christie responded to Bachmann with a letter that Cork described as 'devastating'.[139] It opened:

Dear Larry

Soft words butter no parsnips. (A saying of my nursery days!)

I deeply resent the way all this Murder Ahoy business was sprung upon me. The only prior knowledge I had was that you had advanced it as a suggestion of something you would like to do. The next thing I am informed is that you have actually made an original script and are going to begin shooting in a fortnight! Despite my personal protest, you have decided to go ahead albeit with a form of credit notice to which I have reluctantly agreed.

It is to me a matter of an author's integrity. To have one's characters incorporated in somebody else's film seems to me monstrous and highly unethical. I do not see how you can expect me to feel anything but deep resentment at your high handed action, or to pretend otherwise, and I still feel it questionable that you really have the right to act as you have done.

In this, you will understand, I am simply putting before you my own personal point of view.[140]

While *Murder Ahoy* was enduring the lion's share of negative attention, thoughts were also turning to a film adaptation of *The ABC Murders*, which the press claimed would feature

This was 'Sherlock Holmes in petticoats!' according to the French marketeers.

Zero Mostel as a shabby girl-chasing Poirot. By May 1964, Mostel was off the picture, which was then heavily reworked, as Bachmann tried to repair an impossibly strained relationship with Christie.[141] While the press reported on high-jinks during the filming of *Murder Ahoy*, including seventy-one-year-old Margaret Rutherford being coached by Olympic swordsman Rupert Evans for the climactic duel (her Miss Marple is a fencing champion, of course), the legal details of the MGM deal was being interrogated by Anthony Hicks.[142] By May, it was confirmed that Agatha Christie Ltd would waive its objections to *Murder Ahoy*, but insist on greater control over future films.[143] Anthony Hicks was not optimistic about their proposal, and he was right, as MGM's lawyers resisted any clause that handed substantial control back to the author and her company, although they agreed not to create original stories featuring Christie's characters. The question of original stories became an important point of principle for the author as well as her daughter and son-in-law, and *Murder Ahoy* instilled a sense of distrust concerning filmmakers that would never really go away.[144]

The behind-the-scenes arguments surrounding *Murder Ahoy* are certainly more interesting than the film itself. It presents Rutherford's Miss Marple in a similar fashion to both *Murder at the Gallop* and *Murder Most Foul*, as a comedic and adventurous go-getter, a veritable bloodhound who takes an active part in solving the crime. The tone of the film is firmly established by the opening credits, which feature Miss Marple changing into the naval uniform that so horrified Christie, but seems natural for this interpretation of the character. Comic moments are of a familiar type, including yet another unflattering angle of Miss Marple peering through a window, while blustering men struggle to cope with her confident persona. Meanwhile, Mr (Jim) Stringer has a closer relationship with Miss Marple than ever, as she consistently refers to him by his first name, and he also gets his own comedy subplot with a local tramp. Rutherford didn't want the film to ridicule patriotism, and so insisted that a performance of 'Rule Britannia' by the less-than-tuneful young cast was dubbed by a proper choir.[145]

There are also some familiar faces, including Lionel Jeffries as the exasperated captain of HMS Battledore, who can't wait to be rid of Miss Marple at the beginning ('Who does she think she is? Neptune's Mother?') but is grateful to her by the end. At the film's conclusion he even attempts a romantic proposal, although this time Miss Marple is not the object of the lead male character's affections. Jeffries plays the part almost entirely for laughs, and does his best to steal scenes from the rest of the cast, although he can't compete with Rutherford. This means that his Captain Rhumstone feels at odds with the rest of the (generally underplayed) supporting cast, and so the tone of the film is inconsistent, as it struggles to balance mystery and comedy, which are both at their weakest in this, the final chapter for Rutherford's Miss Marple.

Murder Ahoy was first released in the United States in September 1964, a year before it appeared in Britain, and the reviews were mixed. For some, it was 'one of the best Miss Marple movies, consistently amusing and with an intriguing murder puzzle that won't cause your mind to labor too much', while others argued that 'The humor in *Murder Ahoy* is strained, and the mystery only mildly baffling.'[146] The formulaic

A more traditionally cartoon-style advert from Spain.

nature of the series was either continuing to delight or start-ing to bore. The *Boston Globe* highlighted its local success, where apparently local women at matinee screenings burst into applause after seeing it: 'one of the best of the whole murder series', it argued. 'Just to hear her utter "Splice the main brace" when champagne is served is worth the price of admission.'[147] *Time* magazine felt that the plot was 'nonsensi-cal' and that Rutherford, who had recently won the Academy Award for Best Supporting Actress for *The V.I.P.s* (which she clutches in *Murder Ahoy*'s posters), was simply sent Miss Marple scripts whenever there was nothing better for her to do.[148] The *New York Times* knew not to put any blame in the direction of Miss Marple's creator, however. 'Since this is an original yarn, Miss Christie cannot be faulted, and neither can Miss Rutherford, in the efforts to make light of this somewhat heavy combination of homicide and hanky-panky,' read its

The classic yellow, black and red look for probably the most swashbuckling of all the Italian posters.

review. 'It is, in short, a simple matter of lots of dialogue, only a bit of which is truly funny, and a modicum of action, which is rarely exciting, intriguing, or comic.'[149]

The combination of diminishing critical and commercial returns alongside contract negotiations meant that this was the end of the line for Miss Marple films from MGM. Rutherford was keen to make more, as she told *Photoplay* magazine. 'I don't think I'll ever get tired of playing Miss Marples [sic]', she was quoted as saying, 'in Agatha Christie's stories there's never horror for horror's sake. It's more like a puzzle to be solved – and they're very exhilarating to work in.'[150] The character even made a cameo appearance in 1965's *The Alphabet Murders*, which starred Tony Randall as Poirot. 'I cannot see why they're having such difficulty,' wonders Miss Marple as she passes the Belgian detective, accompanied by the familiar Ron Goodwin musical theme from her films. 'The solution is ABC, to anyone who has half a brain cell.' This was Rutherford's final appearance in the role, although the possibility of a return was discussed for several months after *Murder Ahoy*.

In November 1964, Edmund Cork told Christie that MGM planned to make *The Body in the Library* in January the following year, using the original title and general story line.[151] This did not happen, and Christie's strength of feeling against MGM only grew. This included forwarding letters from fans to her agent, in which they complained about the distortion of the Miss Marple character in the films: 'she is a person to them. They know her.'[152] Cork sympathised but pointed out that Rutherford was too successful to be replaced, and further discussions stalled anyway due to the contractual wranglings.[153] By July 1965, Bachmann informed Cork that no further films were scheduled, although they were still looking into television, but this got no further before MGM's option expired at the end of August.[154]

While there was general unhappiness with MGM, both Christie and her daughter noted adaptations of other authors' work that they viewed with envious eyes. Rosalind felt that it was time for a 'really good series' for television, 'like *Maigret!*', referring to the BBC adaptations of Georges Simenon's books that had starred Rupert Davies from 1960 to 1963.[155] In 1971, Christie was so impressed by the film of *The Railway Children* that she was motivated to write to the author of its screenplay. In an ironic twist, this writer was *Murder Ahoy*'s Captain, Lionel Jeffries, who was a writer as well as an actor. Christie was likely unaware of this when she wrote Jeffries a letter praising his work. 'I have wanted to write to you for some time because of the enormous pleasure that the film of *The Railway Children* gave me,' she told him, 'it was my favourite book as a child and up to the age of 24 at least I still used occasionally to read it. I dreaded going to see the film because nearly always films of one's favourite books are a disastrous disappointed [sic] – but this was so perfectly produced and acted. I gather you are the person to thank for the great pleasure it gave me.' Hopefully Jeffries did not take Christie's final comments too personally, as she also wrote that 'Except for *The Witness for the Prosecution* which was good, all the films that have been made from my stories and books I have hated!'[156]

Christie was so hurt by the changes to her work by MGM that she often recounted her disappointment, even many years after the fact. In 1972 she enthusiastically wrote to a fan to agree with their criticisms. Christie agreed that the MGM films were 'a thoroughly bad bit of work ... Margaret Rutherford was a very fine actress, but she was never in the least like Miss Marple.'[157] When Christie again criticised the films in a 1974 interview, screenwriter Jack Seddon wrote to *The Sunday Times* to have his own say. 'Agatha Christie is of course entitled to her opinion,' he agreed, 'and as one of the two writers responsible for the screenplays so am I. It is

Margaret Rutherford and Agatha Christie in an awkward photo opportunity on the set of *Murder She Said* (1961).

quite true, as Miss Christie says, that the screen Miss Marple was nothing like her own creation,' Seddon conceded, before pointing out 'That Miss Christie "would never advise anyone to go and see them now" comes a little late, as millions already have, no doubt to the great financial benefit of the principal parties concerned – including, I should have thought, Miss Christie.'[158]

After filming *Murder Ahoy*, Rutherford recalled her first meeting with Christie, which illustrated something of the differences between the actor and the author, as well as their similarities. 'We were rather shy of each other,' she recalled, 'different worlds, you know. Hers is the world of observation, mine is the world of speech.'[159]

At Bertram's Hotel
(Novel, 1965)

At Bertram's Hotel is not a puzzle mystery, although the plot does concern the investigation of criminal activities. While eventually there will be a murder that has to be solved, vague discussions of gangs and train robberies are not a strength of the novel. Instead, *At Bertram's Hotel* relies on atmosphere and characterisation for effect, and in doing so it sets itself out as one of the most fascinating Miss Marple books.

The novel opens with some of Christie's most evocative writing, as she conjures up the image of a tiny pocket of London's lost past, at Bertram's Hotel:

ABOVE LEFT: Collins avoided all temptation to feature any hotel iconography on its 1965 jacket for *At Bertram's Hotel*, instead going for a contemporary Sixties feel. **ABOVE RIGHT:** A bloodied key fob on another primarily white dustjacket from Dodd Mead (1966).

If you turn off on an unpretentious street from the Park, and turn left and right once or twice, you will find yourself in a quiet street with Bertram's Hotel on the right-hand side. Bertram's Hotel has been there a long time. During the war, houses were demolished on the right of it, and a little farther down on the left of it, but Bertram's itself remained unscathed. Naturally it could not escape being, as house agents would say, scratched, bruised and marked, but by the expenditure of only a reasonable amount of money it was restored to its original condition. By 1955 it looked precisely as it had looked in 1939 — dignified, unostentatious, and quietly expensive.

Several commentators have pointed out that Miss Marple's past now seems to have become intertwined with Christie's. As biographer Laura Thompson notes, such memories as 'the drive to a matinée in a four-wheeler, the coffee creams at the theatre' are both Marple's *and* Christie's.[160] There is also the appearance of the Army and Navy stores, which Christie recalled in a 1969 interview:

I used to go there with my grandmother. She lived in Ealing and came in a four-wheeler because she didn't trust herself in a hansom. She would ensconce herself in the grocery department and listen to the assistant telling her all the medical details about his wife's goitre. Then we would go to the confectionary department, where we would buy a half-pound box of coffee creams. Upstairs we would have a splendid lunch, to my mind, then we'd get another four-wheeler and go to the theatre. That has always been one of my greatest pleasures, although I'm getting a little deaf for it now.[161]

Nephew Raymond has facilitated Miss Marple's latest trip away from St Mary Mead again, although even his

A familiar face on Biblioteca Ora's first Spanish edition (1966).

'modern' wife Joan is no longer considered to be modern, as so much time has passed since their first appearances. At the hotel, Miss Marple is sometimes annoyed to be treated like an old lady when she feels so much younger. She is particularly frustrated when a cab is arranged for her by doorman Micky Gorman, when she may prefer to walk or get the bus. But even though one guest assumed her to be dead, and asserts that she 'Looks a hundred', Miss Marple is grateful that she has 're-entered a vanished world. Time had gone back. You were in Edwardian England once more.' But youth is not everything, as Miss Marple concedes that she was 'a silly girl in many ways', a description that will also be true of another character by the end of the book. Christie was asked if Miss Marple would be shocked by the permissiveness of the 1960s. 'Not at all,' she insisted. 'The old have been through too much themselves to be shocked by anything. It is the in-between generation, who throw up their hands and go through the motions of being outraged.'[162]

Through the haze of atmosphere and descriptions of Bertram's, it slowly becomes clear that things aren't quite as they seem. The old-world illusion of the hotel starts to feel like just that: an *illusion*, and this is due to more than just the installation of a television lounge that is tucked away so as not to break the period atmosphere. There is confusion over faces that seem familiar and yet aren't quite right, while the arrival of the gung-ho Lady Bess Sedgwick certainly provokes a lot of attention, but she seems out of place in such old-fashioned and sedate surroundings. Bess is a famous face, known for her adventuring and glamorous lifestyle as well as her multiple marriages. Another visitor to the hotel is Bess's daughter, Elvira Blake, but the two are estranged. Elvira's interests are cared for by the trustees of her late father's estate, and as she approaches the age of twenty-one, the young woman is starting to wonder about the ramifications of coming into a very large sum of money.

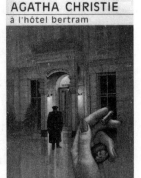

The book is full of intriguing and well-drawn characters, with dialogue and inner monologues making them memorable. Even the minor players in the story stand out as real people, from Mr Bollard the jeweller to Dr Stokes, who has actually been struck-off the medical register. Stokes is briefly involved in the story when one of the residents of the hotel, Canon Pennyfather, goes missing.[163] Pennyfather is a forgetful man who makes a mistake with the date of a conference he is due to attend, and consequently ends up caught up in the affairs of a criminal gang. For a moment, the clergyman seems to come face to face with himself, a confusing moment that neatly sums up the book, with its premise of uncertain appearances, as does the fact that even Miss Marple is revealed to have made a mistaken identification.

Tom Adams' 1968 cover, as used on Club des Masques' French edition.

The exact nature of the crime to be uncovered is not clear for most of the book, which mostly follows the adventures of Elvira and Bess, with their mutual attraction to racing driver Ladislaus Malinowski, who is later chief suspect in a murder that has a surprising motive. Elvira and Bess have a curious relationship, and the reader may expect there to be some revelation of mutual subterfuge; this would not be the first time that two characters who seemed to have an uneasy or hostile relationship were actually secretly working together. But this does not happen, and instead the complex nature of their relationship

Pocket Books' surreal lime green paperback from 1971.

remains open for interpretation, as Bess seems to have little interest in her daughter, which Elvira is resigned to. It is odd to have the characters interact so little when they are both visitors to Bertram's, but at the end of the story there is an indication that Bess cares more for her daughter than she was ever happy to admit.

The real star of the novel is Bertram's itself. It has often been argued that the hotel was based on Brown's Hotel in Mayfair, while Dorothy Olding thought it might have been the Connaught in the same area. The hotel is not a direct reproduction of any particular establishment, but Christie certainly based many details on Flemings Mayfair, to the extent that, when she sent the draft off to her agent, Cork ensured that changes were made so that the connection was not too obvious. Mindful that Flemings is in Half Moon Street, he changed Bertram's location from Crescent Street to Square Street, while suggesting that the name Capello was too close to the name of real-life Flemings proprietors Manetta (in the final book, the owners are the Swiss Hoffman brothers).

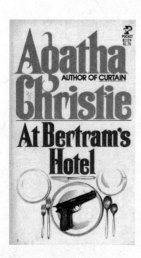

The 1977 Pocket Books paperback.

One person who believed the hotel to be Brown's was *Lord of the Rings* author J. R. R. Tolkien, who was inspired to stay in the hotel after reading the novel, where he encountered his own mystery: the sound of footsteps in the corridor. Deciding to investigate, he then found himself locked out of his room.[164]

Perhaps as befits a more modern novel, albeit one laced with heavy nostalgia, the ending is much more open than Christie would have allowed in an earlier decade. This is not a traditional closed-circle whodunnit and the novel ends with emotional revelations rather than proven facts that will close the case. In fact, evidence is so thin on the ground that it isn't clear how the guilty party will be caught. Although Miss Marple's instinct is certainly correct, the reader does not get to witness the criminal being brought to justice. This troubled *Good Housekeeping* in America, which bought the serialisation rights and felt that there needed to be more concrete evidence that the character would not escape scot-free, and that they would have psychiatric help and guidance, along with 'some hint' that they were 'salvageable', perhaps by indicating that the murder was an accident, and that they will remain under court supervision for quite some time.[165]

Room keys with a twist by Martin Baker (1985).

Christie made several notes relating to *At Bertram's Hotel* in the early stages of its development, although as John Curran has pointed out, they do not show much in the way of progression. This seems to have been quite a straightforward novel for Christie to write, and when the manuscript was received in February 1965, few changes were needed, although telephone numbers were amended to ones that the Post Office reserved for fictional use.[166] Olding requested clarification on how Miss Marple knew about the relationship between Bess and Elvira, but otherwise seemed happy, while Billy Collins phoned Christie personally to say how enthusiastic the publishers were about the new novel.[167]

Before the serialisation deal was made with *Good Housekeeping*, Christie's agents had secured an even more lucrative arrangement with *Reader's Digest*. However, they were unaware of the extent to which Christie opposed the publication of her novels in a single abridged volume. Edward H. Dodd Jr of Christie's American publisher Dodd Mead even made a transatlantic phone call to Cork to try to find a way to convince the author, but she would not be moved, despite Dodd writing her a pleading letter.[168] In Britain, the story

Woman's Own once again featured Hilda Barry as Miss Marple.

was published by *Woman's Own* in November and December 1965 and was accompanied by striking colours, particularly the fashionable orange and purple of the era. As with their serialisation of *A Caribbean Mystery*, the magazine featured a series of specially-taken photographs of key characters. This included a return for Hilda Barry as Miss Marple, which made her only the second actor to have appeared as Miss Marple in more than one story.

'Agatha Christie is really astonishing,' stated the *Times Literary Supplement* in its review, following the novel's publication on 15 November 1965. 'She is an old lady now, and her gentlewoman detective, Miss Marples [sic], an older one; but, unlike too many of her contemporaries she capitalizes instead of concealing the facts. So *At Bertram's Hotel* is an old-lady book, about old Miss Marples receiving the present of a holiday in an exquisitely old-fashioned London hotel and discovering (this is what one might call the Moral) that nostalgia is dangerous and to cash in on it a safe cover for depravity. Miss Christie has lost none of her toughness.'[169] The *Evening Standard* considered that Christie seemed 'ill-at-ease with her court of villains', although the review commended the hotel atmosphere, while Francis Iles of the *Guardian* thought that the book 'can hardly be called a major Agatha Christie, for in spite of the presence of Miss Marples [sic] the denouement really is too far-fetched. But does the plot matter so much with Mrs Christie? What does matter is that one just can't put any book of hers down.'[170] Maurice Richardson in *The Observer* felt that 'This one is a bit wild and far-fetched, but it's got plenty of the phenomenal zest and makes a seasonably snug read.'[171] Far-fetched or not, the book managed to sell an impressive 50,000 copies by Christmas.[172]

Although *At Bertram's Hotel* was the last new Miss Marple story of the 1960s, the character continued to make appearances elsewhere. In 1965 *The Mirror Crack'd from Side to Side* was read by Olive Gregg on BBC radio, with *Bertram's* following in 1966, read by Sheila Mitchell.[173] In the United States, there was demand for a new short story collection featuring Miss Marple, especially considering the success of the Margaret Rutherford films. Although Christie did not write the new introduction that Dodd Mead wanted (a letter from Miss Marple was suggested), *13 Clues for Miss Marple* was published in 1966. Perhaps a new introduction may have been a good idea, in order to remind readers that Christie was still active in the field, as a review of the book in the *Courier Post* referred to her as 'the late author'.[174] More repurposed Miss Marple subsequently appeared in 1967, as Dodd Mead brought out *Murder in*

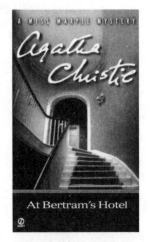

At Bertram's Hotel

Signet's US paperback, one of the first to bear the trademark signature (2000).

our Midst, which put *The Body in the Library*, *The Murder at the Vicarage* and *The Moving Finger* into one volume. 'It is quite surprising how the Miss Marple tales, once secondary to Hercule Poirot, have stood up over the years far better than those of the Belgian wonderman', argued the *Los Angeles Times* in its review.[175] The 1960s had been Miss Marple's decade, and this meant that not only was she more prominent (both on page and screen), but that her strengths were more frequently assessed by critics and readers alike.

The 1960s saw ever-increasing interest in Christie not only as a person and writer of popular mysteries, but also as a respected author whose works required dissection and intelligent consideration. Requests for interviews continued to be made, and occasionally Christie consented to them, especially when it came to the respectable broadsheet newspapers and illustrious international publications. She was asked if she would be interviewed for a Japanese newspaper, which was seeking conversations with notable persons includ-

ing Fidel Castro, Robert Kennedy, Benjamin Britten, Salvador Dali, Noël Coward, W. Somerset Maugham, Arthur Miller, Jean-Paul Sartre and Dr Martin Luther King Jr. 'For once I am not averse!' Christie responded, 'Japan prints my books beautifully', but she was worried that they might want 'too much philosophy'.[176]

Christie was not interested in straightforward accounts of her life, and in 1964 she sent one 'tiresome' request to Patricia Cork to respond to: 'Make clear I have no wish for a biography of myself ... I write books to be sold and I hope people will enjoy them but I think people should be interested in books and not their authors!!'[177] However, Christie was 'indifferent' about

HarperCollins' 2008 signature cover by Julie Jenkins.

evaluations of her work, such as one suggested by American scholar Gordon C. Ramsey in 1965.[178] Later the same year, Ramsey penned a celebration of the author, which was published in the *New York Times* to coincide with the American book publication of *A Caribbean Mystery*. Ramsey particularly commended the character of Miss Marple, stating that 'by following the psychological parallels that each case suggests, she is able to solve the mystery, simply by using common sense and her knowledge of human nature. Herein lies the greatest reason for Mrs Christie's (and Miss Marple's) success. Human nature, as we all know, does not change, no matter what the developing technology of our scientific society may present that is new and different.'[179] Indeed, Miss Marple really had become an increasingly significant calm point in a stormy sea, as the world changed around her.

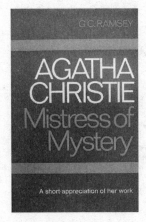

Collins' UK hardback of G. C. Ramsey's 1967 celebration of Christie.

In her eighth decade, Christie had shown that she could both continue the traditions of the past while forging ahead with new ventures. These may not have always ended well for her personally, as she was particularly hurt by the battles with MGM, but she was commanding respect commensurate with both her popularity and her skill. The precise puzzle construction of earlier decades was no longer such a priority as Christie instead emphasised characters and relationships of all kinds, as well as meditations on modern society. As time moved on, so Christie allowed more of herself to seep into the books. The 1970s would offer a reflection of the author's own perspective on a changing world, and there were still some surprises left for Miss Marple of St Mary Mead.

CHAPTER FIVE:

THE
1970s

Agatha Christie continued to be fascinated by modern life at the turn of the 1970s, and although she enjoyed reading fiction from a range of genres, the author was inevitably asked about her views on contemporary crime writers. 'It is part of my homework,' she acknowledged, 'just to check that I am not about to trespass on their ground, with an idea already germinating in my mind. But I don't enjoy them very much, I'm afraid.'[1] One person whom she did single out for praise was New Zealand's Ngaio Marsh, but on the whole Christie existed in her own bubble, with her popularity so exceeding her contemporaries that any comparisons seemed almost worthless.

OPPOSITE: Miss Marple depicted in fashionable mauve with matching carry case – the *Woman's Realm* serialisation of the last Marple book to be penned by her creator (1971).

IL GIALLO MONDADORI 1239

MISS MARPLE: NEMESI

Agatha Christie

The image of Margaret Rutherford outlived her film tenure and continued to appear on international book covers (1972).

While Christie had always resisted comparisons between herself and Miss Marple, as she got older she seemed to be increasingly fascinated by unsolved criminal cases. One notable example was the poisoning of Charles Bravo in 1876, which Christie mentions in three novels across her final fifteen years of writing.[2] The British lawyer took several days to die but refused to indicate the source of the poisoning, leading to widespread speculation but no conviction. In October 1968, *The Sunday Times Magazine* ran a feature on the crime, and Agatha Christie adopted the role of Miss Marple as she presented her own solution to the case, using the sort of reflection on a second-hand story seen in the meetings of the Tuesday Night Club more than forty years earlier. Somewhat typically for Christie, she believed that the guilty party was a doctor, a profession to be treated with suspicion by readers of her novels. She even used her own knowledge of human nature to support her thesis, including people noticing apparently 'secret' relationships:

> I remember, when I was a child, my grandmother saying of a Mrs F ... 'Such a nice woman, Colonel L ... is an old friend of her husband who asked him to look after her. There is, of course, nothing wrong about it, everybody knows that.' I bet there was! And I bet that deep down, people knew it all right.[3]

When it came to Miss Marple herself, the spectre of Margaret Rutherford continued to loom over the character, which annoyed Christie. She complained that the films appeared on television ('Have had very nice letter from a woman who says she had to turn off *Murder Most Foul* because it was such an awful travesty of dear Miss Marple') and reiterated that her own Miss Marple was quite unlike the actor ('She is tall and thin - not stout').[4] Christie also worked towards her annual Christmas books, although 'I can't imagine why I do so much', she said in 1969. 'Especially as I say "This is the last one I'll ever write" whenever one is finished. The family say "You always say that" and I say "No, this time I really mean it." You get into a habit and once you're in a mould of doing a thing - and consider you do it reasonably well, shall we say - you want to go on doing it.'[5] Now that Christie was much closer in age to Miss Marple (indeed, by some calculations even older than the character), she increasingly used the character less as a plot-solving device, and more as a conduit for her own observations.

Although Christie was starting to find it more difficult to work, due to periods of ill-health, she never lost the urge to create more stories. In her ninth, and last, decade this would include the final outings for Miss Marple. 'As for running out of ideas, I don't think I shall,' she said, 'but I may run out of application!'[6]

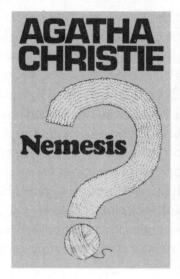
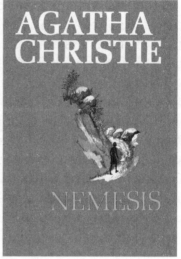

Nemesis
(Novel, 1971)

Although not the final Miss Marple book to be published, *Nemesis* was the final story featuring the character to be written by Agatha Christie. It is a fascinating novel, and one that has sharply divided readers over the years. John Curran is one person who has argued that 'it is not a great detective novel,' but 'considered solely as a novel it is a revelation', and indeed its engagement with characters and their relationships makes it a standout Agatha Christie for many, and one that has been positively re-evaluated in recent years.[7] By now, Christie generally enjoyed writing her standalone thrillers

ABOVE LEFT: A peculiarly space age finish was applied to the first Miss Marple book of the 1970s with metallic silver and bright pink inks (1971). The knitted question mark became an enduring motif for Agatha Christie's Marple. **ABOVE RIGHT:** A black-and-white drawing of a lonely figure was the centrepiece of Dodd Mead's first edition (1971).

and mysteries the most (she stated that working on 1967's *Endless Night* was 'Much more fun than writing something with Poirot or Miss Marple') and perhaps this was because such stories didn't require close adherence to the puzzle mystery mould of old.[8] This might also explain why, as with *At Bertram's Hotel*, the focus of *Nemesis* is more on atmosphere and character than clues and detection.

However, this doesn't mean that the process of writing *Nemesis* was an easy one. Over the years many critics have suggested that when Christie began to dictate her novels there was a corresponding looseness of her plots. Christie acknowledged that this method 'encourages you to be much too verbose' and that 'There is no doubt that the effort involved in typing or writing does help me in keeping to the point. Economy of wording, I think, is particularly necessary in detective stories. You don't want to hear the same thing rehashed three or four times over. But it is tempting when one is speaking into a dictaphone to say the same thing over and over again in slightly different words.'[9] Nevertheless, the surviving typescripts of *Nemesis* show exactly how much work was undertaken on some novels once returned from the typist. Christie extensively edited and reworked the book, including the addition of many pages of handwritten material. It is clear that she studied it closely, and worked to avoid repetition, although she wasn't always entirely successful.

The story itself is in part a sequel to *A Caribbean Mystery*, in which the wealthy Mr Rafiel referred to Miss Marple as 'Nemesis'. He has now died, and Miss Marple receives a posthumous letter from her former 'ally', in which he asks her to investigate a crime. The crime itself is not specified, but there is the promise of £20,000 (equivalent to nearly a quarter of a million pounds in 2024) should Miss Marple undertake the investigation, although it is not yet clear what is to be investigated. This vague premise for detection means that *Nemesis* is initially a meandering mystery, but Miss Marple soon finds the right path, with an invitation to join a tour of English country homes and gardens, where she meets some characters on the coach who may well be suspicious. On the journey she is invited to stay with Lavinia Glynne and her two sisters, Clotilde and Anthea Bradbury-Scott, and following discussions with them, the nature of the mystery starts to take shape. It transpires that a young woman named Verity Hunt was murdered some years previously, and Mr Rafiel's son, Michael, was accused of the crime. Clotilde had adopted Verity, and the trauma of her loss is made clear to the readers and Miss Marple.

A Tom Adams painting adorned Pocket Books' first US paperback in 1973.

When we meet Miss Marple, she is still being attended to by Cherry Baker, who first appeared in *The Mirror Crack'd from Side to Side*. Miss Marple is a reader of *The Times*, even if it isn't as good as it was, in her opinion, as her eyes wander mostly to the announcements of 'Deaths'. Miss Marple is happy to undertake her own investigations, even if it means travelling twenty-five miles by taxi, as she insists that 'My health is really very good' (while acknowledging that she is slightly deaf and has eyesight troubles), and although her age is once again not specified, she considers passengers who are around seventy to be rough contemporaries of her own, which means that she now considers herself to be nearly two decades younger than Christie stated when writing *4.50 from Paddington*. Miss Marple seems to enjoy her sleuthing and travelling, and even recounts part of *The Body in the Library* to two of her fellow coach passengers. She also has no time for dawdling or sentiment, in a slight toughening of the character compared to *At Bertram's Hotel*. When awaiting some facts, she becomes irritated: 'For goodness' sake, tell me something,' she snaps, while she holds no truck with the idea that 'an unhappy childhood' and a 'bad environment' may partially explain the actions of criminals. As one person says, she has 'a very fine sense of evil'.

It is easy to pick fault with some elements of the novel, and many of the most obvious problems could have been minimised by Collins' editors. The lack of editorial intervention is arguably evident on the very first page, in which a lengthy single sentence dominates the second paragraph of the book. There are also time-consuming diversions, which potentially would have been more difficult to alter, such as the meeting with Esther Anderson (*née* Walters), Mr Rafiel's secretary, which provides no helpful information even if there are some interesting asides from Miss Marple. It is also curious that Esther expects Miss Marple to have 'died a long time ago', when the events of *A Caribbean Mystery* are stated to have taken place only a year earlier. Collins' editors did correct some more egregious issues, however, such as the question of Mr Rafiel's age, which was stated to be 'nearly eighty' in *A Caribbean Mystery*. In *Nemesis*, Christie originally referred to him variously as sixty-nine, under sixty, and 'not very old'. Similar inconsistencies arose concerning the discovery of a body, stated to occur between three weeks and six months after death at different points; this was corrected for the published version.

In 1974, Tom Adams' UK cover was released by Fontana.

Nevertheless, these inconsistencies and editing issues are only part of the picture. Much of *Nemesis* is strikingly bold when it comes to characters and situations, including some sharp descriptions. The vocabulary on display is

HarperCollins' 1996 cover by Geoff Appleton.

varied enough that even a 2009 study from the University of Toronto, which claimed Christie likely had dementia, acknowledged that the breadth of her language in this novel is almost the same as seen in *Murder on the Orient Express* in 1934 (although *Nemesis* apparently uses twice as many vague or 'indefinite' words).[10] *Nemesis* offers evocative descriptions and lengthy, candid and thoughtful discussions between characters that show insight into the changing world.

A notable example is Chapter Eighteen, in which Miss Marple and her new acquaintance, Archdeacon Brabazon, discuss the modern world in a conversation that covers sex and love, including the distinction between them. The Archdeacon does not believe that sex is wrong, but 'sex cannot take the place of love, it goes *with* love but it cannot succeed by itself'. Even the question of same-sex attraction is nonchalantly discussed by the two characters, whose backgrounds may make us assume that they would be dismissive of such a thing. Although such feelings are couched in terms of a 'crush', rather than anything that may lead to a lasting relationship, they are described as 'a natural part of life'. Love, both agree, can be a dangerous thing, and the Archdeacon recounts a tale in which two elderly women living together (described as both 'friends' and 'a couple') met with tragedy when one murdered the other: 'I saw the devil looking out of her eyes,' the killer explained. Not all of modern life is embraced, however, and one of Christie's bêtes-noire rears its head: long-haired students, especially those taking part in demonstrations.

Love underpins *Nemesis*, which is the most intimate Miss Marple novel. The question of what love can mean, and what it can do, is crucial to the solving of Verity Hunt's murder. The clues to the identity of the culprit, such as they are, are reinforced enough that many readers will spot them with ease, but this is almost secondary. This is not a puzzle mystery, it is a meditation on crime and love, and the selfish effects of both. At the end of the novel, there is a complex discussion of the death of Verity, in which Miss Marple shows that she understands the actions of the murderer but is certainly not approving of them. 'I am in my own way an emissary of justice,' she claims, and ensures that the murderer's arguments are swiftly shut down and they are taken into custody, with the assistance of her own 'guardian angels'. Nevertheless, Miss Marple concedes that 'I don't suppose there can be any agony so great as what [the murderer] has suffered all this time … living in eternal sorrow.' Miss Marple cites the power of 'frustrated love' as a crucial motivating factor, but never allows the victim to be forgotten: 'I'm sorry for Verity because of all that she missed, all that she was so near to obtaining. A life of love and devotion.'

Miss Marple is so astute and confident that her manner worries some of the men concerned with the case, with the Home Secretary describing her as 'The most frightening woman I ever met.' The Assistant Commissioner simply describes her as 'So gentle – and so ruthless.' As for her reward from Mr Rafiel, Miss Marple is quite direct. Asking for it to be placed into her current account, she tells the solicitors that 'I'm going to spend it, you know. I'm going to have some fun with it.' Just for a moment, the two men then see in her a glimpse of a girl, 'young, happy, going to enjoy herself.'

The signature cover by Julie Jenkins (2008).

Early notes for the book included some different ideas about the nature of the relationship between characters. On one page, she suggested 'Mr R[afiel]'s son / not his son / His wife had a lover – she dies – son unsatisfactory'. This was

The 2011 paperback cover for publisher Wm. Morrow.

followed by a different option that concentrated on the three sisters. 'One of them had a child ... a son? - daughter? Called niece or nephew.' She also suggested that the initials C.L.A. could have significance: these are the first letters of the sisters' names in the book, as well as the ancient Greek Fates, sisters of Nemesis, called Clotho, Lachesis and Atropos. Christie also sketched out details for all of the novel's characters in the style of Miss Marple's journal.[11] The notes (on plain paper rather than in her notebooks) often refer to her progress on the dictaphone, showing the extent to which Christie edited while she worked, and then extensively revised the material received from her typist.

Christie carried out many of the revisions to *Nemesis* over June and July 1971, at which point she was also recovering from a broken hip, and ended up hospitalised at the same time as Margaret Rutherford, who coincidentally broke her leg on the same day. According to one newspaper, Christie walked on the hip for a week before realising it was fractured.[12] Passages removed by Christie included a further explanation of Miss Marple's unusually methodical approach to detection in this novel, as she uses the aforementioned journal to record her investigations and thoughts. 'The whole trouble is that I didn't do my homework properly,' she thinks in one removed section. 'I must make a logical appraisal of this whole problem.'[13] This makes it sound a little like Miss Marple has been liaising with Hercule Poirot, or - at least - reading up on her Sherlock Holmes. Christie also spent some time thinking about quotations that she wished to use, musing 'Biblical?', before opting for an extract from the Book of Amos ('Let justice roll down like waters ...').[14] One entire page was cut when Christie realised that she had already included the information earlier; in a sad irony, it included Miss Marple getting annoyed with herself for her failing memory. A village parallel was also dropped, in which a packet of pins attached to some tape was found in a gooseberry pie for apparently no reason. [15]

During editing, Christie asked for help in tracing the provenance of two poems she wished to use, by Thomas Chatterton ('Rose white youth …') and Beatrice Harraden ('Ships that pass in the night …'). She was also sent a proof copy of the book's artwork, which depicted a question mark made out of a knitted shawl and a ball of wool: an excellent concept for the cover design of a Miss Marple book. Billy Collins suggested that the final version should be more ragged in appearance (to make it clearer that it's knitted), but otherwise thought it 'ingenious'. [16]

When it came to serialisation and international sales, some difficulties were encountered, at least in part due to

'Why did the girl die?' Miss Marple in the *Woman's Realm* serial, illustrated by Len Thurston (1971).

the feeling that Christie's 1970 thriller *Passenger to Frankfurt* was a weak book, even though it was a commercial success and received some good reviews. Her Swedish publishers wondered if the next Christie was worth pursuing, but were assured that *Nemesis* is 'an extremely good traditional Miss Marple mystery story', and that 'this is no time to get cold feet about Agatha Christie'.[17] Phyllis Westberg at Harold Ober Associates was frustrated by the lack of a serial sale for the book, even though she came close. *McCall's*, *Cosmopolitan* and *Redbook* magazines all had no opening for the story, while *Ladies' Home Journal*'s readers liked it but were overruled by their editor for reasons unknown.[18]

In the UK, *Woman's Realm* serialised the story, beginning in September 1971. The first instalment depicted a watercolour of a short and bespectacled Miss Marple dressed in mauve, with matching carry case. Edmund Cork wrote to Christie to say that he anticipated strong sales for the book, while he also wrote to Collins to ask that they no longer use photographs of the author due to her strong aversion to them, as she was especially sensitive about her appearance as she got older.[19] American publishers Dodd Mead were also asked to stop sending on fan mail to Christie directly, and there were signs that the author was starting to feel overwhelmed. By December, Christie confessed that 'One quarter of an hour's Xmas shopping exhausted me – most years I have enjoyed it.'[20] Her purchased presents included a cuckoo clock for her great-granddaughter and 'apparatus which fills the air with noise' for great-grandson James Prichard, who more than forty years later would become Chair and CEO of the company that bears her name.

Collins published the novel on 18 October 1971, with Dodd Mead following a month later in the United States, and reviews were mostly positive. 'Just as there are people who believe Christmas is not Christmas without snow, there are those who think it is not full value without a new Agatha Christie,' proclaimed Australia's *The Age*. 'It seems hardly necessary to say it, but the story is suitably baffling, the characters neatly limned, the narration as smooth as a good Christmas port.'[21] For the *Daily Telegraph*, 'Miss Marple and her author are right back on form', one of several reviews that referred to an improvement since *Passenger to Frankfurt*.[22] The *Leader Post* even argued that 'It is no exaggeration to say she seems to have been getting better with the years', although the *Guardian* felt that it was 'Not a Christie classic but the old hand is aston-

The current cover by Bill Bragg (2022).

ishingly fresh and the mixture as relaxing as a hot bath.'[23] For Maurice Richardson in *The Observer*, *Nemesis* is 'Not one of her best, perhaps, but remarkably inventive, quite worthy of the Picasso of the detective story.'[24] Contrarily, the *Courier Post* insisted that 'This book marks the passing of an era - a time when Agatha Christie wrote compelling, absorbing mysteries ... *Nemesus* [sic] is a bore. And Miss Jane Marple ... should be retired with all due honours.'[25]

Christie herself was unsure about the book, as she confessed in a letter to a fan: 'I am glad that you enjoyed *Nemesis*. I was rather worried about it when I had finished writing it, but on the whole people seem to have enjoyed it very much - and after doubts at first, I enjoyed writing it once I was getting towards the end.'[26] While Christie was finding the process of writing much more difficult than she had in the past, there is no denying her claim just a couple of years earlier that 'I've lasted very well; I must have stamina.'[27]

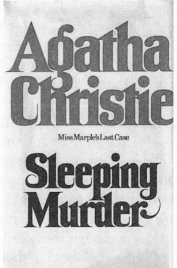

Sleeping Murder
(Novel, 1976)

On 12 January 1976, Agatha Christie died at her home in Wallingford, Oxfordshire. The 1973 novel *Postern of Fate* was the last that she wrote; unfortunately, this somewhat rambling and repetitive book exposed the difficulties she was having with coherency and focus. Rosalind had asked Billy Collins not to push her mother for another novel, while others working at the publisher were acutely aware that the author was now struggling: 'The trouble with Agatha is, as you know, that on certain days she is all there and on other days she is only half there,' said one Collins employee in April 1974.[28]

ABOVE LEFT: *'Miss Marple's Last Case'* – a shocking subtitle on a shocking-pink jacket for the UK's final Christie novel in 1976. **ABOVE RIGHT:** Dodd Mead's more sober cream-coloured jacket for America's *Sleeping Murder* (1976).

Nevertheless, the same year she considered writing 'a semi-ghost story or book built round the White Horse of Uffington' and, in late 1973, she wrote an article and poem (neither published at the time) that reflected on both her youth and old age.[29] 'One of the interesting things about Life is not insistence on being youthful – it is being your age!' she argued. 'Life is a highly interesting journey. It consists of a travel not so much through space as through TIME.' Reminiscences included 'My canary in its cage near my cot', 'swimming in the sea', and 'Long walks on the moors', but the abiding impression is of a woman who was content to accept that her life was drawing to a close.[30]

In summer 1975 a syndicated newspaper article informed the world that Christie would not be writing any more novels: 'Agatha Christie has been murdering people for 55 years, and the time has come for the killing to stop.'[31] By now, it was common knowledge that Christie had two book manuscripts 'in reserve' that she had written some decades earlier, and the expectation was that they would be published posthumously, although this was not an obligation. The first book, *Curtain*, had been gifted to Rosalind, who decided to publish the novel in 1975, a few months before her mother's death. The other, *Sleeping Murder*, was owned by Max, and although he was permitted to publish the book whenever he liked, as Christie's spouse the tax situation was much more complicated, and it was not financially expedient for it to be published in her lifetime. *Sleeping Murder* was mostly written in the 1940s (see 'When did Agatha Christie write *Sleeping Murder*?' on p. 255) and both Christie and Max returned to it a few times over the years, both out of curiosity and to investigate how it might be used. In 1952, Christie was informed that while Max could sell the book outright, there were potential tax ramifications due to their joint income.[32] It may be no coincidence that the following year arrangements were made so that *A Pocket Full of Rye* would benefit the British School of Archaeology, which was perhaps a result of Max being unable to directly profit from the book he owned. At this point, the novel was called *Murder in Retrospect*, but this title had already been used in America for the 1942 Poirot novel *Five Little Pigs*, and so an alternative was needed. A few years later, Christie confessed that she never cared for this alternative title (although it was used for the book's fifth chapter) and offered new suggestions: *Sleeping Death, Let Sleeping Murder Lie, Sleeping Murder* or *Dead Yesterday*. She preferred the last two, and particularly *Sleeping Murder*.[33]

In 1950 Christie had returned to the novel some time after beginning work on it. 'As I seem to be well forward with books for the moment – two still to come out, I thought I might as well go over *Murder in Retrospect* thoroughly, as a lot of it seems to date very much,' she told Edmund Cork. 'I've removed all political references etc, or remarks which seemed to echo the trend of the time. The scene of it must remain laid in that period, as so much of the action depends on servants (plentiful then) and ample meals etc! It's more catchwords and particular phrases that seem to make a book seem old fashioned. I've now tried not to make Giles or Gwenda particularly colloquial which I think will leave it quite all right. In another ten years I can run over it again if I'm still here!' Having apparently not looked at the story for some time, Christie reflected that 'On rereading it I think it's quite a good one. I'm not sure I haven't gone down the hill since then!'[34]

'Goodbye, Miss Marple' was the translated title in Italy and elsewhere (1976).

More discussions about the book followed every decade or so. In 1964, the name on the title deed was formally changed to Christie's new choice of *Cover Her Face*, a quote from the John Webster play *The Duchess of Malfi*, which features in the novel. It seems that neither Christie nor Cork were aware that P. D. James had published her debut book with the same title in 1962. Ten years later, Christie couldn't remember if the new title had been agreed on, and suggested *She Died Young* as another possibility.[35] A copy of both the novel and the deed was prepared over summer and sent to the Mallowans. Once more, Max investigated if he could sell the book, perhaps on the proviso that any purchaser would not publish it until after Christie's death. After some consideration, it was decided that this would only raise a fraction of the book's value, and the idea was abandoned. Following Christie's death, publication of the book was rapidly agreed on, with a typescript received by Collins on 18 March 1976, at which point it was still called *Cover Her Face*.

Unlike *Curtain*, *Sleeping Murder* is not explicitly a swansong for its lead detective. It opens with a particularly memorable mystery, which then segues into more traditional 'murder in retrospect' territory, as Miss Marple helps to solve a crime from many years earlier. Twenty-one-year-old Gwenda Reed has arrived in Britain after living in New Zealand for many years and she is searching for a marital home ahead of the arrival of her new husband, Giles. Gwenda thinks she has found the perfect property in Dillmouth, Devon, only to be unsettled by a series of curious coincidences. The novel initially moves quickly, and Gwenda seems to share some of Christie's desires and memories, such as apples by a bath (here for decoration, but for Christie a convenient place for the fruit that she munched while bathing), a nursery with floral wallpaper,

Tom Adams was the inevitable choice for the UK paperback (1978).

Bantam Books' US paperback used the Tom Adams art.

and a garden reminiscent of Ashfield, Christie's childhood home in Torquay. An original and exciting mystery is then established, as Gwenda becomes unsettled by the fact that she keeps expecting to find items, which are then uncovered during the course of the house's refurbishment. Steps to the garden, a covered door, and old wallpaper are all exposed exactly where Gwenda expects or requests them, which seems impossible. Christie then segues into some brief fantastical ideas: 'Wild fragments of explanation whirled round in her head. Dunne, Experiment with Time – seeing forward instead of back ...'. The Dunne referred to is J. W. Dunne, who had written a popular book about time, a subject that seemed to intrigue Christie in the early 1940s, as she also read *The Mysterious Universe* by James Jeans. She rhapsodised about it to Max, including the idea that time 'is like a cinema film run backwards' and 'we could move through it either way'.[36] *Sleeping Murder* does not take such a diversion, however, and by the third chapter Miss Marple has provided a simple solution, suggesting that Gwenda had briefly lived in the house as a child after all.

Bantam's 1977 paperback celebrated the book's bestseller status.

Gwenda's memories of witnessing what may have been her stepmother's murder are then revealed when she goes to the theatre to see *The Duchess of Malfi*, and her recollections include the creepy suggestion that the killer had 'monkey's paws'. Gwenda and Giles investigate, and enlist the help of various people, including the brother of Gwenda's missing stepmother, Dr James Kennedy. Together, they are determined to find out whether Gwenda's stepmother, Helen, simply disappeared of her own free will or was murdered by a figure from the past. Unravelling the truth takes some work, and although Miss Marple is on hand (as Giles is a cousin of the Wests, although the specifics of the familial connections are not shared), it is the young newlyweds who do much of the work. Raymond is described as well-known ('rather than popular'), while Joan is still an artist. Raymond also describes his aunt as 'a perfect Period Piece', which indeed she would have to be if she were 'Victorian to the core', as he also states. Miss Marple is keen to help solve the mystery and manages to convince Dr Haydock to prescribe sea air in order to bring her to Dillmouth. Although the doctor thinks it is 'likely to be the end of you', he cannot stand in Miss Marple's way.[37] While Miss Marple won't take his advice, she administers a similar warning to the young married couple, in which she suggests that they should let sleeping murders lie: 'There are times when it is one's *duty*,' she clarifies. 'But you must realize that this murder is very much in the *past* ... are you really sure, that you are wise to dig it all up again?'

A 1980s hardback edition reissued as a Crime Club Classic.

It may be significant that Christie contemplated using either Poirot or Tommy and Tuppence as detectives for this case, and it would be easy to see the latter pair investigating it.[38] In fact, Giles and Gwenda's adventuring spirit has a hint of the private detectives, and one can certainly imagine Tuppence running up the back staircase and confronting the murderer with a jet of soapy water, as Miss Marple miraculously manages at the novel's conclusion. Prior to this, some readers may note connections between this story and others by Christie. These include the appearance of an elderly lady who asks '*Is it your poor child ... behind the fireplace*', just as happened in 1961's *The Pale Horse* and 1968's *By the Pricking of My Thumbs*, both written quite some time after *Sleeping Murder*. The novel also contemplates the role of 'X' in the murder, an unknown element, just as 'X' is used to describe the murderer in *Curtain*. Some of these similarities struck readers of the time, and one even wrote to Collins to ask if it had been a deliberate final joke, or mystery, for her readers.

There was a great deal of interest when the typescript of *Sleeping Murder* was dusted off and readied for publication in 1976. Christie's death had provoked an outpouring of tributes, both public and private; in Italy, the writer Nico Orengo even penned a short piece in which Miss Marple reflected on the loss of both Poirot and her creator.[39] Many of those who had known Christie in both personal and professional capacities took the time to write to the family with their condolences. A notably touching letter came from her American publisher, Edward Dodd, who wrote to Max: 'It must be very sad for you, and lonesome, to have Agatha gone. It is sad for all of us except that we can rejoice that she led such a warm, joyous, and productive life.' Dodd went on to reminisce about 'those parties in New York when Charles Laughton embraced Agatha as if he were playing a love scene from Shakespeare. And the one at the Century when she sat like a Queen, in a big armchair and the publishing world of New York came to pay her homage… Oh, they were all good times.'[40] A more public discussion of Christie's work and legacy came in the 1977 book *Agatha Christie: First Lady of Crime*, edited by H. R. F. Keating, in which many of the writer's contemporaries wrote essays on core aspects of Christie's work. Christianna Brand wrote about Miss Marple, and was sent a pre-publication typescript of *Sleeping Murder* to ensure that her contribution was up to date. Brand had already finished her essay, but now updated it, noting that Christie allowed Miss Marple to survive her final case: 'Perhaps she could not bear to kill off her own grandmother'.[41]

1992's US paperback released by Harper.

Sleeping Murder first appeared in the United States, as it was serialised in the *Ladies Home Journal* in July and August 1976, which was followed by Dodd Mead's book publication in September. In Britain, it was published by Collins on 11 October 1976 in the UK, with a striking purple cover and the additional subtitle 'Miss Marple's Last Case', which was sometimes retained for later editions. This subtitle annoyed some readers, a handful of whom complained to Collins that the story cannot be Miss Marple's final case as it features Colonel Bantry, who was dead in 1962's *The Mirror Crack'd from Side to Side*. In recent years the suggested reading order for Miss Marple stories has changed, and both

Geoff Appleton illustrated the 1996 HarperCollins cover.

Agatha Christie Ltd and HarperCollins now place *Sleeping Murder* after *The Moving Finger*, aligning it with the period in which it was written. This also helps to separate the book from *Nemesis*, which features an almost identical motive for murder and disposal of the body.

As a finale for both Miss Marple and Christie, *Sleeping Murder* was almost critic-proof, but it fared reasonably well in reviews anyway. *The New Yorker* judged it to be 'A very satisfactory farewell performance', while Maurice Richardson in *The Observer* felt that it was 'well up to the needle-sharp old spinster's average'.[42] The *Times Literary Supplement* was a little less sure: '*Sleeping Murder* has all the virtues of Agatha Christie's work: a coherent plot, firm and purposeful narration, and a pleasant, light and agreeable style. On the other hand, the red herrings are not as convincing as they might be, and the murderer's identity is not too difficult to discover – even for a reader without Miss Marple's long experience of life.'[43] The *New York Times Book Review* was similarly guarded: '*Sleeping Murder* is not among her most skillful works, but it displays her personal sense of what she calls "evil," of murder as an affront and a violation and an act of unique cruelty. She was not an imaginative or original enough writer to explore this, but when Marple tells us here that "it was real evil that was in the air last night," Christie makes us feel her curious primitive shiver.'[44] New Hampshire's *Valley News* probably best reflected the thoughts of many Christie readers in its review, which acknowledged that 'A true Christie fan will receive *Sleeping Murder* with mixed emotions. How lovely to have a new Miss Marple as good as any written in the old days, but how sad that this is the last. Trite but true, no one today writes mysteries like Agatha Christie.'[45]

In 1970 Christie wrote to a Japanese fan and scholar who had wondered about the finer details of Miss Marple's life. 'I can only tell you that Miss Jane Marple does not exist in the flesh and never has,' Christie responded. 'She is entirely a creation of my brain. I have developed her slowly, adding a few characteristics from time to time. She is entirely a person in her own right, not anyone seen, observed, or noticed.'[46] Christie continued to resist any suggestion that she and Miss Marple were alike, although 'fringe friend' Nigel Morland felt otherwise, as he recalled that the author 'was a very kind, very modest, and genuinely original woman in as much as she was not aware of what a charmer she really was. She was never "clever" or superior but very sweet – I always thought there was a great deal of the real Agatha Christie in Miss Marple.'[47] Christie was asked how she wished to be remembered in a century, and simply responded that 'I would like it to be said that I was a good writer of detective and thriller stories'.[48] As for a description, she resisted 'Queen of Crime': 'I prefer being referred to as the Duchess of Death,' she said with a chuckle.[49]

When did Agatha Christie write *Sleeping Murder*?

Agatha Christie wrote *Sleeping Murder* during the 1940s. If you wish to know more, then you should prepare yourself for an avalanche of dates, contradictory evidence and a dose of speculation, in order to help us try to answer one question: when did Agatha Christie write *Sleeping Murder*?

Sleeping Murder is often discussed in the same breath as *Curtain*, but Poirot's finale has a helpful paper trail that pins its composition down to late 1940 and early 1941. *Sleeping Murder* is altogether less clear-cut. In her autobiography, Christie claims that both books were written 'during the first years of the war', but there are problems with this assertion.[50] Firstly, *Sleeping Murder* refers to the events of *The Moving Finger* (first published in 1942) and John Gielgud appearing in *The Duchess of Malfi* (which happened in 1944–5), while her notebooks include details of the plot under the headings 'Plans Sept. 1947' and 'Plans Nov. 1948'.[51] And yet, we know that there was a book called *Murder in Retrospect* (an early title for *Sleeping Murder*) that was assigned to Max in October 1940, and in a 1950 letter Christie indicates that she had just re-read and modified the typescript of *Murder in Retrospect* for what appears to be the first time in several years and mentions that 'In *another* ten years I can run over it again if I'm still here!' [my emphasis], indicating that around a decade had passed since it was written.[52] Let's look at this timeline …

'You oughtn't to be here.' A centenary edition illustration by David Matysiak (1990).

One problem that occurs when researching *Sleeping Murder* is its title, as it was consistently

Miss Marple as she appeared in the *L.A. Times* in 1941, drawn by Arthur Sarnoff.

referred to as *Murder in Retrospect* until 1964. Some online sources claim that there is evidence that *Sleeping Murder* existed by March 1940 because *Murder in Retrospect* is cited on a statement relating to typing costs, but a page of corrections for *Murder in Retrospect* from the same year reveals that this typescript was, in fact, *Five Little Pigs* (which was called *Murder in Retrospect* in America).[53] This muddies the waters, but also starts to give us a possible explanation for what then happened. In June 1940, Edmund Cork flagged up the looming tax issues in America with Christie and suggested that the publication of *Murder in Retrospect* should not be delayed, and just a day later it was agreed that a deed assigning copyright in *Murder in Retrospect* to Max would be drawn up. The most sensible conclusion to be made here is that Max was originally assigned ownership of what became *Five Little Pigs*. This makes even more sense once it is realised that there was never a requirement for the book to be published posthumously. My suggestion is that the plan had been for *Five Little Pigs* to be published immediately and owned by Max, only for this to coincide with Christie's tax problems in the United States. Indeed, when referring to sending the story to *Collier's* magazine in early 1941, Cork mentions needing Max's permission ('if your husband has no objection'), showing that it was expected that the story he owned would be published fairly soon.[54] In late 1940, Christie's tax problems really became a concern, and the author had difficulties extracting money from the United States as a result. Clearly, this was a bad time to expect her husband (whose tax duties were linked with his wife's) to make money from one of her books. In 1949, Cork noted that this 1940 deed had a supplemental note, which read 'not proceeded with in view of new American Income Tax Demand'.[55] I suggest that at this point the decision was made for Max to retain ownership in *a* book called *Murder in Retrospect*, but that this would no longer be what is now known as *Five Little Pigs*. Instead, the deed (finalised on 14 October 1940) would remain the same, but the book to which it refers would be a different story with the legal name *Murder in Retrospect*; this is similar to what happened with 'Greenshaw's Folly' the following decade.

In the United States, *Five Little Pigs* was serialised from September 1941 as *Murder in Retrospect*, but it isn't clear when Christie began work on *Sleeping Murder*. The dates in the novel itself don't help, especially as it was edited in order to be reasonably timeless; a mention that the gardener had worked at the house in 1920 only gives the vaguest sense of period, for example. Meanwhile, Dr Haydock has a similar role in both this book and the short story 'The Case of the Caretaker', written in 1940 or 1941, and so it might have followed that Christie was continuing this thread. But how can we reconcile this with her dated plans in her notebooks? The key may be the fact that Christie continued to revise the book over time. The 1947 plans simply say 'Cover her face (Helen)' and could refer to revisions for the book, or even just a new title. However, the 1948 notes refer to some of the basic elements of the story. This has led to John Curran to suggest that *Sleeping Murder* was actually written as late as the 1950s, although a recently rediscovered 1950 letter from Christie indicates that it cannot be later than the 1940s.

Cork wrote to Christie in 1949 to tell her that the deed would not be subject to death duties, as more than five years had passed, while pointing out that 'the title *Murder in Retrospect* was not used in this country, and might apply to quite a lot of your books, I think we ought to consider the possibility of utilising it for a later story, say your penultimate one.'[56] There seems to be an indication here that *Curtain* was expected to be her final book, if this could be published as her penultimate one. When a member of Collins' staff sent Christianna Brand a copy of the book's typescript in June 1976, she noted that her understanding was that it was written after *The Body in the Library* (first published as a serialisation in 1941), but there is no indication of where she got this information from.[57] As *The Moving Finger* followed the following year (and features events referred to in *Sleeping Murder*), this raises the intriguing possibility that these two stories were written concurrently, as Christie had done with *The Body in the Library* and *N or M?*.

It is plausible that work was started on *Sleeping Murder* in around 1942 (after *Five Little Pigs*), with Christie returning to it several times to both update and alter it, most notably in 1950. It is difficult to reconcile this with her 1948 notes, unless we are to believe that Christie simply forgot that she had already used these elements in her unpublished book, or that her revisions were more extensive than usual towards the end of the decade. This is unusual but not impossible. The fact of the matter is, we just don't know for sure. Agatha Christie has left us with one final mystery.

A Murder is Announced (Play)
(Stage Play, 1977)

Agatha Christie's ongoing theatrical successes continued to be a draw for producers even when the author was no longer able to pen new plays herself. Interested parties had been delighted with the success of the new tour of *Murder at the Vicarage* starring Barbara Mullen, which began in February 1975, and from July 1975 found a home in London, first at the Savoy Theatre and then at the Fortune Theatre, by which point Avril Angers had taken over the role of Miss Marple.. The adaptation by Moie Charles and Barbara Toy had continued to find success in the years since its 1949 premiere, and even made it as far as German television, where Inge Langen played Miss Marple in 1970. As *Murder at the Vicarage* was one of the 'reserved titles'

ABOVE: Dulcie Gray was a major star of stage and screen when she took on the role of Miss Marple aged just 61 (1977).

Inge Langen (left) was just 45 when she played Fraülein Marple in ZDF's TV adaptation of the *Murder at the Vicarage* play, *Mord im Pfarrhaus* (1970).

still owned by Christie personally, it made the author a good amount of money, which probably explains why she agreed to another adaptation of a Miss Marple book from the list.[58] Christie had considered dramatising *A Murder is Announced* herself, and this was cited as a reason to ward off those who wished to adapt it in some way, including a 1953 request to make it into a radio play.[59] Christie never got around to this, making it a prime candidate for another writer to bring to the stage. By the time the play appeared in the West End, Christie had died, but such was her power that even a story originally published in 1950 had strong appeal for the theatre-going public, giving an early indication of the strength of her legacy.

A Murder is Announced was produced by Peter Saunders, whose most famous collaboration with Christie was *The Mousetrap*, but the script from Leslie Darbon is far removed from the original author's best theatrical work. The play is set in the nebulous concept of what the dramatist calls 'Christie Time', which immediately robs the story of its specific and

Dulcie Gray in the Miss Marple costume designed for her by Anthony Holland (1977).

powerful post-war context. It also necessarily reduces the cast of characters (meaning the unfortunate loss of Hinchliffe and Murgatroyd, two of the most memorable characters in the Miss Marple canon), and locates the whole story in Miss Blacklock's home, Little Paddocks. Comic relief is uneasily provided by Mitzi, whose war-torn background remains awkward and distasteful, perhaps even more so when played out on stage for audience laughter. Elsewhere, there is little indication that any character particularly cares about what is going on, and not much sense of drama. The production plays out like a spoof of Christie, but without any insight; it feels like Darbon doesn't really understand what the story has to say about characters and society, as the script focuses on the mechanics of the mystery without wondering why anyone should care, meaning that it never convinces as a drama about real people.

A Murder is Announced opened at the Theatre Royal in Brighton before transferring to the Vaudeville Theatre in London on 21 September 1977. Julius Green, historian of Christie's plays, describes the adaptation as 'pedestrian' and takes aim at the play's producer: 'Saunders, of all people, should arguably have been more respectful of Christie's dramatic legacy'.[60] Although *The Stage* commended Darbon as 'a skilful adapter' and the production as 'irresistible', the *New York Times* offered a pithy review of the production, headlined 'Not So Much a Whodunit as a Whydoit'.[61] The review highlighted the fact that Christie's talents should not be underestimated and could not be replicated easily. 'What Darbon misses is Christie's compulsiveness,' wrote Benedict Nightingale, 'her canny ability to intrigue and grip and not

Prunella Scales, as she appeared 30 years later as Mrs MacKenzie in ITV's *A Pocket Full of Rye*.

let go.' Nightingale rightly pointed out that after the murder occurs, 'The atmosphere, never exactly electric, returns to waxen normality. Nothing happens here: nothing that matters, anyway.' Nightingale gave limited praise to Dulcie Gray's Miss Marple, but otherwise the actors (who included Dinah Sheridan as Letitia Blacklock) did not impress: 'it might have been easier to sustain an interest in the play's denouement if we had felt that one or two of the cast had themselves wanted to find it out ... As it is, the solution comes so casually, so anti-climactically that there is not the slightest danger of my breaking the reviewer's code and giving it away. I cannot, I fear, remember what it was.'[62]

The play ran successfully in the West End for a year, closing in September 1978, and has been revived several times, with tours reaching as far as Australia. In 1982, enquiries were made by one Robert Cusack of a New York theatre company, who wished to stage a musical version of the story, but this didn't make it off the ground.[63]

Miss Marple had a strong showing in 1977, as *Sleeping Murder* continued to sell well, helped by a reading of the novel on BBC Radio 4 by Prunella Scales, beginning on 20 June. The press noted continued interest in 'Christieana', which even included an original radio story by A. R. Rawlinson called 'The Detectives', in which two avid readers of Christie create a private world in which one half of the couple plays Miss Marple, and the other Hercule Poirot; this was read by Martin Jarvis as the *Morning Story* on Radio 4 on 9 August 1977. Meanwhile, readers craving more original Miss Marple from her creator would have just one more chance to read a story or six that they might not have encountered before, as Collins readied one final selection of Miss Marple tales.

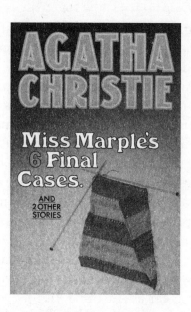

Miss Marple's Final Cases
(Short Story Collection, 1979)

There was no 'Christie for Christmas' in 1978. Following 1976's *Sleeping Murder*, 1977 saw the publication of Christie's keenly anticipated autobiography, but this seemed to be the end of the road for the annual Christie book. Nevertheless, the staff at Collins dutifully combed through lists of the author's stories to try to find something that could be considered 'new' material for her many readers. Eventually they settled on seven short stories that had not been collected in any of Christie's standard British collections; of these, two were standalone supernatural tales, while five were Miss Marple mysteries. Collins were aware that this was a slim volume

ABOVE: Collins Crime Club went solo with Miss Marple's 6 *Final Cases and 2 Other Stories*, a concoction of short stories that had been collected by Dodd Mead in previous short story editions (1979).

indeed but felt that there was sufficient public interest to put them in a new book, to be called *Sanctuary and Other Stories*. In March 1979 this was changed to *Miss Marple's Final Cases*, which made the most of the volume's lead sleuth, but concerns about the Trades Description Act may explain why, by June 1979, it had become the awkwardly titled *Miss Marple's 6 Final Cases and 2 Other Stories*, with *Miss Marple's Final Cases* in notably bolder text; many later reprints have simply used the shorter title. The sixth Miss Marple story was a last-minute discovery, as 'Miss Marple Tells a Story' was missed when the list was first compiled, while some other uncollected stories, such as 'Problem at Pollensa Bay' (investigated by Parker Pyne) were noted but not included.

The collection's first story, 'Sanctuary', has one of the best openings of any Agatha Christie short story.[64] It revisits Chipping Cleghorn, where *A Murder is Announced* took place, and reintroduces Bunch, the vicar's wife and goddaughter of Miss Marple. One day, Bunch is getting ready to sort out the church's flower arrangements when she finds a dying man on the chancel steps, illuminated by coloured light from the stained-glass windows. The man manages to say 'Sanctuary ... Please, *please*', but despite the best efforts of the vicarage and local doctor, he cannot be saved. Bunch's suspicions are aroused by the prompt arrival of the dead man's relatives, and she feels that there is a mystery to be solved here: 'I think I ought to go and see Aunt Jane,' she declares. Miss Marple, here described as a 'sweet old lady', ties her investigation in with some bargain hunting, including the likes of 'a prewar quality' face towel (at this stage, one wonders which war). The story's strong opening leads to a more perfunctory resolution, which suffers from the fact that characterisation

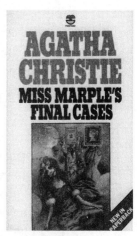

Tom Adams' last Christie cover – Fontana's 'Continental Edition' (1980).

Miss Marple in search of buried treasure, as depicted in *The Strand* in 1944.

is limited in these shorter mysteries, but 'Sanctuary' is nevertheless a satisfying mystery.

The story had its origins in late 1953, when Christie let her agent know that she was considering making a contribution to Westminster Abbey's restoration appeal. This would be in the form of a short story to be auctioned to the highest bidder. Edmund Cork wrote to the Westminster Abbey Appeal Fund to confirm the donation on 11 Jan 1954, and just nine days later the story arrived from the typist.[65] In America, the story was sold to *This Week* for $3,500, while in Britain the Amalgamated Press paid one hundred guineas for it to appear in *Woman's Journal*. The story's appearance in *This Week* (in two parts, beginning on 12 September 1954) resulted in an unusual coincidence, as the magazine elected to publish the story under the title 'Murder at the Vicarage', apparently unaware of Christie's earlier novel. Apologies were made, but nobody seemed to mind too much. This version featured watercolour illustrations, as did *Woman's Realm*'s publication the following month, which also included a note that Christie had donated the 'considerable' fee for the story to the Abbey.

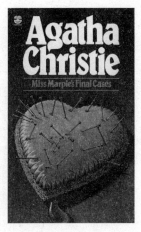

Fontana's new-look cover for 1983.

The next story is 'Strange Jest', which Christie originally called 'The Case of the Buried Treasure'.[66] 'Strange Jest' first appeared in *This Week* on 2 November 1941, and was one of four Miss Marple stories that Christie had been commissioned to write for the publication, although for reasons unknown only this one and 'Tape-Measure Murder' appeared, with the other two syndicated to various newspapers the following year. When it appeared in *The Strand* in July 1944, it used an approximation of Christie's title ('A Case of Buried Treasure'), accompanied by a picture of an inquisitive Miss Marple.[67] For this short mystery, a young couple has been referred to Miss Marple by the actress Jane Helier ('she's absolutely *marvellous*', she assures them) as they try to locate a fortune that has been left to them by a mischievous uncle. The couple are unsure ('Behind Miss Marple's back, Charmian made a sign to Edward. It said, *She's ga-ga.*') but willing to try anything. Miss Marple invokes village parallels to help her find the fortune, and offers some old-fashioned turns of phrase into the bargain; modern readers may not be familiar with the terms 'gammon and spinach' or 'All my eye and Betty Martin', but they will follow Miss Marple's argument that things should not be taken at face value in this neat and light story.[68] Christie's original version, as published in *The Strand*,

Miss Marple startles Scotland Yard in *The Strand*'s 'Tape-Measure Murder', appearing under Christie's original title 'The Case of the Retired Jeweller' (1942).

includes extra character touches, such as the description of Jane Helier as 'pretty dumb at everything outside acting'. More shockingly, in this version the young couple's initial consultation with Miss Marple takes place in the quietest room of the house: the bathroom. Miss Marple then finds herself sitting on the lavatory (albeit with a closed seat) while hearing all about the buried treasure; this makes her blush 'in an old-fashioned way since she had been brought up never to mention lavatories, much less hold social gatherings in one'. Other printings move the scene to a small sitting room.[69]

'Tape-Measure Murder' first appeared in *This Week* on 16 November 1941, although this title is something of a spoiler, unlike Christie's original ('The Case of the Retired Jeweller'), which was used when published in *The Strand* in February 1942. In this story, Miss Marple seems to be a little more like her earlier appearances before she was softened, as she is said to be described as 'vinegar-tongued' by some. Nevertheless, her attention to detail will be essential for the solving of this crime, in which a woman is found murdered, with her apparently unemotional husband the prime suspect. Of course, the solution is not so simple, and although many readers may correctly work out the truth, Christie plays fair with her placement of clues in a story that relies on clearly drawn characters. Inspector Slack cannot help but question some of Miss Marple's more intuitive conclusions, but receives a 'pitying smile' in return, for human nature is Miss Marple's speciality. 'People don't leave fingerprints and cigarette ash nowadays,' insists Slack, when asked about clues at the crime scene, but Miss Marple correctly deduces that this is 'an old-fashioned crime'. The real-life Dr Crippen is mentioned as a point of comparison with the suspected husband, as is Miss Marple's Uncle Henry ('a man of unusual self-control'), but it is Miss Marple's questioning of the facts that leads her to the solution.

When a list of stories was drawn up for this collection a question mark was raised over 'The Case of the Caretaker', as it was noted that the story is very similar to the 1967 novel *Endless Night*. After some consideration, it was decided that this shouldn't be a barrier to its inclusion, and although the stories are indeed similar in both premise and solution, they also demonstrate one of the strengths of Christie's writing. In *Endless Night*, the characterisation and growing uneasiness mark it out as one of her masterpieces, while 'The Case of the Caretaker' is a short, sharp, twisting story that makes an immediate impact. It opens with an unusual premise, as Miss Marple is laid up in bed after catching the 'flu and given an unusual prescription by Dr Haydock. She is unusually depressed ('I can't help feeling how much better it would have been if I had died'), and to help her recuperate the doctor asks her to

1989 centenary livery for Fontana.

read a manuscript that he has written, based on true events, and to see if she can work out the ending. The story concerns a young couple, Harry and Louise Laxton, who are trying to settle into village life in St Mary Mead but keep encountering a mysterious woman who used to live in a house that was pulled down and replaced by the couple's new home. Louise worries that they have been cursed, and these worries seem to come true when she is killed in a horse-riding accident. Miss Marple manages to work out what really went on, and her suspicions are confirmed by Dr Haydock.

The premise of Miss Marple commenting on a story in which she was not directly involved is reminiscent of most of the cases in *The Thirteen Problems*, and the result is that she is a peripheral figure. However, there is a different version of the story in which she is more involved. In 'The Case of the Caretaker's Wife', the premise of Miss Marple reading a manuscript has been dropped, and instead she is an active participant in the story. The exact reasons for these two different versions of the same mystery are unknown, but 'The Case of the Caretaker's Wife' was eventually published in John Curran's book *Agatha Christie's Murder in the Making* in 2012.[70] The better-known version, 'The Case of the Caretaker', was first published by *The Strand* in January 1942.

'The Case of the Perfect Maid', which first appeared in *The Strand* in April 1942, is exactly the sort of story that works best in a magazine. It is engaging and has an interesting solution, although it doesn't stand up to much scrutiny. The story concerns the maid Gladys (not the same one who featured in *A Pocket Full of Rye*), who has been dismissed by her employers for apparently stealing a brooch, which she insists she did not do. Even when the jewellery

Jeff Cottenden's photo cover (2002).

is returned, Gladys knows that the cloud of suspicion will prevent her from finding new employment. Miss Marple doesn't care for the 'bouncing, self-opinionated' Gladys, but also doesn't believe that she is a thief, and so decides to find out what has gone on. Gladys's ex-employers are two sisters, and they seem to find an excellent replacement for her. This 'perfect maid' then disappears, having stolen from the flats where they live. While Miss Marple acknowledges her own lack of formal education (taught by 'just a governess, you know', just like Christie herself), she manages to outwit the culprit by providing clear evidence to the police. For Miss Marple, rescuing Gladys's reputation is almost as important as solving a crime: 'I'm not going to have one of our village girls' character for honesty taken away like that!'

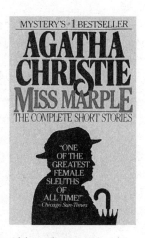

Although *Miss Marple's Final Cases* did not appear in the US, it paved the way for *The Complete Short Stories* in 1985 and this bestselling Berkley trade paperback in 1986.

The final Miss Marple story in the collection is 'Miss Marple Tells a Story', which had been written for the radio in 1934 as a last-minute replacement for 'In a Glass Darkly', a supernatural short story about a premonition that also features here.[71] The other supernatural story is 'The Dressmaker's Doll', which Christie dropped into her agent's office unexpectedly in December 1957, as she suddenly felt compelled to write it.[72] With Miss Marple as the collection's title character, these extra short stories may be welcome 'free' additions, but the result is a volume that doesn't feel cohesive. In later years, 'Greenshaw's Folly' has been added, which means that readers need only purchase this and *The Thirteen Problems* to get the full collection of the twenty original Miss Marple short stories.[73]

Miss Marple's Final Cases was published in October 1979, and as the stories were already in American collections, it did not appear in the United States. It was distributed in Canada, though, which created a problem as the rear of the dustjacket proudly stated that the stories were 'never previously published in volume form on this side of the Atlantic', which is geographically untrue in that country. Swift apologies were made to the Canadian distributors, and the book's jackets were narrowly saved from being pulped in order to avoid a costly and time-consuming reprinting, despite being incorrect. The cover was even noted by some reviewers. 'The dustjacket designers are being coy with the latest Agatha Christie collection,' stated the *Calgary Herald*. 'The title, *Miss Marple's 6 Final Cases*, is printed so the six disappears', noted the reviewer (the '6' was printed in a light grey, rather than the sharp white of '*Miss Marple's Final Cases*'). Nevertheless, 'They're vintage Christie'.[74] 'At least two of the stories are over 40 years old, but they are still good,' acknowledged *The Birmingham Post*, while *The Times Literary Supplement* considered the book alongside another posthumous collection, *Fen Country* by Edmund Crispin: 'The contents are, admittedly, scrapings. But what barrels are being scraped!'[75]

But what of Miss Marple's final thoughts as imagined by Agatha Christie? In March 1974, the author was conferred with the Award of Excellence by the Popular Culture Association, and Christie wrote a grateful letter in response:

> I am tempted to imagine how three of my characters would have reacted, and I think that Hercule Poirot, who adored flattery, would have been best at expressing himself in a bombastic way and would certainly have said that your appreciation was 'epatant'. This attitude of conceit would have found a proper corrective in Miss Marple, who would have received the news with an enigmatic smile in silence, and would perhaps have reflected that much of her

success had come to her in the manner of Wordsworth's poem: 'through recollection in Tranquility'. Tommy and Tuppence in their young days would have accepted praise with Philistine enjoyment and each would have congratulated the other.[76]

This seems to have been the last time that Christie put herself into the mind of her main detectives, all of whom debuted in the 1920s. Christie had served her creations well, and they would find a resurgence in popularity in the following decade, thanks in no small part to television. After a bumpy start to her screen adventures, fans of Miss Marple would soon be able to watch what is often considered to be her definitive portrayal, by Joan Hickson – but not before a couple of less successful attempts to bring the character to life.

MISS MARPLE

CHAPTER SIX:

THE
1980s and 1990s

n 1974 Hercule Poirot finally had his first major on-screen success, with the film of *Murder on the Orient Express* starring Albert Finney and produced by John Brabourne and Richard Goodwin. The film did well both critically and commercially and, perhaps more significantly, was largely seen as a success by Rosalind Hicks, who now controlled many of the decisions relating to her mother's work alongside her son Mathew Prichard. Inevitably there was call for a follow-up, with *Death on the Nile* as the first choice; this film was released in 1978, with Peter Ustinov taking on the part of Poirot. But even before Poirot's second outing made it to cinemas, Brabourne and Goodwin had plans in mind for

OPPOSITE: At 78, Joan Hickson was the oldest actress ever to take the lead in a major television series, featured here on the BBC's first series sales brochure.

Miss Marple. However, this was not to be the only attempt to bring Miss Marple to the screen in this era, as the years following Christie's death saw a new concerted effort to find a definitive portrayal of the character.

The Mirror Crack'd (Film)
(Film, 1980)

There had been occasional interest in *The Mirror Crack'd from Side to Side* from filmmakers since its 1962 publication, perhaps because of its focus on a star of the silver screen. In 1974, theatre producer Michael Harvey of New York enquired about the rights to make a film of the story, first contacting Edmund Cork, and then Christie directly, which resulted in a memorable response from the author: 'I am allergic to the making of films from my books.'[1] Christie's 'allergy' softened only a little after the success of *Orient Express*, but following her death more screen adaptations were readied, with press reports in October 1977 revealing that Helen Hayes was lined

ABOVE: A promotional portrait of Angela Lansbury as Miss Marple (1980).

The UK film poster.

Fontana's tie-in
paperback (1981).

up to take on the role of Miss Marple for two television movies for Warner Bros.[2] The titles were stated to be *A Caribbean Mystery* and *The Mirror Crack'd*, although it would be six more years before Hayes appeared in the former, during which time the latter had already made it to the big screen. The decision to transfer this novel to the cinema screen rather than television seems to have been made pretty swiftly, as by July 1978 a script of *The Mirror Crack'd from Side to Side* (using the full British title) was prepared and distributed to interested parties, and in November it was announced that filming would begin in the spring of 1979.[3] This script was by British screenwriter Jonathan Hales and it adheres closely to Christie's original story, but it was not the version used for the final film.

In April 1979 it was revealed that Angela Lansbury was to play the part of Miss Marple in the movie, which it was now hoped would be filmed in autumn the same year. However, the success of Lansbury's run in *Sweeney Todd* on Broadway meant that the producers had to choose between a new Miss Marple and delaying the production, which is what they chose to do. What could not have been foreseen was that this delay would allow for some recuperation time for Brabourne, who had been on the boat that was exploded by the IRA in August 1979, killing his father-in-law Lord Mountbatten (also King Charles III's great-uncle and 'Honorary Grandfather'), as well as Brabourne's mother and one of his sons. Nevertheless, Brabourne remained committed to the picture, despite the injuries he sustained. One of the decisions by the producers was that Hales's straightforward script needed an extra bit of Hollywood polish, and they brought in Barry Sandler to sharpen up the dialogue, although his revisions became more extensive. Sandler's additions included the film's memorable opening, in which Miss Marple solves a fictional murder in a film being watched by the residents of St Mary Mead. The addition of this sequence also allowed for a spoof of whodunnit tropes as they watch *Murder at Midnight* (which is not a real film), while firmly establishing Miss Marple's deductive powers. Hales's original script had introduced Miss Marple more simply, showing her gardening (and correctly assessing the motives of her daily helper, Cherry),

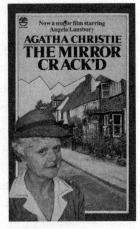

An early export paperback (1980).

and then going to buy knitting needles. This script also had her solve the small mystery of a shop assistant's missing list: 'Still sharp as a tack, our Miss M!' says the shopkeeper. Sandler's revisions also ensured that Miss Marple made it to the Gossington Hall fête, although she has to leave early; in Hales's script she is injured beforehand and so cannot attend (as in the novel). Sandler particularly relished the opportunity to increase the cattiness of the dialogue between stars Lola Brewster and Marina Gregg-Rudd; Hales offered 'After such a long lay off! It's bound to seem strange', but Sandler added more bitchy dialogue, such as 'Chin up, darling… both of them.' Hales had also opted to make the final death a murder (which Miss Marple doesn't criticise), as had been alluded to in the original novel.[4] Both versions of the script also included a scene in which the photographer Margot Bence confesses that she is the abandoned adopted daughter of Marina Gregg; this relationship was in the original novel but ended up being cut from the final film.

In February 1980 it was announced that Natalie Wood was to join the film, playing Marina, but apparent scheduling conflicts (or, some claim, a disagreement over star billing) meant that, by the end of March, she had been replaced by Elizabeth Taylor, who hadn't made a picture for several years, and hadn't had a hit for several more.[5] Other cast members were also announced, including Tony Curtis, Kim Novak, Edward Fox and Rock Hudson. Filming then began in May 1980, and continued for ten weeks. Locations included the Kent village of Smarden, which was paid £4,000 for the inconvenience of a film crew turning the metaphorical clock back to 1953 (making the movie more of a period piece than the novel). This included the painting out of street lines, but the local publican was particularly happy to see the increase in trade from stars and technicians alike. 'I love a good pint of draught beer in a pub and maybe a cold plate of beef or ham round the bar,' claimed Rock Hudson. 'The British are always so polite.'[6] Originally several members of the cast had stated that they wished to stay locally during filming, although once the lack of amenities became clear most then opted to commute from the Savoy in London instead. One exception was Novak, who 'rode her bicycle everywhere and lived on apples'.[7]

The shoot went smoothly, although the filming of the fête sequences were delayed by eight days due to unseasonably poor weather, and Elizabeth Taylor (famously late to film sets) traded efficient performances that kept the film on schedule for gifts from the producers, including a designer coat and antique clock.[8] The film was budgeted at $6.5m, but surprisingly cost a little less once production wrapped. This was not a large amount of money for Hollywood; in fact, in real terms it was only half of what had been spent on *Death on the Nile* two years earlier. This was a deliberate strategy on the part of the producers, who wished to reduce the costs of the Christie adaptations. 'The budget is not colossal, and when you see what's up on the screen, I think it's a bargain,' stated Goodwin,

The French poster used the Tom Adams book cover – and misspelt 'Landsbury'.

although some critics felt it was a false economy given the appeal of the international settings of the Poirot films.[9] The desire to reduce budgets (following a period of considerable inflation in Britain) probably explains why this story, based firmly in the South East of England, was preferred over the exotic destination required for *A Caribbean Mystery*.

Guy Hamilton was selected to direct, a role that he would retain for the next Poirot film *Evil Under the Sun*, in 1982. Probably best-known for his work on the action-packed James Bond films, including *Goldfinger* (1964), the choice raised some eyebrows, but Goodwin pointed out that 'Guy is a magnificent technician, and with this sort of film, that's exactly

The US film poster highlighting the film's starry cast..

the kind of director you need … With a complicated narrative, he's got to know how the scenes relate to each other.'[10] Others on the production thought that he was probably selected because of his long-established career as a director, which would put some of the bigger stars at ease. Certainly, Hamilton didn't take part due to any particular love of the material. 'On the face of it, it's not the sort of film I'd go and see,' he told one interviewer, while informing others that he didn't enjoy Agatha Christie books, but was attracted by the humour in the (revised) script.[11] Several cast members were similarly critical of Christie when speaking to the press, giving the general impression that nobody was particularly excited by the production: 'Christie to me is too predictable even if you don't know who the murderer is,' grumbled Tony Curtis to a local newspaper.[12] Taylor admitted that she signed up to the film because it only needed her for six weeks. While she enjoyed Christie's oeuvre more than Curtis, she didn't seem to particularly care for this mystery: 'It also happens that I adore detective stories,' she told *The Times*. 'Richard [Burton] and I used to read them in bed: we had a copy each and when we got to page fifty or thereabouts we both wrote down the name of the murderer. I'm glad to say that I invariably beat him, which drove him mad. I remember reading *The Mirror Crack'd* when it first came out in 1962. OK, so perhaps I agree with you that it wasn't one of the best Agatha Christies, but it has possibilities. Maybe the film is better than the book.'[13] Nevertheless, Taylor was happy to play Marina: 'My part is wonderful in its diversity. It has humour, pathos, chewing up the scenery – an actor's dream in one small part.'[14]

One thing that all involved were curious about was how Lansbury would play Miss Marple, especially given how memorable Margaret Rutherford's performance had been. The *Guardian* even called their article on the making of film 'The exorcism of Miss Rutherford', in which Richard Roud argued that the problem with Christie films is that 'their makers don't believe in them. They think of them as enjoyable rubbish … Miss Christie's world may be artificial, limited, implausible, but she, I am sure, believed every word she wrote, and the result is that we do too.'[15] For Guy Hamilton, 'Margaret Rutherford was a divine clown but no more Miss Marple than flying to the moon', while Angela Lansbury confessed to not seeing Rutherford play the part, although she was aware of her interpretation.[16] 'Miss Marple was a quiet, still person, not at all the figure of fun that Margaret Rutherford made her,' Lansbury argued. 'She really was an Edwardian maiden lady. You know, rather proper. I don't want to say that she's a bit of a snob. But she was, really. I didn't want to play her in that way so I've made her a broad-minded, extraordinarily perceptive and subtle person.'[17] Lansbury was aware that concerns over Rutherford's portrayal made the custodians of her estate extra sensitive about the character being played straight and

Angela Lansbury in her 'old age' make-up on location in the village of Wrotham.

confessed that 'I would have enjoyed making Miss Marple a little more batty myself, but Agatha Christie didn't necessarily approve of that.'[18]

Lansbury was fifty-four years old during filming, but aged up for the part: 'I look exactly as I shall when I'm 70,' she claimed, although in truth she would look rather better, especially given the unconvincing grey wig she dons for the movie.[19] When offered the part, Lansbury claimed that she 'nearly fell off the end of the phone – I really was amazed – in the first place that they'd thought of me, and in the second place because it happened to be something I'd thought perhaps one day I might play. I just felt that as a character she would be pretty good for me to latch on to.'[20] Lansbury acknowledged that she struggled to always find the best way to play the sleuth. For her, 'I certainly want to suggest that Miss Marple has a very eager mind and that she has an understanding of humanity based on a detailed knowledge of her own village, St Mary Mead. I've also made one or two very tiny changes from the book in order to try and heighten the character: for instance, she now does crossword puzzles all the time instead of knitting.' In terms of her costume, Lansbury was keen to make it old-fashioned, but 'I had to abandon the idea of wearing a stiff whalebone corset for the sake of her posture because you could see it sticking through the costume like some prehistoric animal's rib-cage.' Most controversially, Lansbury insisted on her own character touch: 'I also thought it would be helpful if she did one particular thing while she was thinking so that the audience would always know the old grey cells were ticking over,' she said, referencing Poirot. 'I felt that, as an Edwardian woman, she would do what my own grandmother did and always smoke a cigarette after dinner ... I did it during tests but no one liked it. Even Agatha Christie's daughter said: "I hope you're not going to smoke – Miss Marple would never do that!" I know they're all wrong, so I'm desperately searching for some other signal to let everyone know I'm thinking.'[21]

Although Lansbury enjoyed taking part in the production, she wasn't happy with the final film; her official biography claims that the star found it unwatchable, although she seemed to warm to it in later years.[22] One of the problems with the film is its lack of atmosphere, not helped by the placing of the story in 1953, which means that it doesn't acknowledge the creeping modernity that underpins the original novel. The result is a straightforward but somewhat flat interpretation of a good mystery, which pales in comparison to the surrounding Poirot pictures, and much of the blame must be laid at the door of director Guy Hamilton. The opening spoof of an old whodunnit could only really work if the movie that follows was markedly more fresh and exciting; as it is, it reads as an unintentional lampooning of itself.

A Hungarian edition, which focused on the Hollywood stars rather than Miss Marple (1998).

Despite being a great actor, Lansbury never truly seems to be comfortable playing the part of

Miss Marple. She isn't present often enough to feel important (she doesn't even get to speak to Elizabeth Taylor) and isn't allowed to shine, while she is also hampered by her poor 'old age' make-up. The whole film feels mannered and unreal, while Hamilton doesn't display any flair for humour, even when assisted by the likes of Kim Novak camping it up wherever possible. Despite being only 105 minutes long, the film drags, and misses the chance to tell a genuinely engaging story that taps into the psychology of an impulsive and emotional murderer with a fascinating backstory.

Lansbury suggested that 'People are getting sick of gratuitous violence. They want a return to law and order.'[23] Nevertheless, having first been released in the United States in December 1980, when it appeared in the UK in February 1981 the film was often reviewed alongside the British gangster movie *The Long Good Friday*, which did rather better with critics and audiences.

'*Murder in the Mirror or Stupidity is Dangerous*': Scherz's edition from 1980 included the book's full German title – and a photo from *Death on the Nile*.

There was another Royal Gala Premiere, with the Queen and the Duke of Edinburgh in attendance; the charity event raised £45,000, and attendees received a programme and menu printed on reflective 'mirror' paper. There was a great deal of tie-in publicity, which included a hugely condensed retelling of the story in *Woman's Own*, which reduced the entire plot (including solution) to a mere five pages.[24]

A few critics were kind about the film: *Variety* thought it was a 'worthy if more leisurely successor' to the Poirot films, while another critic called it 'a first-rate Miss Marple outing and a delightfully entertaining film for any season', and *Time* felt that 'the good lines make *Mirror* more fun to watch than it has any right to be'.[25] Others did not hold back from their criticism. 'As a film, if truth be told, it's mostly awful, but it also has an awful fascination,' stated the *Financial Times*: 'For all its over-dressing it's a yawning, ludicrous void of a film'.[26] Others seemed shocked by the lacklustre direction, with Hamilton criticised as 'uninspired', with the result of a 'stale-looking old-fashioned movie', while one was so surprised by his 'sluggish' direction that they wondered if a reel was missing at the end, when the movie reaches an abrupt climax.[27] For Douglas Slater in *Film Illustrated*, the movie was 'an uneasy compromise between the '30s of the previous films and the '60s of the book … [1953] is an almost impossible period, since it doesn't have a definite style. The costumes are left looking tacky rather than glamorous.' Slater also took issue with the dialogue and music, stating that: 'These cumulative failures on points of detail detract from the atmosphere the film should create, the quality of which should make it as watchable as Agatha Christie is readable.'[28] In summary, the *Daily Express* bemoaned that 'It all seems a waste of time and talent.'[29]

Although the film performed reasonably well in some markets, the American box office of $11m was cited as a disappointment in the press.[30] Nevertheless, as late as summer 1981 there were still plans for another Miss Marple movie. Lansbury had signed a three-picture deal, with the idea that they would alternate with Poirot adaptations. The plan had been that Lansbury would film *At Bertram's Hotel* after appearing in a new Stephen Sondheim stage musical production of *Sunset Boulevard*; neither happened.[31] However, Lansbury would soon be solving mysteries again on screen, but this time on television. Despite insisting that 'I wouldn't want to be known as Miss Marple. I wouldn't want to be known as anything,' her characterisation of Jessica Fletcher in the CBS series *Murder, She Wrote* (1984–96) would soon become intrinsically linked with the actor, as the series succeeded where *The Mirror Crack'd* had failed.[32]

Helen Hayes as Miss Marple
(Two Television Movies, 1983 & 1985)

In the late 1970s, Rosalind Hicks informed the Agatha Christie Ltd board that she felt that the time had come for them to take television more seriously. Historically, the company (and Rosalind personally) had been suspicious of the medium, and repeatedly declined requests for small screen adaptations of Christie's works, including proposed Miss Marple series in both Britain and the United States earlier in the decade. The success of the *Murder on the Orient Express* film and a keenness to continue the visibility of Christie's works after her death contributed to the decision to engage with promising producers. In America it was Warner Bros who entered into a discussion with Agatha Christie Ltd, and in late 1977 it was claimed that they would be making Miss Marple adaptations

ABOVE: Helen Hayes as Miss Marple in *Murder with Mirrors* (1985).

for network television, starring Helen Hayes, the first lady of American theatre. According to one newspaper report, Rosalind told producers that 'There is one actress in America who can play Miss Marple – Helen Hayes', although if this were ever the case then her opinion was to change.[33]

Under the guidance of Alan Shayne, the President of Warner Bros Television, the company began making Christie adaptations for CBS in 1982, with a production of the 1939 standalone mystery *Murder is Easy*. Like all the Christie television films made for the company, this adaptation moved the action to the then-present day and cast American actors alongside their British counterparts. Notably, this included Helen Hayes in a small but important role, playing a character not unlike Miss Marple. Although it had taken years to agree that a Miss Marple novel could be adapted by the company, Hayes was still in the frame when a title was finally selected: *A Caribbean Mystery*. A first draft of the script was delivered on 1 August 1982, written by married couple Sue Grafton (author of the popular 'alphabet series' of crime novels) and Steve Humphrey. The script retained the core elements of the

Maurice Evans as Major Palgrave (1983).

Barnard Hughes as Mr
Rafiel (1983).

story, with some omissions (such as the Major's glass eye) that simplified the story and production, which was essential given the tight schedule of just three weeks for filming. In the revised draft some of Miss Marple's characterisation was subtly changed; originally she was first seen as a nervous passenger in a taxi, but in the final version she is introduced as a mean tipper at the end of her journey from the airport.

Production took place not in the Caribbean but in Santa Barbara, California, where the weather was not always kind thanks to intermittent downpours and chilly temperatures that meant some of its actors made use of thermal clothing where possible. The script was adapted to the location as needed, with filming helmed by Robert Michael Lewis, an experienced TV movie director who also worked on a non-Marple adaptation, *Sparkling Cyanide*, the same year. Hayes was initially concerned about the amount of dialogue she was required to learn but, as a fan of Christie's work, insisted that Miss Marple was a part that she had always wanted to play. Nevertheless, she was acutely aware that there was already a Miss Marple screen legacy to contend with: 'as for Margaret [Rutherford], I adored her,' she told one newspaper. 'I rolled in the aisles watching her. The thought of following in her amazing footsteps terrifies me. And I wouldn't even go to see Angela [Lansbury] – I don't want to be haunted by her.'[34] Hayes was joined by some familiar faces from the world of television and film, including Barnard Hughes as Mr Rafiel and Jameson Parker as Tim Kendall, while British actor Maurice Evans played the part of Major Palgrave.[35]

The finished production never quite escapes the sense that it is being pulled in different directions, with the lure of the Agatha Christie name (and her plotting) not always complemented by a cast of variable effectiveness. Key characters are depicted as young and somewhat brash, with their characterisations sometimes veering into obnoxiousness through performances. The mystery unfolds in a sedate manner, as characters get to know each other via a trip to a local market and suchlike, before heading towards an abrupt climax, where there is also a hint of romance for Miss Marple (another character moment added after the first draft of the script). The production's star performer is one of the best indications of the film's uneasy compromises, with Hayes adopting an accent that is somewhat mid-Atlantic: 'I hope I won't offend anyone by not sounding very English,' she said.[36] There is also the issue of the location, as all the stock footage and steel-drum bands in the world cannot give a true sense of the Caribbean when shot elsewhere. This isn't helped by the direction, which is never dynamic and occasionally ill-judged, notably with an awkward 'freeze frame' of the key characters. Hayes is an amiable presence and presents Miss Marple as someone we might like to spend time with, even when she has to endure a 1980s makeover for her hair in order to track down more clues. As a detective, she can sometimes seem weak (notably when confessing that she has no idea who the next victim will be), but at least Miss Marple is a more prominent part of the mystery than in *The Mirror Crack'd*.

When Rosalind Hicks saw the final film, she was not impressed, especially as she had been assured by Alan Shayne that Miss Marple would be as English as possible. One example was Miss Marple's exclamation of 'Oh, my!', which Rosalind considered to be an American turn of phrase ('Oh, dear!' was her suggested replacement), while she also ensured that Miss Marple would certainly not wear trousers, as seemed to be an early suggestion. Americanisms aside, for Rosalind the 'biggest disappointment' in the film was Helen Hayes:

I know she is a bit old but she is a good actress. I felt she could have put a bit more sparkle into the character. She was quite frankly dull and also very American. You promised me that you would take some notice of my criticisms of the American phrases in your script like … Mailing a letter (we post it), things like that, but nothing was done at all. I do believe that Miss Marple should be English! … It was a good story and the plot was all there but I'm afraid it seemed dull.[37]

Shayne did not agree, feeling that both Rosalind and Mathew wanted 'an old, rather fey, maiden aunt rather than a feisty, strong, capable woman like Helen', and he far preferred the 'feisty' Hayes. 'They got their way in a long series that was

Romancing the mystery – a CBS advertisement for its TV premiere (1983).

done in England,' he noted later, 'but I found Joan Hickson not as interesting playing Miss Marple as Helen was.'[38]

Critically, *A Caribbean Mystery* was fairly well-received upon its CBS transmission on 22 October 1983. The *New York Times* noted that, rather than Rutherford's 'determined dottiness', Hayes imbued Miss Marple with 'gentle perkiness' in a production that 'has its engaging moments'.[39] The *Philadelphia Inquirer* judged that '*A Caribbean Mystery* is full of false leads and red herrings. But Hayes is such a charmer you may not mind. She could probably read a telephone book and draw a sizable crowd.'[40] Certainly, Hayes had added a stamp of quality to the television film that audiences seemed to find irresistible, as it did much better in the ratings than anyone had expected; even against the stiff opposition of *The Love Boat*, it managed to rank as the twenty-ninth most watched programme of the week on American television. CBS were delighted and immediately wanted more, so Alan Shayne called Mathew with what he thought was good news:

Shayne rang up and said 'We're in the money, Mathew, CBS want to sign up for sixty one-hour versions of Miss Marple on American network television!' ... I said to him, 'Hang on Alan, there aren't sixty Miss Marple stories.' He said, 'Oh, don't worry about that, we'll invent our own!' And I said look, we don't do that. He said, 'You're not serious?' and I said yes, I am. And he said 'well, can I come over and talk to you about it?' ... Anyway he did come over, and we did talk and he presented his case. All of us actually, not only my mother, were adamant that this was not the way we wished to go ... Literally, within a few months, *Murder, She Wrote* appeared ...[41]

However, this was not the end for Miss Marple on American television. Although Rosalind was not happy to

Helen Hayes with John Mills as Lewis Serrocold and Bette Davis as Carrie Louise (1983).

license a further Miss Marple novel to Warner Bros, this was not entirely within her control, thanks to her mother's generous gift three decades earlier. 'My mother got quite angry with me because I owned *They Do It with Mirrors* and I sold that to Alan,' remembers Mathew Prichard. 'As far as I remember I wanted to buy quite an expensive sculpture at the time!'[42] And so it was that Helen Hayes returned to the role for a second (and final) time in a production that used the American title of the novel, *Murder with Mirrors*.

Perhaps mindful of Rosalind's criticisms of creeping Americanisms in *A Caribbean Mystery*, *Murder with Mirrors* is a far more British affair. Not only is it set and filmed in England, but the cast is populated by an excellent array of well-known British actors, including the likes of Leo McKern,

John Mills and Frances de la Tour. The production, adapted by George Eckstein and directed by Dick Lowry, makes great use of its British locations, thanks to the fact that it was financially advantageous to film in the country. Viewers are treated to key tourist shots, from Trafalgar Square and the Houses of Parliament to Harrods. The script itself makes some sensible changes, including making Miss Marple friends with the murder victim, although it loses a sense of the geography of Stonygates (Brocket Hall in Hertfordshire), which is important to the solving of the crime in the book, and an essential element of the misdirection core to the mystery. The production also adds a rather over-the-top crashing of a car (which then explodes), which is the sort of action sequence that was almost a requirement of American network dramas at the time. Hayes's accent is even more eccentric than in *A Caribbean Mystery*, but she commands the screen and is more ably supported by the rest of the cast this time. At one point she even performs lines from *Macbeth* on stage, in a scene more fitting for the actor than Miss Marple. The production also saw the return of composer Richard Rodney Bennett to the world of Agatha Christie, following his exemplary work on *Murder on the Orient Express*.

The most notable coup for the production was in its casting of film legend Bette Davis as Miss Marple's old friend Carrie Louise. Alan Shayne had been encouraged to offer the part to Davis, but immediately tried to get out of the casting when he not only saw how ill she was (she was recovering from both a stroke and a mastectomy), but also discovered how difficult she could be on set. Shayne begged Davis's agent to allow him to release her from the picture, but to no avail. Davis claimed that the script was 'the first film of any intelligence that has come my way in some time', and that 'my life would have no meaning if I didn't work. It keeps me going. Aside from my grandchildren, of course, working is my life. I may tell

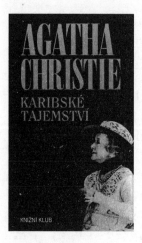

Ironically, Bette Davis found her way on to this Czech reprint of *A Caribbean Mystery* in 1995 as Miss Marple, using a still from *Death on the Nile*.

you that it was scary not working for so long.'[43] Davis initially stated that she would not play the part of an unwell woman, until she was quietly reminded of her (financial) need to work. The production did its best to help, including shooting Davis as sympathetically as possible, but her illness was so apparent that a line explaining her appearance was dubbed in later. The script was also tweaked, giving some of the character's dialogue to other actors. Davis was unimpressed. 'Am not over the shock of my best scene being cut plus my lines given to McKern plus some to Miss Hayes!!' she wrote to Shayne, in a letter signed off with a smiley face. 'Didn't she have enough?'[44]

Although Helen Hayes was a highly respected actor who was, by all accounts, both professional and kind on set, Davis did not wish to make any friends during filming. In his autobiography, Shayne recalled that on the first day Hayes greeted Davis with 'How are you Bette? I'm so glad we are working together.' Davis was unmoved. 'Look,' she said, 'We're going to be here for days, and there's no point wasting our breath saying "Hello" and "How are you?" every time we see each other. Let's just do our work.' According to Shayne, 'To my knowledge, the two ladies never spoke again.'[45] The two stars of stage and screen were required to do a joint interview, but even then Davis did not speak to Hayes, and seemed to give answers that were deliberately prickly. While Hayes gushed in appreciation of Christie's works (claiming to have read all her novels), Davis was unmoved. 'I don't read them. I don't do them,' she said, referring to the mystery genre generally, before being reminded that she did 'do' a mystery in *Death on the Nile* seven years earlier.[46] Hayes remained gracious in response, happily telling reporters stories that cast Davis in a positive light, such as when she apparently completed a lengthy scene in one take, telling the crew that 'If you want a thing well done, get a couple of old broads to do it.'[47] For Hayes, this was to be her final film role and having read the original novel, she expected light work, as 'Miss Marple doesn't have all that much to do'; she then discovered that her role had been expanded during scripting: 'it's taking too much out of me at eighty-four,' she confessed.[48]

Broadcast on 20 February 1985, *Murder with Mirrors* found some success and performed reasonably well in the ratings, although the press seemed to be tiring a little of the recent Agatha Christie productions. 'Red herrings fly in all directions, but the going was more than a little talky and a little bit stodgy in the early parts,' stated *Variety*: 'In print, Christie seems to maintain her hold on readers; on tv, it seems to get increasingly harder to shuck the old-fashioned feeling while doing an adaptation of a Christie script.'[49] The casting was the main talking point, with kind references to Davis's frailty from some, with the *New York Times* noting the casting as a highlight as it claimed that 'the quality of the production is rather exceptional'.[50] Some reviews also alluded to another production, which had the potential to steal the thunder of these American TV movies; on the other side of the Atlantic, Joan Hickson's Miss Marple had arrived ...

Joan Hickson in
Agatha Christie's Miss Marple
(Television Series, 1984–92)

The possibility of the BBC making a Miss Marple television series first surfaced in the early 1970s. In 1970, the corporation approached Christie's agents at Hughes Massie with the possibility of adapting thirteen of her stories for the screen, which may or may not have included Hercule Poirot, Miss Marple, or any of her other running detectives. The request was firmly declined, as Christie was 'anti-TV' and not interested in giving the BBC the rights for any dramatisations.[51] Four years later, producer Pieter Rogers tried again, suggesting that Barbara Mullen was now the right age to play Miss

ABOVE: Joan Hickson as Miss Marple. According to various obituaries, her fellow-actors would come to refer to her as 'justice in a hand-knitted cardigan'.

Marple on screen (having recently reprised the part in the stage revival of *Murder at the Vicarage*), and he requested a meeting with the author to discuss the possibility, promising 'all the care the BBC could bestow upon the production'.[52] Privately, Rogers was not optimistic, and indeed nothing came of the approach. Christie made her opinions about television clear when writing to Edmund Cork that 'my books are written as books and I do not relish the idea of adapting them to television'.[53]

By the early 1980s, things were different, as, following Christie's death, there had been tentative movements into the world of adaptations on British television. A handful appeared on ITV, the country's only commercial broadcaster at the time. These included *Why Didn't They Ask Evans?* in 1980, followed by *The Seven Dials Mystery* (1981), *The Agatha Christie Hour* (1982, adapting various short stories) and Tommy and Tuppence in *Partners in Crime* (1983-4). These adaptations stuck closely to the original texts, which meant that Rosalind Hicks started to feel reassured that television could adequately present her mother's works for audiences. She was also keen that no producer should feel that they had a monopoly on a character, and so while she had permitted adaptations of later Miss Marple novels for the productions starring Angela Lansbury and Helen Hayes, she kept the earlier stories in reserve for a potential British series. In early 1983 Brian Stone, the Christie estate's agent, contacted the BBC to see if they were interested in making a ten-part Miss Marple series, which would constitute three novels (each in two parts) and four short stories, with Agatha Christie Ltd as co-producer (a role that they did not adopt in the end). The BBC were very keen, and it fell to David Reid, Head of Series and Serials, to assign a producer to the programme. Guy Slater had recent experience with period dramas, having produced the first two seasons of *Nanny* (1981-2), set in the 1930s, but initially he was not particularly excited by the prospect of producing a Miss Marple series. However, upon re-reading some of Christie's work, he changed his mind. Slater recalls his realisation that 'actually she's bloody clever. These are extraordinary stories, the range of her imagination was fantastic. And they were dark; underneath the narrative, there were characters who were very twisted and had backgrounds and histories.'[54]

Slater was unimpressed with some of what he had seen of the recent television adaptations: 'I thought these are just the producers and directors saying, gosh, aren't we clever? Let's take the piss out of Christie, and it didn't seem to be the right way to approach it.' Along with David Reid, he went to dinner with Rosalind and Anthony Hicks and found that they got on well: 'She was a stubborn lady, but I grew to love her and Anthony, who made me laugh so much.' These good relations would continue throughout the production, perhaps in part because although the series had a prestigious air with excellent attention to detail, the stories and characters remained the most important elements. Mathew Prichard had recently bemoaned that television companies were using Christie's stories as vehicles for period visuals, rather than focusing on the mysteries; he wondered if viewers of *Partners in Crime* remembered Tuppence's hats more than the plots. Slater's interest in the characters and stories of Christie therefore chimed with the thinking of her family. A rare occasion when Slater could not agree with Rosalind concerned philosophy and human nature rather than any practicalities. 'The debate that Rosalind and I had was about her mother's conviction that there is a primal evil force and *my* profound belief that that we're born as people and that evil is inculcated,' says Slater. 'In other words, that it's nurture rather than nature. Of course, Miss Marple has a profound sense of ethics and morality, but she also seems to understand what leads people to darkness.'

With the preparation of a new series came the all-important question of casting. Slater had been thinking of a particular actor with whom he had worked on *Nanny*: Celia Johnson, probably best known for her leading role in David Lean's *Brief Encounter* in 1945. 'There was great charm in her,' he remembers, while also acknowledging the draw of a known name starring in the series. Johnson died suddenly in April 1982, which was more than a year before formal discussions began between Agatha Christie Ltd and the BBC, indicating that there had been thoughts about the series for some time. Slater's next choice was another person who had appeared in *Nanny*: Joan Hickson.[55] David Reid was initially unsure, as Hickson wasn't a household name, but came around to the suggestion and agreed that Slater could offer her the role. 'Oh, I couldn't possibly do it,' she told Slater when he called her with the idea, 'I wouldn't know how to begin to do it!' Nevertheless, she was soon convinced, and in August 1983 Slater wrote to Rosalind to pass on the news that 'Miss Marple addict' Hickson was free and interested. He also took the opportunity to outline his intentions for the series while some final contractual issues were ironed out:

I do, I think, have some idea how important Miss Marple is to you and I would only say that when/if we get the go ahead I can promise you two things. Firstly I will aim for perfection: and secondly I will consult you all along the line. I cannot promise that everything you want can be done but will give my word that it will be taken very seriously and that I will make every effort to accommodate you.[56]

For the first series of Miss Marple, it was agreed that the BBC would adapt *The Body in the Library*, *The Moving Finger* and *A Murder is Announced*, all quintessential Miss Marple titles. It had already been decided not to adapt short stories after all, at least initially, and Slater remembers that 'Rosalind sent me [*The Thirteen Problems*] and said you can have the rights to all these. She was very sweet to, but I really thought they were too thin for an hour.' As it happened, German television was interested in the Miss Marple short stories in 1983, although plans didn't get very far.[57] Mathew Prichard recalls that initially his mother was not keen to offer a fourth novel to the BBC, which resulted in them opting for *A Pocket Full of Rye* instead, as the rights were not owned by Agatha Christie Ltd at the time.[58] Because of its different ownership, the inclusion of *Rye* in the series created difficulties for the company as it meant that any sales of the series would need to have payments split in a complicated manner. As a result, Slater was offered *The Murder at the Vicarage*, *4.50 from Paddington* or *Sleeping Murder* as alternatives. Slater decided to stick with *Rye*, and the lawyers simply had to deal with the resulting paperwork.[59] By October 1983 a deal was drawn up and signed, granting the BBC the rights to

Original art from the iconic title sequence by Paul Birkbeck.

adapt the four novels, with a healthy budget of £350,000 per episode.[60] Funding was supplemented by the Seven Network in Australia and the Arts and Entertainment Network (A&E) in the United States, who were credited as co-producers. Seven Network had no creative input, while A&E gave some feedback but were not heavily involved; for the most part, the co-producers simply provided early funding in return for some domestic distribution rights and on-screen credits.

The first writer to be approached by Slater was Trevor Bowen, who had scripted two episodes of *The Agatha Christie Hour* in 1982 and was an old friend of the producer. Bowen remembers that at the time the screen image of Miss Marple was 'dominated by this image of Margaret Rutherford', whose 'character overwhelmed the interest in the actual story'.[61] He was therefore very pleased to learn that Slater told him that 'we're trying to do it by taking this text seriously, as literature ... I thought that was a very good idea.' Bowen was especially thrilled to learn that Joan Hickson had been cast in the part: 'I remember thinking quite distinctly "I think this is going to last rather a long time, you know." And so it turned out!' For the first series, Bowen scripted the opening mystery *The Body in the Library*, and the closing adaptation of *A Pocket Full of Rye*. The former was in three episodes of around 55 minutes each, while the latter was two episodes, and both producer and writer agree that the shorter length was generally better. 'We were indulging ourselves, I think,' remembers Bowen, while Slater concedes that 'they could all have come in on two', but remembers that, at the time, audiences expected a slower pace. There was also the significant issue that the series was expected to adhere closely to Christie's original novels, and scripts were being inspected closely by Rosalind in particular. This wasn't without precedent; in 1983, ITV's adaptation of P. D. James's novel *Death of an Expert Witness* ran for seven hour-long episodes (including commercials), making *The*

Fontana's *The Body in the Library* cover (1985).

Body in the Library seem positively zippy by comparison. James's novels were often substantially longer than Christie's, but both series indicated a new desire to treat crime fiction with the respect afforded to other literary adaptations.

When Rosalind received Bowen's script, she was initially quite critical, more because of its tone and small details than its overall construction, although she also felt that 'there are far too many policemen!'[62] This was an early indication that Rosalind was happy for the series to deviate from the source material when needed, as the abundance of policemen was a fault of the original novel, not the new script. She suggested removing Sir Henry Clithering from proceedings and recommended further deviations from the novel in order to reduce the cast of characters and show a closer adherence to police procedure ('It can't be necessary to have four policemen to arrest Basil Blake'). Rosalind was also concerned that Colonel Bantry was made to look foolish rather than sympathetic, and then listed issues with the dialogue and other points throughout the script, from questions of how people addressed and knew each other ('If you must have Sir Henry Clithering too he does know Miss Marple and she knows him, they wouldn't ignore each other'), to the practicalities of day-to-day life ('Mrs Bantry would certainly not knock on her husband's door'), which showed her excellent grasp of character and logistics. Slater replied, agreeing with some points, which resulted in changes to the rehearsal scripts; this included removing an early dream sequence as well as brief appearances from Miss Wetherby and Miss Hartnell gossiping about the murder, and having Dolly rather than her husband call in Miss Marple. A firm but cordial system of discussions had been successfully established.

Director Silvio Narizzano was assigned to *The Body in the Library*; for both practical and stylistic reasons, it was decided to give each adaptation its own director, as the schedules were long, and there was a desire to make each adaptation feel distinctive, rather than having a restrictive 'house style'. Narizzano was best known for the films *Georgy Girl* (1966) and Joe Orton's *Loot* (1970), both of which were strongly situated in the then-present day, showcasing both the swinging and seedy sixties. 'I think Silvio directed it rather like a movie, and it had a kind of darkness that that the others didn't,' remembers actor David Horovitch. Horovitch had called his friend Guy Slater to enquire if there were any parts suitable for him in the new Miss Marple series, only to be told that he'd already been cast as Detective Inspector Slack, who would reappear four more times across the series. Slater himself recalls that Narizzano was a 'deft, cheeky subversive director', with 'a great sense of style'.

The new series, and Hickson's casting, was announced to the press in March 1984, and filming commenced on 25 May following rehearsals. Shooting began at the 'Majestic Hotel', represented by Bournemouth's Royal Bath and Marriott Highcliffe hotels, with interiors shot at the former, and exteriors at the latter.[63] Among the cast members assembled was Horovitch, who remembers the series being 'terrific fun from beginning to end'. For him, working with Joan Hickson was a highlight of the series, although she had concerns over playing a leading role in her late seventies. Slater recalls Hickson's repeated refrain of 'Send me to Denville Hall!' whenever she lost confidence, referring to the performers' retirement home. Horovitch remembers the first day of filming: 'She was terribly, terribly nervous, and remained nervous really, throughout the whole thing. "I can't do this, I don't know why I'm doing this …" And then, as soon as the camera rolled, she was absolutely wonderful.'[64] Hickson was aware of the screen legacy of Miss Marple, and insisted that 'I am anxious not to send her up on any way, but to play her straight.' For Hickson, Miss Marple was 'multi-faceted – shrewd, unobtrusive, extremely determined, and full of surprises.' Although the star name in the series, she did not want the character to dominate the screen, preferring to depict Miss Marple 'not as hurtling along with the action of the plot, but rather as watching, listening, waiting and picking up clues that the experts from the Yard fail to spot'.[65] Rosalind came along to the set to see some of the filming, and assured Slater that 'I liked Joan Hickson. She had a good voice and expression and I'm sure she will make a great success of Miss Marple.'[66]

It was decided to set the series at some non-specific point in the late 1940s for this first set of adaptations, and the tone was set by the title sequence drawn by Paul Birkbeck, which depicted sinister corners of superficially cosy village

Another beautiful drawing from Paul Birkbeck's title sequence.

life. Slater's intention was to show 'an idyllic English village bathed in sunshine – a cloud goes across the sun and the village suddenly appears malevolent, frightening'.[67] The effect was enhanced by Ken Howard and Alan Blaikley's memorable score, which switches from bombastic to disconcerting as the pictures hint at darkness.

This first adaptation's excellent cast includes Gwen Watford as Dolly Bantry, while even smaller roles are filled with notable and recognisable names, such as Valentine Dyall as Lorrimer the butler. It's notable that although the series takes the subject matter seriously, there is still plenty of humour, neatly established by the Bantrys' conversations in bed early in the episode. Narizzano also made visually striking directorial choices: for example, Miss Marple contemplating the case while on a funicular is an unscripted relocation. The overall impression is one of confidence, not only in the work of the cast and crew, but also in the original material. The story is allowed to speak for itself, and this includes some of the more practical issues with the crime, which are presented as written. The explanation of how the dead body arrived at Gossington Hall is shown as a flashback, but one member of the BBC's Programme Weekly Review Board wondered if a dramatisation of the murder itself should have been supplied. For writer Bowen, this was a deliberate choice, as he preferred the closing conversations to speak for themselves: 'I distrust flashbacks greatly, it strikes me that you haven't plotted it right if you get too many of them.' Guy Slater confesses that, for him, 'It didn't occur to me ... damn it, I want to go and do it again!'

The Body in the Library was extremely well received by most critics when transmitted across three consecutive nights from 26 December 1984. *The Listener* declared it 'all quite preposterously,

The figure in the window...

impossibly enjoyable', while the *New York Times* claimed that 'Once hooked, you won't be able to turn it off', particularly commending the cast.[68] Complaints were few, although elsewhere in *The Listener* Phil Hardy didn't seem to have been paying attention when he claimed that 'script and design combine to reinforce the empty *Dad's Army*-type nostalgia of Christie's original novel'.[69] The BBC's own feedback systems were positively effusive. One member of the corporation's weekly review board described it as 'the best Agatha Christie production he had seen', with others calling it 'first-class' while commending the director and writer along with Hickson.[70] Members of the public were quizzed for the BBC's Television Audience Research Report, and were just as positive, scoring it 78 out of 100 (above the average of 75 for British dramas), with particular praise for the production values and acting. The audience immediately took Hickson to their hearts, and even before transmission the *Radio Times* speculated that Hickson could become the 'definitive' Miss Marple, while over half of the panel gave her the highest possible rating, confirming the magazine's hunch.[71]

While *The Body in the Library* had been a largely straightforward affair, production of *The Moving Finger* was a little more troubled. Julia Jones was enlisted to adapt the novel, but the result was deemed unsatisfactory and the script was extensively reworked by director Roy Boulting, with input from Guy Slater. Due to the brevity of Miss Marple's appearance in the original story, her role was necessarily expanded, ensuring that she is local to Lymston (as Lymstock is renamed) for almost the duration of the mystery.[72] In contrast to Narizzano's background on the previous production, Boulting was very much of the old school. A well-known and respected name in British film, he and his twin brother, John, had produced and directed many of the country's classic films in earlier decades, perhaps most notably 1948's *Brighton Rock*, and their elder brother Sydney (aka Peter Cotes) was the first director of *The Mousetrap*. Slater had approached Boulting following what he called 'a lunatic brain wave', as they had worked together in the theatre, but it soon became clear that he wanted to direct on his own terms. 'I had to accept the brevity of the schedule,' Boulting told the *Radio Times*, '110 minutes in five weeks. Didn't do it, of course.' Slater remembers Boulting as 'quite a difficult man, but we became friends', and speaks warmly of the 'old-fashioned' but 'well shot' result. In a joint interview with his brother John, Roy stated

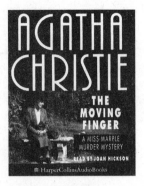

The Moving Finger didn't get a tie-in paperback, but in 1998 Joan Hickson read the book on cassette.

that he felt that 'skilled though [Christie's] writing is, the characters are stereotyped and the stories are written to a formula', but 'I enjoyed this as a challenge – either to divine the depths to which television can sink, or to scale the slopes on which one can ascend to greater glory.' His brother was more dismissive: 'Anyone who agrees to do Agatha Christie should be justifiably condemned.'[73] This was a particularly interesting argument given that, in 1954, the brothers had shown an interest in making a film of *The Mousetrap*.[74]

Roy Boulting's background in film perfectionism came at a cost. Donning a boiler suit throughout the production (apparently due to advice from the late British director Anthony Asquith), he would happily wait for the light to be exactly right. When reminded that the BBC did not have the flexibility nor the resources of the film industry, he simply asked his producer 'Are we doing this for you or for the accountants?' Inevitably, filming overran, and several scenes had to be cut to try to keep close to the schedule. The main casualty was a sequence in which Gerry and Megan go to London.[75] In the final episode, this is represented through a series of photographs, but they were scripted as full scenes, in which Gerry takes Megan to the hairdresser before he goes to the doctor ('Into your tender hands, I commit this unhappy creature!'), then they go clothes shopping at a department store and finally eat at a restaurant, having enjoyed 'a perfect day'. The loss of these scenes and some other trims resulted in shorter episodes than normal, partially covered by an extended reprise in the second part and a reshuffling of scenes, which moves the inquest to the end of the first episode rather than the beginning of the second. This alteration required a little dubbing in post-production to explain the new timeline, and results in the odd situation where Miss Marple is hanging around outside the Symmington house on the night of the inquest. As originally scripted and shot, this scene took place on the day of the murder.

Despite its production problems, *The Moving Finger* cements the strengths of the series. Humour is well-presented, mostly in the relationship between Miss Marple and Superintendent Nash (Geoffrey Davion), which allows the elderly sleuth to be neatly sarcastic. The script has Nash

A poster for the US release of the first series on PBS's Channel 13.

'staring unwaveringly at Miss Marple' as he 'considers the implications' of information that she has obtained from a key witness; 'Perhaps you never asked her?' she wonders in a lightly barbed manner. While he tries not to agree with Miss Marple's suggestion that he finds her irritating, his description of her as a 'nosy old bint' was scripted but did not make the final programme. This second *Miss Marple* proved that the series could convincingly and entertainingly present an almost entirely new cast of characters for each adaptation and ensure that the viewers were interested in what happened to them. Rosalind was pleased with the result: 'I enjoyed *The Moving*

Finger very much particularly as I know you felt it was the weakest one,' she wrote to Slater. 'I thought the script was good and it had a lot of humour and although I know Joan Hickson thought she looked untidy she was very good and brought out a lot of Miss Marple in a short time. I have to say that the policeman seemed a bit too grand this time but at least there was only one of them!'[76] Following its transmission on 21 and 22 February 1985, the BBC Programme Review Board thought it 'beautifully produced' and 'like a 1950s movie at its best'.[77] The audience's Appreciation Index rose to a high 81, with the first part being seen by 14.3 million people, and reviews consistently praised Joan Hickson. 'It would be hard to think of a British actress better equipped to assume this famous role,' argued Herbert Kretzmer of the *Daily Mail*.[78]

'I never thought he'd do an Agatha Christie,' says Guy Slater of Alan Plater, the respected screenwriter who adapted *A Murder is Announced* for the series. Plater was interested in the challenge and sent the producer a description of how he intended to break down the book by episodes, while also asking many questions of the production. This included when it would be set (Plater considered it important that it remained just postwar), and where it would likely be filmed. He also observed that Christie considered the middle classes to be an 'evil' and 'seedy' institution, while also providing excellent parts for women.[79] When breaking down the story, Plater noted its complexity, which he found to be a difficult but enjoyable challenge. He had to provide corrections to his own scripts as he wrestled with the plotting of the clues and acknowledged that it would be impossible to have Miss Marple become an impressionist at the story's conclusion, assuring Slater that he would find a better solution. For the screenwriter, it was important to focus on Miss Marple where possible, even though she hardly appears in the first of the three parts.

Fontana's *A Pocket Full of Rye* cover (1985).

Described in the script as 'swamped in knitting and a deep armchair', she is a presence from the beginning, subtly observing key events. One observation cut from the final episode, in which she notes that 'I suppose everything leaves a scar', neatly summarises some character motivations.

Initially, Rosalind was a little unsure about the scripts, as she was worried that it was 'too full of facetious remarks and jokes which are easy enough to play but can be distracting'.[80] She also wondered about the change of Mitzi's name to Hannah; Slater explained that it was felt that 'Mitzi' could sound comical, and indeed she is taken a little more seriously here than in both the novel and the earlier adaptation for the stage. Once Rosalind met director David Giles and saw the cast, she started to feel reassured. It is understandable that she might have been concerned that the script could be played for laughs, including moments where Miss Marple deliberately underplays her intelligence or even appears a little silly in order to find out more information. This is evident when she insists 'I've never seen a real bullet hole' in order to investigate the scene of the crime more fully. When played intelligently by Hickson, this moment simply reveals more of Miss Marple's understated cunning.

A Murder is Announced was filmed in two blocks, from 30 July to 25 August 1984 and then 3 to 28 September. Giles assembled an exemplary cast, including Ursula Howells as Miss Blacklock, with whom he had worked on the wildly successful television series *The Forsyte Saga* in 1967. Initially, another member of *The Forsyte Saga*'s cast had been pencilled in, Margaret Tyzack, but she would instead appear later, in *Nemesis*, while Martin Clunes was in contention for the part of Patrick Simmons, which went to Simon Shepherd. John

Castle took on the role of Detective Inspector Craddock, with a pre-*Inspector Morse* and *Lewis* Kevin Whately as Detective Sergeant Fletcher; Castle's Craddock is a serious and unemotional man with a twinkle in his eye. Even small parts such as waitress Myrna (Liz Crowther) are perfectly played and convincing as real characters, while the emotional gut-punch of the murder of Murgatroyd (Joan Sims) is reinforced by the strength of her relationship with Hinchcliffe (Paola Dionisotti), such as when she teases her about her recollections of the crime ('he certainly didn't say please!'). Unfortunately for Sims, the discovery of Hinchcliffe's body did not go according to plan when a 'stupid' Red Setter refused to take an interest in the actor lying on the wet ground, even when she was smeared with chicken liver paste.

One surprising incident concerning Joan Hickson occurred in the middle of filming, when her daughter discovered a long-forgotten letter in her attic. The letter was from one Agatha Christie in 1945, who had seen Hickson on stage and stated that she'd like 'you to play my "Miss Marple" one day'; Hickson was delighted to rediscover this unexpected vote of confidence.[81] Christie's instinct was excellent, as the British viewing public soon fell in love with her depiction of the character. Broadcast between 28 February and 2 March 1985, the Audience Reaction report summarised high praise for the serial, with an Appreciation Index of 87, the highest of any British television drama that week. As well as the cast, the respondents singled out the production's attention to detail as another high point; less than 5% of the panel had any negative comments to make at all. The BBC's own Programme Review Board felt that this was the best production yet, and warmly congratulated Guy Slater.[82] In the *Daily Mail*, reviewer Mary Kenny stated simply that 'They've committed the perfect crime series!'[83]

* * *

The final production in this first run of Miss Marple adapted the novel *A Pocket Full of Rye* (with the title tweaked to *A Pocketful of Rye*). For this adaptation, there was a change behind the scenes, as Guy Slater moved from being producer to director, with George Gallaccio (who had been production associate on the first three mysteries) becoming producer, working from a script by Trevor Bowen. Rosalind noted that the script was 'quite good – I know you were worried about it – Miss Marple comes out particularly well I think', but still offered a list of notes to Slater.[84] These included questions of dialogue ('Miss Marple would have said "meet her young man" not "meet her chap"'), as well as the mechanics of plotting alongside characterisation issues.[85] By now, the Agatha Christie Ltd board had seen *The Body in the Library* and were feeling enthusiastic about the series, much to the relief of all involved.

A Pocket Full of Rye is one of Christie's nursery rhyme murders, in which the rhyme provides a recurring motif and (usually) some link with the crimes committed. Slater's direction embraces this, as he makes use of the tune at key moments to reinforce the title.[86] Both the script and performances emphasise the social commentary of the book, including characters wondering precisely how large a 'lodge' should be (relating to the family's large country house), as well as simple questions of relationships between the upper-middle classes, their servants and the police. Deference is on display, but none of these characters are pushovers. Perhaps the one exception is the unfortunate maid Gladys, who falls victim to a particularly horrific death in which where she is pegged out on a clothes line. Annette Badland played the character, and almost four decades later she still fondly remembers the

Fontana's *A Murder is Announced* cover (1985).

production. 'When I was auditioning for it, they were concerned because they thought it should be a young girl,' she recalls, and indeed other auditionees were much younger, including a twenty-year-old Kathy Burke.[87] However, Slater was so impressed by Badland's performance that she was cast, despite being thirty-four at the time ('that's the glory of being an actor!'). Badland was aware that this was Slater's directorial debut, and noted his enthusiasm, while she also got on well with Joan Hickson, who would take herself off at lunchtime to sleep in her car. Although Hickson insisted that she wasn't like Miss Marple ('I'm just an old character actress, dear'), Badland remembers her fondly in terms that could describe the fictional sleuth: 'tenacious, [and] a part of her character was the tenacity, and the dedication to something, the kind of pursuit of truth in the storytelling.'[88] Badland and Hickson worked together to establish a connection, because although they shared very little screen time the characters knew each other well. As for her death scene, it was both 'disturbing' and 'a great deal of fun'. She enjoyed considering Gladys's motivation as a fully rounded character: 'Agatha Christie isn't superficial. That's the great thing, it comes from genuine human desires and anxieties.'

Slater enjoyed the experience of directing, which included challenges related to the locations during filming, which began on 8 October 1984. He remembers that Thelveton Hall in Norfolk was used 'for lots of interiors [but] It had no front drive and had no [boundary] walls. And so we actually built some magnificent walls, which you could only shoot from one side because it was too expensive to make double sided!' Elsewhere, there was a problem with Miss Marple's cottage. From the first episode, Nether Wallop in Hampshire had doubled as St Mary Mead, and this included the cottage. Two were used, one for exteriors and one more practical residence (actually the old vicarage) for interiors. Unfortunately, the

BBC Enterprises' Series
Two flyer.

owner of the latter property was deeply unhappy with the disruption caused by the initial filming and refused to allow the BBC to return. A pleading letter was sent, but in the end the cottage interior had to be reconstructed as a set.[89] Gallaccio remembers the cottage as 'the big bugbear' of location filming but sympathises with homeowners who can't foresee the disruption of a crew of forty people traipsing through their house.

The BBC's Programme Review Board wondered if this story had been a little 'thinner' than the previous three, and in some ways they may be right. It certainly focuses on character dynamics rather than incident, and much of the interesting action necessarily takes place off screen. Nevertheless, the cast was again commended; star of the moment Peter Davison took the part of charming Lance, while even the small but significant part of Rex Fortescue is played by the respected thespian Timothy West. The cast also play into the simmering hints of sexuality that recur throughout what is in many ways one of Christie's most overtly adult novels, and the themes of class and sex are foregrounded in the production.

Although *Miss Marple* had mostly run smoothly as a production, by the time filming wrapped on *A Pocketful of Rye*, tiredness was creeping in. For the first time, Hickson had to sometimes make use of cue cards, which in turn restricted the editing choices available to Slater. Nevertheless, she was in remarkably good health, and even the BBC Programme Review Board considered that 'there were many series in her yet'.[90] On the other side of the camera, Guy Slater had decided that one series was enough for him, much to the disappointment of Rosalind, who had encouraged him to speak to Brian Stone about licensing more of Christie's novels for a second run of Miss Marple. Slater conveyed his apologies but was happy to leave the programme in the safe hands of George Gallaccio as permanent producer from now on. Rosalind had even floated the suggestion of a Poirot series at the BBC, but Slater thought he was 'too cold a fish as a character to sustain a series'.[91] Hickson finished the run happy with her portrayal. 'I had a lovely time playing Miss Marple,' she said, 'I'd love to do some more – but I'm so old now that they'll have to hurry!'[92]

By the spring of 1985, all parties were keen to make more Miss Marple adaptations, and the BBC requested ten more episodes. In May, George Gallaccio wrote to Rosalind to open conversations about a second run, having already met with Brian Stone.[93] He assured her that Guy Slater would still be an adviser in the early stages, and revealed that he still had hundreds of letters from well-wishers to which he needed to reply. The series had been such a success that it spearheaded the BBC's attempts to sell its content abroad; in the case of Miss Marple, this even included the Chinese market, which rarely imported British television programmes, while *A Pocketful of Rye* was projected on British Airways long-haul flights.[94] For this second series, Gallaccio suggested four novels (each in two parts) and then two short stories of a single episode each: 'The Case of the Caretaker' and 'A Christmas Tragedy'. He assured Rosalind that Hickson was keen to return, and despite Rosalind's concerns about her age, 'I think we can feel confident that our Miss M. will stay the course because of the pleasure she takes in the role.'[95]

Plans to film the short stories did not get far, and only the four novels moved into production, which took place in two blocks. The first comprised *The Murder at the Vicarage* and *Sleeping Murder*, filmed between March and July 1986. Hickson was keen to resume playing the part and was rewarded with a fee that was more than twice as much as she had been paid for the first four productions. This was fair, as not only was her performance a significant reason for the series' success,

AGATHA CHRISTIE

Miss Marple's Final Cases

READ BY JOAN HICKSON

Not on TV, but Joan Hickson's readings of the Miss Marple short stories became enduring audiobook bestsellers (1990).

but she was also a considerable draw for other high calibre actors who wished to work with her. In *The Murder at the Vicarage* this included the likes of Paul Eddington, playing the crucial role of Leonard Clement, the vicar. The crew returned to Nether Wallop, led by director Julian Amyes and working from a script by Trevor Bowen. One person who was pleasantly surprised to return was David Horovitch, who did not expect to be playing the part of Inspector Slack again as he assumed the character was a one-off. Hickson particularly enjoyed playing against Horovitch, and Bowen even began to think about a Slack spin-off series that would have relocated him to the seaside at retirement. Horovitch remembers being consistently impressed by the fellow cast members, while he found Amyes's direction to be notably different to Silvio Narizzano's (who had originally been pencilled in to direct this adaptation as well).[96] While Horovitch thought that Narizzano was 'a bit dark and a bit heavy [although] it was very good', he felt that Amyes's direction better fitted the superficially 'cosy feeling' of *The Murder at the Vicarage*.

One significant change for this second run of episodes was a new title sequence, which closely mirrored the original but with new drawings that were now in colour. This was partly in order to set up the fact that the period was moving on to the more colourful 1950s, while there had also been some dissatisfaction with the moving curtains effect in one of the shots in the original titles. Otherwise, it was pretty much business as usual for the series, although there was one significant indication of the programme's high status. Although *The Murder at the Vicarage* was written and shot as a two-part story (with the cliffhanger occurring when the defaced painting is discovered), the BBC decided to air the mystery as a single film in its prestigious Christmas Day slot. The adaptation was an excellent choice for such treatment, as it exemplifies much of what is typical of Miss Marple mysteries. The production ensures that much of the social commentary and humour from the novel is retained and even though some of the practicalities are changed (with French windows substituted for a lobby in the crucial study), the basic mechanics of the mystery are unaltered. The inclusion of a flashback may have been a partial response to the Programme Review Board's comments on the first series that noted their omission. They are particularly important here as they allow the audience to see precisely what Miss Marple witnessed while the murder

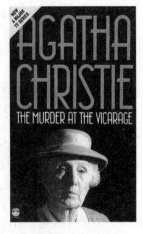

Fontana's *The Murder at the Vicarage* cover (1986).

was committed, and so they give her deductions more weight. In a scripted but deleted exchange, Miss Marple states that 'I don't think it's at all obvious, although I dare say I do know who did it', and so she proves to be right. As Slack begrudgingly admits, Miss Marple has 'an ear for gossip and a talent for a bit of blind guesswork'.

The archetypal Miss Marple mystery proved to be yet another hit, following high anticipation, stoked by a swift repeat run of the first series, and even a spoof appearance of the character in *The Two Ronnies* (alongside Poirot), in which the comedy duo investigated 'The Teddy Bear Who Knew Too Much', while *The Russ Abbot Show* featured its own comedic 'Miss Marbles'. Joan Hickson was interviewed for a plethora of magazines and newspapers throughout the year, as the press repeatedly wondered why it had taken so long for the wider public to fall in love with her. Hickson gave several interviews, although she refused to appear on popular television chat show *Wogan*. She told the *Daily Telegraph* that Miss Marple 'must be a little unobtrusive, even though she knows everything that is going on and takes everything in', and recounted to the *Radio Times* that, regarding Miss Marple, 'I love her dearly. I think she's a wonderful woman with very high standards and a very clear outlook on life. I'm devoted to her.'[97] Fans of the series also had no need to fear her advancing age: 'I think retirement is fatal'. Upon transmission, many reviewers took *The Murder at the Vicarage*'s quality for granted ('predictably a delight') and used it as a stick with which to beat the rest of the Christmas television viewing.[98] As the BBC's Programme Review Board noted, Miss Marple was 'a Rolls-Royce of a programme'.[99] The wider industry agreed, as Joan Hickson was nominated for a BAFTA for this performance.[100]

Sleeping Murder's emphasis on a young married couple means that this next production feels fresh after the close-knit communities mostly seen to this point. Writer Ken Taylor made the wise decision to bring in Giles (John Moulder-Brown) to accompany his wife Gwenda (Geraldine Alexander) from the beginning. Indeed, Gwenda really has the starring role in the production, and Geraldine Alexander remembers the production fondly. She recalls lengthy discussions about Gwenda's New Zealand accent: 'It made her more "other" and because she lands in this English village. It makes them more open in a way; curious and less restrained.'[101] Alexander appreciated the active part that Gwen played in the story: 'she laughs and enjoys things'. For her, being able to drive a story that was shot with such care is 'my favourite thing in the world'. The production's attention to detail included carefully-designed costumes: 'the clothes were all made for me. It was absolutely brilliant, all really thought through.' Once more, it was the series' lead who

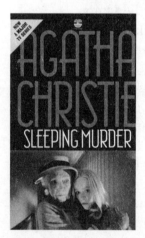

Fontana's *Sleeping Murder* cover (1986). This is how it was on the original, with misaligned corner flash 'Now a major TV series'.

seems to have inspired such care and attention from those around her. 'Miss Marple had a lot to do with Joan, and the same with Poirot, because you've got these great central characters who are really brilliant actors who've been around and it radiates out from there. They're holding that standard very high.'[102] Four decades later, Hickson has 'really stayed in my head ... She was absolutely perfect for it. I had a scene when I'm crying in bed. She's just quietly watching actively, really listening. It's all about just being there, and she taught me that; she was just so alert.'

Perhaps the only international book cover to depict Hickson's Miss Marple – Italy's *Sleeping Murder* (1986).

In terms of the story, there is a slightly hysterical tone to some aspects of *Sleeping Murder* that seems out of keeping with the earlier Miss Marple adaptations in the series, although some of it is effectively sinister. Nevertheless, while the situation is naturally distressing for Gwenda, the music and some of the direction (by John Davies) tends towards the melodramatic, which marks this out as quite different to the understated tone seen in the earlier episodes. Elements of the mystery (particularly the identity of the culprit) are also reasonably easy to solve, although this is a fault of the original novel as well. Some scripted moments were later dispensed with, perhaps to obscure more of the mystery: this included a plan to intercut Gwenda's trip to the theatre with flashbacks to the events of 1937. Broadcast on 11 and 18 January 1987, a few reviewers wondered if this Miss Marple mystery was a little slow in parts, but for the most part notices remained positive, and Hickson's 'listening' acting was praised by the Programme Review Board.[103]

The next adaptation saw another respected writer drawn to the series, as Jill Hyem took on *At Bertram's Hotel*. Hyem

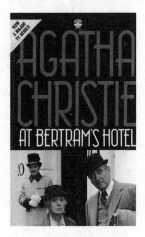

Fontana's *At Bertram's Hotel* cover, featuring George Baker (1986).

was probably best known for her work on the acclaimed series *Tenko*, which depicted female prisoners of war in Singapore. Gallaccio had also worked on the series, and so knew Hyem, whose scripts were well-received by both producer and Rosalind. In a sign that she understood the realities of television, Rosalind wondered if there was 'Too long before violence' in the script, and raised various other queries, including the procedure for catching a flight in the 1950s and the likelihood of Miss Marple using the word 'doppelganger'.[104]

Mary McMurray was chosen to direct, having forged much of her career at Granada Television. An excellent choice, McMurray's direction successfully maintains the claustrophobia of the hotel setting while also opening out the story enough to make it feel dramatic. Much of the story is a meditation on a changing world, which is not particularly televisual, but the atmosphere that is so crucial to the novel is successfully created. Women were (and remain) very much in the minority when it came to directing films and television, and McMurray recalls that 'You just didn't get hired, and sometimes the worst offenders were women producers ... I could never quite work out why.' McMurray embraced the 'pretty generous' shooting schedule, and on a recent rewatch was struck by how much action each scene required, with actors and supporting artists needing to move around the hotel while eating, drinking and talking. The series leaned heavily on the BBC's famous expertise with period dramas, and having costume and makeup departments that were able to cope were important to McMurray's production. Many of the hotel's interiors were filmed at the University Women's Club in Mayfair, where the crew constructed a new reception desk, 'and when we finished, they asked if we would leave it. So we did!' The requirements for the hotel dictated this portmanteau approach to location hunting (the exterior was located in Essex Street, Temple), which also included the interiors of a building then owned by the BBC, which is now The Langham hotel (near to Broadcasting House). McMurray fondly remembers Hickson, who didn't complain even when she had to walk up several flights of stairs for filming; at the end of the day, Hickson would reward herself with a glass of The Famous Grouse whisky.

Actors Joan Greenwood and George Baker joined the production, playing Selina Hazy and Chief Inspector Davy. Familiar faces from the big and small screens, both contributed to the high quality of the production, although Greenwood was distressed when an accident at home caused a minor delay to the production. Baker's appearance would have significance for his future career, as it directly led to him playing the part of Inspector Wexford for a long-running series on ITV. 'I was editing in Ealing quite late on in the process,' remembers McMurray, 'and John Davies, the director who was about to do the first [of *The Ruth Rendell Mysteries*] stopped me in the corridor. He said that he'd seen he'd been walking past and he'd heard George doing his rural policeman act, and he asked me what George was like as he was thinking of casting him ...'

Although it is one of the less conventional Miss Marple stories, critics still admired *At Bertram's Hotel*. 'Seldom can dear old Agatha's computerised tales have been accorded such Rolls-Royce treatment, or so splendid a cast, even unto the peripheral characters,' said the *Daily Telegraph*, following the adaptation's transmission on 25 January and 1 February 1987. 'The period touches are laid on with such lush and loving care that you'd sign for a week at Bertram's without a second thought, except that it would be impossibly expensive.'[105]

At Bertram's Hotel was the last story of this second series to be filmed, across six weeks from 5 October 1986, but it wasn't the last to be shown. Nemesis was filmed earlier, in August and September, probably in order to catch good weather as the story demanded more exterior filming as it concerns a coach tour. Quizzed by the press, Hickson remembered a tour of her own, this time with a theatrical troupe, probably when performing in Appointment with Death in 1945. 'Agatha came on tour with us,' she remembered. 'She was very charming and shy and didn't talk much. But she was also very generous – I remember she gave me some tea, which was rationed then.'[106]

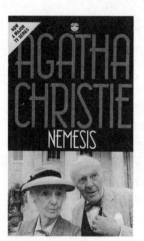

Fontana's Nemesis cover (1986).

Trevor Bowen returned to script Nemesis, which was directed by David Tucker. 'He was a bit of a handful, David,' laughs George Gallaccio. 'That was a fun one. I really like old actors and, particularly with the women we had, that one had all my favourites.' Indeed, the cast included such venerable names as Margaret Tyzack, who played Clotilde Bradbury-Scott, and was most recognisable for her roles in The Forsyte Saga and I, Claudius, which were arguably the BBC's most prestigious drama serials of the 1960s and 1970s respectively.

It was another happy production, but not without its difficulties due to the range of locations, taking in Oxfordshire (where the crew stayed in Wallingford, Christie's home during the later part of her life), Gloucestershire, Wiltshire, London and Devon. This resulted in some of the crew putting together a special celebratory booklet at the end, entitled 'You Survived Nemesis!', which included a cheeky song reflecting on their travels: 'Left my toothbrush at Tetbury / My underwear at Andover ... The BBC said, "Have a thirties trip with me / Drinking cocktails called Miss Marple's cheeks!"'

One of the locations included Burgh Island off the coast of

Devon, although it wasn't chosen for its well-known Agatha Christie connections.[107] It was simply a suitably grand location for the dying days of Jason Rafiel, who (in the books) Miss Marple had first encountered in *A Caribbean Mystery*, which had not yet been filmed. The reason for this was straightforward, as the rights to that novel were not available to the BBC at the time, and nor were *The Mirror Crack'd from Side to Side* and *They Do It with Mirrors*. This was due to the adaptations starring Helen Hayes and Angela Lansbury earlier in the decade. The result is that no real thought was given to the fact that Mr Rafiel might have to stage a miraculous recovery in later years; 'it was in nobody's mind at all,' confesses Gallaccio.

One happy incident on location was the eightieth birthday of Joan Hickson, which was celebrated during filming at Woodstock, Oxfordshire. Locals got a view of the action, as did some travelling tourists who pestered the star for autographs. 'I haven't a clue why they do this,' Hickson told the local paper, 'I'm not at all clever really. I'm no good at all at solving puzzles. I just like to do the odd crossword.'[108] Later, she spoke to the *Daily Mail*, where she revealed a little of her politics, which were somewhere to the right of Miss Marple. 'She isn't prissy,' Hickson said of Miss Marple. 'She knows all about vice – nothing shocks her while I am rather shockable. It's all too damned easy to divorce now and I feel strongly that a child should have two parents and it must have discipline or it is lost.'[109]

Nemesis benefits from an excellent script that reworks the original novel to make it suitable for television. It is much more direct about the central mission, while less convincing elements are changed, such the unwieldy murder weapon of a boulder, which is substituted with a falling bust of William Shakespeare. A new nephew for Miss Marple is also inserted, called Lionel Peel (Peter Tilbury), which means that Miss Marple has someone to talk to early on; he does not appear to be the same character as Miss Marple's stamp-collecting young great-nephew Lionel who is mentioned in the short story 'Strange Jest'. The death of Mr Rafiel is now a strong opening hook, and Miss Marple is almost immediately put on the trail of the mystery, unlike in the novel. Character work is superb, including the amusing appearances of Rafiel's solicitors, as well as the varied members of the coach tour. Bowen remembers being particularly impressed by Joanna Hole as tour guide Madge, who 'invented this this constant flurry of not really quite knowing what she's doing, and it worked beautifully. It was very funny and sweet.' Alongside these amusements are darker moments, most significantly the exceptional denouement, in which the actor playing the murderer gives one of the greatest screen performances in any Agatha Christie adaptation. While love is undoubtedly the key motivation, Miss Marple is unmoved, pointing out that Verity is now 'a rotted corpse and there's no one to kiss her awake'.

Broadcast on 8 and 15 February 1987, the BBC's Programme Review Board simply described *Nemesis* as 'marvellous' and 'beautifully directed'.[110] There was a keenness to continue Miss Marple, with Gallaccio writing to Rosalind in October 1986 to state that he was interested in adapting *4.50 from Paddington* the following year as a 'special film', noting that 'I know Joan would be happy to keep Miss Marple alive.'[111] All involved were conscious that this was the last available Miss Marple novel (at the time), and that speed was of the essence given Hickson's age. Terms were agreed, with Bowen returning for writing duties, and the adaptation was filmed in August and September 1987, helmed by director Martyn Friend. Locations included Marylebone Station (standing in for Paddington thanks to

The cover for the *4.50 From Paddington* sales brochure.

its period look) for the all-important departure of the titular train, the temporary closure of which upset sports fans who were delayed on their journeys as a result.[112]

Bowen's script strives to make the audience more interested in the victim than the novel achieved, as we see her almost cross paths with Mrs McGillicuddy after a visit to church, while Friend's direction reminds us that the murder would take place in darkness at that time of year, which brings additional atmosphere. Horovitch's Inspector Slack returns, replacing Inspector Craddock because actor John Castle was unavailable. The relationship with Hickson's Miss Marple is as delightful and pronounced as ever, as Slack struggles to hide his annoyance with Miss Marple's sleuthing. Friend's direction subtly moves the action away from any sense of cosiness, as befits a novel written in the second half of the 1950s that opens with the brutal strangling of a young woman, in a sequence that Horovitch remembers as one of the most effective of the whole series: 'I just think it's terrific. It could be Hitchcock.' Bowen also remembers the finished product being 'atmospheric and good', and indeed the drama often leans into horror movie staples, especially the dramatic music that accompanies the discovery of a body in a sarcophagus placed in a cobweb-draped outbuilding. Both director and writer manage to effectively differentiate between each of the brothers, including the use of some distinctive costumes and musical motifs. Dr Quimper's character is also fleshed out, as he is now depicted as a champion of the new-fangled National Health Service, and so surely an all-round good guy.

One issue with 4.50 from Paddington has always been that its most exciting and dramatic moments take place at the very beginning, and the rest of the novel struggles to match up to it. This adaptation works hard to keep the attention of its audience, with sequences including Miss Marple as a passenger in a fast car ('Thank you very much, that was exciting!') and,

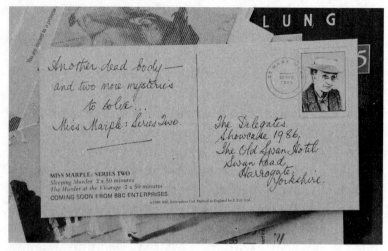

A Series Two promotional postcard.

towards the end, the landing of a plane outside Rutherford Hall. Bowen was grateful that Gallaccio allowed him the indulgence of concluding a love story with such a grand gesture, as he felt the characterisation was important. He was sadder to see that one scripted moment of humour was lost, however: 'At the end, when the villain has been named and the young fighter pilot has crashed through the glass to go and arrest him, Slack turns up, slaps a handcuff on him and says gotcha. What I wanted him to do was to put his hand through the open window and put the handcuffs on, then realise that he couldn't actually get out of the car!'

Broadcast on Christmas Day 1987, *The Times* wrote of the production that 'the magic of Joan Hickson as Miss Marple never fades. It acts as an embalming fluid upon an England that never was.' Commending it as a standout of the Christmas Day schedule, Henry Stanthorpe considered that 'the sight of *The 4.50 from Paddington* [sic] steaming in at 8.15 was like that of a distant billowing sail to Robinson Crusoe.'[113] Hilary Kingsley of the *Daily Mirror* concurred, arguing that 'The appeal of the series must be due to clever scripts, impeccably acted', and that 'This was the best yet.'[114] In the run up to transmission several newspapers quoted Hickson and others who pointed out that this was to be the last Miss Marple of the series, due to the unavailability of the other titles (Hickson blamed 'the Americans'). Hickson was still basking in the positive glow of the critical and popular reactions to her performances and stated that she would never retire. She was boosted by the award of an OBE from Queen Elizabeth II in November, and the next month had dinner with the monarch, who told Hickson how much her family enjoyed watching *Miss Marple*.

While the future of *Miss Marple* was in doubt, other Agatha Christie possibilities were suggested, as Rosalind pointed out that ITV had only the rights to the Poirot short stories at this time, and the BBC might be interested in adapting some of the novels featuring the Belgian sleuth. This didn't happen, but when it came to Miss Marple, Gallaccio was 'determined to complete them all', and 'never lost hope', although Hickson was starting to hint that perhaps she was less keen to continue than she had been. With the remaining three novels unavailable until the rights reverted, a new possibility was discussed for Christmas 1988: an adaptation of the Miss Marple short story 'Death by Drowning', expanded to a full feature-length production. The BBC approached Brian Stone in September 1987, and asked for a swift decision. Mathew Prichard wrote to the Agatha Christie Ltd board with his thoughts. Noting that it is 'a very short story', Mathew understood that 'it has the intrinsic character studies necessary for television, though I seriously wonder whether it could possibly run for one hour fifty minutes.'[115] He also pointed out that it was not one of the loosely linked 'storytelling' mysteries in *The Thirteen Problems*, and that there was next-to-no chance of getting Hickson to do the rest of the stories in the collection anyway. He recommended that they licensed the rights to the BBC, and Rosalind and Brian Stone had lunch with Trevor Bowen to discuss the prospect. Rosalind was more circumspect than Mathew, and initially Bowen was less sure if he could make the story work, but he then wrote to Stone after spending some time plotting out a potential script. After adding extra characters (to act as suspects), Bowen was also:

> able to introduce a good "impossibility" about the crime to which Miss Marple is able to provide a solution, and the whole thing is turning into a good, complex tale with plenty of surprises and twists. Of course a good deal of this input is my own version of what I hope and believe Miss Christie would have approved of ... What matters most it seems to me is that at the heart of [this story and *Nemesis*] is a blind sexual jealousy of sufficient violence to do murder. In fact, I am quite sure now that in terms of plot, action and character we have all the ingredients of a first rate film which will run naturally to 100 minutes.[116]

Despite Bowen's best efforts, the decision was made not to proceed with 'Death by Drowning', and so there was no new Miss Marple for 1988. Hickson stated that she was not interested in returning, saying that 'The BBC had already pencilled the remaining one into their filming schedule, assuming I would do it. But they rather jumun. I spoke to Agatha Christie's daughter and she agreed with me entirely.'[117]

Despite Hickson's reservations, however, when the rights to *A Caribbean Mystery* became available, she was tempted back into the fold. This production would help to kick off 1990's Agatha Christie centenary celebrations, with the new film scheduled for Christmas 1989. By July 1989, Gallaccio let

Rosalind know that Bowen was working on the script, and that they would film at the Coral Reef Club in Barbados, where she and her mother had stayed in the late 1950s; this was a happy coincidence, as the location had been selected simply by chance. Bowen successfully argued that he needed to visit the locations and local villages so that he could write the script effectively, and so he joined Gallaccio and director Christopher Petit for a recce prior to the commencement of filming on 6 September, with interiors then recorded at Ealing film studios back in London. Gallaccio informed Rosalind that the hotel had changed very little, and they even found Christie's name in one of the old guestbooks. The hotel was still run by the same proprietors who had greeted Christie and Rosalind three decades earlier, and they found old photographs to help the production team when dressing the location to look as it would have in the 1950s. Petit later wrote that, on this recce, 'we realised that Christie hadn't invented anything. It was all there', and also that he had accepted the offer to direct on the strength of Hickson's performances.[118]

Hickson told *Hello* magazine that 'The heat was tremendous. We were working with the temperature in the nineties most of the time. But the other problem which had us very worried for a time was that we were bang in the path of Hurricane Hugo, which was heading straight for us. Luckily it turned north, so we were safe, although we were held up on the island for a few extra days.' Despite weather worries, most of the cast and crew enjoyed the tropical climes, and some even enjoyed feeding the local wild monkeys at breakfast.

BBC Television's promotional brochure for *A Caribbean Mystery*.

A Caribbean Mystery was the last of the tie-in book covers (1989).

Nevertheless, Hickson once again informed the press that 'it's going to be the last. It's good to end on a high note.'[119] Hickson was joined by Donald Pleasence as the resurrected Jason Rafiel, another indication of how Hickson's presence encouraged high calibre actors to join the production. The location filming makes the adaptation feel quite different from the rest of *Miss Marple*, complemented by music that is fitting for the Caribbean setting, with its steel drum take on the series' theme. When the happy cast and crew returned to London, BBC Two programme *Behind the Screen* followed some of the production. '[Miss Marple is] much nicer than I am, I think,' Hickson told the programme, 'she's just a little lady living in a village really, but she knows everything that goes on, and nothing that could happen could ever shock her, she knows it all'. One person who was a little less happy was Bowen, who felt that it was one of his weaker scripts. 'I did a little bit of what I think should have been done,' he remembers. 'The Bajan people [people of Barbados] are much more interesting than they're allowed to be. I was desperate not to condescend.'

The Christmas Day broadcast of *A Caribbean Mystery* was slightly spoiled by ITV's attempt to sabotage the screening by repeating the Helen Hayes production two weeks earlier, but appreciative audiences still lapped up the unquestionably superior new version. By now, Hickson was slowing down quite considerably, but she enjoyed reading the audiobooks of the Miss Marple stories, many of which were recorded at her home. Attempts were made for her to complete the canon on audio even after the television series ended, but her poor health became clear in her later readings. Nevertheless, she did manage to complete the Miss Marple novels on television, as 1991 and 1992 saw the production and broadcast of the two remaining novels, which had now become available. These were *They Do It with Mirrors* and *The Mirror Crack'd from Side to Side*, both directed by Norman Stone, working from scripts by Trevor Bowen. 'By then I think she was too old,' admits Mathew Prichard. 'I remember going to the filming and they had some policeman who forgot his line six times running and Joan, who is word-perfect, eventually said "Come along my dear! This won't do, I'm getting old and I can't be doing with all these takes just because you can't remember your lines!"'[120]

'Foul play is just around the corner...' The BBC's sales brochure for They *Do It with Mirrors*.

Less than a year after Hickson had insisted to the press that she would not return to Miss Marple, newspapers reported on the filming of *They Do It with Mirrors* in June 1991. The previous month there had been cause for concern when Miss Marple's straw hat and handbag were found to have gone missing; neatly, Hickson herself helped the production team locate the items, which had been loaned to Torquay Museum for display. After the striking imagery of *A Caribbean Mystery*, even some of the publicity for this new production conceded that the story was not one of Christie's best. 'No, this story isn't my favourite,' Hickson told the *Telegraph* magazine. 'Well, I haven't got a favourite. I'm afraid I'm a superficial actress, I can't bear anything like the Method. I embark like a butterfly and then I fly away.' Gallaccio also told the magazine that 'We had a lot of trouble with this book. It doesn't make sense. We took out Inspector Curry and put in Inspector Slack because he's very popular.' Horovitch himself noted that 'There's one less murder in the film than in the book – I did wonder whether the BBC rations the number of people who can be killed at Christmas.'[121] Indeed, the 'missing' late murder is now an injury, which itself was an addition after the first draft (in which the character survived uninjured), presumably in order to add drama to the final act. Horovitch remembers enjoying

Slack's new character trait, as an amateur conjurer: 'It was delightful, and I thought entirely characteristic of Slack, that he would have a hobby like that.'

This time, the production was greeted less warmly than in earlier years. Even at the BBC, there was a sense that this was not one of the stronger adaptations, which may explain why it was shown on 29 December rather than in the prestigious Christmas Day slot. Once more, ITV attempted to put a dent in the ratings of the production, this time by repeating an episode of *Agatha Christie's Poirot* at the same time; the series starring David Suchet had launched to great acclaim in January 1989, and both series showed the extent of public interest in Christie's works, even more than a century after the author's birth.[122] The plot of *They Do It with Mirrors* may be weaker than some, but perhaps the adaptation was most affected by the lacklustre visuals that a wet summer and rather unexciting country house have to offer, in a story that doesn't have a strong opening hook of some of the other Miss Marple mysteries. There is still much to enjoy, and the excellent casting of Jean Simmons as Carrie-Louise is a masterstroke, while it is a pleasure to see Miss Marple in a bustling London on her way to the Savoy, with atmospheric use of fog and lighting at night to add visual variety.

The production also goes to lengths to emphasise the importance of psychology and individual interpretations of appearances, as discussed following a visit to a dance early on (and, more obviously, through Slack's interest in conjuring). Bowen's script used descriptions from the book throughout, and an unfortunate loss from the final film was a scene in which Miss Marple discovers two of the 'delinquent' boys dancing to Elvis, clearly situating the story on the cusp of a new era. Despite the fresh ingredients of the 'delinquents' in the mystery, one critic argued that 'It was just the same old story with a little light relief...Too many characters and not enough wit can make Miss Marple's work a trifle tedious.'[123] Lynne Truss in *The Times* bemoaned the fact that 'the identity of the murderer, when revealed, must be *interesting*', which she didn't believe to be the case here.[124]

Christmas 1992 saw the final *Miss Marple*, with *The Mirror Crack'd from Side to Side* shown on 27 December. This last production became something of a reunion, with Slack returning (and promoted to Superintendent) along with Ian Brimble's Sergeant Lake, who had accompanied Slack since the first episode. Also appearing were

The Mirror Crack'd from Side to Side sales brochure.

Inspector Craddock and Dolly Bantry, while writer Bowen made his second appearance as Raymond, Miss Marple's nephew (following *A Caribbean Mystery*).[125] Filmed between April and June 1992, the screenplay clearly states the year to be 1960, which neatly concludes Miss Marple's progress through the 1950s. Claire Bloom took on the significant role of film star Marina Gregg, and Gallaccio recalls 'she was perfect, we had a lovely time'.

While the Angela Lansbury adaptation had shied away from the social commentary and changing world so important to the novel, here it is placed front and centre. Dolly's delight that her new lodge has a washing machine is both funny and believable, while the script also makes a point of saying that Miss Marple is older and frailer than before, although if anything Hickson seems a little more sprightly than in the previous film. The draft script retained Miss Marple spraining her ankle after giving out some unwelcome advice to Gladys in the Development, but the final version substituted this for a broken

Sphere's Joan Hickson cover transformed the sales of Anne Hart's book in 1990.

Joan Hickson and David Suchet at Agatha Christie's 100th birthday celebrations in Torquay on 15 September 1990.

shoe as she is startled by a passing motorbike. This means that Miss Marple makes it to Gossington Hall for some of the festivities, even if she has to leave before the murder occurs. The fête itself is particularly well shot, as the different events jostle for the attention of the audience as well as attendees. Another change between drafts meant that Miss Marple now visits the set of Marina's film, which is charmingly incongruous and a welcome addition. Here she is accompanied by Craddock (who was originally scripted to visit the set alone), who now states that Miss Marple is his aunt.[126]

Agatha Christie's Miss Marple was an unusually happy television production. 'I remember us having a cricket match, cast versus crew,' says Horovitch. 'I've never done that on anything. That was really good fun, even though I was out first ball to one of the sparks!' Similarly, Gallaccio remembers the series extremely fondly: 'As far as my career is concerned it has been the one of the best things I've ever done, or was associated with in any way. It was really a pleasure to be part of that.' These thoughts were echoed by both Mathew and Rosalind, who particularly felt that Hickson had been an exceptional custodian of Miss Marple. 'I'm really sorry that my grandmother never saw [the series],' says Mathew. Hickson reflected on the fact that she would no longer play Miss Marple. 'I shall miss her, oh, I certainly shall,' she said. 'I really do like Miss M. The more I have played her, the more I have grown to like her. I do so admire her. She is a good egg. And I have so much enjoyed making the series.'[127]

June Whitfield as Miss Marple
(Radio, 1993–2001 & 2015)

While the 1970s saw a more sustained effort to bring Agatha Christie's stories to the screen, the 1980s saw Agatha Christie Ltd become more open to the prospect of bringing the author's works to the radio in a dramatised fashion. There had been several requests for full cast adaptations over the years, but these had been routinely declined in favour of single-voice readings. A breakthrough of sorts occurred in 1985 when Maurice Denham starred as Hercule Poirot in *The Mystery of the Blue Train*. This particular production was not considered to be a success, and so producer Enyd Williams was brought on board to direct a new Poirot, this time played by Peter Sallis *in Hercule Poirot's Christmas* for 1986. Sallis didn't feel comfortable in the role, and the following year

ABOVE: June Whitfield in a photoshoot for Radio 4's *Miss Marple*.

saw John Moffatt make his debut as Poirot in *The Murder of Roger Ackroyd*. Moffatt's Poirot was well-received, and he played the part for the next two decades, with scripts by Michael Bakewell, who had also dramatised the stories that starred Denham and Sallis. With one success in hand, it was natural that the BBC would then turn to Christie's second major sleuth, Miss Jane Marple.

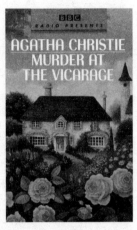

Murder at the Vicarage was released on cassette in America in 1997.

Enyd Williams had long enjoyed reading Agatha Christie's work, even when others were dismissive about the quality of her writing, and so enjoyed the chance to work with writer Michael Bakewell on the radio dramatisations. For Williams, the distinction between adaptation and dramatisation is an important one, as she points out that not only does dramatising mean that 'it comes straight from the book', keeping much of the original text intact, but that 'the fee for a dramatisation is a darn sight more than a fee for an adaptation!'[128] Inevitably, first thoughts concerned the casting of Miss Marple herself, and Williams was keen to emphasise the initial impression that the character was a 'fluffy old lady'. The producer was particularly drawn to the description of Miss Marple wearing a pink scarf as a shawl in *A Caribbean Mystery*, in which she 'seemed to be a very sweet old lady, which was the cleverness of course'. Williams spent some time thinking about potential actors, until she woke in the middle of the night with an inspired idea: June Whitfield. Whitfield was well-known to audiences; she was most recognised for her work in comedy on both television and radio, where she appeared in the likes of *Hancock's Half Hour* and as one half of the titular duo *Terry and June*. The fact that she was already a beloved figure made her perfect for this superficially 'fluffy' character that Williams was going for, and in 1992 she was entering a career renaissance as Mother

The 1996 BBC Radio Collection audiobook *At Bertram's Hotel*.

in Jennifer Saunders' comedy *Absolutely Fabulous*, where she starred alongside Joanna Lumley, later to play Dolly Bantry on television.

Whitfield greatly enjoyed playing Miss Marple and would often cite it as one of her happiest working experiences, even turning down other jobs so that she could continue in the role. She recorded the first dramatisation, *The Murder at the Vicarage*, in September 1993, and coincidentally the following month saw the broadcast of her appearance on light entertainment television show *The Generation Game*, in which she briefly impersonated Margaret Rutherford's take on the character. Broadcast on BBC Radio 4 in five parts beginning on 26 December 1993, *The Murder at the Vicarage* was a great success. This included the casting, with the likes of Imelda Staunton, Nigel Davenport and Richard Todd joining Whitfield, with Francis Matthews as the Reverend Leonard

Clement. 'Everybody had loved it,' remembers Williams, 'it really was an unexpected success.' More Miss Marple was commissioned, and it soon became clear that there was every chance of completing the twelve novels.

As may be expected for a series bearing her name, the role of Miss Marple was necessarily increased where possible. This included using the character as narrator as well as detective, which allowed her inner thoughts to be heard as well as giving the character a sustained prominence. For *The Murder at the Vicarage* this had the effect of displacing the reverend who narrates the novel, with Miss Marple taking centre stage instead. Meanwhile, the likes of *The Moving Finger* brought Miss Marple into the story much earlier than was the case in the novel, lest Whitfield be reduced to little more than a cameo, while some familiar voices recurred across the series as needed, including Ian Lavender as Chief Inspector Craddock and Pauline Jameson as Dolly Bantry. The requirements of radio storytelling meant that some necessary changes were made; for example, in *They Do It with Mirrors* the layout of the house is de-emphasised (a floorplan is supplied in the novel), while a significant letter becomes a telephone call.

The series is perhaps most remarkable for the way that it simply and effectively presents the original stories as written, while ensuring that the mysteries still work for an audio medium. Miss Marple's narration helps to cultivate an intimate atmosphere and insight while the mysteries retain Christie's clear characterisation and motivations, thanks to Michael Bakewell's skills with dramatisation. Miss Marple often sets up the intrigue of the story with her own narration at the beginning, while elsewhere some exciting mystery is alluded to, such as when *Sleeping Murder* (the last of the novels to be adapted, in 2001) opens with Gwenda wondering if her new house is haunted. Radio may also be the medium

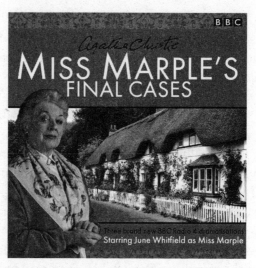

Three final cases, released on CD in 2015.

in which Miss Marple's talent for mimicry is most believable (especially for an actor of June Whitfield's skills), as heard in *A Murder is Announced*.

Fourteen years after *Sleeping Murder* was broadcast, June Whitfield returned as Miss Marple with three more mysteries, this time scripted by Joy Wilkinson and directed by Gemma Jenkins. Wilkinson had already dramatised several Christie novels for radio, including *And Then There Were None* and *Endless Night* and, along with producer Mary Peate, suggested that Miss Marple could have her last hurrah on the radio, using *Miss Marple's Final Cases*. Radio 4 were keen to ensure that Whitfield returned for any new production, and the actor readily agreed. By now, both the character and Whitfield herself seem a little more frail. Miss Marple is both depressed and ill at the beginning of 'Tape-Measure Murder', which is followed by 'The Case of the Perfect Maid' (which BBC radio had already adapted in 2003 as 'The Case of the Perfect Carer', in a production that modernised the story and removed the character of Miss Marple) and 'Sanctuary', with a sprinkling of 'The Case of the Caretaker', which is now a story that Raymond West (played by Raymond Coulthard) is writing. Other familiar characters also returned, including both Inspector Slack (Stephen Critchlow, replacing John Baddeley) and Bunch (Rose Cavaliero, replacing Molly Gaisford). Gemma Jenkins remembers that the connections between the stories was a deliberate choice: 'Joy did it in such a way that it feels like you're in her world and they're interlinked, rather than three separate cases.'[129]

While the trio of episodes had been designed to give Miss Marple a finale that had been denied her by Christie, Whitfield was keen to ensure that Miss Marple was still the character she knew. 'Having played the character and being so familiar with her she was really keen that we in no way portrayed her as a character who was close to death,' explains Jenkins: 'She didn't feel that Miss Marple would be somebody who would be in any way neurotic or scared about that, so she wanted to bring that very much into how she portrayed the character, that it was about her strength of spirit and love of life. That was largely due to her understanding of human nature and ability to see patterns and solve crimes.'

For Enyd Williams, it was June Whitfield who was the key to the ongoing success of the series. This included the fact that other actors were keen to work with her, which resulted in some illustrious casts, as well as the fact that Whitfield had genuine dramatic range. 'It wasn't all lightness and fun and comedy,' Williams recalls, 'certainly not.' Particularly memorable is the closing scene of *The Mirror Crack'd from Side to Side*, in which Miss Marple reflects on the death of a key character with a performance that 'really brought tears to everybody around her. She played Miss Marple with the complete truth.'

CHAPTER SEVEN:

THE
Twenty-First Century

n the early part of the twenty-first century, work was afoot
to reinvigorate the Agatha Christie brand. In 1998 the
company Chorion bought a 64% stake in Agatha Christie
Ltd, and they were keen to see a return on their investment.[1]
In part, this concerned Christie's books, as there was a feeling
that the physical products could be improved, leading to a
rebranding exercise that included increasing the quality of
the typesetting and new cover designs that would have an
appeal beyond the core group of readers. Both publisher
HarperCollins (formerly Collins) and Agatha Christie
Ltd were concerned that their research showed that many
readers would be embarrassed to be seen reading Christie

OPPOSITE: The noughties ushered in not one but two Miss Marples,
in a television series which proved so successful that producers had
to resort to writing the character into other Agatha Christie stories to
extend its run.

Miss Marple illustrated by Christopher Brown on a 2003 Folio Society edition.

books, and the rebranding aimed to make her works appear more sophisticated and literary. Part of this rebrand was the adoption of the now-ubiquitous Agatha Christie signature, which was modified from Christie's handwriting.

Chorion had little experience with literary estates, and so brought in Phil Clymer from the BBC to spearhead their work reinvigorating Agatha Christie for a new millennium. Clymer impressed Agatha Christie Ltd chairman Mathew Prichard with his honesty, as he revealed that he did not initially consider himself to be a particular fan of Christie's work, but he remembers that he 'spent the weekend reading Christies and was really shocked at how good they were. She was absolutely so clever. And she was playing fair.'[2] Clymer was a perfect example of the potential (rather than existing) market for the author's works, who needed a little encouragement to read some Christie. However, the brand was more than just the books, and new ventures in film and television were also important to keeping Agatha Christie's works visible more than two decades after her death. One early attempt was to make a new Tommy and Tuppence series, but although scripting began, it didn't make it to screen. Meanwhile, a new Poirot venture appeared in the United States with an updated retelling of *Murder on the Orient Express* for television in 2001, while thoughts also started to turn to Miss Marple. A decade had passed since Joan Hickson's final appearance, and it was felt that the time was right for the spinster sleuth to return to screens.

Geraldine McEwan and Julia McKenzie in *Agatha Christie's Marple*
(Television Series, 2004–2013)

In the early 2000s, Agatha Christie Ltd spoke to a number of companies about the prospect of a new Miss Marple series, including the BBC, which had shown early interest in a new venture despite the fact that they were still regularly repeating their earlier adaptations. For Agatha Christie Ltd, it was of primary importance for any new venture to get the casting right, and some time was spent mulling over potential names. A gentle canvassing of big names such as Maggie Smith and Judi Dench revealed that some stars may have been interested in a one-off film, but not an ongoing series. There had been some thoughts about a Miss Marple movie, and for a while

ABOVE: The Two Marples, McEwan and McKenzie, in a post-series marketing image.

it was felt that both the character and such big names would be better kept in reserve until the possibility of a big screen venture had been fully explored. Nevertheless, Phil Clymer met with a range of potential companies who had shown an interest in making a Miss Marple television series. ITV offered an excellent deal that would see them make eight Miss Marple films over the course of two years, with an option for more, showing substantially more commitment than the BBC were willing to offer, and so ITV secured the rights.

Producers Damien Timmer and Michele Buck had recently been brought on board to helm *Agatha Christie's Poirot*, and so it was natural that they were also asked to take the reins of *Agatha Christie's Marple*, which would be made by ITV Studios. Finding a new Miss Marple was relatively straightforward. 'My first idea was always Geraldine McEwan,' says Clymer, although other actors were also considered and even auditioned for the role. They included Gemma Jones, who was Mathew Prichard's favourite, but he accepted Clymer's argument that the actor was simply too similar to Joan Hickson.

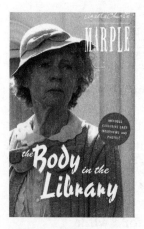

All four Season 1 adaptations were accompanied by tie-in paperbacks (2004).

It was important that this new series had its own identity, and it was in no one's interests to simply replicate what had gone before. 'It was Geraldine that had everything we wanted,' argues Clymer, 'and also she was an icon. She'd played Ophelia opposite Olivier! People were in awe of Geraldine.' McEwan's status meant that recruiting high profile guest stars to perform opposite her became much easier than it might have been for a standard ITV drama, helped by the fact that her late husband had been Principal of RADA and so she had relationships with acting talents across several generations.

When the series was announced to the press in late 2002, it was at the peak of rivalry between the licence-fee funded BBC and commercial channel ITV. The head of drama at Granada (one of the ITV regions), John Whiston, used the new series to criticise the corporation. 'I genuinely believe the BBC's heart isn't in popular drama and it never has been,' he told the press. 'In other words, ITV has been doing what the BBC is lavishly funded to do.'³ *Agatha Christie's Marple* was held up as an example of the commercial broadcaster's attempts to make popular but prestigious productions, and in the case of *Marple* this also relied on international sales to help to boost the budget.

For the first season of *Agatha Christie's Marple*, four novels were chosen, with *The Body in the Library* adapted by the acclaimed playwright Kevin Elyot, *The Murder at the Vicarage* and *4.50 from Paddington* by Stephen Churchett, and *A Murder is Announced* by Stewart Harcourt. Elyot and Churchett frequently returned as the programme developed, and Clymer felt that these two writers offered the perfect balance for the show as the producers envisaged it, 'with Kevin's ability to explore the dark side and absurdity, and Stephen to root it into a real place with real people'. The first run clearly sets out what this new series of *Marple* is intending to do. It is bright, breezy and almost brash in its stylings. This isn't a world of subtlety, it's a place where Christie's stories can be told for a modern audience on a major television channel, with a particular eye on encouraging people who wouldn't consider themselves to be fans to dip their toe into the world of Agatha Christie.

One place where this attempt to find new audiences was made clear was in the casting, where names and faces familiar to ITV audiences were heavily featured. This meant that, from a storytelling perspective, the issue that the most famous actor often ends up being the villain in a whodunnit could be avoided as the casts featured so many well-known names. In *The Body in the Library* alone, there are the likes of

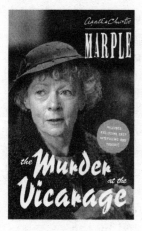
The Murder at the Vicarage tie-in.

well-established and highly esteemed actors such as Ian Richardson and Simon Callow alongside those less well-known for 'straight' acting, such as David Walliams (then best known for comedy series *Little Britain*) and Jamie Theakston (primarily a radio and television presenter). Initial reports stated that the series was aiming even higher, with *Variety* claiming that Tom Hanks was in the frame. An ITV spokesperson denied the reports, suggesting that 'Miss Marple has, in fact, got her beady eye on a few of Mr. Hanks' contemporaries, although a good detective never reveals her hunches until the mystery is finally unravelled'.[4] Meanwhile, the most attention was paid to Joanna Lumley, whose casting as Dolly Bantry was one factor in opening the series with *The Body in the Library*, the second Miss Marple novel. Reflecting on the difference between Dolly and her character in outrageous comedy *Absolutely Fabulous*, Lumley remarked that 'unlike Patsy, Dolly is essentially good and moral in a way that women were in the 1950s. Nowadays if you were married to a boring man, as Dolly is, the advice would be to leave him or take a lover. But in those days you just got on with it.' For Lumley, Christie 'lives on not because an eccentric fan club decrees it, but because people all over the world still pick her up and think: "My God, I must read the next one!"'[5]

In this first adaptation, Dolly and Miss Marple are set up as a double act, to the extent that some viewers may be sad to realise that Mrs Bantry will not be a permanent fixture of the series (although Lumley returned for *The Mirror Crack'd from Side to Side* several years later, by which point Julia McKenzie was playing Miss Marple). However, this Miss Marple is a fiercely independent figure. Unlike the most famous previous screen versions of the character, McEwan's Marple does not rely on any recurring detective characters with which to spar. Instead, she is very definitely the star of the series. 'We wanted to get away from the whole tweedy, village spinster on a bicycle image,' stated McEwan, perhaps thinking of *Murder, She Wrote*'s cyclist detective Jessica Fletcher more than Miss Marple. 'She's a very independent woman who is living her own life. At the same time she loves people and is fascinated by them – whether they're involved in a murder or not. She is completely open-minded and non-judgmental. She's witty and likes a laugh but also takes the problems of others seriously. She's a flirt, too, which I rather like, and has an attractiveness that transcends age.'[6]

This flirtatious Miss Marple is a person who both understands and has experience of love and sex, as she is given a new backstory in which the audience learns that she had loved a married man who died during the First World War. Miss Marple's 'sexy side will stun her fans', announced the *Daily Mirror* shortly before the first episode was broadcast, and indeed the idea of her lost love surprised many viewers who had read the original stories. Most of this story was established in the second episode, *The Murder at the Vicarage*, which Clymer cites as one of his favourites of the run. The lost love 'was a Stephen Churchett thing', he says of the late screenwriter, 'and beautifully done. We needed to give her a life. We needed to help our audience understand how you can feel, how you can be in love, and the pain, and how those things can change you as a person. That was a big deal for us. It's all part of humanising her, because it's all about that emotional intelligence that very often wins the day.'

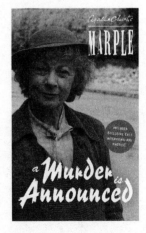

The third HarperCollins tie-in.

McEwan was aware that changes and additions 'might well be controversial for the diehard fans, but hopefully they will keep an open mind to the fact it is being made in 2004.'[7] Here was a television programme that was acutely conscious that it needed to appeal to a contemporary television audience in the twenty-first century. While the setting of the series in the past was an important element, even the period setting is made in broad strokes; this is almost a Technicolor version of England; a take on the post-war world of circa 1950 that looks as stylised as many of the films of the period, rather than the historical realities. This approach is embraced in the styling of many characters, including Miss Marple herself, whose costume is almost caricature-like in its slightly exaggerated representation of an old lady of the period, and certainly miles away from the Victorian depicted in the early stories, or the smarter look of Hickson. This is a representation of Miss Marple that makes her less thoughtful and quiet, but more adventurous and fun.

Adventures and fun are certainly the type of content that any mainstream broadcaster will want as part of their programming in order to appeal to large audiences. These are adaptations that have only around 95 minutes of screen time

4.50 – Murder, she said. . .?

per novel, and so stories and characters are inevitably condensed and simplified to fit the mould. There is also a new sense of structure that is more in line with modern television; many episodes open with a flashback to earlier events, which set up the mystery or a character's backstory in an intriguing way. Whereas Christie's stories were mostly linear, here the language of television requires an immediate hook for floating viewers, meaning that (for example) *The Body in the Library* has a literally explosive start, as we see the dropping of a German bomb during a dinner party.

One of the most talked about elements of *Agatha Christie's Marple* became the inclusion of overtly gay characters and subplots in several of the stories. In some cases, this merely meant making the implicit relationships more explicit; for example, Hinchcliffe and Murgatroyd in *A Murder is Announced* are now established as a romantic couple (with Murgatroyd now a family friend of Miss Marple's), which is how many readers interpreted them in the original novel. Elsewhere, the opportunity was taken to reflect relationships as seen in the twenty-first century, including a lesbian couple in *The Body in the Library*, whose relationship is not revealed until the final act, and certainly adds a new dimension to a sequence in which one of them helps a teenage girl to get changed.[8] Clymer states that there was no particular intention to shock: 'We were trying to present a world that's more recognisable as our world rather than as "Christie world". It didn't seem that big a deal to us, it seemed a much bigger deal to some of the audiences.' It certainly makes sense that a writer such as the late Kevin Elyot, a gay man whose plays such as *My Night with Reg* focused on queer lives, should want to make more of these aspects of British society that were rarely addressed by Christie. For those working on the series, the most important thing was to make the series an attractive proposition for modern television viewers. 'One of the challenges was, without alienating the existing constituency, to bring in more people into the party, in a sense,' says Clymer. 'I think we did. More people watched because of the casting and the way ITV scheduled it, a real solid Sunday night booking.' The 'shock' decision to make such alterations also resulted in some helpful attendant publicity, while it also meant that even die-hard Christie fans could never be quite sure whodunit until Miss Marple's final explanation.

When the series debuted on 12 December 2004, a 'solid Sunday night booking' is precisely what was delivered, with well over eight million viewers, which was maintained the following week.[9] Inevitably, critics were divided about a new take on such a well-known and much-loved character, and the producers were blamed for what some critics saw as unnecessary meddling. In an article headlined 'Who needs this thoroughly modernised Miss Marple?', David Stephenson in the *Sunday Express* complained that 'The truth is that television producers just can't leave anything alone. Audiences and readers alike love Agatha Christie because of the great stories and Marple's dry wit. *Poirot* is pitched just right. *Marple* should be pitched into the long grass.'[10] After three episodes, Christie biographer Laura Thompson made similar complaints in the *Daily Telegraph*: 'When Agatha Christie wrote detective fiction, she knew absolutely what she was doing. *Marple*, unfortunately, thinks that it knows better. It sees Christie as no more than a resilient framework around which all kinds of liberties can be taken; you can almost hear the cocky television executive saying: "Cheers, thanks for the outline, Agatha love – now we'll take over."'[11] Elsewhere, some critics embraced this fresh take on Miss Marple, while the series was successful internationally, and was even nominated for a Primetime Emmy Award. Positive critics included Paul Hoggart in *The Times*, who said of McEwan that 'She is different, but wonderful in her own way', and that the revisiting of such a well-known character 'is a dangerous conundrum. Most devotees probably want the escapism of the stylised past ... Well, of course, there were lesbians during post-war rationing, and perhaps Agatha Christie would have worked them into her plots in a different climate, so why not?'[12]

In summer 2005, production reconvened for the second season of *Agatha Christie's Marple*, with the first three episodes broadcast in February 2006, and the final film shown two months later. The first two adaptations are a good example of the varied ways that the series would go on to adapt Christie's works. Kevin Elyot's *The Moving Finger*, broadcast second, is heavily stylised at times thanks to Tom Shankland's distinctive direction but retains the core plot beats from Christie's original. This even includes Jerry Burton's narration and foregrounding as protagonist, in an early sign that perhaps the production was trying to find ways to ease the burden on seventy-three-year-old McEwan, who had been such a dominant presence in the first run, with the resultant long shooting schedules. This followed a less conventional adaptation of *Sleeping Murder*, which was an example of how the series was returning with the confidence to make more radical changes to the original works in order to repurpose them for a particular audience. In Stephen Churchett's script, the most striking example is the addition of a comedy theatrical troupe called 'The Funnybones', which allows for some broad performances from popular names such as Dawn French (whose character resides at a house called 'Dunlaughin') and Martin Kemp. *Agatha Christie's Marple* had rarely opted for subtlety, but this was a sign that the series wanted to be punchy and attention-grabbing for audiences who might join in primarily to see the beloved comedian or an ex-Spandau Ballet singer. Perhaps the best indication of the movement from inference and subtext to more overt storytelling is that the crucial line from the Duchess of Malfi is no longer 'Cover her face, mine eyes dazzle. She died young.' It is now the more on-the-nose 'strangling is a very quiet death'.

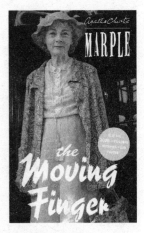

'New for 2006': *The Moving Finger* tie-in.

Agatha Christie's Marple had been such a commercial success in its first run that thoughts were turning to the future of the series, and it had always been clear that there was every chance that it would need more material than could be provided

The last of the McEwan tie-in books was *Sleeping Murder*.

by the twelve Miss Marple novels. Phil Clymer remembers that 'We were always going to parachute her into other stories. Agatha does kind of recycle stories; to her credit they're hard to spot but [sometimes] it's basically the same car with different wheels.' As it was not permissible to create entirely new Miss Marple mysteries, a way had to be found to involve Miss Marple in stories written for other characters. Stewart Harcourt adapted the Tommy and Tuppence novel *By the Pricking of My Thumbs* for Miss Marple to investigate, although the original investigators still appear. Miss Marple forms a detective duo with Tuppence (Greta Scacchi) while Tommy (Anthony Andrews) is away on MI6 business for most of the episode. The production may not feel like a traditional Miss Marple mystery, with its hints of fairytale fantasy, but it remains a jolly and exciting adventure, as McEwan leans into the quirkier end of her characterisation, as well as emphasising her confidence; not since Margaret Rutherford might an audience have expected to see Miss Marple standing on the back of an American GI's jeep as it careers down the road.[13]

The second and third seasons play with reinventions that riff on a theme from Agatha Christie, but increasingly move into their own world of the television series, rather than a depiction of Christie's original stories for the screen. *Agatha Christie's Marple* was now its own entity, known for its all-star casts and strong characters, settings and incidents. Stephen Churchett's *The Sittaford Mystery* was the final adaptation of the second run, with its snowy setting acting as a neat contrast to the more typically summery films seen so far. Here, the changes were the most radical yet, going far beyond simply dropping Miss Marple into the mystery of a murder in a cut-off house. Names are swapped, backstories changed, and the murderer's identity is altered. By now, not all of the series' writers were particularly concerned about fidelity, and instead wished to create their own entertaining productions; one privately stated that he enjoyed annoying some Christie fans with his changes. In some ways, *The Sittaford Mystery* is typical of *Agatha Christie's Marple*, as it offers a broadening out of what was a smaller scale mystery. This includes flashbacks and new characters, although its mass of elements sometimes distract from the core mystery rather than complement it. The adaptation also features the series' recurring preoccupations, in which real-life people of the period appear as characters in order to situate the programme more clearly in the 'real world'; in this case it is Winston Churchill, played by Robert Hardy.

As with the second series, the third run of *Agatha Christie's Marple* included two Miss Marple novels and two others in which she did not originally feature. The original Marples bookend the series, with Tom MacRae's *At Bertram's Hotel* as the opener in September 2007, followed by Stewart Harcourt's adaptation of *Ordeal by Innocence*. However, there was then nearly a year until Kevin Elyot's *Towards Zero* was broadcast, in August 2008, with Stephen Churchett's take on *Nemesis* not arriving on ITV screens until January 2009. By this point, many episodes were broadcast outside of the UK first, but this wasn't due to any concerns at ITV, although viewing figures had dropped to closer to five million. The simple reason was that *Marple* was an expensive series, and for accounting purposes the money was only considered 'spent' by ITV once the programme was broadcast, making the programme a good choice to be delayed until later when money was tight.

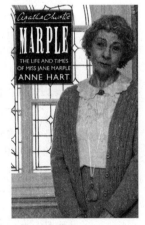

Anne Hart's biography also got a tie-in cover in 2005.

In this third season, *Ordeal by Innocence* sees

Miss Marple as an old friend and employer invited to a wedding, and it manages to insert the sleuth into a non-Marple novel in an effective and reasonably organic way, keeping to the original mystery fairly closely. Similarly, *Towards Zero* has Miss Marple take on many of the duties of the original novel's investigator, Superintendent Battle. However, both *At Bertram's Hotel* and *Nemesis* extensively rework the Miss Marple novels, indicating that the choice of an original Marple novel was no indication of the production's fidelity to the source. For *At Bertram's Hotel*, this includes the addition of a subplot about twins, which mirrors a theme of the original novel: that appearances can be deceptive. This adaptation also includes a further attempt to give Miss Marple a younger companion, as had happened with Amanda Holden's Lucy Eyelesbarrow in *4.50 from Paddington*, which was such a success that Phil Clymer suggested that the character be revisited somehow. This was vetoed, but Martine McCutcheon's depiction of a maid called Jane is as close as television has yet come to 'Young Miss Marple', as she shares duties with McEwan not only during the investigation, but also during the final explanatory speech, which is always exhausting for lead actors in Agatha Christie dramas. For *Nemesis*, new characters are introduced, meaning that we get to see Raymond West (Richard E. Grant), while Agnes and Clotilde are now sisters of a different type, in an alteration that uses heavy-handed symbolism: they are now nuns.

By the third season, Geraldine McEwan was starting to tire of working on the series. The schedule was heavy, and she was dissatisfied with some elements of the production, including the lateness of some of the scripts. As an experienced actor and star of the show, she could also be demanding, and this led to friction between her and some of those working on the production. For Clymer, this was just an example of McEwan's dedication to her craft. 'I loved Geraldine, she was a great actor,' he recalls. 'She was finding it very hard work. She wasn't easy because she set very high standards for herself; she came from a background where she expected everyone to have those high standards.' Speaking at the launch of what would be her final run as Miss Marple, McEwan recalled that originally 'I was filled with trepidation. Joan was a hard act to follow. But I decided to be Marple my own way, as lighter, flightier and with a twinkle ... Miss Marple has become very special to me and transformed my life ... I find myself walking down the street knowing exactly how Miss Marple would react to any situation that comes up.'[14] Despite her fondness for the character, McEwan decided that the third season would be her last.

While McEwan's time as Miss Marple had come to an end, the series was still in good health, and so it was immediately decided to recast the role. It was felt that it was best not to let news of the change of actor worry the higher-ups at ITV, and so casting was quietly undertaken so that a new Miss Marple could be presented as a *fait accompli* alongside news of McEwan's departure. Many names had been suggested for the series ever since the initial casting, including Susan Hampshire, Anna Massey, Barbara Flynn and Pauline Collins, but following the filmed auditions there was a clear front runner: Julia McKenzie. Focus groups were shown the footage and reported that 'she encapsulates the key Marple-like qualities' by 'Appearing to be unassuming "little old lady" but disguising a fierce intelligence and tenacity, balanced with warmth, kindness and vulnerability.' The series had found its new Miss Marple, with an actor who needed to encapsulate precisely these qualities, as well as being able to star in a physically demanding series.

HarperCollins published two new tie-ins for the new Marple (2009).

Julia McKenzie remembers that there seemed to be a long gap between her filmed audition and confirmation of the role, but that events moved quickly once all was confirmed. On hearing the news, she replied that 'Well, I'll have to sit down, my knees have gone a bit funny!' Despite being on holiday in New Zealand, producers immediately sent her a script for *A Pocket Full of Rye*, adapted by Kevin Elyot: 'I flew back and I was on camera in a week and a half maybe,' remembers McKenzie, 'so a lot of choices had to be made very early on.'[15] Having studied the script on the plane, McKenzie was aware of the scale of the production she was joining, and that the existing scripts had been prepared for her predecessor. Nevertheless, her Miss Marple would be her own character, and this included a new wardrobe. 'I knew I wanted to look as though she'd had clothes for a long while,' she says, but there was little time to consider too many options. 'I probably wouldn't have gone quite as baggy. I'm not saying I didn't

Joan Collins as Ruth Van Rydock in Series 4's *They Do It with Mirrors*.

agree with it, but I was rushed into it somewhat and my only qualm was I wanted a different hat! If you ever look at the first episode, I've got the hat I wanted, and after that I have the hat the producer wanted, which I felt made her too noticeable. I liked the soft little trilby that she'd had on the wardrobe for a couple of years.'

Although a minor detail, the issue of McKenzie's hat in some way sums up the difficult struggle of the series, in which an unobtrusive person must also be the star. McKenzie is a highly experienced actor, but even for her the character of Miss Marple presented a challenge. 'The difficulty with playing it – and it is difficult, very difficult, almost the most difficult thing I've ever done – is that she's the person that's least likely to solve [the crime] when you see her, but that person is leading a series, so you have to be a little bolder than you might. I tried to play it ordinary and let the others turn cartwheels.' This ordinariness is an effective contrast with McEwan's depiction, and helps to establish Christie's original conception of Miss Marple as an observer above all else. McKenzie noted that the character was the one person who had to simultaneously show that she was working out the crime, while also not revealing too much to the audience:

and so she can't be entirely truthful with everything or she gives everything away. If you look at any other detective, they've always got cohorts. In fact, I have to say I liked *Poirot* better when it had the other two characters in it, the relationships between them. But she's on her own, and wherever she goes, there's a murder. It's not like she's Poirot, who's [asked to] investigate the murder. So don't invite her, because someone's gonna get killed! It's a fantasy, of course. But that doesn't make it easy to play it in a real way and that's all I tried to do, to make a nice person, essentially English. Essentially of her period.

The period itself caused some issues for McKenzie, who remembers that 'I wanted to make her aware of the fifties, but not always approving, just about managing.' McKenzie felt that Miss Marple was sometimes treated like an old lady of 1930 rather than 1950: 'It just makes her slightly different. That's quite a lot, twenty years.'

McKenzie was aware of the screen legacy of Miss Marple, including her immediate predecessor, but she was not looking to replicate any earlier performances. 'Well, Geraldine was a very particular actress, very wonderful actress and her theatre career was fantastic. But she's quirky. Miss Marple *can* be quirky, but Geraldine was playing off her basic self. I played off *my* basic self.' Even now, it was Joan Hickson who was still casting the longest shadow. 'She was super,' says McKenzie. 'It was such a true performance. Really ace. I don't have that in me, so I couldn't [replicate it]. I think everybody who's ever played Marple feels that Joan Hickson was *it*. Absolutely *it*.' Shortly before her first episode was shown, McKenzie told the press that there had been a brief correspondence between

The second Julia McKenzie tie-in book (2009).

Miss Marples when the role had passed between actors: '[Geraldine McEwan] wrote to me and I wrote back. But we haven't actually met, and we've never worked together, which is a strange thing. She said she was pleased it was me and I wrote back and said it would be hard to replace her, and all the things you would expect. But I think it must have been very hard for her to give the part up. But it is tremendously hard work. If you're not feeling quite up to scratch – I think she had a little hip problem, I'm not sure, or something like that. If you see Marple walking up a hill once, you've done that twelve times in filming. It's quite wearing when you're older.'[16]

Production on Julia McKenzie's first series

of *Agatha Christie's Marple* began with a read-through at Pinewood Studios on 25 February, with filming *on A Pocket Full of Rye* then taking place for a month from 2 March 2008. McKenzie particularly enjoyed working with director Charlie Palmer, who put the actor at her ease, as she tried to build up her own take on Miss Marple: McKenzie was inspired by one of the lines in her first script, 'which was something like "all evil must be punished", and that was the driving force really,' she remembers. McKenzie was aware that not all the adaptations that she was in were drawn from Miss Marple stories, and

A French DVD release of *The Blue Geranium*.

this meant that her role could differ quite substantially from her usual quiet and thoughtful character. Stephen Churchett's script of *Murder is Easy* added Miss Marple to a village setting that seems suitable, although when she reveals the details of an incestuous rape during the denouement (not a part of the original novel), the series is pushing the character to the limit of what she may expect to discuss.

These first two episodes were broadcast in the UK in September 2009, more than a year after production; when the first episode debuted, McKenzie sent McEwan a bouquet of flowers to show that she understood the difficulties of giving up such a big part. Paul Rutman's adaptation of *They Do It with Mirrors* was then shown on New Year's Day 2010, having been filmed in September 2008. The series continued to capitalise on its distinctive identity, showcasing its starry cast, including the likes of Joan Collins and Brian Cox. This was followed by *Why Didn't They Ask Evans?* adapted by Patrick Barlow, which was filmed in August 2008, but wasn't shown by ITV until June 2011, after the fifth run of *Marple* had been broadcast. Perhaps this was because the film is such an anomaly, as Miss Marple is parachuted into a runaround adventure (passing herself off

Greenshaw's Folly expanded from a novella to a full-length episode.

as the governess of spirited young Frankie) that is quite unsuited to her quiet methods of detection. Such inconsistencies were noted by the series' star, who enjoyed the production, but felt that it portrayed Miss Marple in a different way to the rest of the programme. 'I liked that because she was trying to keep up, she wasn't going to be an old lady with [younger characters]. But it wasn't in the writing after that.' With such a quick start to her work on the series, McKenzie didn't get the chance to really establish the character as well as she would have liked: 'They were all so different to me because they're all by different writers, all by different directors. Sometimes there would be a line in the script and you think, "this isn't her, I can't do that." There are several things I would like to have changed, but I didn't feel I had the power to do that.'

A fifth season of *Agatha Christie's Marple* went into production in mid-2009, and this time the series debuted with a non-Marple novel, *The Pale Horse*, scripted by Russell Lewis, shown by ITV on 30 August 2010. Once more, this does not feel like a natural mystery for Miss Marple to investigate, and both this run and the final sixth season adapted so many different types of stories that it barely seems to be the same series from episode to episode as it moves from the semi-supernatural antics of *The Pale Horse* to the more lightweight capers of *The Secret of Chimneys*. Adapted by Paul Rutman, McKenzie enjoyed working with Stephen Dillane for the latter film, and speaks warmly of the high-quality actors with whom she got to work throughout the series. *Chimneys* was one of Christie's earlier novels, while by the end of the final run of *Marple* she would appear in an adaptation of one of Christie's later novels, the psychological thriller *Endless Night*, a story that could scarcely be more different. McKenzie herself had suggested *Crooked House* would be suitable, and it would certainly have been interesting to see Miss Marple wrestle with the family dynamics seen in that memorable mystery. There is a fine line between variety and lack of cohesion, and the series sometimes struggled with this. In part this may have been due to some key members of the production team working on other series, while Chorion had entered a difficult financial period, which meant that the series did not always receive the close attention that it had been granted previously.

The fifth and sixth seasons did finally exploit some of the long-neglected Miss Marple short stories, however, with *The Blue Geranium* (adapted by Stewart Harcourt) and *Greenshaw's Folly* (by Tim Whitnall). Both necessarily added material to the original stories to make them suitable for two hours of television, but by now the series was adept when it came to expanding parts of the narrative and introducing new subplots. *The Blue Geranium* puts Miss Marple in the centre of the plot, unlike the original story where she was simply hearing the tale second-hand, and Miss Marple is now so involved that she gets to reveal the truth in a courtroom to the presiding judge. McKenzie was not keen on the way that a village parallel was expressed in this setting: 'If I'd had the power I would have said, "this doesn't sit",' she says. 'It was about one of her neighbours, Mrs "Somebody"'s knitting and she's talking to a judge and saying, "well, it was like [her] knitting, it was very tangled". I could see that happening twenty years before, but when they brought it into the fifties, only a nutcase would say that to a judge! That's the sort of thing that did not gel with me very much and you do find it very hard to act it.'

For *Greenshaw's Folly*, extra material included

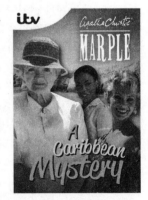

The production moved to Cape Town to film this story.

the insertion of elements from another Miss Marple short story, 'The Thumb Mark of St Peter'. Extra clues, murders and subplots were added to the story, which enabled television viewers who were not readers of Christie to experience some Miss Marple mysteries that would be new to them. One unavoidable element of any adaptation was the lengthy denouement, in which Miss Marple has to explain all. McKenzie recalls that 'you dreaded it. [The camera] is on you while other actors sit around playing their parts and reacting. But, of course, getting bored to death with you because you're the only thing!' When one of her co-stars once fell asleep during the filming of such a sequence, McKenzie sympathised. McKenzie also enjoyed working with Joanna Lumley in *The Mirror Crack'd from Side to Side*, which concluded the fifth series. 'She's everything you think she is and more,' McKenzie says, 'she's so lovely. She could see that I perhaps wasn't quite as confident as I might have been, and she wrote me such a supportive lovely letter; that was tremendously kind.'

The final season of *Agatha Christie's Marple* featured only three adaptations, opening with *A Caribbean Mystery*, the last Miss Marple novel to be filmed for the series. Although broadcast in June 2013, Charlie Higson first wrote a script for the adaptation in early 2007, with budgetary reasons the likely explanation for the delay. Production decamped to South Africa to film the 'Caribbean' sequences where, just as had happened with both previous screen treatments of the mystery, the crew were hit by some bad luck. 'Dreadful weather,' remembers McKenzie, 'and of course, we were in Cape Town, which is exquisite. So beautiful. I was treated very well, and it was wonderful, a marvellous experience. But [when] doing one of the big dinner scenes where everybody's outdoors, they propped up stuff to keep the rain off us, but it collected up there so much, the whole lot caved in on us!' One highlight of the trip was an evening dinner for the cast and crew which allowed everyone to dress up, and McKenzie was thrilled to learn that the chief camera operator didn't recognise her when not in her usual Marple garb. For this adaptation, Higson kept fairly closely to the original story, but inserted the character of Ian Fleming, who meets the ornithologist James Bond (played by Higson himself).[17]

The series soundtrack by Dominik Scherrer was finally released on CD in 2020.

With the broadcast of *Greenshaw's Folly* and then, at the end of 2013, Kevin Elyot's adaptation of *Endless Night*, it seemed that *Agatha Christie's Marple* had come to a natural end. *Endless Night* struggled to introduce Miss Marple into a narrative that requires her to be so close to a young couple that she almost becomes their stalker, so awkwardly does she intrude on their lives.[18] There were no more Miss Marple novels to adapt, and although several short stories were available, there didn't seem to be the same interest in continuing the series that there had been. Conversely, the BBC was now interested in taking on some of the other Christie titles, which meant that there were other avenues for adaptation beyond this series; *Endless Night* was exactly the sort of title that could have benefited from the treatment that the corporation would give *And Then There Were None* in 2015. For McKenzie, the time was right to say goodbye to Miss Marple. 'When it finished that was it and I thought, "I won't go back to it. It's very hard and I'm not getting younger." I was taken out to lunch by one of the producers who didn't actually say "would you do another one?" but sort of said "we're thinking of maybe doing one for Christmas..." and I said, oh dear, I don't think I'd be up for that.'

Agatha Christie's Marple had faced an almost impossible task initially, as it operated in the shadow of Joan Hickson's portrayal of the character, but it cleverly established itself as very much its own series. While existing die-hard fans have often baulked at the changes made to Christie's stories for the series, the colourful and stylised productions attracted new audiences, thanks in no small part to the casts of recognisable faces who appealed beyond the existing pool of Agatha Christie readers. It would have been a fruitless exercise to simply attempt to replicate what had gone before, and now that two decades have passed since the programme's debut, there are many fans of Christie who were first introduced to her work through *Agatha Christie's Marple*, and grew up with Geraldine McEwan and Julia McKenzie's takes on St Mary Mead's sleuth.

Reinventing Miss Marple

Although Miss Marple may be a quintessentially English creation, and a woman whose roots in Victorian culture are essential to her character, there have been repeated attempts to bring the character to life in ways that break her free of St Mary Mead. Miss Marple has been seen around the world on screen, sometimes in productions directly licensed by Agatha Christie Ltd, but often in productions that are less official. In 1983, Ita Ever played a Rubik's Cube-playing version of the character in the Soviet Union's *Secret of the Blackbirds*, directed by Vadim Derbenyov (aka *The Blackbirds Mystery*, an adaption of *A Pocket Full of Rye*).[19] Sometimes the clash of cultures may seem a little odd, including a Soviet castle standing in as an English country house, but the production makes great

ABOVE: Susie Blake had a successful run as Miss Marple in a touring production of *The Mirror Crack'd from Side to Side* in 2022-23.

Ita Ever in a Russian version of *A Pocket Full of Rye* (1983).

attempts to situate the story in then-contemporary Britain, including original location filming in London. Most striking is Ita Ever herself, who gives a strong performance as a charming and confident Miss Marple, who adroitly sees the path to the truth. Extra action is added to supplement the action, including a bomb being placed in Miss Marple's handbag, making for an original and effective take on Christie's story.

An essential part of Miss Marple's character is her placement in society, as she is overlooked by those in authority due to her status as an older unmarried woman. As such, it's interesting to see how other countries rework the role of an older female lead detective. 2003's *Shubho Muharat* (*The First Shoot*, directed by Rituparno Ghosh) adapts some of the basics of *The Mirror Crack'd from Side to Side*, but places it within Indian culture in this Bengali language film. Acclaimed actor Raakhee Gulzar plays Ranga Pishima, this film's version of Miss Marple, who, like the original character, is an aunt, but here is altogether more maternal, perhaps due to Indian society's stronger emphasis on the importance of strong familial relations. Miss Marple's unerring ability to deduce what is really going on remains present in this version of the character, as indicated by the film's dedication:

> To those Miss Marples who have guessed what's wrong when their sons skip school feigning an upset stomach, but have remained silent ... To those Miss Marples who have guessed what's wrong when their daughters return from their in-laws with blotchy eyes, but have remained silent.

The film itself is more of an extended homage than a close adaptation, and this is typical of many international adaptations that are influenced by both the works of Christie and the character of Miss Marple.[20]

In the last twenty years, Japan has explored Miss Marple mysteries a few times. The charming anime series *Agatha Christie's Great Detectives Poirot and Marple* (2004–5) adapted several Miss Marple stories, including the novels *4.50 from Paddington* and *Sleeping Murder*. More interestingly for Marple devotees, the series provides rare screen adaptations of several Miss Marple short stories, namely 'Strange Jest', 'The Case of the Perfect Maid', 'Tape-Measure Murder', 'Ingots of Gold', 'Motive v Opportunity', and 'The Blue Geranium' (the only one to have been seen on screen elsewhere, as part of *Agatha Christie's Marple*). Kaoru Yachigusa voices the gentle Miss Marple in these lively and faithful adaptations, which add Miss Marple's great-niece, Mabel West (daughter of Raymond, and so a different character to the Mabel of 'The Thumb Mark of St. Peter'), as the series' narrator and protagonist, who moves between assisting Miss Marple and Poirot with her pet duck Oliver. Animation is a perfect way to present some of Christie's more visual murders, particularly as it allows for a fair

Raakhee Gulzar as the Bengali Miss Marple, Ranga Pishima (2003).

Veteran Japanese actor Kaora Yachigusa voiced the anime Miss Marple (2004-5).

obscuring of secret or double identities, and the programme is both charming and well-made.

Live action television adaptations of Christie in Japan have been lavish and well-publicised affairs, although Miss Marple does not always feature.[21] In 2018's *Night Express Train Murder* (*4.50 from Paddington*), Miss Marple is replaced with the character Toko Amano, described as 'a successful police officer and professional in risk management'.[22] The story had earlier been adapted alongside *The Mirror Crack'd from Side to Side* and *A Murder is Announced* (2006-7), investigated by Junko Mabuchi (played by Keiko Kishi); a mystery-loving older woman who is more clearly reminiscent of the original Miss Marple. Miss Marple was then absent from 2018's adaptation of *The Mirror Crack'd from Side to Side*, and 2019's *A Murder is Announced*, lavish productions that relocate the stories to modern-day Japan.[23] In South Korea, the publicity for the 2018 series *Ms Ma, Nemesis* indicated that it features a local version of Miss Marple, but the character is quite unlike Christie's creation in several ways; Ms Ma is a mother who has been wrongly convicted of the murder of her ten-year-old daughter, and sets out to find the truth. Along the way, the character (played by Yunjin Kim) adopts the identity of mystery writer Ms Ma and finds herself in the centre of several storylines that revisit elements of Miss Marple novels, to greater or lesser degrees. These include the titular *Nemesis*, as well as *The Moving Finger*, *The Mirror Crack'd from Side to Side*, *A Murder is Announced*, *The Body in the Library* and *At Bertram's Hotel*. Initially, there were some at Agatha Christie Ltd who, instinctively, were concerned about the premise of a Miss Marple-type character in prison for murder at the beginning of the series, but as they heard more about the series, they became more willing to see this new take on the stories. Although superficially quite unlike Miss Marple (Yunjin Kim was only forty-four years old when the series was made), Ms Ma shares her passion for knitting, and, more significantly, her dogged determination to find out the truth through a perceptive reading of the people she meets; it's just that here she meets them in modern-day South Korea, not in St Mary Mead of the twentieth century. The series has more in common with Christie's character and stories than the French series *Les Petits Meurtres d'Agatha Christie*, which since 2009 has adapted many of the writer's mysteries in a production that uses its own detectives and often just presents elements of the original mysteries. The majority of the Miss Marple novels have featured in the series, which has moved from the 1930s to the 1970s, with different mismatched detectives for each era.

Yunjin Kim (centre) in South Korea's 2018 series *Ms Ma, Nemesis*.

One recurring project that has so far failed to see the light of the day is *Young Miss Marple*, which was originally announced in 2011, with Jennifer Garner attached to play the sleuth.[24] Garner was keen on the project, but it repeatedly

Maria Amelia Monti as Miss Marple on stage in Italy

stalled, despite a script being written by Mark Frost that reinvented Miss Marple as a quiet Californian bookseller. In 2015 a similar project was announced again, this time with David Wolstencroft as writer, for the CBS network. This series failed to materialise but rumours of a younger version of Miss Marple have persisted ever since.

However, when yet another Miss Marple series was announced in 2019, to be produced by *Big Little Lies*' Bruna Papandrea, there was no longer any mention of a young version of the character. As Agatha Christie Ltd's CEO and Chair James Prichard points out, there is a middle ground between the two, and he has suggested that a Miss Marple in her early sixties might be an interesting perspective. 'The world is ready for a Marple series,' he believes, 'and I think it is time to do something really first rate and first class.' Although he acknowledges the strengths of Joan Hickson's portrayal, Prichard thinks that Hickson's age gave a particular perception of the character: 'There is that feeling in people's heads that Miss Marple was always very old. And actually, I think if you read the books, particularly the earlier ones, I don't think she's *that* old, and she's certainly not inactive. You see a far more active, interesting, dynamic woman than maybe we imagine. I think that's something that could be explored.'[25] Although Prichard specifies that there are no current plans to make a *Young Miss Marple* series, at least until an older version of the character is reintroduced to the viewing public, this hasn't stopped some producers considering it.

Agatha Christie stage productions have proven to be such a continued success that more titles have been added to the portfolio for touring companies, including a couple of Miss Marple adaptations. In Italy, Edoardo Erba adapted *They Do It* with *Mirrors* in 2018 for a production that starred Maria Amelia Monti as Miss Marple in a faithful production; James Prichard was particularly impressed with the character's appearance in this production, which showed her as an older woman who still had energy and zest. In Britain, Rachel Wagstaff's adaptation of *The Mirror Crack'd from Side to Side* premiered in Salisbury in March 2019 before a short tour. A new tour of the play then premiered in September 2022, and in both instances the part of Miss Marple was played by the superlative Susie Blake, but the productions

Yuki Amami as Toko Amano in Japan's 2018 version of *4.50 from Paddington.*

were not identical. The original version made more of the character of Larry (added for this production), a lost love of Miss Marple who was shot for cowardice. The staging and production design was also quite different, although both were effectively choreographed, with the hard-working cast rarely off stage. Even Miss Marple's costume was altered between runs, as her appearance in trousers for the first tour reverted to a more traditional skirt for the second run. For the most part, the stage version of the story moves between Miss Marple's cottage and Gossington Hall, meaning that although Miss Marple necessarily misses some of the key action (as in the novel), she is most definitely the anchor for the production, as other characters share their thoughts and perspectives with her. As one reviewer pointed out, 'The play concentrates on relationships as much as events, which seems right for what is perhaps Christie's most poignant story.'[26] The result is a thoughtful production that fleshes out the character of Miss Marple while sticking closely to the original story. Given the play's success, it seems unlikely that this will be the final new adaptation of Miss Marple for the stage.

Marple: Twelve New Stories
(Short stories, 2022)

In 2014 *The Monogram Murders* was published, a new Poirot novel written by best-selling author Sophie Hannah, and inevitably many fans wondered if Miss Marple would be next to get the treatment, but there were no immediate plans. Hannah felt that her loyalty to Poirot ruled out her writing for Miss Marple too, while Agatha Christie Ltd and HarperCollins were keen not to simply replicate the earlier approach. Several possibilities were discussed over the years, but the time didn't feel right until, one day, HarperCollins publisher David Brawn made a suggestion. James Prichard remembers that 'We had

ABOVE LEFT: HarperCollins' UK hardback had a minimalist design by Holly Macdonald focusing on the book title, with the twelve contributors' names relegated to the spine (2022). **ABOVE RIGHT:** The US jacket from William Morrow was painted by Holly Ovenden and continued a floral theme from her 2002 paperback reissues.

one of our annual reviews with HarperCollins in the UK and, at the end of the meeting, David Brawn said: "What do you all think about the idea of doing a collection of short stories, with different authors, for Miss Marple?" We all looked at each other and went "David, you have not mentioned this to any of us, but it's a brilliant idea!"'

A decision was swiftly made to have Miss Marple return to her roots with a collection of short stories by a diverse group of women writers, who not only had different backgrounds but were associated with different genres of writing. When approaching these writers, the most important thing was that they should have a passion for writing Miss Marple. 'I think pretty much everyone we approached wanted to do it,' says Prichard, and indeed one was so keen that she immediately sketched out her story despite considerable commitments elsewhere. Bringing in writers who were not all best known for crime fiction had two perceived benefits. The first was that they could bring a fresh perspective on a well-known character; secondly, it was hoped that such writers would help to introduce new readers to the world of Agatha Christie, as their

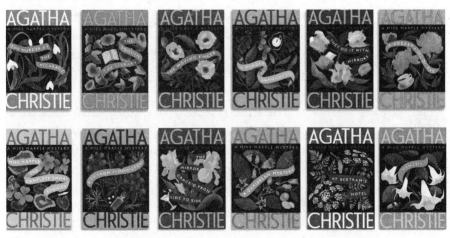

The William Morrow paperbacks, designed by Holly Ovenden (2022).

fans would hopefully be keen to read their contributions to the new collection. There was no 'star' writer of the collection, as each author was expected to bring something new to the world of Marple.

Initially, there were thoughts that the new collection might follow a particular structure, perhaps replicating the Tuesday Night Club of *The Thirteen Problems*. However, it was soon decided that this would be too constrictive and complicated. Instead, the new authors were furnished with a short but important list of rules to adhere to, but otherwise left to get on with their work, with the expectation that the stories were not to be pastiches; instead, the hope was that they would feel like both Christie and the author. These rules were straightforward, and included a request that the mysteries be set between the years 1927 and 1971 (which saw the publication of Christie's first and final Miss Marple stories, excluding the posthumous *Sleeping Murder*), which immediately ruled out any 'Young Miss Marple' exercises, as well as the death of the sleuth, while it was also stipulated that Miss Marple should not meet Poirot, and nor should she have any love affairs. Inevitably, there was some nervousness attached to

the project, and so it was a great relief when the first story arrived (Ruth Ware's 'Miss Marple's Christmas'), which was immediately seen as proof that the new Miss Marple volume had every chance of being a success.

The final selection of authors also took Miss Marple into the present day, not by means of time travel, but because many of the writers took the opportunity to be more explicit about attitudes and elements of society that may have been left more implicit in Christie's writings. This means that certain prejudices are both acknowledged and engaged with, including in

The Indonesian edition from Gramedia (2023).

Alyssa Cole's 'Miss Marple Takes Manhattan' and Jean Kwok's 'The Jade Empress'. Both rely on the reader's understanding of widespread societal attitudes, including problematic ones, to inform their knowledge of the situations and even help them to solve the mysteries. Both also show an active Miss Marple, still making use of Raymond's generosity to see the world, as she visits both New York and Hong Kong. These travels invoke memories of *A Caribbean Mystery*, which, in turn, influences Dreda Say Mitchell's 'A Deadly Wedding Day'. This story sees Miss Marple as a guest at a wedding, having been invited by Miss Bella, a friend from St Honoré.

The Polish translation from Wydawnictwo Dolnoslaskie (2023).

The pairing of two old ladies, one English and one African Caribbean, gives Mitchell the chance to compare cultures: 'Agatha Christie put her stamp on this wise older woman who is a real figurehead for single women who are postmenopausal, which I am now,' the author told *The Sunday Post*. 'Christie always had a male character who dismissed Miss Marple because of her age, whereas Miss Bella is from the Caribbean community where we almost revere older people. Christie did that with Marple by making her the smartest person in the room. That's not usually how we think about women of a particular age in our society. She's a fabulous character.'[27]

Other stories in the collection feel as if they might have been lifted from Christie, albeit with their authors' own takes on character, motivation and style. Natalie Haynes' 'The Unravelling' is exactly the sort of story with a twist that might have featured in *The Thirteen Problems*, while it also makes use of its author's expertise in its retelling of a Greek myth, something that Christie also referenced. In Val McDermid's 'The Second Murder at the Vicarage', meanwhile, the reader can delight in becoming reacquainted with the exasperated and

The Guinness World Record-breaking *Complete Miss Marple*, published in 2009, leatherbound with its own wooden carry case.

rather unlucky Reverend Clement, who is quite put out to find a stranger dead in his home. Much thought was also given to the ordering of the stories in the collection, to ensure the book felt balanced with a good rhythm, with Lucy Foley's 'Evil in Small Places' eventually picked as the opener, partly because it both embraces and reworks traditional Marple elements, as the character visits an old friend and solves a murder, which leads to a conclusion that may surprise those who believe they understand the usual pattern of Miss Marple investigations. The ordering also means that the stories subtly follow the seasons, starting in autumn and finishing in late summer.

Coincidentally, two authors considered writing a Christmas story, with Ruth Ware's 'Miss Marple's Christmas' winning the cordial battle, as she proposed her premise first. This story acknowledges the wider world of detective fiction, as a Dorothy L. Sayers mystery inspires criminal actions in a pleasingly small-scale and effectively constructed tale. Other authors push in different directions from the world of Miss Marple and St Mary Mead, as in Naomi Alderman's 'The Open Mind', which serves as a foray into the world of academic research of 1970 and gives the Marple universe its first mention of a 'computing machine' in a story that is a neat contrast to more traditional village antics.[28] Locating a story around St Mary Mead is not necessarily an indication that the reader should expect the familiar, however, and surprises are in store in Leigh Bardugo's 'The Disappearance'. Meanwhile, Kate Mosse's 'The Mystery of the Acid Soil' is a tale that is cleverly plotted and benefits from strong char-

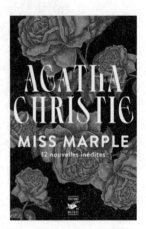

acterisation of Miss Marple, as one might expect from a fan, which Mosse certainly is. Mosse had previously written an introduction to a complete collection of Miss Marple stories, which is officially a record-breaker as the thickest book in the world (at 4,032 pages its spine is over a foot long), and was one of the first to be approached for the project. 'Miss Marple is one of those exceptional characters in fiction, in that she is an old woman who is there on her own terms,' Mosse told an interviewer; 'she gets to solve the mysteries because old women are overlooked'.[29] In Mosse's story, there is no doubt that Miss Marple remains a formidable figure with a sharp mind even as

The French edition from Editions du Masque (2023).

she ages, a sentiment that was continued in the marketing of both this collection and new editions of the original Miss Marple books, which used the tagline 'Never Underestimate Miss Marple'.

Elly Griffiths' 'Murder at the Villa Rosa' supplies another type of Miss Marple mystery, with a case that emphasises her kind nature and desire to help those around her, this time in Italy (with the setting partially inspired by Griffiths' Italian father), in a story that plays with mystery conventions. Another side of the character is also seen in Karen M. McManus's 'The Murdering Sort', which stylistically is perhaps the least like Christie, with its use of present-tense and inclusion of Miss Marple's spirited great niece Nicola, granddaughter of Raymond West, as its protagonist. It was a deliberate policy to include stories by best-selling authors of books aimed at young adults, with both McManus and Leigh Bardugo appealing to readers who are often of an age where they first experience the world of Agatha Christie. It seems that the principle of Miss Marple will work almost anywhere, and the character's appearance in Cape Cod shows a charming relationship between the now surely very elderly Miss Marple and her extended family.[30]

The new Miss Marple collection was published in September 2022 as *Marple: Twelve New Stories*, after many discussions about potential titles, from nursery rhymes to Shakespeare and Tennyson quotes, but none felt as iconic as the simple statement of Miss Marple's surname. The accompanying publicity included a promotional edition of the St Mary Mead parish newsletter that even featured a rock cake recipe, as per Natalie Haynes' story, while the audiobook mirrored the written collection by featuring a different reader for each story, each of them as impressive as the roster of authors, including Miriam Margolyes, Alison Steadman and Adjoa Andoh. Only a few final tweaks were made before publication, including, after heated debate, the removal of a use of the f-word; fans will be relieved to hear that it was not uttered by Miss Marple herself. 'I think one of the things that I loved about the whole thing was everyone I spoke to actually had a different favourite,' says James Prichard, 'and that's part of the fun of it when you've got twelve different authors who are

The Spanish edition from Espasa (2023).

To help promote the new book, 2022 also saw the publication of the first Agatha Christie wall calendar.

taking on one character.' The collection certainly achieved its aim for diversity, both in terms of the authors but also the stories they told, which meant that there was something for everyone. *The Times* described the collection as 'half treat, half carpet-bag curio', which perhaps it will be for many readers, although precisely which half is 'treat' and which is 'curio' will differ between individuals.[31] More simply, the *Guardian* called it 'a testament to the enduring power of Christie's imagination', while it was also testament to the popularity of both the world of Agatha Christie and Miss Marple, as the book became such a bestseller that the publisher struggled to keep up with the pre-Christmas demand.[32] It seems that Miss Marple is more popular than ever.

ST MARY MEAD
PARISH AND VILLAGE NEWS

September, 2022   No. 1   Price: Free

MISS MARPLE IS BACK

SIGHTINGS IN MANHATTAN AND HONG KONG

Agatha Christie's iconic detective is back – and she has not one, but twelve new mysteries to solve.

Miss Marple's crime-solving spree will transport her from our quiet little village of St Mary Mead to the bustling streets of New York, to the sun-soaked Italian Riviera and beyond.

She may be an unassuming old lady, but nobody knows better than Jane Marple the wickedness that lurks around every corner . . .

FROM FLORA TO FOUL –
HOW WELL DO YOU KNOW YOUR POISONOUS PLANTS? PG 17

READ EXCLUSIVE EXTRACTS INSIDE

PUT YOUR DETECTION SKILLS TO THE TEST PG. 25

EPILOGUE

Miss Marple's Next Cases

'I don't know why people should want to write about me,' said a typically self-effacing Agatha Christie, and perhaps Miss Marple would feel the same.[1] However, once Miss Marple was released into the world from her imagination, Christie could have no control over the extent to which the reading public took the spinster sleuth of St Mary Mead to their hearts. Christie notably never displayed the irritation with the character that she had with the more prolific Hercule Poirot and suggested a preference for Miss Marple when questioned. However, she was always keen to ensure that we understood Miss Marple as a symbol for a particular type of old lady, and certainly not a character rigidly based on one person, whether Christie herself or one of her grandmothers. Perhaps it is the fact that Miss Marple has so much of her life that is unexplained and unexplored that has allowed readers to fill in the blanks and create their own Miss Marple in their head, whom they may associate with a favourite aunt, grandmother or neighbour. Certainly, Miss Marple has consistently received an outpouring of love from readers that is unusual for any fictional character. Miss Marple is a favourite of readers because

OPPOSITE: The cover of the 28-page 'parish magazine' released to promote *Marple* (2022).

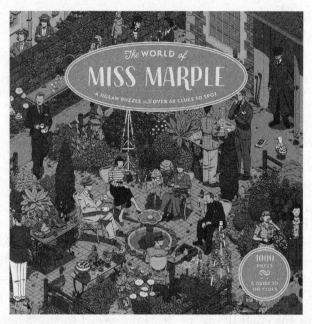

The official Miss Marple jigsaw puzzle, illustrated by Ilya Milstein and published in 2024 by Laurence King, was an immediate bestseller, demonstrating that the public's appetite for the character is undiminished.

she quietly but firmly stands up for the power of good, while defeating wickedness.

But what next for Miss Marple? James Prichard acknowledges that Miss Marple has always been a little in the shadow of Poirot, but has a desire to see a new prestigious screen production that would give her a new prominence. 'Whether that's in TV or film, that's a debate,' he explains, 'but I think Marple deserves that kind of treatment. She needs her moment.' Perhaps it is time for Miss Marple, the quiet older lady in the corner, to take her place in the spotlight.

KEY NAMES

Dame Agatha Christie – born Agatha Miller in 1890, died in 1976. Married Archibald Christie in 1914; separated in 1926, divorced in 1928. Married Max Mallowan in 1930; they remained married until her death. Also known as Lady Mallowan (from 1968); awarded a DBE in 1971. Alongside the sixty-six detective novels that made her famous, Christie was author of more than two dozen plays, over 150 short stories and many poems. She also wrote six novels under the name Mary Westmacott (these focused on relationships between characters rather than crime), and two books under the name Agatha Christie Mallowan (one non-fiction, one a religious-themed collection of short stories and poems). Christie had one child, Rosalind Hicks, born 1919.

Archibald ('Archie') Christie – Agatha Christie's first husband, and father of Rosalind. Born 1889, died 1962.

Sir Max Mallowan – Agatha Christie's second husband. Born in 1904, died in 1978. A notable archaeologist, knighted in 1968. Married Barbara Parker in 1977.

Rosalind Hicks – Agatha Christie's only child, born in 1919. Married **Hubert Prichard** in 1940, who was killed in active service in 1944. With Hubert she had her only child, Mathew Prichard, who was born in 1943. Rosalind married **Anthony Hicks** in 1949; they remained married until her death in 2004.

Mathew Prichard CBE – born in 1943, son of Hubert Prichard and Rosalind Hicks, and Agatha Christie's only grandchild. Retired Chairman of Agatha Christie Ltd, succeeded by his son James Prichard in 2015.

James Prichard – Chairman and CEO of Agatha Christie Ltd since 2015. Agatha Christie's great grandson.

William ('Billy') Collins – Born 1900, Christie's publisher for many years. Christie and Collins became friends, and Collins read a eulogy at Christie's funeral in 1976. He died later the same year.

Edmund Cork – Agatha Christie's agent from 1926 to 1978.

Charlotte 'Carlo' Fisher – Christie's secretary for many years, and governess to Rosalind.

Lord (George) Hardinge – A senior publisher at Collins for many years, Hardinge often provided the early reader's reports on Christie's works and was an admirer of both Christie and the mystery genre. He became a Lord in 1960 upon the death of his father, and left Collins to work at Macmillan in 1968.

Harold Ober – Agatha Christie's American agent for much of her career (died 1959).

Dorothy Olding – Agatha Christie's American agent from 1959.

Brian Stone – Agatha Christie Limited's agent following Edmund Cork's retirement in 1978.

SELECTED BIBLIOGRAPHY

The list below is by no means an exhaustive selection of worthwhile books about Agatha Christie and Miss Marple, but are titles that readers may find interesting, and often expand on topics only touched upon in this book.

Aldridge, Mark, *Agatha Christie on Screen* (Palgrave Macmillan, 2016)

_____, *Agatha Christie's Poirot: The Greatest Detective in the World* (HarperCollins, 2020)

Barnard, Robert, *A Talent to Deceive* (Dodd Mead & Company, 1980)

Bayard, Pierre, *Who Killed Roger Ackroyd?* (Editions de Minuit, 1998)

Bernthal, J. C. and Evans, Mary Anna (eds.), *The Bloomsbury Handbook to Agatha Christie* (Bloomsbury, 2023)

Bernthal, J. C., *Agatha Christie: A Companion to the Mystery Fiction* (McFarland & Company, 2022)

_____, *Queering Agatha Christie* (Palgrave Macmillan, 2016)

Chandler, Raymond, *The Simple Art of Murder* (Vintage Books, 1988)

Christie, Agatha, *An Autobiography* (HarperCollins, 2011; first published by Collins, 1977)

Curran, John, *Agatha Christie's Complete Secret Notebooks* (HarperCollins, 2016)

Edwards, Martin, *The Golden Age of Murder* (HarperCollins, 2015)

Gill, Gillian, *Agatha Christie: The Woman and her Mysteries* (Robson Books, 1999)

Goddard, John, *Agatha Christie's Golden Age* [Vols I & II] (Stylish Eye Press, 2018 & 2021)

Green, Julius, *Agatha Christie: A Life in Theatre* (HarperCollins, 2018 [revised ed.])

Gregg, Hubert, *Agatha Christie and All That Mousetrap* (William Kimber & Co., 1980)

Haining, Peter, *Agatha Christie: Murder in Four Acts* (Virgin Books, 1990)

Hart, Anne, *The Life and Times of Miss Marple* (HarperCollins, 2019 [revised ed.])

Harkup, Kathryn, *A is for Arsenic: The Poisons of Agatha Christie* (Bloomsbury, 2015)

James, P. D., *Talking about Detective Fiction* (Faber and Faber, 2010)

Keating, H. R. F., *Agatha Christie: First Lady of Crime* (Weidenfeld and Nicolson, 1977)

Keating, Peter, *Agatha Christie and Shrewd Miss Marple* (Priskus Books, 2017)

Merriman, Andy, *Margaret Rutherford: Dreadnought with Good Manners* (Aurum Press, 2009)

Morgan, Janet, *Agatha Christie: A Biography* (Collins, 1984)

Osborne, Charles, *The Life and Crimes of Agatha Christie* (HarperCollins, 1999 [revised ed.])

Palmer, Scott, *The Films of Agatha Christie* (B. T. Batsford, 1993)

Prichard, Mathew (ed.), *Agatha Christie: The Grand Tour* (HarperCollins, 2012)

Rutherford, Margaret and Robyns, Gwen, *An Autobiography* (W. H. Allen, 1972)

Saunders, Peter, *The Mousetrap Man* (Collins, 1972)

Shaw, Marion and Vanacker, Sabine, *Reflecting on Miss Marple* (Routledge, 1991)

Shayne, Alan and Sunshine, Norman, *Double Life* (Magnus Books, 2011)

Thompson, Laura, *Agatha Christie: An English Mystery* (Headline, 2007)

Worsley, Lucy, *Agatha Christie: A Very Elusive Woman* (Hodder & Stoughton, 2022)

ENDNOTES

The following archives are referenced in the notes:

ACA   Agatha Christie Archive, Christie Archive Trust, Wales
BBC   BBC Written Archives Centre, Caversham
BOD   The Bodley Head Archive, University of Reading
HC   HarperCollins Archive, Glasgow
HMA   Hughes Massie Archive, University of Exeter

INTRODUCTION: MEET MISS MARPLE

1   In the short story 'The Bloodstained Pavement'.
2   Christie, Agatha, *An Autobiography*, p. 436 [henceforth *An Autobiography*].
3   Christianna Brand in H. R. F. Keating, *Agatha Christie: First Lady of Crime*, p. 197.
4   Agatha Christie [henceforth AC] to Edmund Cork [henceforth EC], 14 January 1971 [ACA].
5   AC to Yasuo Suto, 22 August 1970 [HMA].
6   Sometimes renamed Christine Vole.
7   Christie's father died in 1901, when Christie was eleven years old.
8   AC to Yasuo Suto, 22 August 1970 [HMA].
9   AC to Mrs McMurphy, 11 August [unknown year]. As reproduced at http://www.friendsofmarplestation.co.uk/agatha-christie.html. For more on Marple Hall, visit https://www.marple.website/local-history/marple-hall.html.
10   AC to Yasuo Suto, 22 August 1970 [HMA].
11   *An Autobiography*, p. 433.
12   *An Autobiography*, pp. 434–5. If Christie's recollection is correct, then the timing is tight, as Miss Marple first appeared in December 1927, with *Alibi* (the play based on *Ackroyd*)

actually debuting later than this in May 1928. However, the rights to make the novel into a play were sold in April 1927 (Green, Julius, *Agatha Christie: A Life in Theatre*, p. 73) and so it's not unreasonable to believe that the changes to Caroline's character happened at the same time that the idea of Miss Marple formulated in Christie's mind.

CHAPTER ONE: MISS MARPLE'S EARLY MYSTERIES (1927-38)

1   This is one reason why it would not be fair to say that Patricia Wentworth's Miss Silver, another older female detective, was any direct influence, despite some claims that Christie copied Wentworth's idea. Miss Silver made her debut in a 1928 novel – the year after the first Miss Marple story, but two years before Miss Marple first appeared in a novel.

2   AC to Christianna Brand, 12 October [likely 1960, but no year specified], private collection.

3   Ibid.

4   Lucy Worsley, who has convincingly summarised the likely sequence of events, argues that this honesty may well have been in part due to the upcoming divorce between Agatha and Archie Christie, where custody of their daughter Rosalind would also be decided.

5   *Daily Mail*, 16 February 1928.

6   AC to Christianna Brand, 12 October [likely 1960, but no year specified], private collection. The writing is sometimes difficult to decipher: 'and now long after' may be 'then long after'.

7   Puerto de la Cruz now holds an Agatha Christie festival every other year, to honour one of its most famous visitors. It is also the inspiration for 'The Man from the Sea', a Mr Quin short story that ranks among her very best. The house in which the story takes place still stands proudly above the beach today.

8   *Pall Mall Gazette*, 20 January 1922.

9   *An Autobiography*, p. 435.

10   When published in the United States in *Detective Story Magazine*, most of the short stories were given new titles – this one became 'The Solving Six'.

11   *An Autobiography*, p. 435.

12   Ibid.

13 Ibid, p. 436.
14 Ibid.
15 Ibid, p. 40.
16 This is also a reminder of how much younger 'old' people were before the late twentieth century. Sixty-five is now seen as positively sprightly, and a normal working age.
17 *An Autobiography*, p. 243.
18 Ptomaine poisoning could be the result of 'bad' or damaged tinned fish; bulging tins were a sign that their contents may be 'off', possibly to the point of being dangerous.
19 *An Autobiography*, p. 436.
20 These changes appear to have been made by the magazine, as the United States publication of the story the following year in *Detective Story Magazine* mirrors the text of the story as published in *The Thirteen Problems* four years later, demonstrating that the changes weren't made specially for the book. Unfortunately, the original typescript does not survive. This story was also published in the 1929 book *The Best Detective Stories of the Year – 1928* (aka *Best English Detective Stories of 1928* for its US edition), and in this case it was this, *The Royal Magazine*'s version of the story, that was included – more information is available at the excellent Collecting Christie website: https://www.collectingchristie.com/post/collecting-the-first-miss-marple-story-in-a-book. *The Royal Magazine* version also includes an extra incorrect conclusion for Joyce, who immediately assumes that the murdered woman's companion 'was young and beautiful' – 'I am right, am I not?' she asks Sir Henry. 'No, my dear young lady, for once you are wrong,' he replies. This version also spells the companion's name 'Clarke', not 'Clark'.
21 Renamed 'The Solving Six and the Evil Hour' for *Detective Story Magazine*.
22 Namely (**SPOILER**): what causes the victim to fall over? Miss Marple supposes a tree root, which would surely be obvious to at least one observer on the night. The murderer must have been very quick thinking indeed to take advantage of this chance opportunity.
23 Renamed 'The Solving Six and the Golden Grave' for *Detective Story Magazine*.
24 Polperran is probably a play on the real Cornish town of Polperro.

25 Of course, it may be that Raymond's marriage to Joyce does not go ahead as planned, and he finds another artist to be the object of his attractions – this time called Joan. The first reference to Joan is in 1934's 'Miss Marple Tells a Story'.

26 Interview with Francis Wyndham in *The Sunday Times*, 27 February 1966 [Henceforth 'Wyndham interview, 1966'].

27 Renamed 'Drip! Drip!' for *Detective Story Magazine*, with the subtitle 'A Story of The Solving Six'.

28 Which, in Cornwall, is properly pronounced 'Mouze-ull'. We can therefore infer that Rathole is pronounced 'Rat-ull'!

29 Morgan, Janet, *Agatha Christie: A Biography*, p. 316.

30 Renamed 'Where's the Catch?' for *Detective Story Magazine*, again with the subtitle 'A Story of The Solving Six'.

31 *An Autobiography*, p. 436. Despite its claimed ridiculousness, it is the only one of these first six stories to retain its original title for *Detective Story Magazine* in the United States (albeit with the additional subtitle of 'A Story of The Solving Six').

32 AC to Yasuo Suto, 22 August 1970 [HMA].

33 Originally published in newspaper *The Star* on 14 May 1928, it was reproduced as part of *Murder, She Said: The Quotable Miss Marple* (HarperCollins, 2019).

34 Christie seemed to have something of a fixation on Mrs Jones as an everywoman name, as the name features in two of these six stories as well as the aforementioned 1928 article.

35 Possibly an antecedent of this classic, frequently revisited, plot in the television series *Murder, She Wrote*, itself partially inspired by Miss Marple.

36 *An Autobiography*, p. 436.

37 This parallel was suggested to me by Gray Robert Brown.

38 AC to Allen Lane, 26 July 1930 [ACA].

39 Ibid, 13 September 1930 [ACA].

40 Ibid, 13 September 1930 [ACA].

41 British newspapers taking the story as a serialisation include the *Gloucester Citizen*, which began printing it from 19 August (the day after the *Chicago Tribune*), shortly followed by the likes of the *Hull Daily Mail* and the *Leicester Evening Mail*. These British serialisations used the title 'Who Killed Colonel Protheroe?' The precise date of the novel publication is revealed in a letter from Collins to Christie's secretary, Charlotte 'Carlo' Fisher, dated 18 July 1933 [ACA].

42 John Curran also suggests 1929 in *The Complete Secret Notebooks*

(p. 176). Christie wrote seven more Miss Marple short stories as well around this time, which were published in magazines between 1929 and 1931 – these are discussed in the section on *The Thirteen Problems* (1932) (see pp. oo–oo).

43   This includes the famous picked shrimps, although since 'The Tuesday Night Club', Miss Wetherby seems to have taken ownership of the disappearing items, which were previously Mrs Carruthers' problem.

44   In *The Body in the Library*.

45   AC to Yasuo Suto, 22 August 1970 [HMA].

46   Christie's corrections for G. C. Ramsey's book, undated c. August 1966 [HMA]. There is a Downshire in Berkshire, which may explain the confusion.

47   Specifically the third season's 'The Days Dwindle Down', 1987.

48   Originally published under the title 'At the Crossroads', in the United States this short story was eventually collected in the 1950 book *Three Blind Mice and Other Stories*, but the UK had to wait until 1991, when it was published in *Problem at Pollensa Bay and Other Stories*.

49   *An Autobiography*, p. 433.

50   Itself largely written between 1950 and 1965.

51   *An Autobiography*, p. 434.

52   Ibid, pp. 434–5.

53   *Belfast Telegraph*, 15 September 1970.

54   *Daily Mirror*, 15 October 1930; *Times Literary Supplement*, 6 November 1930.

55   *Yorkshire Post*, 24 November 1930

56   *The Observer*, 28 December 1930

57   *The News Chronicle*, 14 October 1930

58   *New York Times*, 30 November 1930.

59   *The Brooklyn Citizen*, 30 November 1930.

60   *The Beatrice Daily Sun*, 25 October 1931.

61   Dorothy L. Sayers to AC, 19 November 1930 [ACA].

62   Ibid, 20 December 1930 [ACA].

63   Date stated in a letter from Collins publishers to Charlotte Fisher, 18 July 1933 [ACA].

64   Introduction to Penguin edition, 1953. The Penguin edition of the book elevates Miss Marple's status, as she is incorporated into the title – *Miss Marple and the Thirteen Problems*.

65   Introduction to Penguin edition, 1953.

66   Although Ms Helier shares her forename with Miss Marple,

there is no possibility of confusion as the generational divide allows only the actress to be referred to by her first name.

67 *An Autobiography*, p. 27.

68 Catherine Brobeck of the *All About Agatha* podcast was a particularly strong proponent of this theory, and originated the term 'Dark Marple'.

69 *Daily Mirror*, 13 June 1932.

70 The story had the spoilerific title 'The Resurrection of Amy Durrant' when published in *The Story-Teller Magazine*, February 1930. The magazine published 'A Christmas Tragedy' as the second of these six stories, with this story as the third, presumably because issues dated January 1930 would be in shops during the festive season. The final three stories were also re-ordered – 'The Herb of Death' (March), then 'The Four Suspects' (April), and finally 'The Affair at the Bungalow' (May). **SPOILER:** The switched identities is a significant element of *A Murder is Announced*, which is partially set in a house called 'Little Paddocks', and which is also the given address of the dead woman and her companion in this story.

71 This was given the name 'The Hat and the Alibi' in *The Story-Teller Magazine*.

72 Foreword to Penguin edition, 1953.

73 The BBC serials were designed to raise money for The Detection Club, a society for the best writers of the genre. Each writer contributed a chapter or two, and they were organised by Sayers. Christie's two chapters of *The Scoop* have also been printed under the titles 'At the Inquest' and 'The Weapon', but those I have used are the originals, as recorded by the BBC's paperwork and information for radio listings.

74 Morgan, Janet, *Agatha Christie: A Biography*, p. 200.

75 Charlotte 'Carlo' Fisher to AC, 4 October 1931 [ACA].

76 *The Edinburgh Evening News*, 6 June 1932.

77 *Western Morning News and Daily Gazette*, 6 June 1932.

78 *Daily Herald*, 23 June 1932.

79 *Manchester Guardian*, 2 September 1932.

80 *Courier-Post* (New Jersey), 4 March 1933.

81 *Times Literary Supplement*, 8 September 1932.

82 Correspondence with the author.

83 Foreword to Penguin edition, 1953.

84 J. R. Ackerley to AC, 12 September 1932 [BBC Agatha Christie Talks 1930–58].

85   Ibid, 20 October 1932 [BBC Agatha Christie Talks 1930–58].

86   AC to J. R. Ackerley, 26 October 1932 [BBC Agatha Christie Talks 1930–58].

87   J. R. Ackerley to AC, 23 February 1934 [BBC Agatha Christie Talks 1930–58].

88   AC to J. R. Ackerley, 26 February 1934 [BBC Agatha Christie Talks 1930–58].

89   J. R. Ackerley to AC, 27 February 1934 [BBC Agatha Christie Talks 1930–58].

90   Charlotte Fisher to J. R. Ackerley, 27 March 1934 [BBC Agatha Christie Talks 1930–58].

91   This is in an article concerning Christie's new play for radio, 'The Yellow Iris'. *Radio Times*, 31 Oct 1937.

92   The issue related to the placement and naming of two doors within the story. Letters also show that Christie was away when the live broadcast was scheduled to take place.

93   *Richmond Times*, 22 March 1936.

94   Harold Ober [henceforth HO] to EC, 9 Jan 1936 [ACA].

95   EC to AC, 4 September 1936 [ACA].

CHAPTER TWO: THE 1940s

1   See https://www.collectingchristie.com/post/la-bantam for more information about the different editions of this rare book, and a background to them. The stories collected were 'The Blue Geranium', 'The Companion', 'The Four Suspects', 'A Christmas Tragedy', and 'Death by Drowning'.

2   EC to AC, 10 September 1940 [HMA].

3   In Britain, these stories were eventually later collected in 1979's *Miss Marple's Final Cases*, and are discussed in more depth in the section dealing with that book (see pp. 00–00). Christie delivered the first two stories on 31 October 1940 ('The Case of the Retired Jeweller' and 'A Case of Buried Treasure'), with the other two following on 6 November ('The Case of the Caretaker' and 'The Case of the Perfect Maid'). In the event, *This Week* seems to have only published the first two of these, with the others syndicated in newspapers the following year.

4   EC to AC, 28 May 1942 [HMA]. Christie suggested being given a special commission to write articles on the area for magazines, which would allow her to travel to the area.

5   *An Autobiography*, p. 510.

6   Ibid, pp. 509-510.
7   This book, and its convoluted history, is covered in the 1970s chapter (see pp. 00-00).
8   *An Autobiography*, p. 489.
9   Foreword to Penguin edition, 1953.
10   Ibid.
11   Ruby's name would appear to be a reference to Ruby Anne Keen, a young woman whose murder by strangulation made headlines in 1937.
12   *Pall Mall Gazette*, 20 January 1922.
13   *An Autobiography*, p. 313.
14   Foreword to Penguin edition, 1953.
15   Ibid.
16   Interview with Marcelle Bernstein in *The Observer* magazine, 14 December 1969 [Henceforth 'Bernstein interview, 1969'].
17   Ibid.
18   *An Autobiography*, p. 341.
19   As quoted by Laura Thompson in *Agatha Christie: An English Mystery*, pp. 384-5.
20   EC to AC, 18 October 1940 [HMA].
21   The version currently available is complete.
22   Morgan, Janet, *Agatha Christie: A Biography*, p. 323.
23   William Collins [henceforth 'WC'] to AC, 5 January 1942 [HC].
24   Mary Jane Glennan of *Coronet Magazine* to AC, 30 October 1942 [HMA].
25   *Hampstead and St John's Wood News and Golders Green Gazette*, 4 June 1942; *The Knoxville News Sentinel*, 22 February 1942.
26   *The New York Times*, 1 March 1942.
27   *The Gazette* (Montreal), 21 March 1942.
28   *Times Literary Supplement*, 16 May 1942.
29   *El Paso Times*, 26 April 1942. *The Tampa Tribune*, 18 October 1942, and *The Vancouver Sun*, 11 April 1942, all declared the story to be Christie 'at her best' in different reviews.
30   *The Observer*, 17 May 1942.
31   *The New York Times*, 1 March 1942.
32   L. P. Hartley is probably best known for the 1953 novel *The Go-Between*. *The Sketch* published many of Christie's early Poirot short stories in the 1920s.
33   *The Sketch*, 3 June 1942.
34   EC to HO, 10 March 1941 [HMA].

35   Foreword to Penguin edition, 1953.
36   Bernstein interview, 1969.
37   Foreword to Penguin edition, 1953.
38   Interview with Nigel Dennis in *Life*, 14 May 1956.
39   Foreword to Penguin edition, 1953.
40   E. W. Stein to AC, 1 April 1942 [HMA].
41   Wyndham interview, 1966.
42   Foreword to Penguin edition, 1953.
43   HO to EC, 23 May 1941 [HMA].
44   Christie was asked to prepare it so it could be published in instalments of 8,000, 6,000 and then 5,000 words. EC to AC, 2 January 1942 [HMA].
45   AC to EC, 6 January 1942; EC to HO, 14 Jan 1942 [HMA].
46   The title was also shortened slightly to *Moving Finger* for both American and British serialisations.
47   EC to AC, 4 December 1942 [HMA].
48   This was because Collins' file copy of the book was destroyed during the war, and so an American edition from Grosset & Dunlap was used as the basis, as it erroneously claimed to be unabridged. This seems to be the first time that Christie's British agent realised that the serialised version had been used for the United States book.
49   EC to AC, 10 April 1942 [HMA]. It seems that this magazine also received the second copy of the typescript originally intended for Ober in the United States.
50   *The Sketch*, 28 July 1943.
51   *Oakland Tribune*, 1 November 1942.
52   *The Atlanta Constitution*, 1 November 1942.
53   *The New York Times*, 18 October 1942; *Sunday Call-Chronicle* (Pennsylvania), 7 February 1943.
54   *Courier Journal*, 6 December 1942.
55   *The Gazette* (Montreal), 17 October 1942.
56   *The Observer*, 13 June 1943.
57   *Times Literary Supplement*, 19 June 1943.
58   *An Autobiography*, p. 520.
59   Radio schedules show that the programme was broadcast between 12 and 16 January, depending on region, although it may have debuted earlier than this as the listings are not comprehensive.
60   *Albany Democrat Herald*, 14 January 1942.
61   Curran, John, *Agatha Christie's Complete Secret Notebooks*,

p. 388 [henceforth 'Curran']. Although undated, other stories outlined in the notebook include 1957's *4.50 from Paddington* and 1956's *Dead Man's Folly*, making the 1950s the most likely period. In 1960, the novel was also on the list of 'Reserved' titles that film studio MGM were not allowed to adapt for the screen, as Christie was considering dramatising them for herself. (Also in the 'Reserved' list were titles that had already been dramatised, either by Christie or others.)

62   Green, Julius, *Agatha Christie: A Life in Theatre*, p. 240.
63   EC to AC, 24 December 1942; EC to AC, 18 September 1944 [HMA].
64   Green, Julius, *Agatha Christie: A Life in Theatre*, p. 240. Green also gives some background to both adaptors. For those curious, the unusually named Moie Charles was a woman with the birth name of Marion.
65   This and Christie's following comments on the play, all AC to EC, 22 June 1949 [HMA].
66   'The beginning could profitably have shared the pace of the end,' stated Cecil Wilson in the *Daily Mail*, 15 December 1949.
67   Mullen is probably best known as the housekeeper Janet in the BBC television series of *Dr Finlay's Casebook*, which began in 1962.
68   Although they are now referred to as pickled, not picked. I am indebted to Tony Medawar for educating me on the difference!
69   *An Autobiography*, p. 471.
70   At the Playhouse Theatre.
71   EC to AC, 2 January 1950 [HMA].
72   Ibid, 1 May 1950 [HMA].
73   AC to RH, undated 1971 [ACA].
74   *Kensington News and West London Times*, 30 December 1949.
75   *The Observer*, 18 December 1949.
76   *The Sunday Dispatch*, 18 December 1949.
77   *Daily Telegraph and Morning Post*, 15 December 1949.
78   *The Stage*, 22 December 1949.
79   AC to Michael Prichard, 30 March 1968 [ACA].
80   As Julius Green points out, this revival was running when Christie died in January 1976, and so its lights were dimmed in tribute along with *The Mousetrap*'s.
81   Orwell's full essay is available at https://www.orwellfoundation.com/the-orwell-foundation/orwell/essays-and-other-works/decline-of-the-english-murder/.

82   Chandler's full essay is available at https://www.
theatlantic.com/magazine/archive/1944/12/
the-simple-art-of-murder/656179/.

83   This particular depiction of isolated English villages was called
'Mayhem Parva' by Colin Watson in his 1971 book *Snobbery with
Violence*.

CHAPTER THREE: THE 1950s

1   'Strange Jest', 'The Case of the Perfect Maid', 'Tape-Measure
Murder' and 'The Case of the Caretaker': all covered in the *Miss
Marple's Final Cases* section of this book (see pp. 00–00).

2   *Chicago Sunday Tribune*, 30 April 1950. The Poirot stories are
'The Third Floor Flat', 'The Adventure of Johnnie Waverly' and
'Four-and-Twenty Blackbirds'.

3   *Hartford Courant*, 12 March 1950.

4   AC to EC, 3 August 1948 [HMA].

5   EC to HO, 8 October 1948 [HMA].

6   Although *Crooked House* was the next novel published after this
letter (in 1949), evidence points to it having been written in
late 1947 and possibly early 1948 (see Curran, p. 474).

7   Morgan, Janet, *Agatha Christie: A Biography*, p. 270.

8   Interview with Valerie Knox, *The Times*, 1 December 1967
[henceforth 'Knox interview, 1967'].

9   *An Autobiography*, p. 184.

10   AC, 'Note', undated, likely early 1950 [HMA].

11   The correct spelling, as per the first edition and original
typescript, is 'Hinchliffe'. However, some editions and
adaptations change this to 'Hinchcliffe', while Fontana offered
both spellings!

12   This, and subsequent observations about the typescripts of
this and other Miss Marple novels and stories, are based on
the original copies held by the Christie Archive Trust, who
generously allowed me access.

13   Christie's rationale for some of the changes is preserved in a
loose handwritten note housed at the back of the typescript's
folder. Johnnie's new surname means that he is probably
a relative (perhaps son?) of Mrs Butt, who is referred to by
Bunch.

14   **SPOILER:** At this stage, Christie also alters the way that 'Letitia'
Blacklock is referred to – originally, she is often referred to

as 'Laetitia' [sic] in third-person descriptions early in the typescript, but Christie crosses these out and replaces them with 'Miss Blacklock', presumably so that she can't be accused of cheating the reader when the character's true identity is revealed.

15   WC to AC, 12 October 1949 [HC].

16   AC to EC, 16 February 1950 [HMA].

17   This was perhaps not a direct result of Christie's new deal with Dodd Mead, but was indicative of a wider feeling that Christie's works shouldn't be expected to self-generate publicity simply because of her consistently good sales and strong reader recognition. In the United States the novel was serialised later, after a great deal of issues regarding rights, including those in Canada. This was unusual, because magazines and newspapers in the United States usually insisted on being the first to publish internationally, but a special deal was brokered in order to support the London production of *Murder at the Vicarage*. In the event, her American agents didn't even know of the play's existence, and so asked for a copy, although an initially interested producer turned it down once he read it. The American serialisation of *A Murder is Announced* was in the *Chicago Tribune* from April to June 1950.

18   EC to AC, 17 February 1950 [HMA].

19   HO to EC, 9 May 1950 [HMA].

20   EC to AC, 2 March 1950 [HMA].

21   *BBC News*, 'An Agatha Christie birthday cake to die for', http://news.bbc.co.uk/local/devon/hi/people_and_places/history/newsid_8988000/8988240.stm.

22   Interview with Nigel Dennis in *Life*, 14 May 1956.

23   Quoted by Gwen Robyns in *The Mystery of Agatha Christie* (Penguin, 1978), p. 245.

24   James, P. D., *Talking about Detective Fiction*, p. 88. To explain more would be to spoil the story.

25   Ibid, p. 84.

26   Ibid, p. 85.

27   *New York Times Book Review*, 4 June 1950.

28   *Times Literary Supplement*, 23 June 1950.

29   *Weekly Scotsman*, 8 June 1950; *Huddersfield Examiner*, 17 June 1950.

30   *Manchester Evening News*, 13 June 1950; *New Statesman*, 5 August 1950.

31   *The Observer*, 4 June 1950.
32   *The Sunday Times*, 25 June 1950.
33   *Evening Standard*, 10 June 1950.
34   *The Bookseller*, 17 June 1950.
35   *Tatler*, 28 June 1950.
36   *Evening Standard*, 9 June 1950.
37   *News Chronicle*, 9 June 1950.
38   Interview with Nicholas Bull, *Torbay Herald Express*, 4 September 1970.
39   Christianna Brand, *Books of To-day*, June 1950.
40   *Fabian of the Yard* was a successful book and then television series.
41   Margery Allingham in *New York Times Book Review*, 4 June 1950.
42   EC to AC, 20 April 1951 [HMA]; Billy Collins to AC, 11 August 1950
43   Interview with Lord Snowdon, *The Australian Woman's Weekly*, 18 September 1974 [henceforth 'Snowdon interview, 1974'].
44   *An Autobiography*, p. 131.
45   Interview with Nigel Dennis in *Life*, 14 May 1956.
46   AC to EC, 18 August 1951 [HMA].
47   Undated letter, 'Monday' c. January 1951 [HMA].
48   AC to EC, 18 August 1951; AC to EC, 15 September 1951. Christie also changed the name of Emma to Mildred [HMA].
49   AC to EC, 18 August 1951 [HMA].
50   By the time the book was published in Britain in late 1952, Mathew (born 21 September 1943) was nine years old.
51   HO to EC, 28 November 1951 [HMA].
52   Ibid.
53   Ibid, 13 December 1951 [HMA].
54   EC to HO, 18 January 1952 [HMA].
55   Although 1956 saw Christie's pseudonymous alter-ego Mary Westmacott publish the character drama *The Burden* the same year as Poirot investigated *Dead Man's Folly*. Christie's use of the pseudonym had been exposed in 1949, after four of the six Westmacott titles had been published.
56   EC to HO, 18 January 1952 [HMA].
57   EC to Rosalind Hicks [hereafter 'RH'], 29 January 1952 [HMA].
58   HO Associates to EC, 31 January 1952 [HMA].
59   It's difficult to pin down a precise date for the book's American publication, but reviews appeared from mid-September.
60   *The Miami Herald*, 5 October 1952.

61   *Richmond Times Dispatch*, 21 September 1952.
62   *The Daily Oklahoman*, 16 November 1952; *The Albuquerque Tribune*, 26 September 1952.
63   *Punch*, 10 December 1952.
64   *The Sunday Times*, 30 November 1952. Iles was a pseudonym of crime writer Anthony Berkeley Cox.
65   *The Observer*, 30 November 1952,
66   *Chicago Tribune*, 8 November 1954.
67   *Oakland Tribune*, 15 February 1953.
68   AC to EC, 19 February 1952 [HMA].
69   See Curran, pp. 519–523, for the development of the story in her notebooks.
70   Interview with Nigel Dennis in *Life*, 14 May 1956.
71   *Agatha Christie in Close Up*, BBC Light Programme, 13 February 1955.
72   Curran, p. 520.
73   *An Autobiography*, p. 29.
74   EC to AC, 17 September 1952 [HMA].
75   Ibid, 25 September 1952 [HMA].
76   Ibid.
77   Interview with Nigel Dennis in *Life*, 14 May 1956; Snowdon interview, 1974.
78   Wyndham interview, 1966.
79   'The Guessing Game': https://www.agathachristie.com/about-christie/family-memories/the-guessing-game.
80   Wyndham interview, 1966.
81   Snowdon interview, 1974.
82   AC to EC, 3 February 1953 [HMA].
83   Ibid.
84   Ibid, 20 February 1953 [ACA].
85   EC to HO, 6 February 1953 [ACA].
86   HO to EC, 17 February 1953 [HMA].
87   AC to EC, 28 February 1953 [HMA]. Christie mentions adding a small section as well as deleting the epilogue – possibly the letter received by Miss Marple was a new addition. Cork later told Ober that Christie had 'tightened up' the book a little.
88   EC to AC, 13 February 1953 [HMA].
89   Ibid, 4 February 1953 [HMA]. The site is now home to a luxury hotel: https://parklane.intercontinental.com/our-history/. 'We had thought it was rather too exhausting to take Mathew but now my mother has these seats she may want to take him

after all!' wrote Rosalind Hicks to Edmund Cork, 2 March 1953 [HMA].

90   Conversation with the author, 4 January 2023.
91   Reader's report, George Hardinge, 20 April 1943 [HC].
92   WC to AC, 23 July 1953 [HC].
93   EC to AC, 5 August 1953 [HMA]. The dedication was mentioned by the *Daily Telegraph and Morning Post* on 9 November: 'Money is wanted also for a cause connected with architecture of a considerably earlier date – the continued excavation of Nimrud by the British School of Archaeology in Iraq. Towards the work of this school a widely admired writer has made a gift of a novel kind: the copyright of her new book. Entitled *A Pocket Full of Rye*, it is by Mrs Mallowan, wife of Prof. Mallowan, director of the school. The book is to appear today, under the author's pen name, Agatha Christie.'
94   *The Observer*, 15 November 1953.
95   *The Sketch*, 16 December 1953.
96   *Manchester Guardian*, 27 November 1953.
97   *The Daily Oklahoman*, 4 April 1954.
98   *Times Literary Supplement*, 4 December 1953.
99   'Miss Marple Tells a Story' was specially written for the radio, and not an adaptation. It was also single voice.
100 James Langham to Controller of the Light Programme, 28 October 1955 [BBC RCONT1 Agatha Christie File 1 1937-62].
101 See https://coronationstreet.fandom.com/wiki/Clara_Midgeley.
102 *Edinburgh Evening News*, 24 February 1956.
103 AC to EC, undated note headed 'Nimrud Expedition', c. May 1956 [HMA].
104 EC to AC, 11 April 1957 [HMA].
105 Ibid, 1 September 1949 [ACA].
106 EC to HO, 14 August 1950 [HMA].
107 HO to EC, 20 October 1950 [HMA].
108 Ibid, 15 November 1950 [HMA].
109 HO to EC, 6 March 1951 [HMA].
110 Equivalent to around $1,735 and $2,892 in 2024.
111 EC to HO, 16 March 1951 [HMA].
112 Ibid, 18 January 1952 [HMA].
113 HO to EC, 23 January 1952 [HMA].
114 EC to HO, 31 January 1952 [HMA].
115 HO to EC, 17 February 1954 [HMA].

116 Ibid, 27 January 1955 [HMA].
117 Anne Louise Davis at Harold Ober to EC, 16 June 1955 [HMA].
118 Mitzi was played by German actor Christiane Felsmann. The only other cast member apparently not born in Britain was Josephine Brown, who played Murgatroyd; online sources state that she was born in Chicago, although she was based in Britain at some point (as her other credits indicate) and appears to have an authentic accent.
119 Hinchliffe has become Hinchcliffe once more.
120 **SPOILER:** It is Hinchcliffe, not Murgatroyd, who dies in this version.
121 *Daily News*, 31 December 1956.
122 *Kansas City Star*, 6 January 1957.
123 *New York Times*, 31 December 1956.
124 EC to AC, 24 January 1957 [HMA].
125 HO to EC, 21 January 1958 [HMA].
126 Penelope Gilliatt to AC, 6 October 1955 [HMA].
127 AC to EC, 8 January 1956 [HMA].
128 Ibid, 27 February 1956 [HMA].
129 Ibid, 8 Jan 1956 [HMA].
130 EC to HO, 15 February 1957 [HMA].
131 AC to EC, 8 April 1957 [HMA].
132 The exchange takes place between Miss Marple and Lucy Eyelesbarrow in Chapter 13, as they have tea.
133 Bernthal, J. C., *Agatha Christie: A Companion to the Mystery Fiction*, p. 174.
134 Curran, p. 553.
135 Originally published in newspaper *The Star* on 14 May 1928, it was reproduced as part of *Murder, She Said: The Quotable Miss Marple* (HarperCollins, 2019).
136 Hazel Mary Carron to AC, c. January/February 1959 [ACA].
137 *Guardian*, 25 January 1962.
138 *An Autobiography*, pp. 438-9.
139 Undated note from AC to EC, c. March 1957 [HMA].
140 AC to EC, 8 April 1957 [HMA]. Early American editions of the book retain the 4.54 time for the train in the main text.
141 George Hardinge's reader's report for Collins, 1 March 1957 [HC].
142 HO to EC, 15 March 1957 [HMA]; HO to EC, 15 April 1957 [HMA].
143 Undated note from AC to EC, c. March 1957 [HMA].

144   AC to EC, 29 March 1957 [HMA].
145   EC to Anthony Hicks [henceforth 'AH'], 15 May 1957 [HMA];
      AC to EC, 2 February [possibly 24 February] 1957 [HMA].
146   George Hardinge to Mr Greig, 19 June 1957 [HC].
147   *Birmingham Post and Gazette*, 10 December 1957; *The News and
      Observer* (Raleigh), 8 December 1957.
148   *Manchester Guardian*, 6 Dec 1957.
149   *Western Mail*, 9 November 1957.
150   *The Tatler*, 4 December 1957.

CHAPTER FOUR: THE 1960s

1   AC to EC, 11 January 1960 [HMA].
2   Hughes Massie & Co to L. H. Bowen, undated letter *c.* June 1960
      [HMA].
3   EC to Dorothy Olding [henceforth 'DO'], 24 June 1960 [HMA].
4   AC to EC, 12 April 1960 [HMA]. 'The Case of the Perfect Maid'
      was eventually published in 1979's *Miss Marple's Final Cases*.
5   See this author's *Agatha Christie's Poirot: The Greatest Detective in
      the World* for more details, pp. 239-242.
6   EC to Secretary of the Diocesan Board of Finance, 18 November
      1954 [HMA].
7   *An Autobiography*, p. 513.
8   EC to Messrs Michelmores, 3 December 1954 [HMA]. £1,250
      translates to a little under £30,000 in 2024.
9   James Paterson to AC, 13 December 1954 [ACA].
10   AC to James Paterson, 6 January 1955 [ACA].
11   AC to James Paterson, 14 September 1955 [ACA].
12   HO to EC, 17 May 1955 [HMA]; EC to HO, 25 May 1955 [HMA].
13   EC to DO, 30 June 1955 [HMA]; DO to EC, 6 July 1955 [HMA].
14   EC to DO, 15 July 1955 [HMA].
15   'Greenshaw's Folly' typescript, p. 21 [ACA].
16   Ibid, p. 35.
17   DO to EC, 6 September 1955 [HMA].
18   Stewart Beach to DO, 3 October [HMA].
19   EC to DO, 14 October 1955 [HMA].
20   AC to EC, 27 February 1956 [HMA].
21   Ibid, 10 March 1956 [HMA].
22   *An Autobiography*, p. 513.
23   AC to EC, 9 September 1960 [HMA].
24   AC to Patricia Cork, 1 December 1960 [HMA].

25 AC to EC, 16 September 1960 [HMA].
26 EC to AC, 15 January 1960 [HMA].
27 AC to EC, 20 January 1960 [HMA].
28 EC to RH, 26 February 1960 [HMA].
29 AH to EC, 28 February 1960 [HMA]; EC to RH, 17 March 1960 [HMA].
30 EC to RH, 17 March 1960 [HMA].
31 Even so, most of the money would not go to Christie personally.
32 *News Chronicle*, 12 May 1960.
33 EC to AH, 22 June 1960 [HMA]; RH to EC, 3 September 1960 [HMA].
34 EC to RH, 11 January 1961 [HMA].
35 Rutherford, Margaret, (with Gwen Robyns) *An Autobiography*, p. 176.
36 The equivalent to around £300,000 in 2024.
37 Frequently written as *Murder, She Said* – but there is no comma.
38 Rutherford, Margaret, (with Gwen Robyns) *An Autobiography*, p. 178.
39 Ibid.
40 *The Sunday Times*, 17 November 1974.
41 £100,000 in 1961 is the equivalent to around £1.85m in 2024.
42 AC to EC, 17 September 1961 [HMA].
43 AC to Lawrence Bachmann [henceforth 'LB'], 11 April 1964 [HMA].
44 *Kinematograph Weekly*, 17 August 1961.
45 *The Illustrated London News*, 14 October 1961.
46 *San Francisco Examiner*, 25 December 1961.
47 *Detroit Free Press*, 17 March 1962.
48 Rutherford, Margaret, (with Gwen Robyns) *An Autobiography*, p. 179
49 EC to AH, 6 October 1961 [HMA].
50 This also might explain other repetitions, such as the way that Cherry Baker seems to be introduced more than once in the same paragraph in the first chapter. In the discussion of 'Close', we also learn that Miss Marple's uncle had been Canon of Chichester Cathedral.
51 Bernstein interview, 1969.
52 Ibid.
53 Ibid.
54 Knox interview, 1967.
55 Lord Hardinge to WC, 12 April 1962 [HC].

56 Snowdon interview, 1974.

57 DO to EC, 25 April 1962 [HMA], **SPOILER:** As soon as German measles (aka rubella) was mentioned, Olding (and many other readers of this draft of the story) realised that Marina Gregg had a perfect motive for murder.

58 DO to EC, 11 May 1962 [HMA].

59 Lord Hardinge to Wiliam Collins, 16 May 1962 [HC].

60 Interview with Godfrey Winn, *Daily Mail*, 12 September 1970.

61 **SPOILER:** Specifically, worries that women may be particularly sensitive about the question of German measles in pregnancy.

62 **SPOILER:** All specific references to German measles made prior to p. 289 of the typescript were removed.

63 Lord Hardinge to WC, 13 June 1962 [HC].

64 AC to EC, 31 July 1962 [HMA].

65 Lord Hardinge to WC, 4 May 1962 [HC].

66 **SPOILER:** Once more, the potential ramifications of contracting German measles during pregnancy.

67 **SPOILER:** Tierney had contracted German measles from a fan, and the illness caused her unborn child to have severe disabilities. Cork told Olding that, when it came to the dangers of German measles, it was an incident in the Dutch royal family that was most famous in Britain.

68 Hughes Massie Ltd to Miss Sarajane Beal, 9 June 1964 [HMA].

69 AC to EC, 7 June 1962 [HMA].

70 *Montreal Star*, 8 December 1962.

71 *The Age*, 6 March 1963.

72 *Times Literary Supplement*, 14 December 1962.

73 *Daily News*, 11 October 1963.

74 Margaret Rutherford to AC, 3 November 1962 [CAT]. The story of the relationship between Rutherford and Christie was the inspiration for Philip Meeks' play *Murder, Margaret and Me*, which first appeared in 2012 as a one-woman show performed by Janet Price.

75 Snowdon interview, 1974.

76 AH to EC, 20 August 1961 [HMA].

77 LB to AC, 12 January 1962 [HMA].

78 EC to RH, 24 April 1962 [HMA]; EC to RH, 22 June 1962 [HMA].

79 EC to RH, 22 June 1962 [HMA].

80 Once more, this is a device dismissed by Christie in an earlier Miss Marple mystery.

81 *Daily Mail*, 11 May 1963.

82   *Daily Express*, 8 May 1963.
83   *New York Times*, 25 June 1963.
84   *Oakland Tribune*, 31 December 1963.
85   *Minneapolis Sunday Tribune*, 11 August 1963; *Star Tribune*, 16 August 1963.
86   AC to WC, 14 May 1963 [HC].
87   The contract also excluded newly published works, meaning that *The Mirror Crack'd* and any other new Miss Marple novels were also unavailable.
88   EC to AC, 23 May 1963 [HMA].
89   AC to EC, 24 May 1963 [HMA].
90   LB to AC, 9 July 1963 [HMA].
91   AC to LB, 24 July 1963 [HMA].
92   RH to EC, 8 December 1963 [HMA].
93   AC to LB, 11 April 1964 [HMA].
94   Response to Raymond J. Fullager to AC, 20 April 1963 [HMA].
95   *She* magazine, May 1963.
96   AC to LB, 24 July 1963 [HMA].
97   LB to AC, 30 July 1963 [HMA].
98   AC to EC, 2 August 1963 [HMA].
99   This plot development also allows for more references to Agatha Christie's works by characters, this time both original and adapted (*The Mousetrap* and *Murder She Said*, respectively).
100   *Plays and Players*, August 1971.
101   Notes from meeting between WC and EC, 26 November 1963 [HC].
102   EC to RH, 14 January 1964 [HMA].
103   RH to EC, 19 January 1964 [HMA].
104   AC to LB, 11 April 1964 [HMA].
105   *The Scotsman*, 20 September 1969.
106   *Films and Filming*, December 1964.
107   *Daily Mail*, 24 October 1964.
108   *Boston Globe*, 5 July 1965; *New York Times*, 24 May 1965.
109   *The Montreal Star*, 27 November 1965.
110   Snowdon interview, 1974.
111   Rutherford, Margaret, (with Gwen Robyns) *An Autobiography*, p. 176.
112   *Pall Mall Gazette*, 20 January 1922.
113   *A Caribbean Mystery* typescript, p. 198 [ACA].
114   *Torbay Herald Express*, 4 September 1970.
115   'Il Giallo Mondadori' interview, 1971.

116 Curran, p. 613.
117 *An Autobiography*, p. 433.
118 Notes from meeting between WC and EC, 26 November 1963 [HC].
119 *A Caribbean Mystery* typescript, p. 70 [ACA].
120 WC to EC, 6 February 1964 [HC].
121 DO to Nora Blackborow (EC's secretary), 5 June 1964 [HMA].
122 Lois at Harold Ober Associates to Nora Blackborow, 28 July 1964 [HMA].
123 Equivalent to around $60,000 and £70,000 in 2024.
124 EC to AC, 1 June 1964 [HMA].
125 *The Sunday Times*, 15 November 1964.
126 *The Sunday Telegraph*, 15 November 1964; *Times Literary Supplement*, 19 November 1964.
127 *Guardian*, 11 December 1964.
128 *The Observer*, 15 November 1964; *The Gazette*, 28 November 1964; *The Montreal Star*, 5 December 1964; *The Leader Post*, 28 November 1964.
129 *Daily Independent Journal*, 4 September 1965.
130 EC to AC, 20 November 1964 [HMA].
131 Although often erroneously referred to as *Murder Ahoy!*, the film's title caption does not feature an exclamation mark, and nor does the main publicity material.
132 EC to AH, 6 January 1964 [HMA].
133 Patricia Cork to AC, dated 19 March 1964 [HMA]. Judging by the dates of surrounding correspondence, this is probably misdated, and was written a few days earlier.
134 This and following quotes from AC to Patricia Cork, 18 March 1964 [HMA].
135 'Note to Miss Cork' (signature indecipherable, possibly 'H. Medly'), 19 March 1964 [HMA].
136 AC to EC, 25 March 1964 [HMA].
137 RH to EC, 25 March 1964 [HMA].
138 LB to AC, 7 April 1964 [HMA].
139 EC to AH, 17 April 1964 [HMA].
140 AC to Bachmann, 11 April 1964 [HMA].
141 See this author's *Agatha Christie's Poirot: The Greatest Detective in the World* for more information about the film that became *The Alphabet Murders*.
142 *Daily Express*, 5 May 1964.
143 AH to EC, 7 May 1964 [HMA].

144 For example, Rosalind wrote 'I still feel that they have no right to make original screen plays for films and do not like any suggestion that they have ever had this right. My mother also said she would not sign anything which suggested this.' RH to EC, 14 May 1964 [HMA].

145 *My Home*, August 1964.

146 *St Louis Post Dispatch*, 30 October 1964; *Courier Journal*, 26 November 1964.

147 *Boston Globe*, 19 October 1964.

148 *Time*, 2 October 1964. Rutherford won the Oscar for *The VIPs* (1963).

149 *New York Times*, 23 September 1964.

150 *Photoplay*, December 1964.

151 EC to RH, 20 November 1964 [HMA].

152 AC to EC, January [precise date unspecified] 1965 [HMA].

153 EC to AC, 14 January 1965 [HMA].

154 EC to AH, 16 July 1965 [HMA].

155 RH to EC, 30 November 1965 [HMA].

156 AC to Lionel Jeffries, 20 May 1971, private collection, auctioned at: https://www.dominicwinter.co.uk/Auction/Lot/630-christie-agatha-1890-1976-autograph-letter-signed-agatha-christie-mallowan/?lot=357601&sd=1.

157 AC to David G. Kamm, 29 September 1972 [ACA].

158 *The Sunday Times*, 17 November 1974.

159 *Boston Globe*, 3 November 1964.

160 Thompson, Laura, *Agatha Christie: An English Mystery*, p. 470.

161 Bernstein interview, 1969.

162 Interview with Godfrey Winn, *Daily Mail*, 12 September 1970.

163 A canon by this name had featured in *Murder on the Nile*, Christie's stage adaptation of *Death on the Nile*, but this is a difference character (and a different spelling; in the play it is 'Pennefather').

164 *Amon Hen*, The Journal of the Tolkien Society, issue 13 (October 1974), p. 9.

165 DO to EC, 26 August 1965 [HMA]; Naome Lewis of *Good Housekeeping* to DO, 14 September 1965 [HMA].

166 Receipt of manuscript acknowledged 23 February 1965 [HMA].

167 DO to Nora Blackborow, 29 March 1965 [HMA]; EC to AC, 23 April 1965 [HMA].

168 Edward H. Dodd Jr to AC, 17 June 1965 [HMA].

169 *Times Literary Supplement*, 2 December 1965.

170 *Evening Standard*, 23 November 1965; *Guardian*, 17 December 1965.

171 *The Observer*, 12 December 1965.

172 WC to AC, 21 December 1965 [HC].

173 Mitchell was married to H. R. F. Keating until his death in 2011. Keating was a crime writer and admirer of Christie's works; he was also president of the Detection Club from 1985 to 2000, just as Christie had been for many years.

174 *Courier Post*, 10 September 1966.

175 *Los Angeles Times*, 11 September 1967.

176 AC to EC, 10 March 1965 [HMA].

177 AC to Patricia Cork, 29 February 1964 [HMA].

178 AC to EC, 9 August 1965 [HMA]. Ramsey's book was published as *Agatha Christie: Mistress of Mystery* in 1967.

179 *New York Times*, 21 November 1965.

CHAPTER FIVE: THE 1970s

1 Interview with Godfrey Winn, *Daily Mail*, 12 September 1970.

2 *Ordeal by Innocence*, *The Clocks*, and *Elephants Can Remember*.

3 *The Sunday Times Magazine*, 20 October 1968.

4 AC to EC, 7 September 1970 [HMA]; AC to Yasuo Suto, 22 August 1970 [HMA].

5 Bernstein interview, 1969.

6 *Torbay Herald Express*, 4 September 1970.

7 Curran, p. 657.

8 Knox interview, 1967.

9 *An Autobiography*, p. 341.

10 Available at: https://ftp.cs.toronto.edu/pub/gh/Lancashire+Hirst-extabs-2009.pdf.

11 Notes accompanying the typescript [ACA].

12 *Daily Mail*, 14 June 1971.

13 *Nemesis* typescript, p. 81 [ACA].

14 Notes accompanying the typescript [ACA].

15 **SPOILER**: Also removed was the news that Molly Kendal of *A Caribbean Mystery* is now happily remarried, and received a wedding present from Mr Rafiel.

16 WC to AC, 10 June 1971 [HC].

17 Robert Knittel at Collins to Georg Svensson, 25 June 1971 [HC].

18 Phyllis Westberg at Harold Ober Associates to Patricia Cork, 20 July 1971 [HMA].

19 EC to AC, 2 August 1971/1 [HMA]; EC to AC, 23 August 1971 [HMA].

20 AC to EC, 27 December 1971 [HMA].

21 *The Age*, 20 November 1971.

22 *Daily Telegraph*, 2 December 1971.

23 *The Leader Post*, 6 November 1971; *Guardian*, 4 November 1971.

24 *The Observer*, 31 October 1971.

25 *Courier Post*, 10 November 1971.

26 AC to Dr Gray, 14 September 1972 [ACA].

27 Bernstein interview, 1969.

28 Robert Knittel to Mr S. Phelps Platt Jr, Dodd Mead, 8 April 1974 [HC].

29 AC to WC, 25 March 1974 [ACA].

30 'The Ford Almanac' article and poem, late 1973 (she refers to the year and her being eighty-three years old, and she turned eighty-three on 15 September 1973) [ACA].

31 *Berkeley Gazette*, 30 August 1975.

32 EC to AC, 23 December 1952 [HMA].

33 AC to EC, 17 March 1950 [ACA].

34 Ibid, 17 March 1950 [ACA].

35 Ibid, 17 July 1972 [ACA].

36 AC to Max Mallowan, 14 November [Year unknown, ascribed to the early 1940s] [ACA].

37 At the beginning of the 1940s Christie penned a short story, 'The Case of the Caretaker', in which Dr Haydock prescribed a mystery to Miss Marple (in the form of a manuscript he had written), but he is less happy with any physical sleuthing.

38 Curran, p. 702.

39 Thanks to Marco Asperger Amici for making me aware of this. It can be read at https://radicalging.wordpress.com/2021/01/12/the-queen-is-dead-long-live-the-queen-43-anni-dalla-morte-di-agatha-christie/.

40 Edward Dodd to Max Mallowan, 13 January 1976 [ACA].

41 Brand in Keating, H. R. F., *Agatha Christie: First Lady of Crime*, p. 196.

42 *The New Yorker*, 25 October 1976; *The Observer*, 10 October 1976.

43 *Times Literary Supplement*, 15 October 1976.

44 *New York Times Book Review*, 19 September 1976.

45 *Valley News*, 12 October 1976.

46 AC to Yasuo Suto, 22 August 1970 [HMA].

47 Quoted by Gwen Robyns in *The Mystery of Agatha Christie*, p. 154.

48   Snowdon interview, 1974.

49   *Torbay Herald Express*, 4 September 1970.

50   *An Autobiography*, p. 509.

51   Curran, pp. 706-7.

52   AC to EC, 17 March 1950 [ACA].

53   Statement dated 15 March 1940 [HMA]; 'Corrections in *Murder in Retrospect*' 1940 [HMA].

54   EC to AC, 14 June 1940 [HMA].

55   EC to AC, 1 September 1949 [ACA].

56   Ibid.

57   Elizabeth M. Walter to Christianna Brand, 11 June 1976 [HC].

58   Green, Julius, *Agatha Christie: A Life in Theatre*, p. 555.

59   Hughes Massie & Co to Robert A. Fullard, 29 September 1953 [HMA].

60   Green, Julius, *Agatha Christie: A Life in Theatre*, p. 555.

61   *The Stage and Television Today*, 29 September 1977.

62   *New York Times*, 2 October 1977.

63   Robert Cusack, Artistic Director Academy Arts Theatre Company, New York, to Sara MacLennan, 5 February 1982 [filed with 1969 correspondence, HMA].

64   In the United States, it was collected in 1961's *Double Sin and Other Stories*, as was 'The Dressmaker's Doll'.

65   Christie made many minor corrections to the typescript, including correcting Miss Marple's name: this was not the last time that a typist would call her 'Miss Marples'.

66   In the United States, this was published in 1950's *Three Blind Mice and Other Stories*, as were 'Tape-Measure Murder', 'The Case of the Caretaker' and 'The Case of the Perfect Maid'. *Miss Marple's Final Cases* opted to reproduce the stories and titles as published in the United States, rather than go back to the original texts.

67   Some sources claim that this title was also used for the publication in *This Week*, but in fact it appeared under the title of 'Strange Jest'.

68   'Gammon and spinach' is a quote from the nursery rhyme 'A Frog He Would A-wooing Go'.

69   There are many differences between the version now seen in *Miss Marple's Final Cases* and as reproduced in *The Strand*, including the mention of Mrs Beaton's cookbook (absent from *The Strand*), and the value of the treasure: $25,000 in the book, £4,500 in Christie's original version. At the end of the original version reproduced in *The Strand*, those involved raise a drink

not only to Miss Marple's Uncle Henry, but also the young couple's Uncle Mathew – as well as 'Betty Martin'.

70 Now part of the updated *Agatha Christie's Complete Secret Notebooks*.

71 Both these stories were published in the United States collection *The Regatta Mystery* in 1939.

72 Unsigned note to DO, 17 December 1957 [HMA].

73 'Greenshaw's Folly' also remains a part of 1960's *The Adventure of the Christmas Pudding*. There have also been other 'complete collections' of Miss Marple short stories in more recent years.

74 *Calgary Herald*, 12 January 1980.

75 *The Birmingham Post*, 13 December 1979; *Times Literary Supplement*, 1 December 1979.

76 AC to Mr Browne, 6 March 1974 [ACA].

CHAPTER SIX: THE 1980s AND 1990s

1   AC to EC, 21 January 1974 [HMA].

2   *Los Angeles Times*, 9 October 1977.

3   *Variety*, 15 November 1978.

4   Sandler's script also used the shortened American title, rather than the full British title used by Hales.

5   *Variety*, 13 February 1980; *Screen International*, 29 March 1980.

6   *In Britain*, February 1981.

7   *Daily Mail*, 30 September 1980.

8   Interview with Richard Goodwin, 2017, Canal+ Blu-ray.

9   *Screen International*, 5 July 1980.

10 Ibid.

11 *Photoplay Film Monthly*, October 1980.

12 *Sevenoaks Chronicle*, 5 July 1980.

13 *The Times*, 18 February 1981.

14 *Film Illustrated*, October 1980.

15 *Guardian*, 12 July 1980.

16 *International Herald Tribune*, 23 August 1980.

17 *Evening Post Echo* (Luton), 21 February 1981.

18 *Film Illustrated*, October 1980.

19 *International Herald Tribune*, 23 August 1980.

20 *Sunday Telegraph Magazine*, 19 October 1980.

21 *New York Times*, 14 September 1980.

22 Gottfried, Martin, *Balancing Act: The Authorised Biography of Angela Lansbury* (Little Brown & Co., 1999), p. 248.

23 *The Scotsman*, 24 January 1981.
24 Kati Nicholl adapted this story, which ran in the 21 February 1981 edition.
25 *Citizen*, 26 December 1980; *Variety*, 17 December 1980; *Time*, 29 December 1980.
26 *Financial Times*, 27 February 1981.
27 *New York Daily News*, 19 December 1980; *Washington Post*, 19 December 1980.
28 *Film Illustrated*, April 1981.
29 *Daily Express*, 28 February 1981.
30 *New York Times*, 16 January 1981.
31 *Variety*, 1 July 1981.
32 *International Herald Tribune*, 23 August 1980.
33 *The Globe and Mail* (Toronto), 15 Dec 1977.
34 Ibid, 22 October 1983.
35 The script shows that the Kendals have gained an extra 'l' in their name here (as they also do in the 2013 ITV adaptation of the story starring Julia McKenzie).
36 Ibid.
37 RH to Alan Shayne, 20 August 1983 [ACA].
38 Alan Shayne and Norman Sunshine, *Double Life*, p. 289.
39 *New York Times*, 21 October 1983.
40 *Philadelphia Inquirer*, 21 October 1983.
41 Interview with the author, August 2013.
42 Ibid.
43 *The Globe and Mail* (Toronto), 16 February 1985.
44 Alan Shayne and Norman Sunshine, *Double Life*, p. 292.
45 Ibid, pp. 291-2.
46 *Boston Globe*, 17 February 1985.
47 *Chicago Tribune*, 20 February 1985.
48 Philadelphia Inquirer, 20 February 1985.
49 *Variety*, 27 February 1985.
50 *New York Times*, 20 February 1985.
51 Untitled notes from discussions with Gerald Savory, 22-25 July 1970 [BBC RCONT20 Agatha Christie Copyright 1970-].
52 Pieter Rogers to Nora Blackborough (sic), 15 November 1974 [BBC RCONT20 Agatha Christie Copyright 1970-].
53 AC to EC, 8 April 1974 [HMA].
54 Interview with the author. Unless otherwise stated, all Slater quotes are taken from interviews conducted in June 2018 and September 2021.

55   Hickson's earlier screen connections with Christie included
      not only the role of Mrs Kidder in *Murder She Said* alongside
      Margaret Rutherford's Miss Marple, but also the maid Emmy
      in *Love from a Stranger* (1937) and Mrs Rivington in the 1980
      television production of *Why Didn't They Ask Evans?*.
56   Guy Slater to RH, 31 August 1983 [ACA].
57   Specifically, the titles selected by the German broadcaster were
      'Sanctuary', 'Strange Jest', 'Tape-Measure Murder', 'The Case of
      the Caretaker', 'The Case of the Perfect Maid', 'Miss Marple Tells
      a Story' and 'Greenshaw's Folly'. They were told that the BBC
      may be interested in 'Caretaker' and so they could not have that
      story. Brian Stone to RH, 3 August 1983 [ACA].
58   Although, confusingly, the American rights were owned by
      Rosalind personally; other rights were held elsewhere.
59   D. H .Joss to RH, 31 August 1983 [ACA].
60   The equivalent to over £1.1m in 2024. The series was also
      shot on film, which was a format reserved for only the most
      prestigious television productions.
61   Interview with the author. Unless otherwise stated, all Trevor
      Bowen quotes are from an interview conducted in January
      2022.
62   This and following notes from letter and comments by RH to
      Guy Slater, 17 January 1984 [ACA].
63   I am indebted to the diligent work of Gary Cooper when it
      comes to confirming some of the locations for which there is
      no paperwork.
64   Interview with the author. Unless otherwise stated, all David
      Horovitch quotes are from an interview conducted in April
      2023.
65   *Radio Times*, 22 December 1984–4 January 1985.
66   RH to Guy Slater, 11 June 1984 [BBC T/65/117/1 *Miss Marple: A
      Murder is Announced* Producer's File].
67   Guy Slater to Alan Plater, 23 November 1983 [BBC T/65/117/1
      Miss Marple: A Murder is Announced Producer's File].
68   *The Listener*, 3 January 1985; *New York Times*, 4 January 1986.
69   *The Listener*, 20–27 December 1984.
70   TV Weekly Programme Review Board, 2 January 1985 [BBC].
71   Television Audience Reaction Report on third episode [BBC
      TV Audience Reaction Reports, document TV/84/168].
72   Presumably renamed because villages ending in -stock are
      more common in Hampshire and surrounding counties,

whereas those ending -on are more common in East Anglia, where this adaptation was filmed and seemingly set.

73   *Radio Times*, 16–22 February 1985.

74   EC to RH, 19 July 1954 [HMA].

75   The spelling is 'Gerry' rather than 'Jerry' in this adaptation.

76   RH to Guy Slater, 9 February 1985 [BBC T/65/117/1 *Miss Marple: A Murder is Announced* Producer's File].

77   TV Weekly Programme Review Board, 27 February 1985 [BBC].

78   *Daily Mail*, 22 February 1985.

79   Alan Plater to Guy Slater, 29 September 1983 [BBC T/65/117/1 *Miss Marple: A Murder is Announced* Producer's File].

80   RH to Guy Slater, 28 June 1984 [BBC T/65/117/1 *Miss Marple: A Murder is Announced* Producer's File].

81   Copy of letter from AC to 'Miss Price', dated 21 March [no year], private collection. Generally, Christie's handwriting is not easy to decipher, and this has been transcribed differently over the years. The BBC press release about the discovery stated that the letter read: 'I hope one day you will play my dear Miss Marple', which was a bit of artistic licence. The *Agatha Christie Official Centenary Celebration* (1990) transcribed it as 'I will call you to play my "Miss Marple" one day' (p. 45), which doesn't seem to quite match the handwriting, but is closer than the BBC's efforts! This author reads it as 'I'd like you to play my "Miss Marple" one day'.

82   TV Weekly Programme Review Board, 13 March 1985 [BBC].

83   *Daily Mail*, 2 March 1985.

84   RH to Guy Slater, 6 August 1984 [BBC T/65/117/1 *Miss Marple: A Murder is Announced* Producer's File].

85   Undated note from Rosalind Hicks c. August 1984, headed 'A Pocket Full of Rye' [BBC T/65/118/1 *Miss Marple: A Pocketful of Rye* Producer's File].

86   Sung by Aled Jones.

87   Badland quotes from an interview with the author, April 2023.

88   Hickson quote from *Daily Express*, 24 December 1984.

89   In *The Mirror Crack'd from Side to Side* the interior of the cottage that is used for exteriors is used for some shots. When seen, Miss Marple's back garden is in Crawley, ten miles from the Nether Wallop location of the front of the cottage!

90   TV Weekly Programme Review Board, 13 March 1985 [BBC].

91   Guy Slater to H. S. S. D. Tel, 16 November 1984 [BBC T/65/118/1 *Miss Marple: A Pocketful of Rye* Producer's File].

92   *Press and Journal* (Aberdeen), 2 March 1985.
93   George Gallaccio to RH, 20 May 1985 [ACA].
94   In the days when the same in-flight entertainment was shown to all, although listening to the audio was optional!
95   George Gallaccio to RH, 20 May 1985 [ACA].
96   The rehearsal scripts feature Narizzano's name, not Amyes's, indicating that this was a fairly late change.
97   *Daily Telegraph*, 12 May 1986; *Radio Times*, 20 December 1986 to 2 January 1987.
98   *The Birmingham Post*, 27 December 1986.
99   TV Weekly Programme Review Board, 31 December 1986 [BBC].
100 She was nominated again the following year for *Nemesis*. She did not win either award, although she did win the Royal Television Society Award for 'Best Performance - Female' in 1987.
101 Interview with the author, April 2023.
102 Geraldine Alexander also appeared in the *Agatha Christie's Poirot* episode 'The Tragedy at Marsdon Manor' in 1991.
103 TV Weekly Programme Review Board, 21 January 1987 [BBC].
104 Undated notes on script [ACA].
105 *Daily Telegraph*, 2 February 1987.
106 *Daily Mail*, 14 February 1987.
107 It is clearly the basis for the island in the 1941 Poirot novel *Evil Under the Sun* and, more arguably, often cited as an influence for 1939's *And Then There Were None*.
108 *Oxford Journal*, 7 August 1986.
109 *Daily Mail*, 14 February 1987.
110 TV Weekly Programme Review Board, 11 February 1987 [BBC].
111 George Gallaccio to RH, 2 October 1986 [ACA].
112 *Wembley Observer*, 13 August 1987.
113 *The Times*, 29 December 1987.
114 *Daily Mirror*, 26 December 1987.
115 Mathew Prichard to RH et al, 30 September 1987 [ACA].
116 Trevor Bowen to Brian Stone, 13 November 1987 [ACA].
117 *West Lancashire Evening Gazette*, 19 September 1988.
118 *The Sunday Correspondent*, 24 December 1989.
119 *Radio Times*, 23 December 1989-5 January 1990.
120 Interview with the author, August 2015.
121 *Daily Telegraph Magazine*, 30 November 1991.
122 For (much) more on this series, see this author's own *Agatha Christie's Poirot: The Greatest Detective in the World*.

123 *The Birmingham Post*, 30 December 1991.

124 *The Times*, 30 December 1991.

125 Raymond had previously been played by David McAlister in *Sleeping Murder*.

126 There is no explanation for this new relationship. Perhaps there were simply crossed wires, as Craddock's previous appearance had been under a different producer, director and writer. The reference is in both surviving drafts of the script.

127 *Daily Mirror*, 21 December 1992.

128 All Enyd Williams quotes are from an interview with the author conducted in August 2023.

129 All Gemma Jenkins quotes are from an interview with the author conducted in August 2023.

CHAPTER SEVEN: THE TWENTY-FIRST CENTURY

1 Purchased from Booker, which originally bought 51% of the company in 1968, rising to 64% a decade later. Booker is now a subsidiary of Tesco.

2 All Phil Clymer quotes are from an interview with the author conducted in June 2023.

3 *The Times*, 13 November 2002.

4 *Variety*, 8 June 2005. https://variety.com/2005/scene/markets-festivals/no-evidence-linking-hanks-miss-marple-1117924084/.

5 *The Times*, 11 December 2004.

6 Ibid.

7 *Daily Mirror*, 11 December 2004.

8 J. C. Bernthal offers an insightful analysis of the series' attitudes to queer characters in his book *Queering Agatha Christie*.

9 Numbers fell to a little under six million for *4.50 from Paddington* on 26 December, due to Boxing Day competition from *Sherlock Holmes and the Case of the Silk Stocking* (which achieved almost identical ratings), but mostly rebounded for *A Murder is Announced*.

10 *Sunday Express*, 19 December 2004.

11 *Daily Telegraph*, 1 January 2005.

12 *The Times*, 13 December 2004.

13 The adaptation also allows for a meeting of Miss Marples, as June Whitfield plays the disappearing care home resident Mrs Lancaster.

14   *Daily Mail*, 28 September 2007.
15   Interview with the author. Unless otherwise stated, all
       Julia McKenzie quotes are from an interview conducted in
       September 2021.
16   *What to Watch*, 25 August 2009. https://www.whattowatch.com/
       news/julia-mckenzie-why-my-miss-marple-rocks-200021.
17   In the real world, Christie was not keen on the author. 'I find
       him incredibly boring,' she said in 1974. 'I used to give his
       books as birthday or Christmas presents to my nephews when
       they were very young because they loved anything of that kind.
       Later, they turned to science fiction, which is quite enjoyable,
       and always seems to make sense. I could quite see why they
       would be interested in it. But Ian Fleming I find boring.'
       [Snowdon interview, 1974.]
18   The series missed a trick in not touting this as an adaptation of
       'The Case of the Caretaker', the very similar Miss Marple short
       story.
19   The character later appeared on both television and radio in
       Russia, although it is difficult to confirm details of unlicensed
       productions. Ita Ever herself apparently played Miss Marple
       again in a 1990 television production; according to J. C.
       Bernthal in *Agatha Christie: A Companion to the Mystery Fiction*
       (p. 88), this was an adaptation of *The Body in the Library*.
20   The rise of the internet (and online archives) has also allowed
       for the discovery of snippets relating to other productions
       that are difficult to gain further information about, from an
       apparent Syrian television adaptation of *Sleeping Murder* to an
       Australian radio production of *The Murder at the Vicarage*; there
       is more Miss Marple in the world than can ever be properly
       documented.
21   Many thanks to Haruhiko Imatake for providing me with
       information about these Japanese adaptations.
22   In a further Miss Marple link, Mitsuko Kusabue, who
       plays Suzume Amano (this adaptation's version of Mrs
       McGillicuddy), was the Japanese voice of Miss Marple for the
       second and third series of *Agatha Christie's Marple* starring
       Geraldine McEwan. '*4.50 from Paddington*: A TV Asahi Agatha
       Christie Special'. https://www.agathachristie.com/en/film-and-
       tv/4-50-from-paddington-a-tv-asahi-agatha-christie-special
23   These three stories seem to be particularly popular candidates
       for adaptation in Japan!

24 Such an idea had been discussed for a long time; in the 1990s, there were rumours that Catherine Zeta Jones had been lined up to play a young Miss Marple, who would be a New York photographer.

25 Interview with the author. Unless otherwise stated, all James Prichard quotes are from an interview conducted in June 2023.

26 *Winchester Today*, 2 March 2019. https://www.winchestertoday. co.uk/2019/03/review-the-mirror-crackd/.

27 *The Sunday Post*, 'Meet the author: Crime writer Dreda Say Mitchell on being a part of *Marple: Twelve New Stories*', 22 September 2022. https://www.sundaypost.com/fp/ dreda-say-mitchell/.

28 Although Ariadne Oliver compares Poirot to a computer in the 1969 novel *Hallowe'en Party*.

29 *The Bookseller*, 'Kate Mosse on Agatha Christie', 14 May 2015, https://www.thebookseller.com/features/ kate-mosse-agatha-christie-339388.

30 Cape Cod was also the location where a proposed (but unproduced) 1950s American Miss Marple television series would have been set, and so it seems to chime with the Miss Marple character!

31 *The Times*, 11 September 2022, https://www.thetimes.co.uk/ article/marple-twelve-new-stories-can-any-modern-writer-match-agatha-christie-3b3jq3cov.

32 *Guardian*, 18 September 2022, https://www.theguardian.com/ books/2022/sep/18/agatha-christie-a-very-elusive-woman-by-lucy-worsley-marple-twelve-new-stories-review.

EPILOGUE: MISS MARPLE'S NEXT CASES

1 Interview with Nigel Dennis in *Life*, 14 May 1956.

PICTURE CREDITS

The editor and publishers would like to thank Agatha Christie Limited, the Christie Archive Trust, David Morris at Collecting Christie, Shutterstock.com, and the many book publishers, newspapers, magazines and TV/film companies for their cooperation in enabling us to share a century of Marple visuals and ephemera in this book.

Every effort has been made to trace all owners of copyright. We apologise for any errors or omissions and would be grateful if notified of any corrections.

INDEX

Bowyer, Alan J. 22
Boyer, Charles 187
Brabourne, John 275, 278
Bragg, Bill 53, 117, 183, 245
Brand, Christianna 3, 104-5, 252, 258
Bravo, Charles 234
Brawn, David 376-7
Brief Encounter 301
Briers, Richard 170
Brighton Rock 309
Brimble, Ian 335
Britten, Benjamin 230
Brown, Christopher 346
Buck, Michele 348
Burke, Kathy 315
Burton, Richard 283
Butterworth, Peter 170
By the Pricking of My Thumbs 251, 356

Callow, Simon 350
Cards on the Table 58, 164
Caribbean Mystery, A **201-10**, 228, 231, 237, 239, 278, 281, 289-296, 325, 330-33, 335, 339, 366, 379
Carr, John Dickson 92
'Case of the Caretaker, The' **269-70**, 317, 343
'Case of the Perfect Maid, The' 156, **270-71**, 304, 333
Castle, John 313, 327
Castle, Nick 77, 105
Castro, Fidel 230
Caswell, Leslie 161
Catcher in the Rye, The 207
Cavaliero, Rose 343
Chandler, Raymond 87
Charles III, King 278
Charles, Moie 81, 259
Chatterton, Thomas 243
Chesterton, G. K. 30, 52
Christie, Archibald 1, 25, 202
'Christmas Tragedy, A' **40-41**, 44, 317
Churchett, Stephen 349, 351, 355-7, 363
Clocks, The 206
Clunes, Martin 312
Clymer, Phil 346, 348-9, 351, 353, 356, 358
Cole, Alyssa 378

Collins, Billy 66, 97, 103, 128, 163, 181-2, 192, 197, 208, 227, 243, 246
Collins, Joan 360, 363
Collins, Pauline 359
'Companion, The' **38-9**
Connell, Tom 64
Cork, Edmund 53, 56, 65, 81, 84-6, 92, 98-9, 114-16, 119, 123, 126, 128, 132-5, 138, 140-41, 149, 154, 156-7, 160-62, 164-8, 172-3, 179, 181-3, 186, 191, 197, 210, 214-15, 219, 226-7, 244, 248-9, 256-8, 266, 277, 299
Cork, Patricia, 211-13, 230
Cotes, Peter 309
Cottenden, Jeff 104, 127, 270
Coward, Noël 230
Cox, Brian 363
Cranford 32
Crispin, Edmund 272
Critchlow, Stephen 343
Crofts, Freeman Wills 43
Cronin, A. J. 213
Crooked House 57, 78, 164, 365
Crowther, Liz 313
Curran, John 80, 144, 227, 236, 257, 270
Curtain: Poirot's Last Case 56, 247, 249, 252, 255, 258
Curtis, Tony 280, 282-3
Cusack, Robert 263
Cuzik, David 1

Dali, Salvador 230
Darbon, Leslie 260-62
Darling, Grace 106
Darlington, W. A. 85
Davenport, Nigel 340
Davidson, Andrew 33, 44
Davies, John 321, 323
Davies, Rupert 220
Davion, Geoffrey 310
Davis, Bette 294-7
Davis, Stringer 167, 196
Davison, Peter 316
de la Tour, Frances 295
Dead Man's Folly 147, 158, 161
'Deadly Wedding Day, A' 379
Dean, Basil 80